D0820760

In our holding company and in two of the single family offices I help run, the blueprints of value machines themselves are worth millions of dollars, and can be leveraged in many different industries or asset classes. While most books on the industry focus on statistics or outdated stressing of fee-only models, no other publication dives into the structures that drive value creation for ultra-wealthy families like this text does. In fact when you first start reading the book you will realize it speaks to professionals who are operating on another level in the space. I have hired Carl to speak at our most private and exclusive events for single family offices and $100M+ families and if you read this book you will see exactly why and be glad you spent the time doing so.

Richard C. Wilson is the bestselling author of *The Single Family Office: Creating, Operating, and Managing Investments of a Single Family Office*, Wilson Holding Company, Key Biscayne FL

Carl's book brings a refreshing twist to the valuation discipline. While most equity valuation literature out there focuses on technical and methodological aspects, Carl thinks outside of the box and delves into unique concepts and tools, namely, Governance, Relationships, Risks, and Knowledge (GRRK) and risk Identification, Measurement, Management, and Mitigation (IMMM) that lead to Equity Value Enhancement (EVE). This book is especially useful for valuation professionals who desire to be more than just routine commodity service providers and have a greater calling to become pro-active participants of a holistic advisory team integral to helping companies produce results, reduce operational risk, and leverage on and maximize valuable intangible assets.

Angela Sadang, MBA, ASA, CFA, Director, Financial Advisory Services, Marks Paneth LLP

Carl is a very introspective individual. He approaches family businesses and public companies with a holistic approach; not just a single focus. Having grown up in a family owned business in manufacturing and working with many family businesses, I know firsthand that Carl understands the dynamics inherent in certain family businesses, and that provides true value. Carl has a talent for sizing up a business for its value, challenges, and governance. Having worked with him, he is someone I would love to work with again for his impressive and consistent ability to create value and help businesses grow.

James M. Hill, Chairman of the Private Equity Practice Group, and former Managing Partner, Benesch, Friedlander, Coplan & Aronoff LLP, Cleveland, OH

This wonderful book shines a light on a universal but widely unrecognized truth: value is only created in the networks of relationships, conversations and commitments between people. The failure to look beyond the numbers to cultural and systemic factors goes a long way to explain the dismal record of value destruction in mergers and acquisitions across the globe. Carl's book is essential reading for executives, advisors and investors seeking sustainable value creation strategies.

Paul Sweeney, Managing Director, Berkeley Research Group (UK) Ltd, Berkeley Research Group (UK) Ltd, London UK

While advisors provide advice to their clients, Dr. Carl Sheeler, based on 2 decades of experience and research, targets the advisors so that they can better assist their clients. As a professional appraiser, I fully agree with Carl that GRRK is so important to see what's driving operational performance. I am sure appraisers and other advisors will be able to become trusted advisors and provide the advice that clients need to enhance the value of their businesses after reading this book.

Chengjun Wang, Phd, FRICS, ASA, FCPV, FCPA, Vice-Chairman, Senior Partner, Zhonghe Appraisal Co., Ltd., Beijing PRC

Dr. Sheeler's Equity Value Enhancement *should be a wakeup call for business owners, large corporations and the people who provide a wide range of services to these firms. Sheeler sheds light on the tangible and intangible drivers of business value. His perspective is valuable for both business owners and their advisors. His approach to explaining the many ways business value is misunderstood and miscalculated is insightful and important. He does an exemplary job of establishing a foundation of understanding about the tangible and intangible drivers of business value and then providing the "how-to" approach to accessing and optimizing the benefits of a strong advisory team. The book also clearly articulates the sources of value creation for advisors. For a diverse range of service provides, he trumpets the criticality of differentiating themselves by going beyond their technical expertise to offer valuable perspective and advice, founded on understanding, that can help owners enhance business value.* Equity Value Enhancement *offers vital insight and offers an indispensable learning tool for all business leaders and the professionals who service them.*

Carol E. Robbins, Executive Business Driver & Digitally Savvy Brand Builder

This isn't just another book to stick on the shelf - it is a tool to be utilized. Carl has taken complex concepts and transformed them into accessible, actionable recommendations. What Carl refers to as "technical myopia" costs business owner clients vast amounts of money each year, but it doesn't have to be that way. With the largest transition of generational wealth well under way, Carl's approach to Equity Value Enhancement *is a must read for advisors and business owner's alike.*

Allie Harding, Partner at Orange Kiwi, LLC & PlanforTransition.com

With Carl's book, you find that a basic feature of modern enterprises is the need to create effective intangible assets through unique approaches. As a

professor, I gleaned from this that a business school should help its students identify the intangibles that are not disclosed by a balance sheet. This book opens a new window and shows the reader how to judge the value of a business with innovative thoughts and methods that transcend the typical limitations of valuation analysis.

Haisu Wang, Professor and Director of Research Center of Business Value, Zhongnan University of Economics and Law, Wuhan PRC

Dr. Sheeler's book succeeds in impressing upon the appraisal and advisory community that risk identification and measurement need not be a commodity. The real opportunity lies in establishing a strategy and culture where owners and advisors align their activities to leverage their knowledge and relationships. The book's focus is on the necessity for the often overlooked risk management and mitigation roles. This separates the dabblers from the industry professionals and allows for more lucrative engagements while making a real difference for the owner and investors in both liquidity and legacy.

John K. Paglia, Ph.D., CFA, CPA, Associate Dean & Associate Professor of Finance, Pepperdine University Graziadio School of Business and Management, Los Angeles CA

Carl Sheeler moves past the limiting aspects of valuation analysis by creating the Governance, Relationships, Risks and Knowledge framework. GRRK gives advisors tools that leverage governance into culture, relationships into advisory boards, risks into opportunities, and knowledge into insight. Applying GRRK methods to valuations provides insights and opportunities that advisors should share with clients to grow their businesses, expand their influence within their markets, and grow professional networks that can be new sources of revenue. The business services industry is moving away from hourly rates towards value pricing. Consultants should use this book and elevate service offerings to become deeply trusted advisors who bill on their value and not on their time.

Vito Colombo, Principal, Trügli Consulting, Middle Village NY

Carl Sheeler's work is a fine contribution to the field of applied and practical economics, which at a certain basic level is to understand human behavior. It succeeds because he simply makes sense. This is no easy task, and it is no minor contribution. Sheeler's work is important to advisors and clients alike, as it reminds us to focus on adding value and managing risk in pursuit of excellence by focusing on the relationships and practices that increase the probability of desired and desirable outcomes. This is a book worth keeping off the shelf and on the nearby table to use as a practical guide and reminder of sustained best practices.

Richard Levine, Esq. and Adjunct Prof., Colorado School of Mines, Law and Economics, Evergreen CO

Most business owners believe their value comes from what appears on their financial statements – sales, gross profit, EBITDA or net income. However, all *acquirers buy the future, not the past, and the future is* always *driven by intangibles. In* Equity Value Enhancement, *Carl Sheeler creates a compelling argument for why and how business owners should use A-level advisors to identify and leverage their intangibles to maximize the value of their time, effort and investment.*

Timothy G. Malott, Partner, Shoreline Partners, LLC, President/CEO, ShP Securities, LLC

Equity Value Enhancement *is a must for any business school, private equity firm or investment banking firm worth its salt. Carl takes an esoteric subject, equity valuation, and makes it come alive, in all its facets–well beyond 'the transaction', and carves a path for those who would endeavor to become better at being strategic value architects. His lessons on understanding the differences between value, price, worth and risk are intellectually thought-provoking, motivating, engaging, full of wisdom and fact-based. Frankly, I wish I'd had his book in hand three years ago. An excellent and well-organized read that you'll take to the bank*

Lara Abrams, Managing Member, Lara Abrams Communications, LLC

Exceptional! I wish I had this information when setting up our generational investing plans. What Carl addresses goes beyond practical advice to encompass contrarian viewpoints that every advisor and family member should consider. Attention to focusing on the cost-benefit analysis of the provider-client relationship as a key metric is a valuable consideration too often ignored by those who select a provider based simply on a friend's recommendation. Reading this brought me to the realization that the way to analyze provider-client relationship is not simply by what is offered, but by the value of the provider as a knowledge base on how to preserve and grow equity, from someone with skin in the game, from the very beginning of the provider selection process throughout the length of the relationship.

Bill Townsend, Founder, Best Selling Author, Interminds, Pasadena CA

Over an almost 40 year career I have been an investment banker, an advisor to private equity firm management teams, a company director and an owner of small businesses. Mr. Sheeler's book expertly describes the way to optimize the effectiveness of professionals in each of these rolls (and several more!). I wish I could have read it 40 years ago. I could have avoided lots of on-the-job learning!

Kevin K. Albert, Managing Director, Pantheon Ventures, New York NY

Equity Value Enhancement

The Wiley Finance series contains books written specifically for finance and investment professionals as well as sophisticated individual investors and their financial advisors. Book topics range from portfolio management to e-commerce, risk management, financial engineering, valuation and financial instrument analysis, as well as much more. For a list of available titles, visit our Web site at www.WileyFinance.com.

Founded in 1807, John Wiley & Sons is the oldest independent publishing company in the United States. With offices in North America, Europe, Australia and Asia, Wiley is globally committed to developing and marketing print and electronic products and services for our customers' professional and personal knowledge and understanding.

Equity Value Enhancement

A Tool to Leverage Human and Financial Capital While Managing Risk

CARL L. SHEELER

WILEY

Published by John Wiley & Sons, Inc., Hoboken, New Jersey.

Published simultaneously in Canada.

For general information on our other products and services or for technical support, please contact our Customer Care Department within the United States at (800) 762-2974, outside the United States at (317) 572-3993 or fax (317) 572-4002.

Wiley publishes in a variety of print and electronic formats and by print-on-demand. Some material included with standard print versions of this book may not be included in e-books or in print-on-demand. If this book refers to media such as a CD or DVD that is not included in the version you purchased, you may download this material at http://booksupport.wiley.com. For more information about Wiley products, visit www.wiley.com.

Library of Congress Cataloging-in-Publication Data:

Names: Sheeler, Carl L., 1960–
Title: Equity value enhancement : a tool to leverage human and financial capital while managing risk / Carl L. Sheeler.
Description: New York : Wiley, 2015. | Series: Wiley finance | Includes index.
Identifiers: LCCN 2015035909| ISBN 9781118871003 (hardback) | ISBN 9781119092025 (ePDF) | ISBN 9781119091981 (ePub)
Subjects: LCSH: Human capital—Management. | Capital market. | Value investing. | Risk management.
Classification: LCC HD4904.7 .S4384 2015 | DDC 658.15/5—dc23 LC record available at http://lccn.loc.gov/2015035909

Cover Design: Wiley
Cover Images: Black and White Marbles © iStock.com/stayorgo;
Financial Chart © iStock.com/dblight

Printed in the United States of America

10 9 8 7 6 5 4 3 2 1

There are six heart-felt dedications: to my family, my extended military family, business owners/executives, trusted advisors, my team, and my editor.

My family: *My precious wife, Sara, is the right-brain Shaman who keeps my left brain centered. She's an artist and a blessing. We're not Ozzie & Harriet. We both have been remarried and have five kids between us. There's that love–hate continuum that undoubtedly is exacerbated by work–life imbalance. They mean the world to us both.*

My extended military family: *Both Sara and I served in the USMC and will always have a special kinship to those who have served and their families. A good portion of the net proceeds of this book will ensure that their sacrifice and they are not forgotten.*

Business owners/executives: *The business media and our elected officials often give little notice to these unsung heroes. They may not be Fortune 500 companies, but they brave the odds and are the backbone of the U.S. economy by mastering the management of concentrated risk. Every advantage should be afforded to these companies and their success. This book is for you. You understand values are more than numbers.*

Trusted advisors: *Business owners, heed my praise and admonition. These are top-flight folks whose knowledge and relationships far exceed what they're paid. There are concierge advisors who don't define themselves by their professional titles. Instead they leverage their knowledge and relationships to the advantage of their business clients and fellow advisors with whom they collaborate. They are connectors. They invest the time and resources to develop deep relationships, not solely more transactions. This is why I see myself as a steward, a chief-of-staff, and a "strategic value architect." Trusted advisors who embrace the "it takes a village" notion of collaboration, I dedicate this book to you.*

Kelly, Rafiq and Boxy: *I would not know which day it is, when and who to call, and where to go without your steady reminders. You are my magic ecosystem that frees up invaluable time and the best human capital I have* *had the privilege of knowing. May abundance befall you and yours. God bless.*

Adrienne Moch: *I've been at this for three decades and I am not always able to string the right words to my thoughts to ensure the best balance of communication and intent. If you love purple and Chicago and somebody who edits like no tomorrow, contact Adrienne.*

> *It is not the critic that counts; not the man who points out how a strong man stumbles, or when the doer of deeds could have done them better. The credit belongs to the man who is actually in the arena, whose face is marred by dust and sweat and blood; who strives valiantly; who errs, who comes short again and again, because there is no effort without error and shortcoming; but who does actually strive to do the deeds; who knows great enthusiasms, the great devotions; who spends himself in a worthy cause; who at best knows in the end the triumph of his achievement, and who at the worst, if he fails, at least fails while daring bravely, so that his place shall never be with those cold and timid souls who neither know victory or defeat.*
>
> —Theodore Roosevelt

On April 23, 1910, Theodore Roosevelt, the 26th President of the United States of America, gave this compelling speech in Paris, France. Its wisdom is as applicable today as then.

Contents

Foreword

I have known Carl for 20+ years from the first time he walked me not only to the door of his office, but to the elevator to the lobby and out to my car. I knew this was somebody with whom I would do business. He walks the talk. We've been referring top clients and advisors back and forth ever since.

Philosopher and Nobel Prize winner Albert Camus stated, "Real generosity towards the future lies in giving all to the present." Never before have words jumped off pages of a valuation and equity value creation book and impacted me the way Carl's book has. I'm not surprised. Valuation usually presents itself as an academic exercise, but it is in fact a tool that can change people's lives, and it's about time somebody said so.

The greatest risk of any wealthy individual's life is that they never achieve some significant measure of fulfillment while on this planet—as Carl references from "success to significance."

While success for a few might be defined as the amount of money or assets they accumulate during their lifetime, for most it is the less calculable metrics of having the time to do good in their communities. It is the way posterity will remember their family's name or legacy. Carl's book bridges this gap from this holistic "ecosystem" perspective to that of the families' "constituents"—most often thought of as their advisors and clients but, as he illustrates, much, much more.

The greatest risk for any professional advisor (I am referring to accountants, attorneys, bankers, and financial advisors), assuming they serve wealthy entrepreneurial individuals, families, and Family Offices, is that they will only contribute to wealth preservation by offering common product and services. They will seldom make any measurable contribution to the more hard-to-measure attributes for their wealthy clients (and for that matter, for themselves). Carl's book offers an alternative narrative where all achieve an aligned vision and share in the success.

I am a certified public accountant and my business office is physically located within a multi-family office. Here, we primarily serve two ultra-wealthy families, originating from two brothers and their spouses. They had 6 children who in turn have had 19 children, making us a third-generation family.

While I am a CPA, I do not prepare income tax returns or financial statements, which are the two services most typically associated with being a CPA. I do indeed review income tax returns prepared by other CPAs on our families' behalf, and sometimes also work in other technical areas, such as income tax controversy representation and estate and gift tax planning and reviewing legal documents.

For the most part, I assist my families with matters that might be described as nontechnical, which are typically not associated with being a CPA. I have been serving these families for almost 25 years. I call what I do "family governance."

But as Carl points out, I leverage my knowledge and relationships. This translates into differentiation and a higher level of services, superior clients, and more revenue.

I have known Carl on a professional and personal basis. His grasp of families' governance issues—a charter, its strategy and execution, as well as its value measurement and management—is rarely matched. Family governance means I am available to Family Office employees and owners and members (patriarch, CEO, CFO, etc.), to family members who are not actively participating in the Family Office's operations, and to all of the professional advisors that serve the Family Office and all of its individual stakeholders.

Carl's and my main focus is to remain central to (*consigliere*) all of these associated relationships, so that an open and transparent platform exists. Our main goals here are:

1. Make sure that all of the work that we do is consistent with the families' value and mission statements and culture.
2. Provide all stakeholders (*constituents*) an easy-to-access resource to ask questions and discuss ideas. Help them find and leverage resources they want and, in essence, help in any way we can.
3. Save the valuable time of key personnel in the Family Office or family business who do not want to ask 10 different professional advisors the same question.
4. Look at all of the risks associated with the business decisions we make, with an "outside view" so that we do not have bad surprises.

Also, and not solely associated with my own Family Office services, we counsel CPAs, attorneys, bankers, insurers, and wealth advisors. My focus for wealth advisors is to help them to make the CPAs they interact with heroes to the CPAs' very best clients. This is a different business model than what most wealth advisors use: Most try to reach end-users (aka customers or clients) directly and not through CPAs.

And for CPAs and attorneys, we assist them in becoming the Most Trusted Business Advisor to their very best business and real estate owning clients. This, too, is a different business model than that used by most. Like many advisors, they have a lot of clients, most of which are not of an "A" variety but rather are of "B" and "C" variety, and they focus on doing large volumes of compliance/regulatory work. This is a model for mediocrity.

Carl led a countywide initiative during and after the financial crisis called Strategic Trusted Advisors Roundtable (STAR). STAR addressed these professional deficiencies that culminated in a higher level of connecting of professionals in order that they might provide a more integrated, holistic, and economically more efficient and effective model of doing good for business clients and fellow professionals.

It also succeeded in enhancing the depth and breadth of each member's service offerings, resulting in higher billings and client caliber. It focuses on deeper relationships versus solely technical knowledge and transactions. I remain a board member and cross the bridge to bring broader perspectives than those limited to business alone.

When I present in public, which I do frequently, many CPAs, attorneys, and wealth advisors tell me that they would like to work with Family Offices. I like to point out, in response, that Family Offices exist, at least in part, because the traditional service models used by CPAs, attorneys, and wealth advisors rarely offer enough value to wealthy families and individuals. Thus, as Carl knows, inadequate value is one reason wealthy families create their own Family Office by taking these functions in-house.

Carl Sheeler is this country's most forward-looking valuation and strategic advisory expert. I dubbed him a "strategic value architect"—a fitting moniker. He gives us a choice: "Do good work for your clients, by only focusing on what they want; or, make a significant contribution to improving your clients' lives by helping them with what they truly need. The choice is ours." Until then, and after, it is all GRRK™ to me!

Richard Muscio, CPA, is The Family Office Guy. He is best-selling author of *So, What's Your Play? How Billie Jean, Bobby and Blindness Begat Tolerance*. Richard is a co-host of the "It's Your Money and Your Life" radio show, voted Best Radio Series in San Diego by the San Diego Press Club for 2013 and 2014.

Preface

An investment banker introduced me to her attorney friend who had a client whose trust held shares in a 10-figure annual sales distributor. Most of the equity was derived from her mother's passing. Her mother's brother (her uncle) controlled both the company and her trust. Her uncle retained a national appraisal firm to substantiate an unusually low value both for estate tax purposes and to use the value to negotiate a buyout of her brother's and her shares. Both she and her brother, who had his own counsel, felt they were being slighted. They alleged their uncle was underreporting company performance and assets held. They alleged he had breached his fiduciary duty. They were worried about a drawn-out and costly confrontation with their uncle.

They just wanted what was bequeathed to them. This was a six-figure retention, which would balloon to a seven-figure engagement, which would allow me to acquire a dream ranch that offered equine therapy for both veterans and a retreat for business owners as well as well as solitude for my wife to do her art.

This book starts with this story because it sums up nicely how to distinguish between a "check-the-box" analyst who is evaluated by hourly rates and the expert who understands the premium placed upon wisdom and mastery that solves irretraceable problems. Think of Showtimes' Ray Donovan (Liev Schreiber) as a "fixer" of messes (without the gun).

Compare this with a recent communication with an attorney who had expressed on a listserv she felt the four-figure fee for an appraisal was too high after researching appraisal firms on the Internet. The rationale was the client would "know" the right amount because he would accept the buyer's offer. Why spend the money? Counsel was certain she understood fair market value.

I tried to dissuade her from her premise by using the following example: "If the seller was first offered $100,000, but held out and received $200,000, is this the value of the asset?" It may be what it is worth to the seller, but that is not necessarily the value of the asset. The buyer may have more experience and knows the asset is worth $1,000,000. The buyer would have been willing to pay as much as $800,000. So, the "price" differential of $600,000 ($800,000 – $200,000) was money left on the table. And, if the seller had found out? A flawed premise is a transaction between two parties establishes arm's-length value. The analyst is usually retained to identify value, assuming a reasonable exposure and marketing period with knowledge and access to capital under no duress. The notional investors are typically assumed to be a pool of transactions examining both the buy and sell motivations so intrinsic or synergistic value is isolated.

I used another example: "If legal services fees came to $10,000 and the dispute was over property found to be worth $10,000, would the client have overpaid for the services? Conversely, if the fee was $10,000 and the benefit of the dispute was $1,000,000, has the client underpaid?" The point is there is a difference between value, price, cost, and worth.

The examples illustrate that an hourly rate alone only meets the threshold of cost for services, where the value received may not be understood or appreciated by clients. They may commoditize services and will be resistant to fees if nothing above common knowledge is received. The advisor has a duty to articulate the value provided and not solely the price. Otherwise, the advisor is just as likely to minimize fees for services, making no distinction between good and great services.

The optics of the previous examples is understandable because professional services deliver human capital intangibles. What does good look like? This has long been the case for business valuation services. It is in large part why writing this book was important not only to my practice but to all professions and those who retain our knowledge and relationships.

The valuation community is still evolving. Some professionals and their entrepreneurial clients understand the merits of a well-crafted appraisal report with the associated intellectual rigor and research. I salute those who do and who are willing to pay a premium for quality work. This reinforces competence over commoditization.

For the reader who is an appraiser, she or he may be perfectly happy performing more routine work product. For the balance, I shall demonstrate there is more than simply identifying and measuring risk to benchmark business and equity values.

There is a greater calling to provide equity value enhancement (EVE). This is the premise of risk management and opportunity optimization, and the elevated ability to master disputes where risk is mitigated by both measuring the impact of risks existence and then to assist in their minimization or elimination. This is common in matters of alleged value impairment ("damages" and "discounts").

Our audience is the founders, families, boards, and C-suite of private mid-market through small-cap public companies, private equity, investors, and their trusted advisors. Our goal is to articulate how *governance*, *relationships*, *risks*, and *knowledge* (GRRK) allows the reader to become a *strategic value architect* and a chief-of-staff who not only measures but can manage, facilitate, create, and maximize company intangible assets value through the leverage and alignment of human and financial capital. Only then is real value created above the assemblage of tangible assets.

Why GRRK? Successful businesses and entrepreneurial families often see their concentrated wealth as part of an ecosystem of family members, staff, client, vendor, and advisor "constituents." They do more than consider revenues and profits. They focus on the family's future expectations and harness a culture that goes beyond daily challenges. It's when they are bogged down by the more familiar, yet less productive daily blocking and tackling, that they plateau and often seek to minimize advisory expenditures versus seeking to leverage the advisor's time and talent investment. Protecting their asset becomes defensive versus embracing innovation and remaining on the offensive where reducing risk provides more time and resources to sense and seize opportunity for value growth.

Supersized, stellar growth occurs because these unique executives, founders/families, advisors, and involved constituents foster value creation by harnessing their collective *uncommon* knowledge and relationships (human capital). This is why those who harness the role of steward, chief-of-staff, and/or strategic value architect thrive, not just survive. Since value creation is dynamic, advisors who align with others are most likely to assist in achieving it.

Expressed differently, the wealthy often get richer not solely from hard work and competent concentrated risk management. They access unique opportunities often unknown to others. It affirms the notion of not only what *you* know, but whom you know and what *they* know. This is why "connectors" are much different than one-off isolated advisors

Steward-leaders have a culture and a strategy that assures success. Success is more than wealth. It is earned significance and respect. So, we have to assist in answering, "How are you getting from here to there?" We then identify resource gaps that may derail progress. If we assist in growth and transition, we have a seat at their table—one that is on the same side as the decision makers sit. We ask tough questions and find independent solutions and options. As important, we just don't have a strategic plan. We have a plan that's executed!

Knowledge and resource gaps occur. Sometimes there is a "bubble" or "silo" around and/or between each constituency. This serves to stifle innovation, growth, and profitability while failing to leverage opportunities or mitigate concentrated risk. This becomes evident when thinking is solely tactical and technical. Such thinking is often transactional and commoditized. It contributes to stagnation versus enduring proactive, strategic, and holistic planning that fosters growth.

As I wrote this book, there were significant market forces in play such as changes in capital availability and increased volatility of marketable securities that define in part how risk is measured. These factors do not impede twenty-first century innovations like the cloud or artificial intelligence, biotech, and other advances.

In each case, *risk* and its alter-ego *opportunity* are the cornerstones of how ideas and companies are valued. The difference is many wealthy families are pursuing direct investment with "patient" capital and vying with private equity groups for companies in which former may hold for decades, not just years. This is in part a reaction to the public company share price volatility that is less about company-specific risk and more on the speed and frequency of institutional trades.

To better understand the intellectual rigor to have enterprises and equities properly valued with risks identified that impact price multiples, we must have a certain degree of mastery of how value is created. This book goes to the heart of whether there is an over reliance on simply revenues and profits as well as financial ratios as current measures of company-specific risk. If so, we change the valuation industry discussion from measurement to active management roles needed by fellow advisors and business owners.

Who am I to ask and seek answers to such questions? I see myself less as a business valuation professional and more as a concierge and connector. The latter two allow me to be a strategic value architect and/or a chief-of-staff, as these attributes permit me to harness and align others' knowledge and relationships. (I don't need to be the smartest person in the room; I just need to know where she or he can be found.)

Before we delve into the issues that were the genesis for this book, here is a brief background of why I may be qualified to share my thoughts. During the past 25+ years, I've been engaged in valuing 1,200+ 7- to 10-figure public and private companies in myriad industries for clients ranging from professionals to private equity for what I refer to as the *6Ts*: tax, transfer, transaction, transition, transformation, and trouble (disruption) purposes.

I refer to these matters as either planned or unplanned events. Unplanned are disruptive. I have been a court/IRS-qualified expert on 170+ occasions for tax, partner, shareholder, and third-party disputes and damages matters. During this period, I have been asked to assist hundreds of advisors, family offices/businesses, ESOPs, private equity groups, UHNW investors and public and private businesses to measure, create, manage, and/or defend $50+ billion in company values and counting.

After all this, I'm left with one humbling and overwhelming conclusion about business- and real estate–owning entrepreneurs as well as the trusted advisors who counsel them: We all don't know what we don't know. That may initially seem a bit simplistic, but there's quite a bit of depth behind it—which is the reason for this book.

This book endeavors to address why ultra-high-net-worth ($25+ million) entrepreneurs are able to continue to attain greater wealth through concentrated risk and why both private and public companies and their advisors who focus on more than financial statement measures may have better success. *After all how do you measure persistance?*

Spoiler alert! The UHNW have access to more and better uncommon knowledge. This knowledge truly is power. It is certainly true when it comes to valuation and, specifically, value creation.

SOME SOBERING REALITIES

From the fledging entrepreneur to the seasoned corner-office executive of a global company, growth decisions are made based on "build versus buy." *Build* is organic growth, and *buy* is through merger and acquisition. It comes down to the risks and rewards of the time value of money.

No one chooses to start or acquire a business because they want to fail. Yet, the odds are stacked against even the most capable, regardless of which business path followed. Those who acquire must have adequate understanding of their capital needs (both human and financial) and their optimal utilization. Those who opt to go the angel investor/venture capital–backed route suffer a failure rate north of 90 percent. They often give up equity to their investors and set their sights on achieving hyper-growth as a result of their innovation.

However, those who choose the bootstrapping or "family and friends" funding route face a slightly better but still dismal failure rate near 80 percent within two to five years. They retain their equity, believing their idea will blossom into a sustainable business.

Small businesses ($5 million and lower revenues) have only a 25 percent chance of selling. Larger businesses that are acquired fail to achieve the synergies sought over 80 percent of the time, creating seller's and buyer's remorse. And, within three generations, many family businesses usually cease to exist or have been sold at least 85 percent of the time. Advisors are either part of the solution or observers to these preventable, sobering statistics.

Why do entrepreneurs still pursue the brass ring given these abysmal statistics? They're usually spurred on by the businesses that do succeed—something I call *selection bias* (ignoring the preponderance that fail). Or, they are either unaware of or oblivious to the high potential of failure—something I refer to as *Economic Darwinism.* They believe in themselves and their idea, ignoring all potential naysayers. Their demise is often failing to plan, which is a plan to fail.

What does this have to do with value creation? It should be obvious: Those who have achieved significant value are exceptional in the manner in which their investment is measured and managed. Those who overlook these critically important metrics and actions are more apt to fail.

IMPROVING THE ODDS

It truly does take a village (*ecosystem*) to build and maintain a successful enterprise, whether an operational business or a portfolio of income-producing real estate. The endgame for most is leqacy and liquidity: that is, to sell or transfer part or all of their equity. Most investors in public companies buy and hold stock looking for capital appreciation (growth) and secondarily yield (income).

Ironically, most private company owners/executives do not know the market value of their companies, nor do their advisors. They have to think more like investors in their companies. Building value is an ongoing process of equity value enhancement, not simply managing sales and profits because they're easier to identify.

Savvy business owners will seek advisors who can best help them create value. Other owners will be complacent, accepting familiar over greater capability. Therefore, advisors have a critical responsibility to leverage governance, relationships, risk, and knowledge (GRRK) in client equity value enhancement (EVE). And business owners can foster success based on the advisors they select to counsel them.

As an example, it's important to seek professionals who are able to discern between economics, accounting, and finance backgrounds for a valuation expert. Each background differs, with financial expertise being more than merely generating or reporting numbers. These professionals must understand what produces results and reduces operational risk while elevating intangible value and what causes equity impairments. Arguably, the ideal valuation expert ought to possess a blend of strategy, operations, finance, and human behavior knowledge.

Further, there is a great difference between risks *to* an asset and risks *within* an asset. The prior is often tabled as asset-protection or preservation activity and the latter deals with risks inherent to the asset, its market, and its management.

These considerations would be inherent in any value creation plan. Focus on advisors who are proactive. (Most are reactive.) You may find it eye-opening to ask existing and potential advisors how they differentiate themselves. If you can swap their name or that of their firm with another name, they may not be adequately differentiating the influence of their knowledge and relationships to serve clients.

The ultimate holistic advisory team is likely to focus on elements of governance, relationship, risk and knowledge management and maintenance as a way to create value by leveraging intangible assets. It's not simply a financial capital game. It's a human capital one, too. It's about seeing what's driving operational performance. *Values are more than numbers!*

These are things an accountant, attorney, wealth advisor, insurance professional, or banker individually may not know—and may be unlikely to ask—so that's why a diverse advisory team is optimal. The ultimate advisory team is one that helps a company play an "A" game versus one that benefits from a company client that is playing their "A" game—a symbiotic versus a parasitic relationship.

THE OPPORTUNITY IS THERE

Many privately-held businesses were started by Baby Boomers who were contemplating some exit in the mid-2000s. Then, from 2007 to 2012, we saw the Economic Darwinism: Businesses that underperformed were swept out of the market.

Those that survived picked up the remnants of competitors, as fiat capital (U.S. denominated dollars printed and electronically infused through treasury bond sales keeping the market moving through "Quantitative Easing"). Some thrived. These owners now find themselves looking beyond today's operational realities and starting to conceive a strategy that may include the sale of part or 100 percent of their equity.

The best-case scenario is a sale prepared for and at price/terms that makes the equity attractive to sell and able to produce the net proceeds an investor seeks. Rare, but it happens.

This is where my lament "they don't know what they don't know" is derived. Business owners can be blindsided by issues they or their advisors never saw coming like hyper-inflation from too much quantitative easing or an all-out regional war in the Middle East or the impact of oil or water shortages on their business. I have intentionally designed this book to demonstrate that no single perspective is adequate to create and sustain concentrated wealth.

While there are several underlying issues, the theme focuses on unmet critical needs in the professional advisory communities and in multi-generational entrepreneurial families. These knowledge and resource gaps often dilute rather than create value.

This is exacerbated by transactional, technical, and tactical thinking and language that compounds the disconnect between the advised and the well-meaning advisor. Most advisors favor preserving wealth through legal, tax, financial, and allocation strategies. They use terms like *optimize*. This is an example of doing things right versus doing the right things. Think of the absolutely perfectly dug hole in circumference and depth. Now, what if that perfect hole was unnecessary or in the wrong place?

Exceptional entrepreneurial families have overcome the odds associated with concentrated risk and wealth. Yet, most businesses started without a plan, or the plan is sell more and make a profit.

It stands to reason, they're as unlikely to have a plan when contemplating one of the 6T's. Meanwhile, right now the largest degree of wealth is transferring from the Baby Boomer generation, with the youngest reaching age 50 in 2014.

While families with modest wealth or revenues are not excluded from consideration, the book's focus is on what families have been able or wish to achieve by leveraging their trusted advisors' abilities to scale their company revenues and wealth to $25 million or more.

Governance (issues of culture, codification, and control), relationships (family, business, staff, and advisory), risk (what operational, legal and financial factors are overlooked), and knowledge (internal, external, uncommon, IP, policy/procedure, and human capital) are integral.

The book's eleven chapters illustrates that the letters and concepts of GRRK are interconnected. In the aggregate, their influence dramatically changes pricing multiples and economic benefit, proving that value creation is dynamic.

In **Chapter** 1, we provide some basics about what value is, as a way to lay the groundwork for the information that follows.

In **Chapter** 2, we explore fundamental trusted advisor relationships overlaid with the notion of concentrated risk and the owners who possess these unique esoteric assets. We provide distinct win-win reasons to operate within a purposeful and collaborative framework of relationships and connections that offers unique value beyond technical know-how.

In **Chapter** 3, we speak to business owners, providing them food for thought to assess whether they are working *in* or *on* their concentrated risk (their business), and challenging them to leverage all the resources they have to understand and to build value.

In **Chapter** 4, we address the traditional ways various professionals measure risks through their lenses, beginning with a brief list that's common to their perspectives. This provides evidence of the benefit of involving multiple disciplines and their alignment to ensure the big picture can evolve.

In **Chapter** 5, we focus on the role of governance: what it is, the role culture plays, and a healthy approach to measure, manage, and maximize governance's influence on value.

In **Chapter** 6, we focus on the role of relationships, assessing the various stakeholders, why they are deeply important, and how they can evolve in healthy ways that can lead to value creation.

In **Chapter** 7, we define and discuss the role of legal and financial risks, which are more readily found due to the financial metrics: a "warm-up" for the following chapter. Please remember, the lower the risks, the higher the price multiple; and the higher the price multiple, the greater the value.

In **Chapter** 8, we identify many less easily measured operational risks that also influence human and financial capital.

In **Chapter** 9, we address the role of knowledge, reflecting on how this human capital intangible provides considerable power that can be leveraged when better understood and harnessed.

In **Chapter** 10, we focus on the business appraiser, providing insight into how the importance of this profession is often overlooked and giving tips on what to look for in a seasoned valuator.

In **Chapter** 11, we provide four vignettes to tie together many of the insights and concepts shared within this book.

There will always be those who want the knowledge nuggets from a 30,000-foot view. While we encourage reading this book cover to cover, that may just be my own wishful sentiment. While not all inclusive, here are some of the top take-aways to consider and apply.

Observations

- Book value is seldom a guide to business value. The latter is dynamic and uncertain.
- Businesses are all their assets—tangible and intangible. They both have life cycles.
- The assets hidden below the financial statements often drive equity value.
- Governance, relationships, and knowledge are assets, not line items. They impact risk.
- How a company tracks and measures its assets influences whether value will be created.
- The higher the ratio of sales to fixed assets, the greater the likely value of these assets.
- Value creation occurs when both tangible and intangible assets are well managed.
- Relationships, knowledge, innovation, and culture (governance/strategy) drive growth.

- Risk and opportunity decisions often differ between entrepreneurs and their advisors.
- Risk management must consider internal and external variables in the context of an ecosystem.
- The ecosystem includes constituents whose ideas, insights, and actions must have alignment to be impactful.
- Leadership is not administration. Leaders inspire uncommon knowledge and actions.
- To differentiate a business must be dynamic. It senses, seizes, transforms, and scales. This is achieved through leveraged human capital.
- Optimal levels of employee retention and decision making are indicators of higher values.
- Most businesses and advisors focus on revenues, profits, and taxes—not risk and innovation. One deals with yield and the other capital appreciation.
- Effective leaders integrate risk management and strategy resulting in value creation.
- Navigating risk well reduces obstacles, saves time, and increases opportunities—a huge differentiator.
- Tools and language can provide transparency and clarity. It's what we all want.
- Value can be extracted from and/or offered to others beyond technical know-how.
- Value creation occurs with a strategy that is executed to rethink and recombine all assets.

Questions for Consideration

- What is the company's free cash flow? Is revenue/profit more important than value?
- What is the company's return on equity/assets/invested capital and what changes can have the greatest impact on value?
- How will strategy be communicated, executed, and governed to achieve scalability (growth)?
- What assets and measures are relied upon to weigh risk/opportunity and value?
- What is the articulated and aligned strategy of founders, families, and their advisors?
- What is the vision of the this ecosystem and its constituents?
- What are the resources needed to get from here to there? What are the gaps?
- How will differentiation and measurement be used to leverage assets?

- How will success, wealth, and risk be defined and by who (spiritual, emotional, intellectual)?
- What are the top three issues and how will decisions be made and guidance be sought and offered?
- How can founder, family, and advisors be proactive in a dynamic/uncertain environment?
- Where are the governance, relationship, risk, and knowledge gaps?
- Why is optimal debt to equity mix so relevant?
- What are critical decisions for better planned and unplanned transition event outcomes?
- Which is more important: the strategy or the ability to execute it? Why?
- Where is there clarity and transparency? Where is there not? Why?
- How is legacy and vision established and communicated? What are the disruptions?
- What are the liquidity options and needs? What and who influences these decisions?
- How do founder, family, and advisors see capital (human versus financial)?
- Is leverage achieved from governance, relationships, and knowledge?
- Sharing this journey differentiates you from the 90 percent who simply are part of the herd, choosing to remain with the familiar. There are abundant opportunities out there to create concentrated wealth—as long as value creation is GRRK to you. Read on.

Acknowledgments

After I finished my doctoral dissertation on private capital illiquidity over a decade ago, I thought I'd be done. I have since gone on to be a prolific writer, presenter, and panelist. However, my words would be meaningless without those numerous valuation legends and investment bankers upon whose shoulders I stand and whom I may join.

My bread-and-butter work primarily has been from the legal community, whether it is a trust and estate or transaction matter or some business dispute. It has morphed into more risk management and mitigation advisory services dealing with the 6Ts, where strategy, facilitation, operational savvy, communication, and stewardship skills all have application. I am indebted to these professionals who make the work interesting and are often underappreciated for their ability to shift risk and assist clients in making better decisions.

Often hailed as the most trusted advisor to business owners are accountants who have accepted my work and me despite my not being a CPA. Rather, I have been honored to train more than a thousand such professionals to perform client-taxpayer valuation work or represent the position of the IRS on matters of business enterprise and equity values and discounts. I am grateful for the many, many CPAs who have trusted me with their affluent business owners, C-suite clients, and their families' issues in 6T engagements.

Recognitions are deserved for the many bankers, trust officers, wealth-insurance professionals, private equity groups, family business advisors, family offices, family businesses, and private and public companies' founders/families, owners, and executives. I'm humbled by your trust and commerce, which has served my passions. You put a roof over my family's head. You gave me the voice to share how your interests can best be served and how together we can leverage both human and financial capital to create new value.

Finally, to Keith Hald. Keith was 75 years old when I hired him as a real estate appraiser and then secondarily as a personal property appraiser. He was well into his late 80s when he "retired". Keith passed in August 2015.

He was a WWII veteran survived by a loving wife, Betty, and two adult children. From the bread basket of the United States, Keith was as reliable as a watch and inspired me by example that honest hard work, a good heart, and the love of a good woman are often all the abundance you need.

Thank you all!

About the Author

By no means a natural athlete (or a Mensa member), Carl's journey has been as much the path of a weightlifter as it has been marathoner literally and figuratively. He has taken his successes and failures (both personal and business) in stride and fashioned a lump of coal into diamond-like brilliance. He brings character, color, and clarity to a profession in need of doers and thinkers, not tinkerers.

Combine a doctoral focus in entrepreneurial finance with a veteran USMC combat officer/strategist and corporate operational audit professional and you produce a dynamic valuation advisor who is as much a litigation support (warrior) expert in governance, business, partnership, class, tax, and fiduciary duty disputes/damages as he is a statesman and spokesman for advanced valuation, strategy, and advisory services addressing both private and public company equity and operational risk issues. In short, he is a ***strategic value architect.***

For 25+ years, Carl has performed and reviewed thousands of valuation reports, operating agreements, financial documents, business plans, corporate records, and industry and market data reports as part of the intellectual rigor he applies to each of his engagements. While a formidable IRS and court qualified expert witness with 170+ matters under his anodized brass belt, his passion lies in the elevation of the valuation industry and company values themselves. His contribution is felt with 300+ presentations and authoritative treatises addressing enterprise and equity value and discounting issues as well as his due diligence associated with identifying, measuring, managing, and mitigating concentrated risk.

He is a board member, a certified valuation analyst (CVA), and an Instructor of Great Distinction as recognized by the National Association of Certified Valuators and Analysts (NACVA). He is also a board member and a certified business appraiser (CBA) certified by the Institute of Business Appraisers (IBA) as well as an accredited senior appraiser (ASA) certified by the American Society of Appraisers. He is an active board and/or committee member of for-profit and nonprofit organizations.

While industry agnostic, Carl's knack is unique in identifying and quantifying operational risks associated with intangible assets, such as human capital areas of governance, relationships, risks, and knowledge (GRRK), the premise of this book. More importantly, he is a connector and concierge, where possessing the humility to recommend the right advice by the right person in the right way holds the greatest impact.

Whereas most valuation work product applies a somewhat check-the-box, cookbook recipe approach, Carl is a master chef (more of a meat-and-potatoes guy) who understands and can address why a certain risk factor/value driver exists and what their impact is to the finished dish (valuation work product result).

While the profession is often limited by abiding to more of a technical and transactional mindset, Carl has challenged the profession specifically and the business community generally by raising what seems like simple questions:

> *If we are purported to know what relevant factors influence company specific risk and their influence on value measurement and management, then why are we satisfied with the notion of the lowest fee for service is better? If a physician could tell you when and why you'll have a heart attack and also provide a real fix such that its occurrence would be slim to none, what would that be worth? Given that for most owners the largest asset families will have is the blood, sweat, and tears of a business and equity interest therein, then what are we doing to guarantee this most rare asset remains healthy and there's a strategy to ensure its value is enhanced, not simply preserved? Isn't preservation synonymous with defensive as well as the illusion of control and safety? If so, how, in a dynamic market, fueled by uncertainty, is the value of advisory services and equity enhanced and what is the economic impact when we don't consider and act on these factors?*

Truth be told, I would be happier than a pig in a poke if I spent my remaining days working with families, founders, owners, boards, C-suites, and their advisors turning 8-figure companies into 9- and 10-figure companies and the balance of my time on a ranch surrounded by trees, pastures, and lots of animals.

Perhaps like the Showtime character, Ray Donovan – I'd be a "fixer" of affluent family businesses and small cap public companies adorned with jeans and a plaid shirt saying "Pay what you think I'm worth. But remember, this here ranch is a retreat for both wayward business folks and military veterans looking to find solace. One of you can afford the retreat and the other cannot."

This book offers sometimes subtle and other times not so much guidance that those who are unwilling to think out of the box are doomed to remain in the box. Familiar has its merits, but the fact remains time is not static, so change is inevitable. Lead the change.

If you didn't get value from this book, return it in new condition in 60 days with the receipt; the full purchase price will be refunded, no questions asked. If it has value, please feel free to share. All proceeds received by the author will go to a 501(c)3 which will benefit veterans with combat PTSD through the use of equine and canine therapy.

And if you need a value opinion, GRRK or EVE advisory services, please contact at: carl@carlsheeler.com I'll reply when I'm unchained from my desk.

Author's Vision and Challenge

"Values are more than numbers."

The above statement would at first glance be seen in the context of finance; however, a significant opportunity and challenge exists. Owners' and advisors' human values are just as relevant, if not more so. Both constituencies seek better ways to get from *here* to *there*.

This may be referred to as achieving liquidity to legacy, or success to significance. But where is guidance on the nonfinancial? This higher purpose, or *self-actualization* for Maslow's Hierarchy of Needs fans, is dear to the author. Mid-market business owners are a rare breed who dare to be great. They are the innovation and employment engine for the U.S. economy. They are the unheralded heroes who are seldom recognized in college corporate finance classes or Wall Street media. What to do when they transition from daily blocking and tackling to more time to do what they want?

This book reflects two passions of the author: (1) provide guidance to owners and advisors to leverage human and financial capital while managing risk, and (2) provide respite for those who have served in our U.S. Armed Services—our brothers and sisters in arms. (My wife and I are both U.S. Marine veterans.)

The stats are staggering. Up to 20 percent of those with military service, many who have been on five or more deployments, suffer from combat post-traumatic stress disorder (PTSD). PTSD is not an affliction for which a prescription drug is the simple answer. The operative word is *trauma* and healing can take years. The rate of unemployment, substance abuse, and homelessness is higher for those who have served. Supporting our troops is as important in peacetime as it is when they're deployed, with over 2,000,000 having served in Iraq and Afghanistan since 9/11. Every affected veteran, with care and treatment, can be the human capital that is so elemental to this book.

All proceeds received by the author will go to a 501(c)3. The 501(c)3 will operate at the Two Bears Ranch (see websites at www.dosososranch.org or www.twobearsranch.com) in Colorado, which will be home to rehabilitated dogs and horses. Veterans in the program will benefit from equine and canine therapy. Both the animals and their military care providers will heal and prosper. In addition, residents will have the opportunity to plant and eat from organic gardens, as well as learn business and life skills for transition back to society. The 501(c)3 will be funded by donations, grants, and ranch operations. Ranch revenues will be from equestrian and pet boarding/training, executive and spiritual retreats; and several home sites with acreage will be available for sale. Crowd funding will also be sourced.

If you order this book directly from me at www.carlsheeler.com, you may pay whatever you wish, to include making a tax-deductible donation. If you choose to purchase the book directly from Wiley Finance or from a retailer, consider supporting this cause or visiting the ranch you helped build.

CHAPTER 1

Value ABCs

Yet, knowing how to get there—to create value—still is not common knowledge. The goals of trusted advisors should include helping clients build and create value by ensuring they're aware of how to enhance their intangible assets' value and the options to do so. Advisors must also recognize owners have limited time to shepherd growth, so having a plan is insufficient. Having resources to execute the plan is what's needed. Successful business owners and their advisors already know it's not simply selling more services and products profitably.

Let's be clear from the beginning. Tracking revenue growth and profitability oversimplifies the complexity of an operating business. Doing so fails to examine the influence of invested capital. Invested capital examines both the use and optimization of a company's assets and liabilities (debt and its leverage as well as its risk sharing attributes). Here is a simple example: If a company has reasonable growth and profitability, it does not necessarily follow that it has performed its cash, accounts receivable, or inventory management well. It also follows that if these tangible assets have not been adequately considered, then what about the intangible assets such as human capital (i.e., governance, relationships, and knowledge) where such attributes are not found on a financial statement, but clearly have a significant impact on performance and value?

It stands to reason that most company founders understandably confuse their roles as owner-investors, officers, and employees of their companies. They may not have had the benefit of more rigorous financial training. However, what is the excuse of business advisors of all kinds who have a fiduciary duty that is greater than selling a service or product. For example, how does an owner allocate assets if she or he doesn't have a full understanding of the risks and value of one of their largest assets—the company? How does financial reporting for tax purposes help create more intangible value? How do rates and terms alone impact the overall business in order to be more competitive in its marketplace?

Value is more than a number. The previous paragraphs ought to give pause. If value were as simple as affixing a number based on a universally accepted formula, there'd never be any disagreements between owners and the IRS, between buyers and sellers, and between any other interested parties. This is especially true for private and thinly traded public companies. The most common way to determine value is by gauging the rate of risk (return) associated with an asset's ability to generate free cash flow—and that leaves room for a lot of gray area (whose idea of risk? what period and duration of time?).

Arguably, that is where intellectual rigor and due diligence that looks beyond financial statements and forecasts is required. Mastering operational risk identification, measurement (*benchmarking*), and management are musts.

In *Driving Your Company's Value: Strategic Benchmarking for Value*, Michael J. Mard expresses, "Management must understand that a focus on value creation is a holistic endeavor that is constantly and consistently applied."[1]

Return on invested capital (ROIC) and strengths, weaknesses, opportunities, and threats (SWOT) analysis as well as associated due diligence are important considerations of value building and creation. Such analyses can and should provide benchmarks including soft and hard measures (human and financial capital). An example of a soft measure would be employee morale. A hard measure might be annual staff turnover. Common performance metrics are:

- Linked to strategy
- Clearly defined
- Understandable
- Easily measured
- Few in number
- Reported regularly
- Consistent follow-through
- Openly shared
- Predictive in nature
- Developed by everyone
- Team or unit based
- Tested against behavioral outcomes
- Assessed and modified regularly
- Linked to compensation

So, a value is determined by establishing economic benefit, such as profit, net income, EBITDA, or cash flow. That's the numerator. Let's say it's $10 million. The remaining variables are growth and *risk* or the denominator stated as a percentage.

If the risk measurement was opined to be 25 percent (expected investor return), then the equation would be $10 million/.25 or $40 million in value. The lower the risk, the higher the value.

So, let's apply 20 percent instead of 25 percent to prove this point, of lower risk. The value would be $50 million or $10 million/.20. Stated another way, using 25 percent is the same thing as applying a price multiple of 4× or four times. Using 20 percent is the same as applying 5×.

So, while seemingly straightforward, the tough part is "What is the risk (multiple)?" This issue is at the heart of what drives investor expectations and the difference between skilled research and analytics versus an otherwise expensive, unsupported result. Thus, the lower fee for services does not matter if the value is incorrect or unsupported.

Behavioral finance does play a role in the valuation process. It's more difficult to discern value in private companies, where data is not as easy to come by compared to their public company counterparts. At the center of it all, does the company's upside investment potential outweigh its perceived level of risk?

Therein lies the Achilles' heel of valuation: making assumptions of risk and future economic benefit. It behooves anyone with a stake to ensure adequate empirical factors are considered. This means that while legal and financial issues are relevant, operational and human capital issues are often overlooked and inadequately portrayed—and that omission can significantly impact value.

Keep in mind there are assets that are seen and reported. These are tangible assets. What a business appraiser is most often retained to opine is the unseen or *intangible* asset values. A successful business has an ever increasing part of its value associated with intangible assets, such as, but not limited to, *goodwill*.

A simple illustration is the comparison of public companies Wells Fargo Bank and Bank of America six-plus years after the Great Recession of 2009. The reported price to book value (P/BV) of Wells Fargo and Bank of America was 1.69× and .82×, respectively. This means the former's price multiple is more than twice the latter's.

More importantly, Wells Fargo enjoys intangible value (as an operational primarily asset-based holding company that exceeds 100% of its book value). That additional value is all intangible. This is likely associated with solid client relationships and reputation. Meanwhile, Bank of America's value is actually below its book value as of this book's writing.

This is not good as is suggested by Wall Street analysts who recommend a "Buy" for Wells Fargo and a "Sell/Hold" for Bank of America. Also, the companies' measured volatility compared to the industry/sector, with a 1.0 being the median and over 1.0 being more volatile (*risky*) and below 1.0 being more stable, further proves the point. Bank of America's volatility (*beta*) was 1.59 as compared to Wells Fargo's 0.86.

CAPITAL AND RISK

Company size can be a significant consideration when it comes to risk, especially with regard to securing capital. As you might expect, larger companies usually have more options and better access to the capital markets as well as better rates and terms. A $1 billion company may have funding sources bending over backwards to provide financial support while a $25 million company may need its owner to make a personal guarantee to be considered for a loan/credit facility.

The less risk perceived, the better rates and terms offered. That can pay huge dividends for larger companies, with which capital sources, such as banks, are more likely to share risk. However, size is not an absolute because growth and niche market dominance are examples of factors that could suggest a smaller company may have the potential of less risk and higher value. Sharp company owners have an idea what their company-specific risk rate is and how to spread risk by having debt allowing the lender to share the risk.

Let's use for illustrative purposes only the previous example of the $50 million company with the $10 million net cash flow and an assumed 20 percent risk rate. Let's assume our research of comparable companies indicates the optimal level of debt to equity is 50/50. So, we determined that 50 percent has a 20 percent rate for equity. This would be shown by (1 – .50).20 = .10 or 10 percent allocated to equity.

Let's then say that interest rate from the lending source is 5 percent and since interest expenses are tax deductible, that the combined state and federal tax rate is 40 percent. That means that the true cost of capital is (1 – .40).05 or 3.0 percent. Since debt represents half, we now have our new rate of (1 – .50).03 or 1.5 percent. The 1.5 percent debt rate is combined with the 10 percent equity rate for the *weighted average cost of capital* (WACC) of 10 percent + 1.5 percent = 11.5 percent. This is 42.5 percent lower than the 20 percent rate or risk for equity alone without debt. This improves the market value of invested capital by sharing risk with the note holder.

Remember, the lower the risk, the lower the rate. The lower the rate, the higher the pricing multiple and value.

Finally, assume the $25 million debt allows the company to produce twice the widgets in half the time, reducing labor expenses. So, despite the new interest expense and repayment of principal, the increased profits are $15 million versus the $10 million.

This means the value of the company is $15 million/11.5 percent or $130.5 million (rounded) less $25 million in debt or $105.5 million in value. This is more than twice the $50 million value even prior to finding other areas where risk may be mitigated and/or minimized. This is why as a strategic value architect, it is possible to claim that in as brief as 24 months a company can feasibly increase its value by 100 percent and often more. Obviously, there are myriad other ways to accomplish this either by organic growth or through acquisition as long as synergies are achieved.

Needless to say, overleveraging may result in high sensitivity to declines in growth and inadequate cash flow to service debt. Most seasoned CFOs know leverage is a single arrow in the business's quiver to shift or reduce risk.

Yet, knowing how to get there—to create value—still is not common knowledge. Keep in mind the founder/owner is a rare breed. She or he is thinking "what if" through the opportunity-lens; whereas, advisors often think "what if" through the risk lens. Therefore, the goals of trusted advisors should include helping clients build and create value by ensuring they're aware of how to enhance their intangible assets' value and the options to do so. Advisors must also recognize that owners have limited time to shepherd growth, so having a plan is insufficient. Having resources to execute the plan is what's needed. Successful business owners and their advisors already know it's not simply selling more services and products profitably.

Here's the more surprising issue to make the point. Let's say it takes $500,000 in advisory expenses to achieve this feat of an extra $50 million in value. Who would say "no" to the proposition of for every dollar paid $100 is returned? If a prospect or a client or an advisor says "not interested," then they may not be ready to invest in themselves.

The point here (as will be explored further in Chapter 2 addressing the focus on trusted advisors) is the discussion needs to be reframed from hourly rates (fees for service) to value, milestone success, participation fees, and/or project billing. Otherwise, there is no perceived connection between services rendered and value created. (**Author note:** *I like a combination of project and participation fees as it conveys to the client that I have skin in the game and the client's success is my success.*)

UNDERSTANDING ASSETS

In just the last decade, current theories (such as modern portfolio theory on a global stage) and methodologies about risk and value have undergone more scrutiny, and may be woefully inadequate to ensure that accurate, fully supportable valuations will consistently be produced. Let's look at a common scenario of asset and equity level risk:

> A partnership owns an apartment building, so equity can be unitized into partner interests. This is done so owners hold equity in the partnership versus directly in the asset (the real property). This can be done for business reasons such as smoothing investment jitters by having a minimum holding period, asset protection, and tax avoidance.
>
> So the first question that needs to be addressed is, what's the value of the asset? A real estate appraisal will provide a figure. Sharp business appraisers will want to know more before valuing the equity held in the LLC.
>
> They'll want to know associated tax liability of capital gains (e.g., the building was purchased for $200K and is now appraised at $1MM). This will also provide guidance as to the annual capital appreciation and not simply the income generated. Both are needed to determine total return. Surprisingly, it is common for this information not to be requested. A solid analyst will want to know whether tenants are on month-to-month or multiyear leases, and if any potential liabilities exist (e.g., failing to transfer the title to the LLC) or the manager is older and possessed most of the investment savvy—all risks that can have a negative effect on the equity value. The analyst may also wish to consider the real estate appraiser's assumed debt to equity developed in the capitalization rate as the asset held may not be financed at all (debt free) or is paying an interest rate that is not at market.

So, the first lesson here is to understand the underlying asset level risks before making financial decisions based solely on a real estate's appraised value. The second lesson is that equity level risks that support investor concessions, referred to as *premiums* and *discounts*, are all too often oversimplified by the advisor who requested them as may the business appraiser providing the partnership interest equity valuation services.

The intellectual rigor would have to explore what is the level of direct ownership expectation risk/return of the asset. If the buy and hold is traditionally seven years, what portion of return is derived from growth/capital appreciation and what is from yield/income?

What are the asset class rate/risk norms for this holding period? If the asset is held in a wrapper like a corporation or partnership, how do bylaws and operating agreement provisions impact the equity ownership in addition to the operating risks?

So, an adjustment such as lack of control or lack of marketability discounts without a discussion of investor expectations (risk tolerance/aversion), asset class, pool of likely investors, and holding period is absent the intellectual rigor a skilled business valuator is supposed to consider to demonstrate the adjustment to the impaired equity value makes sense and is well supported.

We'll be spending considerable time in Chapters 7 and 8 on risks at the company level, so suffice to say, more robust reports that address legal, financial, and operational risks will examine client and advisory involvement that can both establish a benchmark value, but also are risk factors impacting the value at the asset, entity, and equity levels.

This would also require not only examining the company against itself, which is referred to as a trend analysis, but correctly utilizing industry comparative data to determine the level of operational performance. Such analysis is often based upon industry and company revenues and/or asset size.

This will be addressed in greater length in Chapter 9 for my appraisal brethren and those relying on and reviewing business appraisal reports.

PLUGGING THE GAP

How does so much get missed in the valuation process and why are so many opportunities to create value overlooked? There is plenty of responsibility to spread around. The appraisal profession could do a better job articulating its offerings and uses. The standards of practice could be strengthened. Business owners and executives could seek an investment in quality advisory services.

In *Cracking the Value Code,* Richard Boulton states: "Boards of directors need information about all assets that drive value so that they can properly discharge their duties of stewardship and governance."[2]

The advisors who most commonly serve business owners could strive to better understand the valuation work product and its utility. Peter Drucker, a well-regarded academic and management consultant, states: "If you want to do something new, you have to stop doing something old." Academia could emphasize the importance of private capital markets and methodologies applied in valuing private companies.

However, another plain truth is most trusted advisors—attorneys, CPAs, bankers, insurers, and so on—suffer from technical myopia. They focus on their products and services and assume another professional will take up where they leave off. "It's not my job" and the risk of losing client revenues because of an unwillingness to learn the merits of other advisors plagues most professions.

We're almost all guilty of this and we suffer as a result. Worse yet, the client suffers the most due to the ad-hoc manner information often received from various advisors' lenses. The way to change this is also fairly straightforward: Owners and advisors need to elevate themselves to create better alignment on behalf of company clients' ecosystems with a focus on creating value. That is what a successful strategy is supposed to achieve: enhanced shareholder value.

The bar needs to be raised. Otherwise, as Michelangelo warned, "The greatest danger for most of us is not that our aim is too high and we miss it, but that it is too low and we reach it."

It may be best to put people in the same room at the same time, something that will eliminate conflicting advice and facilitate having robust discussions about value creation strategies and their implementation. As will be shared elsewhere in this book, this often means including family, vendors, and clients as part of the holistic approach that becomes embedded in the company's cultural DNA.

NOTES

1. Michael J. Mard, *Driving Your Company's Value: Strategic Benchmarking for Value* (Hoboken: Wiley, 2004).
2. Richard Boulton, *Cracking the Value Code* (HarperCollins, 2000).

CHAPTER 2

Focus on Trusted Advisors

If an advisor can differentiate by the knowledge and relationships that would allow the business being served to flourish, then the discussion changes when a competitor comes knocking, which they will inevitably do. Your competitor contacts a client and identifies current provider price point. If the client says I pay $250,000 for my annual services, the competitor may offer a $50,000 fee reduction; however, if the client explains his risks are lower, profits are greater, and his value increased by $5,000,000 last year, how many competitors can readily offer a 20-to-1 ($5,000,000/ $250,000) return on the relationship? Very, very few.

Let's set the stage. A current, past, or future client has needs and wants. She or he has beaten the long odds and operates a thriving $125 million company. Has the company grown due to unique skills offered by its provider(s)? Or, have the providers grown their billings due to having the good fortune of serving a company that operates very successfully? Perhaps the company has mastered client, vendor, and staff relationships with a culture of empowerment, cohesion, and community. Maybe it has levered the knowledge of several clients, vendors, and key staff to develop a unique knowledge-based product or service.

For the advisor, a larger client may equate to more complexity and more billable hours or higher commissions. But has anything special been offered to this "A-grade" client not available to other "lesser" clients served? If not, why not? What is the value of fees or commissions for service or product if they are commonly offered by competitors and to all clients?

Examples of going the extra mile may be developing a unique client strategy; introductions to other superior providers in complementary sectors or facilitating strategic alliances with other advisors; invitations to industry-specific conferences; as well as offering a deeper dive into how and why the company operates the way it does and recommended improvements from not only the technical perspective, but a more holistic one.

The point is every trusted provider has a base of knowledge and relationships. If the base is, well, *basic*, it may be sufficient to pay for the kids' education and orthodontia, but is it unique? Does it differentiate? Does it afford a strategic advantage to the client or prospect? Be careful. Don't confuse hubris with humility. What's the glue that binds the relationship?

A good starting point for advisory self-assessment is to determine what percentage of clients are 8- or 9-figures compared to the number of such competitive firms in the market(s) served. Is having one just luck? Likely having 10 or more means the provider is offering something that attracts bigger and better companies.

It's not unusual to see boutique firms with primarily larger clients, so it is not simply the advisory firm size. Conversely, if only one or two clients are this large and the balance are of a smaller size, then what is the advisor's client retention like? Did the larger ones begin as smaller clients and at some point in time moved on to larger (perceived "better") providers?

If the business suspects they have outlived an advisor's usefulness, the advisor–client relationship was simply a technical and tactical one. The advisor loses to a competitor who offers a 20 percent reduction in fees or, nearly as bad, the client prefers working with the familiar, so asks the advisor to lower their fees to at or below that of a competitor. The latter is a master–servant relationship conveying reduced importance of the provider's role. Value in this sad case equates to fees or commission costs for services rendered.

This is the beginning of provider–client musical chairs, which is allowed to persist because many advisors fail to frame the cost–benefit equation in terms of spend versus benefits received. As an example, few like paying insurance premiums, but pity the fool who chose to have inadequate coverage and is looking at a seven-figure out-of-pocket spend to cover a loss. We always suggest the advisor educate the client that the premiums are X and the coverage is Y. If a claim is Z and the total premiums paid to date is $10X$ and the claim is $100X$, then the insurance investment makes sense as a business hedge. More importantly, and seldom considered, is an optimally insured company will almost always have a superior value to one that is not. In part, it's intuitive as management understands it is hedging the risks associated with unforeseen losses.

So, if the company value goes from A to B and the cost of the hedge is 1/20 or 1/100 the increased value, it ought to be a straightforward business decision. The same issues hold true for all advisors who are in the risk management and intangible assets (knowledge and relationships) as a service business. It is insufficient to simply offer core services like legal, tax, financial, banking, and insurance, because competitors can do this already.

We all must provide a premium whether it is perceived or not. Golf outings and wine and dine are not premiums. Finding unique ways to provide solutions to challenges or sourcing new opportunities for the business owner whether they are directly related to the provider's core offerings or not *is* "value add." The most successful advisors act as concierges, where clients go to them for advice whether the issue is their specialty or not. Solid advice and stewardship wins trust.

And having stellar advisory relationships cements that trust with fellow advisors and clients, making the advisor the go-to resource. Now that's value add. It takes more effort but provides a deep divide between the client and the remaining me-too advisory competitors.

This really comes down to either leading the herd or comfort with being part of it. Being part creates the sense of safety in numbers. Most choose to work for others as a result. Showing up is not the same thing as doing more. So, explore that chasm between what the business owner really needs and what you're offering. It may be they need a different optics than that of the professional with whom they are working. If the advisor feels that may threaten the business relationship, perhaps that says more about priorities and performance.

It's a given an owner has wants and needs that require relief. If he or she primarily has providers who are unwilling to sit on the same side of the table as he or she does to share their "are you feeling me" concerns, there is no empathy. However, once the advisor is perceived as having skin in the game, a deeper relationship can be established. Frankly, this is where fees become secondary to benefits gained.

Ed Russ, chief marketing officer of Grant Thornton, put it succinctly: "*What makes a good rainmaker? The ability to put yourself in the other person's shoes.*"

Going the extra mile is not always a comfortable decision to make, especially if the relationship is nascent. Consider the alternative if your advice is perceived as a temporal client cost center just ready to be jettisoned. However, if advisor can differentiate by the knowledge and relationships they posses that would allow the business being served to measurably flourish, then the discussion changes when a competitor comes knocking.

Be the advisor that doesn't simply show up at continuing education and professional conferences to collect business cards and mingle. That is what the majority do. Attend venues that will up your "A" game and that of your clients. Better yet, attend client industry conferences. Seek to speak at and participate in relevant industry niches. Even better, be on the planning committee or on the industry's association board. This added effort provides access to new client-centric knowledge and relationships.

This is a combination of efforts most competitors will be unwilling to replicate due to the time and talent hurdles. Yet, it means less competition, more income, and fewer clients with larger more lucrative matters where everyone wins. (Which is more preferred, generating $25 million in revenues with 2,500 clients or 25?) Don't dilute services by being the jack-of-all-trades-and-master-of-none. Such fundamental decisions can increase your own firm's price multiples by 20 percent or more while providing more time to deepen the quality and quantity of client services.

Frank Ohlorst expresses in *Big Data Analytics: Turning Big Data Into Big Money* that an underpinning assumption is that advisors and company leadership embrace the importance of data analytics and research.[1] Knowing why revenues and profits occur *in detail* with the ever-growing complexity of information and the pressure to apply technological leverage means value can only be realized when risk analysis and return on investment are central considerations.

Further, Mike Schultz's book, *Professional Services Marketing*, has an entire chapter titled "Networking, Relationships, Trust, and Value," which stresses that engagements can and should be broken down into stages even if you have the absolute understanding of the need and the perfect solution.[2]

Why? Trust. How does trust get earned? Through relationships, not transactions. If you don't believe relationships are important, consider how most wealth advisors are well-schooled in the art of putting clients at ease so they'll trust their firm with their assets. Yet, a Fidelity Investments 2013 study found 70 percent of widows fire their spouses' financial advisors within 12 months of their husbands' deaths for the following reasons:

- Didn't listen
- Condescending
- Didn't look at me or ask my opinion
- Didn't understand my fears or goals

This is why an entire segment of GRRK is dedicated to this important human capital asset, which includes focus on relationships by and between advisors and business owners.

While I refer to this as optics, the perception of the decision maker is paramount, which can be demonstrated by hourly rate aversion. *(Is it really the fees or the sense of not perceiving value is derived for the fees?)* What is the correlation with the fees charged and the solution or opportunity found? That's the calculus of the owner who writes the check.

The governance, relationships, risks, and knowledge (GRRK) content in this book focuses on how to build and enhance company value. It is applicable to a wide audience, including business owners, C-suite executives, investors, board members, bankers, private equity groups, academics, future entrepreneurs, and trusted advisors.

In this chapter, we speak specifically to the professionals who can play a vital role in enhancing the value of their clients' businesses (and their own)—or do just the opposite. We address how such services should provide differentiated and win-win reasons for clients to operate within a collaborative framework of connections that offers unique value. This differs from simply being technically astute. Since most business owning clients do not know what good professional services looks like, they'll either select the least expensive provider or, more frightening, one who may be charging for his or her own learning curve, but has strong relationship building skills.

Do you really want to lose business to a competitor who is nice but incompetent? If not, how are you creating a cohesive relationship?

Keep in mind: Clients are often overwhelmed with keeping the wheels on their proverbial economic buses and have frequent advisors soliciting them for new business. As such, they and their key staff often have limited time to think outside of their daily company operations, much less "the box" of new ideas. Without external insights, they're doomed to remaining in the box.

This best use of client time leverage could be the domain of trusted advisors. My goal is to make the reader the *most trusted advisor* (MTA) or know what one looks like as best as possible. If among your first questions without adequate information on another advisor is, "What are your fees?", *Stop!* How about obtaining adequate input of what needs to be known and requesting a sample work product or background of representative clients, not just fees charged.

The germination of the idea for this book started with a frustration shared by many advisors I've known for 20+ years. The issues we confront existed back then and remain. They are the economic cycles that create professional advisor engagement ebbs and flows.

Anecdotal evidence such as the number of enrollees in MBA programs and the number of professionals joining associations seems to correlate with the strength of the business environment and economy—clearly reactive behavior. (In other words, "I'm flush with business, so I don't need to attend my association meetings or pursue valuable knowledge" seems shortsighted as these business cycles will always occur.)

Reactive behavior, especially in a crisis, is seldom good. In 2008–2009, many professional advisory firms began to lay off what they perceived to be nonessential personnel or firms divested entire departments (such as law firms jettisoning trust and estate or workout departments). The result? Full partners of many advisory firms lost the benefit of leveraging the skills of junior associates or support staff.

Eliminating expenses, when done prudently, requires surgical skill—not a dull knife. While uncomfortable, it requires revisiting strategies and tactics despite it being easier to track expenses than examining operations.

In the short run, personnel cuts may result in an increase in profits, but over the long run, if little to nothing has been done to ensure revenues increase, then the problem hasn't been resolved. Arguably, cutting into muscle while trying to remove fat suggests an ineffective organization to begin with, regardless of the economic climate. Ultimately, it may be determined that there were human capital gaps in the way advisors were serving the market that were masked when good commerce could be had. This is ironic, when advisors are asked to provide similar guidance to their underperforming clients when stuck in slow-growth mode.

A fundamental change is required so professional services firms are not solely reactive to the marketplace; albeit, this is often perceived as "safe." One of the ways to do that is to know how intangible assets such as goodwill are created, something that's attributed to the firm as much as the firms' individuals.

More than at any time previously, wealth, law, banking, insurance, and accounting firms expect their associates who wish to be on the partner-equity track to have mastered technical skills while also increasing their book of business (aka, keep the doors open with clients that partner-track associates have secured). This is a double-edged sword that is also twice as hard to hone.

When associates have the entrepreneurial attributes needed to garner new clients, the firm needs a compelling reason to retain these staff rather than their striking out on their own. This, too, is becoming more pervasive as millennials seek work–life balance. Frequent staff (human capital) departures fractures service offerings and makes it more difficult to obtain growth funding.

Fear not: Business owners and my family office friends will share that since obtaining credit facility (debt financing) from traditional banks has become more difficult post–Great Recession, they need the brain power of advisors more than ever to make their capital go further.

The wisdom contained within these pages for trusted advisors is based on some basic tenets that should be shared—things learned over three decades of observation. At the top of the list are the following two:

1. It's generally understood that the education required to become a professional regardless of discipline seldom prepares one for how to be an entrepreneur or intrapreneur. Plus, most seek steady paychecks while their clients do not share the same security. This creates a disconnect.

2. There's a significant technical bias and fondness for knowledge unique to a specific discipline, but the ability to articulate and demonstrate its benefit to others without requisite people and business skills is at best challenging. The tools and language must be at the clients' and complementary advisors' comprehension level.

The second point requires further emphasis, because if one is unable to understand what the professional does or the guidance she or he is recommending and under what circumstances, the ability to refer or act on advice is very difficult, and even more so when there are numerous subspecialties offering differing guidance.

As a simple example, an accountant who does audit work may do limited attestation or administration work. A transaction attorney may have limited exposure to tax, trust, and estate issues. So, it is incumbent on both the advisor and those with whom he or she complements that there is an understanding and appreciation of the work performed and value provided.

What's important to recognize is that clients, or potential clients, may not understand these concentration subtleties. Lumping together all CPAs or attorneys in one general group demonstrates limited knowledge or no effort to make important distinctions. The takeaway here is this: Trusted advisors are usually very aware of the distinctions within their professions (i.e., an accountant, a financial professional, and an economist are not the same), but those who use and refer their services may not know the difference. Add to that the unknown advisor competency level and consider the clouded perspective of the client.

This "confusion" also holds true within the business valuation sector. I'm just as guilty as most think I only perform complex 8- to 10-figure company equity valuation advisory and litigation support services. My passion and true calling is applying governance and strategy to build and create equity value enhancement by often acting as a chief-of-staff that aligns fellow advisors and business owner optics and options. This allows us to create metrics and collectively identify resource gaps, then facilitate filling these gaps so plans can be executed in order to deliver significant value add such as doubling equity value in 6 to 24 months. In short, I'm not *just* another business appraiser generating average appraisal reports.

Then there is the confusion created by some who offer a work-product called "appraisal reports." Those focused on banking, business brokerage, accounting, business coaching, or life insurance may have access to software that generates company valuation results, or they apply rules of thumb that lack the intellectual rigor expected of a seasoned, full-time accredited business appraiser. They perceive that no or low cost is somehow benefiting their client. This is why I create a wide berth around the practitioners who do this and emphasize that enterprise and equity valuation mastery should be to the level of a strategic value architect when millions are at stake. This architect is not only one who can identify and measure risk, but one who knows how to manage and mitigate risks that allow owners and advisors more time to pursue opportunities and elevate the value of their companies.

The fellow advisor who perpetuates value creation is doing a service to his or her clients, the advisor's profession, and the professionals with which he or she collaborates. Better still, he or she is benefiting the client or prospect by reframing a discussion based upon value creation, not simply cost.

THE PATH TO BEING THE BEST

What can be done to ensure clients receive the best services where fee is a secondary consideration? The initial onus is on potential clients, who must take adequate time and be sufficiently diligent to understand advisors' roles and offerings.

As multiple advisors are often in play, this warrants respect of each discipline and assurance that their advice is integrated and aligned—plus it can provide real value well above and beyond simply the fees for services purchased. Advisors are strongly encouraged to schedule breakfasts and lunches to spend time with clients even when the clients lack of contact might suggest everything is going well. They'll always share insights that were unknown, which further deepens the relationship and opportunity to be of further service (more billings/commissions/fees). If the lament is insufficient time, then more staff support or fewer lower-margin clients may be a viable option in order to spend more time with better clients.

Similarly seek out contemporaries you know to deepen your understanding of what they do and how they do it. Reciprocal curiosity will follow. Also seek contemporaries your clients and you may not know—an activity that creates new relationships and new knowledge that's beneficial to the provider, the firm, and clients served.

Attending professional events is also a good idea, and in this realm there are two paths that can be chosen:

1. Events that are focused on your own discipline, primarily motivated by ensuring receipt of continuing education credits, and secondarily by the opportunity to network with peers
2. Events focused on complementary professions (i.e., an accountant goes to a legal function or an attorney goes to a function for accountants highlighting tax issues), a strategy that provides greater insights and opportunities borne out of new relationships and new knowledge.

Think about this: Attorneys who meet with peers from complementary disciplines or with other trusted advisors three to five times a week would have 100 to 200 new possible relationships over the course of a year. This can create a real win-win situation, as they may receive referrals from those confident in their skills and with whom they developed a rapport. They also have a broadened referral pool, which can benefit clients who need specialized skills.

Having the humility and people skills to take this path can be challenging and time consuming. And, making the time to build quality relationships means kissing some frogs along the way. About an average of one day a week ought to be allotted toward business development (connecting/networking), which happens to come to roughly three hours per person 150 times.

Let's do the math. Your hour is worth $500 and you spend an hour for lunch and/or breakfast. So, at least one-third and as much as two-thirds of the meeting time would be meals that would be had anyway. Let's assume 250 hours of billable time annually equates to $125,000. If 150 new professionals are met and 90 percent are not up to par, this still means 15 quality relationships per annum. If your average engagement is $10,000 and each relationship refers one assignment, you're at or near breakeven in year one. What about years two, three, and so on?

Now consider the number of relationships attorneys (or any other professional) would have over 10 years if they continue to make this kind of concerted effort. This is how many successful professionals build a multimillion-dollar practice. So, when would be a good time to get started?

As many smart business professionals will share, they've got to eat anyhow. There is a sizable caveat. Professional services are relationship-oriented businesses. Technical and tactical will attract mostly transactions.

Like any courtship, an expression of interest by coming prepared by knowing a little about the person you're meeting beforehand and arriving on time (always confirm a meeting the day before) and having insightful questions and vignettes of challenges make the meeting memorable. It provides an indication of how you'd comport yourself with their clients, too. Learn with whom the other professional commonly does business and who refers him or her in. If there's chemistry, offer to make introductions to fellow professionals who may add a real benefit and new commerce to each person you meet and to whom your refer.

Collecting business cards is not the goal. Timely follow-up and reinforcing how you may help a fellow professional will make most meetings memorable. Courtships flower when we share. They wither when we only take.

QUESTION YOURSELF

Are there things advisors can do to enhance themselves and their practices? Of course—here are a few questions advisors could be asking themselves with respect to attending professional events:

- Are you taking the time to research the panel or presenters so you can seek to develop a rapport with these thought leaders?
- Do you strike up conversations during breakouts with people you don't know?
- Are you speaking to the people sitting to your right and left?
- Do you have plenty of business cards and take notes on ones you receive?
- Do you ask conversational questions like "What path took you to your current profession?"—which is a lot different than merely asking "What do you do?"
- If you exchanged cards with someone, did you follow up with a quick email highlighting one or two things that person shared—professional or personal?
- Do you follow up with panel members or presenters, thanking them for their insight and asking for their thoughts or ideas on something you're struggling with or thinking about?

Many advisors will answer the previous questions with "no"—they don't research presenters or panelists, they rarely strike up conversations with new people, and they seldom follow up. What is the point of attending a lunch, conference, or presentation if no follow-up takes place? When you calculate the time expended, it arguably could have been better used.

Admittedly, this behavior does require some advisors to get out of their comfort zone (I'm included), but those who are relationship focused understand the significant benefits engagement can provide. Relationship-focused advisors network with others and gain clients. In a way, your relationships and those possessed by those whom you know is your barter as much as your knowledge. It's the card played to develop rapport, trust, and then business. And trust, especially with larger matters, takes time. Technical skills are usually assumed.

Think of high school and the bell curve. If there was equal distribution, there would be a flat line. There is a reason it is referred to as a bell curve, as there is often a concentration toward the middle. The ends are at the *A*s and *E*s with more *B*s and *D*s and the most *C*s. We can't all be *A*s. We know from school this tends to be the case. So, what does an "*A*" professional look like?

What if an *E* has the ability to present as well as an *A* with little of the technical ability? So, we accept the herd is in the majority (like we all think we're good drivers), and the minority looking to distinguish themselves is nearer to the fewer *A*s.

While to some extent it's a numbers game, few tend to have mastered the relationships (qualitative) and technical (quantitative) expertise necessary to garner steady referrals. There is one guarantee of doing nothing or only emphasizing technical skills and a tactical approach. You may earn enough to pay the bills, but it's insufficient to scale a book of business and leverage growth, much less advise business owners on how to do so.

TAKING IT TO THE NEXT LEVEL

In the previous discussion, the venues and topics have been decided for you, and you can choose whether to attend, and then whether to follow up. A more advanced method for developing new relationships is not just inviting someone to a meal or graciously accepting invitations (you have permission to be selective; in fact, it's advised), but consider broadening the table by having each of you invite someone else—literally doubling the potential benefit you and your professional advisor's guest receive. As an example, an attorney may ask an accountant to lunch. When the attorney brings a life insurance professional and the accountant invites an investment banker, the opportunity for relationship building has the potential to be significantly enhanced. (Allow for 1.5 hours if more than two are attending the meeting.)

Why is it important to do more than network? Being a *connector* is an art form unto itself. It requires a different mindset, more akin to being a farmer planting seeds that will later be sown as opposed to providing ad-hoc tactical and technical-rich transactions—eat what you kill.

CASE IN POINT

When I met two people who shared a love of surfing—a banker and a partner in a firm that helps CPAs and financial professionals deliver more value—I didn't just introduce them. I invited them and their wives to have dinner with me and my wife, an activity that went a long way toward developing rapport and building a relationship that ultimately provided many new business opportunities for them.

A connector focuses on sharing knowledge and relationships with others; this is foremost in his or her mind. They share this human capital. The higher the quality of these relationships, the more sought after the connector becomes as his or her gravitas becomes further elevated. She and he have to not dwell on those who fail to reciprocate or thank . . . as difficult to do as it might be.

What does that look like? As mentioned earlier, researching the people you meet to understand their personal backgrounds and interests as well as the types of business relationships they seek is the beginning of a relationship "A" game. As an example, if I'm a trusted estate attorney and I meet a CPA, this is what should be going through my mind: "Whom do I know who would benefit from being introduced to this CPA and may provide benefit to the CPA as well?"

In other words, our currency is much more than technical knowhow; it's relationships and the knowledge derived from them. This obviously requires having a deep and wide bench in multiple disciplines, where issues like gender, age, personality, firm size, experience, and location may be filtered.

A person's gravitas directly correlates to the professional company one keeps. It's like being an average tennis player seeking to become above average; the only way that's possible is by playing with people who have better skills.

By being a connector, you elevate your status as someone not just looking for a transaction. You become a center of influence. The epitome of such a connector is one who is occasionally contacted for issues not even related to his or her specialization.

CASE IN POINT

After Hurricane Sandy hit the East Coast, I was contacted by the owner of a high-end boutique accounting firm in Southern California who had a number of clients with multimillion-dollar homes that had been severely damaged. You might wonder why he called me, a business appraiser thousands of miles away from where the disaster hit, but there was a good reason. Insurance companies were so backlogged in making estimates and having appraisers value properties that the wait time just to have a claim processed was more than six months.

His "ask" was if I knew of any real estate appraisers who specialized in high-end coastal properties in the tri-state area. I went to my Rolodex, made a few calls, called in a few favors, and within two weeks all his clients had their appraisals. In the short term, this took about 30 minutes of my time, for no remuneration. Within six months, I was provided with several five-figure engagements that I believe were directly the result of the favor I did for the accounting firm's owner. I was asked the fee *after* I was retained.

TABLE 2.1 Twenty-Five Key Inflection Points Where Strategic Advisory Framework (GRRK) Is Prudent

		CXO	CPA	ESQ	Bank	WAdv	FBA
1	Seeking capital	X	X	X	X	X	X
2	Scale growth	X	X	X	X	X	X
3	Increase profitability	X	X	X	X	X	X
4	Increase value	X	X	X	X	X	X
5	Benchmark performance	X	X	X	X	X	X
6	Manage/mitigate risk	X	X	X	X	X	X
7	Enhance governance/culture	X	X	X	X	X	X
8	Greater liquidity	X	X	X	X	X	X
9	Develop strategy	X	X	X	X	X	X
10	Leveraging capital (human/fin.)	X	X	X	X	X	X
11	Vision/legacy clarity	X	X	X	X	X	X
12	Transition planning	X	X	X	X	X	X
13	Due diligence	X	X	X	X	X	X
14	Independent opinion	X	X	X	X	X	X
15	Disruption defense	X	X	X	X	X	X
16	Joint venture/partnering	X	X	X	X	X	X
17	Post-merger integration	X	X	X	X	X	X
18	Pre-merger planning	X	X	X	X	X	X
19	Sustained vision/legacy	X	X	X	X	X	X
20	Brainstorm opportunities	X	X	X	X	X	X
21	Board (re)focus	X	X	X	X	X	X
22	Divesture or ESOP	X	X	X	X	X	X
23	Insurance funding	X	X	X	X	X	X
24	Asset allocation/preservation	X	X	X	X	X	X
25	Learning organization	X	X	X	X	X	X

Note: It is very common for most of these items to be treated with a technical, tactical, and/or transactional perspective, which is often why the expectation and outcome differ. Most require shared perspectives to ensure alignment and optimal results with efficient resource use, thus freeing the CXO to spend more time on vision and strategic issues. CXO—Officers; Bank—Investment/Commercial Bankers; WAdv—Wealth/Trust/Insurance Advisor (Fiduciary); FBA—Family Business Advisor. The "X" indicates the role of the trusted advisors who can actively assist in increasing opportunity and value while lowering risk.

You've probably heard this before: "Givers gain." Admittedly it takes time and there will be a fair number of individuals who will not reciprocate, so it can be somewhat disheartening. However, these are the kind of relationships that are very difficult to lose to competitors—particularly if they use the "what's your fee" card. This is because the savings of time and the caliber of the relationship (and by extension, knowledge) have such a considerable premium for those who emphasize service over cost.

The process is to reduce 20 percent of your current relationships annually—those who are unable or unwilling to circle back and provide feedback and/or those whose caliber is insufficient. These people may contact you for possible business, but because they don't grasp the service-over-fees concept, they're often seeking the least expensive option. They won't place a premium on your knowledge and relationships, despite being the beneficiary of both.

To illustrate all of the opportunities where advisors can collaborate and advise, consider the checklist in Table 2.1 on the previous page.

This chapter raises a core issue and opportunity. How is it possible for those seeking legal, tax, insurance, banking, or wealth management expertise to know what good looks like if it's not articulated and the investment for good service isn't substantiated?

While the term *consigliore* causes many people to think of Don Corleone in *The Godfather*, it means "most trusted advisor," someone who's counted on to provide both professional and personal counsel. They also have to have a high dose of humility to know what they don't know, but the relationships and knowledge to know who does know. I occasionally use the title chief-of-staff or connector.

We addressed how to transform from a technical provider where fees are often the primary driver for selection to a recipient of multiple referrals. Our challenge is whether clients are applying the same methodologies to differentiate themselves and build more lucrative and deeper relationships. In the next chapter we'll explore this further.

NOTES

1. Frank Ohlorst, *Big Data Analytics: Turning Big Data Into Big Money* (Hoboken: Wiley, 2012).
2. Mike Schultz, *Professional Services Marketing* (Hoboken: Wiley, 2013).

CHAPTER 3

Focus on Business Owners

What is the result of failing to leverage advisors in this way? It is untapped knowledge nuggets—nuggets that can have a significant effect on revenue, profits, and value. One of the difficulties that advisors contend with is that much of their advice is geared toward preventing the likelihood of significant disruption (e.g., disputes, audits, or litigation), so it's hard to see the results of their work.

First things first: I believe that David Maister, author of *The Trusted Advisor*, spoke truthfully when he shared the following about business owners:

> *[M]ost buyers of professional services, even relatively experienced ones, are quite aware of a number of risks. There is the financial risk, emotional risk, the risk of lost time, the risk of embarrassment . . . [as a result] the devil you know is better than the one you don't. . . . [Therefore] professionals in a sense sell confidence, security and ease.*[1]

From my perspective, a good advisor asks good questions, and a great advisor has the humility to know she doesn't have all the answers and earns the right to offer advice only after showing interest in the person(s) she is seeking to serve. In other words, great advisors provide and seek answers on behalf of the client's needs.

As noted previously, this book is relevant to a variety of constituencies in addition to the C-suite, owners, and their families. However, the information contained in this chapter is specifically directed to you, the business owner. Be sure to read the prior chapter dedicated to advisors so the challenges and opportunities as well as their biases are understood.

While having held leadership and strategic staff roles in the U.S. Marine Corps, Abbott Laboratories, and American Automobile Association National Headquarters, I have dedicated numerous years as the owner of a boutique business valuation and advisory firm and been a lifelong learner of everything: entrepreneurship, governance, management, finance, operations, and research. I know firsthand the joys and fears of meeting payroll and keeping the lights on. I had the good fortune of being awarded large federal contracts. I was able to expand our practice from local to national. This abundance led to divesting and selling non-core business lines. It provided the means to invest in and develop land. And more recently, I walked the talk and merged my boutique practice with a global business advisory and litigation support firm as a senior equity partner and the global group leader of family office and business strategies.

And, at the writing of this book, I am expanding my entrepreneurial efforts as a conscientious capitalist to fund a ranch that will serve two primary purposes: (1) Provide an executive retreat for owners, their family, and/or staff as well as key advisors seeking strategies to implement equity value enhancement (EVE) services; and (2) Provide equine and canine therapy for military veterans (with focus on homeless) suffering from post-traumatic stress disorder (PTSD). *(We do accept donations.)*

Over the past decade I have honed these experiences to serve the ultra-affluent, entrepreneurs, boards, the C-Suite, private equity, and the trusted advisors of these 8-to-10-figure privately held and small-cap public companies. My focus has been on strategy as well as identifying, measuring, managing, and mitigating (IMMM) risk. Emphasis in this chapter is on building and creating value by leveraging human and financial capital.

Since I have completed 1,200+ engagements, testified as an IRS/court-qualified expert on 170+ occasions, read hundreds of books, and have presented and authored on 300+ occasions in both academia and professional services forums, I feel reasonably qualified to share these observations. My first thought is I am humbled by knowing what I do not know, and my second thought is I'm relieved to know I can and do find answers to the most complex issues that businesses, their officers/owners, and their advisors confront.

Paul Thiel, a billionaire venture capitalist, understands risk. He shared an observation of how he selected winners like Facebook. He related that its founder, Mark Zuckerberg, paid himself $50,000 per year. This was a common attribute for his selections. His reasoning is sound. Most business owners get a taste for the rewards of their efforts and often prematurely supersize their compensation. Doing so provides inadequate cash to reinvest in the business, so scale is almost impossible to achieve. Going on this kind of "stop the instant gratification" diet plagues many business owners. They're not solely to blame. Advisors often focus on the highest economic benefit as defined by cash in their clients' pockets while paying the lowest possible taxes. It is shortsighted and all too common.

After almost 30 years of being a serial entrepreneur with several liquidity events under my belt, I have developed a profound appreciation for what it takes to start, build, and transition successfully from a thriving business. Admittedly, struggling with the work–life balance has torpedoed past spousal and children relationships. The intention of this chapter is to provide tangible takeaways to assist in higher success rates of companies and improved business resource optimization such that equity value is enhanced.

A founder/CEO by his or her nature is somewhat of a contrarian. We dare to go outside most others' comfort zones—that is to say most folks prefer earning a steady paycheck. Conversely, founders wish to be rewarded by managing risk. The sole question is "Should the reward be sooner or later (meaning harvest profits now or replant for a greater financial reward later through a higher company value) or can a balance be achieved?

While Wall Street darlings and disasters garner the majority of the business media attention (as opposed to Main Street companies), academia occasionally recognizes that innovation is often the child of early-stage companies. This "bigger company is better" bias is so ingrained in our system that there is limited representation on Capitol Hill for the needs of mid-market companies that are the primary drivers of new employment and the U.S. Gross Domestic Product. This reality, which is not likely to change anytime soon, does not deter those with entrepreneurial aspirations from pursuing their dreams. It really shouldn't.

During the course of my career, my activities included operational audits, due diligence, governance, strategic planning/execution, risk management, valuation, and litigation support advisory services. The unvarnished truth is many businesses that do fail didn't have to fail and even mature companies can more than double their values in as few as 6 to 24 months.

One of the purposes of this book is to challenge the way some owners think about their businesses. The book's success is measured by the CEOs/owners who transform from being overwhelmed by working in their business to thriving by working on their greatest investment. The latter is where liquidity, legacies, and significance are built. The following provides examples of various planned transition events most owners will prepare to think about to evolve from tactically fighting fires to strategically writing the next chapter in their family and business lives.

It should encourage you to think about all the advisors you may wish to cultivate deeper relationships with in order to get from here to there. It's never too early to start. In fact, some of the most successful owners had a transition plan on day one of their new entrepreneurial endeavor. Conversely, failing to plan assures a plan to fail. Seldom is achieving considerable wealth based upon hope alone. The challenge for most is to acknowledge time, ability, and resource limitations and to leverage your constituents: staff, family, board, shareholders, clients, vendors, and advisors.

Thirty Paths of "Successful to Significance" for Business Owners:

1. Reinvest "spiritual" self in the family to ensure harmony and balance.
2. Pursue a strategy acquiring other businesses and/or assets like real property.
3. Invite a private equity firm to acquire a partial (minority) or controlling interest.
4. Become more actively involved in trade/professional associations to achieve mastery.
5. Learn from your commercial banker and an investment banker how to prepare for a sale.
6. Determine what wealth means to you and how much is enough and why, what, and whose help is needed to achieve this clarity.
7. Hire MBA interns for company grooming and mentorship—be passionate about metrics.
8. Take senior management and their families on an extended weekend retreat.
9. Study leadership from other cultures, religions, and industries. Apply, refine, repeat.
10. Meet with all current advisors (preferably at the same time) and ask what more they can do for the business and you.
11. Meet with new advisors and compare what more they can do for the business and you.
12. Form a deeper relationship with competitors and suppliers and seek collaboration.
13. Learn a foreign language, an art (writing, dancing), a sport, and travel somewhere new.
14. Explore what if you weren't doing what you spend your day doing.
15. Reduce the number of hours spent on blocking and tackling until staff can do your job proficiently.
16. Find a new charity and get involved in more than the board, such as training dogs to assist owners with PTSD.
17. Take one staff member to lunch once a week.
18. Require staff to run meetings and cross-train where possible.
19. Discover immediate and extended family interest in business and groom them early or look inward to staff C-suite or externally if no candidates.

20. Have a workable what-if plan for key family and staff to minimize disruption.
21. Know how to grieve during loss as all wounds seen and unseen need to heal.
22. Take one manager to dine with your family once a month.
23. Take a specialty course at a local university or be an adjunct professor.
24. Have family assist at-risk kids in some meaningful way.
25. Write a letter to the editor of your favorite newspaper or magazine.
26. Research your family tree and be the first to reach out to neglected family members.
27. Once a month celebrate your spouse's and your anniversary.
28. Conquer one fear each year or do something that is humbling and authentic.
29. Refine your life as you don't know your expiration date. Are you living your bucket list?
30. Seek the answer to who you are beyond your family and business roles and live it. The world is replete with owners who miss being "King" or "Queen".

THE ROLE OF ADVISORS

While simple to express, achievement requires the willingness to step away from what may be familiar and pursue that which may be best. It's a marathon, not a sprint. It starts with the first step. Trusted advisors should be there along the way.

If properly vetted and questioned, trusted advisors can provide insights and recommendations as to how they can best serve business owners. Owners often experience the frustration associated with not knowing or feeling sometimes alone—unable to get out of their own way—and unsure others can be relied upon.

Unfortunately, it's common that owners don't adequately tap into the resources their advisors can bring—but this occurrence is often not their fault. The burden is largely that of the advisor, who may fear risking a business and monetary relationship by perhaps persuading or dissuading an owner to take advice that was not solicited. That fear is often justified.

A common mindset owners often embrace is "lead, follow, or get out of my way" and they often prefer asking for forgiveness rather than permission. Then there is the expense of advice. The issue of expense is a strawman in that most advice is to minimize risk so a more costly consequence is not experienced. It is akin to insurance, but paying premiums is never fun until a claim is filed.

Some business owners prefer their own counsel because they're taking all the risks—but they may fail to see their own self-imposed limitations. They may also seek support from those whom they employ. What is the risk to a staff member to share an alternative view? While the burden may be on advisors to be more proactive, it's ultimately the owner who determines whether advice is to be acted upon and considered an expense or an investment. An interesting study was done supporting the idea that the wisdom of the crowd is usually better than that of an individual, hence the notion of committees and councils may be wise to build consensus and cohesion when big decisions when a crisis isn't facing the company.

So, what is strategic advice worth if it increases the performance and reduces the risk of what is likely an owner's most valuable asset? Can the client wait the two years to see the result or are there milestones that indicate enhanced performance along the way? Expectations must be set. This takes a team.

Having an organization comprised of motivated and collaborative individuals can create a firm of the future. The first self-examination is the one facing owners in the morning when they look at themselves in the mirror. To some extent, they have to trust their own judgment when selecting staff, and the same holds true with respect to retaining advisors.

Would you keep personnel who are familiar but whose work is mediocre? Would you if they were family members, or an advisor? Familiarity may provide comfort, but it can come at a great cost. First, what constitutes average and superior performance?

THE COST OF BAD ADVICE

Some owners lament that advice costs too much. A response may require reframing the discussion. Granted, bad or poor advice may be worthless at best and catastrophic at worse. Mediocre advice can put a bad taste in an owner's mouth such that he is less likely to seek counsel due to less-than-wonderful experiences.

A simple question requiring a more difficult response is as follows: "Has the company grown as a result of the advice it has received or has the advisor benefited by the company's growth?" If the latter is true, the company may have outgrown the given advisor's usefulness or has not sought to exploit the advisory firm's breadth and depth of services.

It's highly recommend that owners gather their advisors together for an all-hands meeting at which time they can verbalize company challenges and opportunities—and effectively give notice that they're seeking cohesive engagement and guidance. This is the beginning of formulating a strategy that permits owners to achieve equity value enhancements by leveraging the knowledge and relationships provided by their advisors.

This can be in the context of developing a roadmap that notes where the company is today, resource gaps, and where the owner envisions navigating the company. The seasoned advisor will also recommend considering the input of the company board, key staff, family, clients, and vendors.

Owners should not only seek counsel from family, staff, and peers. Owners must be able to articulate and ask for guidance on how to get to where they envision going. Each advisor will have his or her take—colored by experience and professional background, which should be carefully weighed. There's no harm in also considering second opinions or asking for clarification to advice that has been given.

Most advisors are prone to using language and tools that are common to their own profession but may be not fully clear to an owner—and this is compounded when multiple advisors are consulted, especially if their advice differs. Either one internal or external person should be charged with clarifying information so owners/officers can understand the counsel provided in order to make informed decisions.

THE VALUE OF LEVERAGED KNOWLEDGE

Another point of this book is for owners to recognize that to achieve equity value enhancement, they must leverage intangible as well as tangible assets.

Intangible assets are those that can't be seen, but they have a distinct impact on business performance and value. They are governance, relationships, risks, and knowledge (GRRK). Much of this has to do with having a strategy to leverage outsized results from human and financial capital.

As it pertains to advisors, it's important to leverage their relationships and knowledge. Are you only talking to your accountant to do year-end tax planning? Do you only reach out to your business or tax attorney when an activity requires their assistance? If your answers are "yes," you need to revisit leveraging your relationships with advisors and the knowledge they possess.

Skilled accountants will recognize many operational business issues that can be addressed by them, an outsourced CFO, or another business advisor. This may include your friendly business appraiser, who can benchmark value and provide recommendations to increase profits, reduce taxes and risks, and enhance value significantly in many ways the owner may not have considered. This why I said "Value is more than a number." Some CPAs may introduce investment bankers with relationships with funding sources such as private equity groups. Each advisor may have his or her entourage of trusted advisors. It's good to tap into their knowledge, too.

What is the result of failing to leverage advisors in this way? It is untapped knowledge nuggets—nuggets that can have a significant effect on revenue, profits, and value. One of the difficulties that advisors contend with is that much of their advice is geared toward preventing the likelihood of significant disruption (e.g., disputes, audits, or litigation), so it's hard to see the short-term benefits of their work.

A few ways an attorney can add value is to suggest changing the structure of the company, recommend a change in how equity is held, and improve existing or draft new agreements. These actions could immediately reduce risk, save money, and continue to do so in the future. While the attorney receives fees for services, what would be the impact if updating agreements and bylaws cost $25,000 and reduced risk so equity value increased by $5 million? This is a 200-to-1 return.

Clearly, most attorneys are in the risk-shifting business. They may be able to provide guidance in establishing policies, and codify many of the company's intangibles (goodwill, relationships, and intellectual property, for instance), thereby protecting the company and owner from unforeseen problems in the future.

More simply, it's not unusual that having a good accountant and legal professional may increase the value of a business by 20 percent or more based on the counsel they provide and the counsel sought by the owner. Owners may wish to weigh the illusion that sage advice equates to giving up control and autonomy. If anything, solid advisors can provide the ability to prioritize activities that optimize company value while contemporaneously protecting it from loss and freeing time to act on strategy that uncovers new opportunities instead of daily dragon slaying.

How would you define your relationship with your trusted advisors? What yardstick are you using to evaluate them? If you ask yourself when paying the bill what you're getting for their counsel and are unsure, it might be time to ponder what you are asking from them and whether you are solely receiving technical guidance. Instead of thinking, "What's this costing me?" owners should be asking, "What value am I receiving for what I'm paying?"

A few years ago a wealthy client was weighing whether to switch her investment account to a different wealth advisor. When asked what prompted the decision, she replied the account had lost 15 percent of its value in 2008. My response was, given the nature of the account's holdings, the advisor ought to have doubled her fees. She snapped, "Why?!" After being educated about what typical losses for the period were, she was fortunate she was not down 25 percent or more. Arbitrary yardsticks may soothe the pain by creating the sense of control, but wiser folks than I know when to go and when to say "no."

As explained throughout the book, the untapped potential of great advisors should be weighed and employed. It could be the difference between adding an extra $25 million or $500 million to a company's value.

ENGAGING THE BEST

How can you determine whether you have the right advisors? This is more complex and challenging than it might initially sound. At the risk of sounding overly simplistic, if you have an advisor who costs you $1 million and you're not entirely clear what benefits you're receiving from the relationship, it may be time to review.

It's important to recognize that by virtue of being in a technical profession where many years have been invested, it's common for providers to rely on their knowledge. Keep in mind there are many impoverished, brilliant people.

There are many questions owners must answer if an advisory relationship is desired: Will this particular individual be well suited? Would you pay a premium if you knew this was an "A" player? How much more? What basis would you use to make the premium decision?

Part of the challenge for the "A" group is to articulate the difference they offer to individuals who may infrequently use their services. Since the stakes can be in the millions of dollars, wouldn't it behoove the owner (and other advisors) to become as well informed as possible?

I've conveyed that the burden is primarily on advisors to demonstrate their worth, but if you knew you were going to make a significant expenditure on personnel, equipment, or real estate, what degree of research would you undertake to ensure the best possible result? Shouldn't that same due diligence go into making advisor selections?

An indelicate point that must be made is that there are a number of C- and D-level players who have mastered relationship skills enough to overcome technical shortcomings. It is incumbent on owners to remember that they're not looking primarily for a friend, but someone who can have a significant positive impact on their business. It's guaranteed that if you've engaged a "C" or "D" advisor, at best you're receiving weak advice and at worst you're getting poor advice that could affect the business to the tune of millions of dollars—much more than whatever fees are being expended. Worse yet, in the absence of retaining two people at the same time, there is little way to know then whether advice was poor and the impact is compounding.

A cautionary note is needed here. If your advisor can't or won't make a recommendation when one has been sought, her body of knowledge may be somewhat limited and reflects poorly on the advisor's caliber of relationships. It is true that you can tell a lot about someone by the company they keep. Conversely, if they are only willing to provide three recommendations for fear of an adverse outcome by any one selection, they may limit how much skin in the game they have as compared to the owner.

PRACTICAL VETTING SUGGESTIONS

What things should you consider when you're in the market for a new advisor? Here is some food for thought:

1. How many years of experience should your practitioner have so you're paying for wisdom and technical expertise?
2. Should the individual reasonably charge a premium (higher fee)? If a skilled practitioner charges 50 percent higher than another candidate but requires less than half the time to produce a work product, which is the better investment? Mediocre advice on a budget is a bad idea.
3. Don't be attracted to solely generalist practitioners who may be jack-of-all-trades but master of none. This may dilute their contribution.
4. Ask peers and other professionals whom they recommend and why. Their responses can be telling.
5. The best line of inquiry to "A"-level advisors is to first tell them about your situation and the guidance you seek or what they would recommend—and for a justifiable fee, based on timeframe, scope, and complexity.
6. Be comfortable that if the questions you receive from an advisor are insightful and somewhat extensive and deep, you're likely dealing with an "A" player. This type of behavior tends to distinguish between one who's learned and thorough and one who's incapable of making an upfront investment of knowledge and time. A good "A"-level advisor should always provide options and be able to summarize after intake their understanding of the issues and your needs as well as suggested courses of action in a reasonable timeframe to achieve the preferred result.

What does this all mean? Do your homework. Do an online search of a potential advisor and his firm. Spend at least 30 minutes (and ideally more) and you'll be able to get a good idea of who the person is and where the advisor stands in the knowledge food chain. In addition, either ask or determine what percentage of the person's time and career is expended on unique issues that may be impacting your firm or you.

It's a common misconception to look for a deep specialty in too narrow an industry niche. This is because the practitioner may be unable to generate sufficient income. You may be searching for a needle in a haystack. A good example would be seeking a literary expert who specializes in faith-based audio books, when the underpinning issue may be a trade secret (trademark) dispute. As a result, someone who works in the publishing sector with deep experience with myriad issues dealing with trade secrets may be preferred rather than a niche of faith-based publications. Another way to put it would be to seek someone with at least 10 years of experience in trade secret litigation.

Business owners' most trusted advisors should be able to steer them past issues like this. In the scenarios noted earlier, the owner's advisor should have better articulated things the client wouldn't know—to streamline the search process.

A final point would be that if two or three advisors independently recommend the same firm, you probably should go with it. The statistical probability of getting identical recommendations from different sources is fairly low, so when that happens it may be considered a green light to proceed.

SIZE AND SCOPE CONSIDERATIONS

At the risk of offending, retaining a professional from a small firm doesn't mean you aren't hiring the best in class. It may be that an "A"-level practitioner is unwilling to serve two masters, the client and the firm, and prefers to operate as a sole proprietor or in a boutique environment.

Conversely, hiring a medium or large firm may provide somewhat of a coalition and the benefit of multiple insights where a premium may be more than justified. If a partner is involved in name only and a junior associate is performing the work, a premium may not be justified.

While tongue in cheek, it's important to forget everything you've learned on TV or the Internet. Advisors like attorneys and accountants (as well as doctors and law enforcement) seldom have lives as depicted on screen. Much of what goes on behind the scenes is culling through minutiae to determine relevance—a timely and painstaking process that's tedious, but often necessary.

It's no different than having a full medical exam that can consume much time when the best result is finding nothing wrong and the second best is knowing what's recommended based on a the exam's results. This is essentially what advisors do; it's seldom glamorous, but requires research and analytics even when a seasoned professional performs the work and has a pretty good idea of the result.

CASE IN POINT

All pilots, no matter how experienced, must do pre- and post-flight checks using a checklist. The alternative? That one missed thing may have everything to do with the safety of the pilot, passengers, plane, and cargo.

The more information you as the owner can gather and clearly summarize, the better your advisors' understanding and the advice that can be provided. However, a good advisor will want a thorough story, and here are two examples where that is *not* the case:

1. An owner with a "C" corporation tells a prospective CPA he's looking for a new accountant and asks how much that will cost.
2. An equity holder in a business dealing with a disruption (death or dispute) contacts a business attorney saying he needs advice, providing only that information and inquiring about the cost.

In both these cases, the backstory is missing (and the emphasis is on cost rather than quality).

An advisor needs to know the relevant details of the engagement, which can take time—minutes, hours, days, weeks, months, or even years—to uncover. It's common for advisors to require retainers because they don't know the full scope of an issue until they dig into it.

While perhaps familiar and simplified by owners, advisors may realize an issue is more complex than initially determined. In a perfect world, a wise owner would have a top advisor on retainer and speed dial to impart guidance before an important decision is made instead of afterward, when implications emerge that the owner was not aware of beforehand. Unringing a bell is difficult!

SETTING EXPECTATIONS

There are occasions when having an immediate need for an advisor's counsel may trump the need to complete due diligence to find someone ideally qualified to serve. Some advisors joined their profession as a direct result of seeing a family member fail to seek good counsel or having a poor experience they wouldn't wish on anyone, so they are focused on being a valuable resource.

When you engage an advisor to provide a quick fix, once the crisis has passed, it's a good idea to ensure this individual is a good long-term option. And, when you do choose your advisors, it's best to establish expectations early on to create the best working relationship.

For instance, you may expect to frequently call an advisor who, while seeing your relationship as important, often serves multiple clients and therefore has responsibilities she must balance. Unless you've paid a premium for 24/7 access, expecting a response in 24–48 hours is reasonable.

Communications can be streamlined if you leave a message noting the nature of your inquiry, the preliminary amount of time expected to address it, and whom the advisor may wish to call to coordinate a response (another advisor or assistant). This makes the process easier, saves time, and may lower costs.

Advisors also play a role in making communications more efficient, as it takes nominal time to acknowledge receiving an owner's query and ask for some preferred dates and times to discuss the issue at hand. (When scheduling a meeting, it's not enough to say that proposed options don't work; alternatives should be provided or else you can end up in an endless spiral of emails and voice mails. It's also a good idea to provide an meeting agenda beforehand, which allows for preparation.)

Expectations also must be set with respect to billable time and freebies as project fees seldom equate to unlimited hours. It's often the case that advisors call on colleagues to weigh in on a particular issue; when that happens they'll often devote some gratis time, but expecting they dedicate too much conveys an under-appreciation of the person's valuable time and talent.

Any charges an advisor incurs in the pursuit of serving a company's needs are usually going to be passed through, so it's recommended to draft an engagement letter that spells out the exact financial obligations. Also within that letter should be verbiage noting that services will cease if the owner is in arrears.

As a business owner, you have so many things on your plate that you really shouldn't have to worry about your advisors. After all, most are professionals. When you make good choices, based on research and recommendations, you eliminate those worries and can focus, together with your advisors, on growing your business and sleeping at night.

How many of the following types of advisors (where applicable and not all-inclusive) are on your speed-dial or should be?

1. **Business Intermediary**—From business brokers who usually are restricted from selling or buying less than 100 percent of a business and primarily list business for sale. Most listings are $5 million in sales and below. May not proactively seek and market to possible acquirers. Conversely, an investment banker is licensed and may work with a broker and may sell or buy less than 100 percent of business (asset or equity sale). This banker may also source debt funding from traditional (banks) and untraditional means (private investors). Usually transactions are $5 million to $25 million (lower mid-market). Middle to upper ("bulge bracket") mid-market is from $25 million to $1 billion.
2. **Private Equity Group**—Source of direct investment and funding in companies. Usually 100 percent; however, may be controlling or noncontrolling; equity only; debt and equity; debt only; selection by revenue or profit size; geography; industry; and will often have access to investor funds; financial sophistication; and either seek existing management to remain and provide board seats to investor(s) or may leverage acquisition with debt and utilize own staff to manage portfolio company. May also be a family office (highly affluent family with tens, hundreds of millions, or even billions of dollars to invest).
3. **Professional and Trade Associations**—May be an excellent source of strategic partnership and access to best practices/metrics as well as a resource of company founders/CXOs looking to sell or acquire competitive or vertical/horizontal companies to achieve economies of scale; more efficient operations and/or new markets.
4. **Family Business Advisory**—Broad segment of advisors who work with family businesses to examine how to successfully transition from one generation to another if electing to keep business in family or to work with key family members to explore roles prior to, during, and after involvement in a business. Focus is on social and emotional issues, not simply business and financial.
5. **Private Fiduciary/Trust Officer**—May be sought to look after settlors' less liquid assets such as real estate and business interests, where family members may have had little or no involvement in their direct ownership or operation to preserve the wealth and family legacy during life and after death of equity holder(s). May be in conjunction with family member who is named as trustee. By nature of the role, trustees are often much more risk adverse than business founder and less familiar with the esoteric assets, such as an operating business or farm/ranch. There is a large difference being an trust administrator versus a manager of alternative assets. The latter needs to be sourced.
6. **Business Attorney**—If specialist, may focus on formation and common "blocking and tackling" of a company, such as agreements, articles

of incorporation, and bylaws. May spend some time acting as outside counsel and provide guidance when considering buying or selling a company or its equity interest. May help with protecting intellectual property, such as patents and trade secrets. The attorney's suitability may be based upon business size and complexity.

7. **Transaction Attorney**—Usually involved in the due diligence, funding, buying, selling, merging, or divesting of business interests. May spend more time doing so involving real estate. May also help with business structure such as classes of shares and funding. Blocking and tackling that is associated with the risk from the perspectives of buyers, sellers, and funding source(s). Suitability may be based upon business size and complexity.
8. **Tax/Trust and Estate Attorney**—As part of the personal life cycle of owner(s) and business life cycle, often considers risk associated with concentrated wealth of significant business and/or real estate holdings as well as the tax ramifications (income, capital gains, gift, trust, and estate) of planned and unplanned events ranging from succession to disability. May also be involved in disputes with taxing authorities. Suitability may be based upon business size and complexity.
9. **Business Litigation Attorney**—Parties don't always agree or may perform acts that may cause harm to business interests or interest holders, such as, but not limited to, financial loss due to breach of contract or fiduciary duty, and partnership and shareholder disputes. May also be involved in IP lawsuits as well as disputes with regulatory bodies like OSHA and SEC.
10. **Commercial Banker**—Ranges from community bank with small business banking to specialty banks for certain types of business loans, to SBA/SBIC lenders to international banks with significant lending limits and letters of credit for foreign business transactions. Suitability may be based upon business size and complexity. Roles can and should be more than rates and terms.
11. **Certified Public Accountant**—May have former CFO experience. May primarily be compilation and reporting; audit and compliance. May have advisory skills based upon industry specialty or business/family needs. Tax/GAAP reporting focus may be confused with finance, economics, and operations skills by business clients with some CPAs being generalists and others expending most of their time in niche specialization, such as sales and real property taxation or trust administration. A plus if Certified Management Accountant (CMA).
12. **Chief Financial Officer: Outsourced**—Often due to company revenue size or sophistication may have not focused on effective roles of the CFO, such as ensuring adequate financial controls and metrics as well

as accessing and managing capital (treasury/cash management); effective inventory turnover; and other related decisions supporting business operations. Usually most involved in companies with $10 million or below in sales; otherwise, a full-time controller needed.

13. **Bookkeeper: Outsourced**—Commonly found in service-related businesses and also for very successful businesspeople whose personal and financial lives are blurred and need to be managed from personal check writing to consolidation of brokerage accounts.
14. **Insurance Professional**—Ranges from general brokerage from business property and casualty to directors and officers coverage; disability and life coverage as well as special lines, such as cybersecurity. Usually sought for buy–sell agreement funding. May suggest premium finance for high end life coverage or captive insurance when reinsurance and tax implications are ideal for certain companies and industries.
15. **Investment Advisor**—May be a specialist based upon asset class and usually will specifically examine opportunities and make allocations based upon advanced training, such as MBA, CIMA, ChFC, or CFA credential where portfolio may include both passive (public securities) and active assets (real property and operating businesses or business interests). May represent hedge or private equity funds and be paid for assets managed and/or capital raised from investors.
16. **IT Specialist**—If phone and computer systems become integrated due to need to monitor processes or clients, this function will be outsourced until such time as the technology demands within business warrant bringing the specialty in-house where ongoing customization may be sought.
17. **HR Specialist**—May range from outsourced payroll and employee leasing to policies and procedures being put into place and/or audited to ensure state/federal compliance of a safe or proper workplace environment. The role may be used to source new staff or when company is rightsizing current headcount. Brought in-house when issues require more full-time staff and skill levels.
18. **Wealth–Financial Advisor/Planner**—May also provide life and disability insurance and other product sales and occasionally also may be an accountant. May also be part of bank services suite. Often have one or more certifications to assist in the personal financial planning of discretionary income of business owners and/or company employees. As dollar amounts become greater may require more sophistication beyond relationship management using back-office support. Focus tends to be on allocation of equities and debt based upon the investor's risk profile and age. May have knowledge of business and how it impacts allocation of risk of illiquid assets versus control of concentrated risk and ability to

generate considerable wealth. May be intimately involved in important business decisions such as equity transfers or sales.

19. **Six Sigma/Lean Expert**—Quality management and efficiency expertise associated with operational, distribution, and supply chain. Commonly used in manufacturing or sophisticated distribution and warehousing operations.
20. **Business Strategist**—Broad scope from business unit to enterprise-wide examination of long-term objectives not being deferred based upon daily blocking and tackling getting in the way of planning and optimization of resources to ensure future growth.
21. **Board and Governance Specialist**—May work in conjunction with or be in addition to business strategy to ensure there is adequate process and procedure in place that formalizes a company's culture and to ensure operational management is furthering both compliance and strategic objectives. Identifies proper individuals have adequate skills to govern and contribute to the many diverse roles required in an organization from marketing to finance and operations.
22. **Conflict Resolution Specialist**—May be a family business advisor; however, tends to be a specialist who may not seek accommodation between parties, but used to minimize disruption and/or damage to the business itself based upon the roles of the disputing parties, which may include owners, when legal assistance may not be seen as the best alternative to resolve conflict.
23. **Business Advisor/Coach**—Often focuses on specific needs of given client or family who may wish to enhance skill sets in negotiation or problem solving as well as other business and family challenges, such as work–life balance. Acts as sounding board and provides developmental assistance.
24. **Sales and Marketing Professional**—Similar to the above advisor but may work with entire organization to assist in messaging and better promotion and closing of product and service offerings using company staff.
25. **ESOP Trustee**—Usually works in conjunction with ERISA/transaction attorney; accountant and funding sources to establish an employee stock ownership plan, whereby a certain equity percentage of company will be owner or bank funded and subsequently owned by employees over a vesting period. This is to ensure the employees as trust participants are adequately represented and the ESOP is properly administered.
26. **Business Valuation Analyst**—May be associated with an accounting firm or investment banking organization; however, may also be affiliated with a real estate appraisal firm or perform purely independent valuations of companies for tax, transfer, or transaction purposes as well as disputes of equity interests held. IRS/court-qualified and certified

analysts must provide compliant work product with varying degree of intellectual rigor based upon company size and complexity.

27. **Family Office Advisor**—If company generates considerable wealth and/or complexity, the running of the family and its investment of the operating asset(s) may require continuity or transition of the concentrated risk and the family legacy across generations. The larger the wealth and the number of family members and interests, the more likely full-time staff such as investment managers, attorneys, and accountants are needed and the more likely a formal governance structure will be required to transition to a fully family run organization from business to private foundations to co-investment between family members and other affluent families.
28. **Exit Planner**—The planner may solely work with the business owner to contemplate life after business ownership akin to a family business advisor to a business intermediary who may also prepare the business owner and the business for a sale (partial or full liquidity event). They may also be an accountant and/or business valuation analyst. Presumably, independent of whether sale is contemplated or not.
29. **Academic Institutions**—Often an alternative resource of best practices with MBA students who may make recommendations or institute changes to enhance operational performance without the same degree of costs as more seasoned advisors with usually a professor overseeing the deliverables. Skilled students may be offered middle or senior management opportunities based upon their prior work experience and niche specialization to be groomed to be part of the company's executive management team or to even replace the founder when family and staff are not adequate alternatives and a sale may not be contemplated in the near term.
30. **1031 Exchange Specialist**—Many successful business owners will either acquire real property that will be owner-occupied or allocate their wealth across different asset classes. When capital gains taxes are sought to be deferred; management is preferred to be performed by others; or capital is to be leveraged with co-investors; and/or greater income is sought; a 1031 exchange may be a viable option and requires a knowledgeable real estate professional.
31. **Real Estate Broker/Agent/Appraiser**—A real estate listing and selling agent/broker or appraiser may provide insight as to best optimizing the use of the real property assets, which may also include a cost segregation specialist to accelerate the depreciation of the various component values of improved real property, thereby allowing for lower taxes and higher cash flow.

32. **Cost Specialist**—If a company makes thousands or millions of dollars in annual purchases across all operations from phone calls to delivery services or supplies to as esoteric as training reimbursement, the specialist will seek to renegotiate the pricing or credits or will share in the savings for a defined period.
33. **Philanthropy Specialist**—During the life cycle of businesses and owners, there is often one or more causes they wish to support with new or established wealth for personal and tax purposes. The establishment of such entities requires familiarity with the tax rules and operations depending upon whether the entity will be self-directed.

While we dedicate an entire chapter to risks, the following pages provide a useful checklist of some of the most common risks found during our due diligence in benchmarking company value. Thereafter, by harnessing the power of your advisors (among your other constituents) you can develop a successful strategy to managing and mitigating these risks to build and create enhanced company value.

Top 29 Operational Risks Found in 3,000+ Business Valuation Engagements *(Frequency 80% or more often)*:

1. Meeting minutes are boilerplate (90%).
2. No budget or forecasts (80%).
3. No performance metrics /nominal knowledge of market or competitors (80%).
4. No annual review of insurance (90%).
5. No independent and regular independent and qualified valuation (95%).
6. No business, marketing, or succession plans (90%).
7. No strategy (90%).
8. Nominal effort to cull clients (80%).
9. No gain-sharing for innovation (90%).
10. Culture is control oriented, siloed, and tactical (80%).
11. Banking relationship is solely transactional (80%).
12. Board comprised of family, inside directors, and friends (95%).
13. Limited or no involvement in own or client industry associations (80%).
14. Poor knowledge of balance sheet, P&L, and growth norms for industry (90%).
15. No shareholder/key person/buy–sell agreements or not followed (80%).
16. No risk assessments/SWOT analysis (80%).
17. No review of education, experience, age, and health of key personnel (80%).
18. Concentration of clients and vendors (80%).
19. Little to no leverage of trusted advisors (90%).

20. No independent advisory board (95%).
21. Little leverage of human capital (knowledge and relationships) (90%).
22. No effort to identify, protect, and/or leverage intangible assets (80%).
23. Founder, management, and/or advisors have reached growth capacity (80%).
24. No review to optimize capital structure (90%).
25. No supply chain analysis (90%).
26. Nominal cross-training of personnel (80%).
27. Nominal redundancy of key functions (80%).
28. Little or no training budget (80%).
29. Underfunded or unfunded buy–sell agreement (80%).

In this listing, the (%) represents the frequency the deficiency (risk) is found. There are hundreds of such risks and the number of risks triples when the frequency is reduced to 50 percent. Industry and revenue size often have nominal correlation to the number of risks. Professional management and a culture of exceptional performance reduce risks and elevate price multiples and enterprise value. Most of the risks deal with human capital issues. Most of them are not found on financial statements. They have a dramatic influence on intangible value. The greater the focus on governance, relationships, and knowledge by leadership and its constituents, the lower the level of risks and the greater the economic benefit and equity value.

Most common constituents are: bankers—investment/commercial; wealth/trust/insurance advisors; family business advisors; and, of course, attorneys and accountants. These trusted advisors can actively assist in increasing opportunity and value while lowering risk. My role is a chief-of-staff and/or strategic value architect, when staff or advisors have a need for alignment, metrics, and facilitation.

Finally, I have found one constant truth about lifetime learners and their successful organizations. They are well read and thirst for knowledge nuggets.

Following are some (classic and new) recommendations from my own library. I hope they serve you as well as they have me.

David Maister, *The Trusted Advisor*, Free Press, 2000.

Gabor Weinstein, *Poised for Growth: Taking Your Business to the Next Level*, McGraw-Hill, 1997.

Daniel Gross, *Greatest Business Stories of All Times*, Forbes, 1997.

J.W. Marriott, *The Spirit to Serve: Marriott's Way*, Harper Business, 1997.

Morgan Jones, *The Thinker's Toolkit*, Three Rivers Press, 1995.

Francis Hesselbein, *The Organization of the Future*, Jossey Bass Press, 1997.

William Bridges, *Managing Transitions*, Addison Wesley, 1991.

Jim Collins, *Built to Last: Successful Habits of Visionary Companies*; Harper Business, 2002.

Jim Collins, *Good to Great: Why Some Companies Make the Leap and Others Don't*, Harper Collins, 2001.

Joel Arthur Barker, *Paradigms: The Business of Discovering the Future*, Harper Business, 1993.

Michael Watkins, *Shaping the Game: The New Leader's Guide to Effective Negotiating*, Harvard Business School Press, 2006.

C. William Pollard, *The Soul of the Firm*, Harper Business, 1996.

Kevin Freiberg, *NUTS: Southwest Airlines' Crazy Recipe and Personal Success*, Bard Press, 1996.

Steven Covey, *First Things First*, Simon & Schuster, 1994.

Rowan Gibson, *Rethinking the Future*, Nicholas Brealy, 1997.

John Maxwell, *The 21 Irrefutable Laws of Leadership* (10th Edition), Thomas Nelson, 2007.

Dennis Kimbro, *What Makes the Great Great*, Doubleday, 1997.

Thomas Cleary, *Training the Samurai Mind*, Shambala Publications, 2008.

Dale Carnegie, *How to Win Friends and Influence People*, Pocketbooks, 1936.

Marc Lesser, *Zen of Business Administration*, New World Library, 2005.

David Bollier, *Aiming Higher: How Companies Prosper by Combining Sound Management and Social Vision*, Amacom, 1996.

Larry Wilson, *Play to Win: Choosing Growth Over Fear in Work and Life*, Bard Press, 1998.

Ken Blanchard, *Mission Possible: Becoming a World Class Organization While There's Still Time*, McGraw Hill, 1997.

Oliver Wright, *ABCD Checklist for Operational Excellence* (5th Edition), Wiley, 2000.

Oliver Wright, *Class A Checklist for Business Excellence* (6th Edition), Wiley, 2005.

Peter Drucker, *Managing for the Future*, Truman Talley Books, 1992.

Dan Kennedy, *No B.S. (Business Success): The Ultimate No Holds Barred, Kick Butt, Take No Prisoners, Tough and Spirited Guide*, Entrepreneur Press, 2004.

Alec Fisher, *Critical Thinking*, Cambridge University Press, 2001.

C. Richard Weylman, *The Power of Why*, Houghton Mifflin Harcourt, 2013.

Harvey MacKay, *Swim with the Sharks without Being Eaten Alive*, William Morrow, 1988.

NOTE

1. David Maister, *The Trusted Advisor* (New York: Touchstone, 2001).

CHAPTER 4

Risk in the Eye of the Beholder

Owners who want to increase the value of their businesses must think specifically about what they're doing to make that happen—rather than having an attitude of how profit can be paid in compensation and salary. Remember the point of Paul Thiel. The company's board and corner office has a fiduciary duty to maximize shareholder value.

This requires long-term thinking and a strategy to support value growth versus more instant gratification. This is in large part why executives are often provided stock options in lieu of higher salaries. For private companies not wishing to give up equity and/or control, they can offer phantom stock or nonvoting stock to key staff.

In order to instill the strategic framework that flows to every employee and externally from the company, businesses must cultivate extraordinary cultures. Such cultures embrace innovation and being dynamic. This is because the market is not static, so serving it can't be, either.

It's all about *optics*. One of the greatest challenges regarding risk is that different constituencies (owners, advisors, family, staff, shareholders, board members, clients, and vendors) are often focused on different risks. Each has a specific, sometimes narrow, perspective on risk. In this chapter we look at how various disciplines render opinions about risk and opportunity through their own lenses. These optics are primarily associated with mid-market companies, which the Wall Street Journal defines as those with annual revenues between \$50M and \$1B. I have included lower mid-market as well as small-cap public companies as they share common issues outlined in this book: the need to leverage both human and financial capital and ensuring management executes on a strategy with performance metrics that include enhanced shareholder value (return on invested capital).

As expressed elsewhere, a key thesis of risk identification, measurement, management, and mitigation is that it is a shared role of the company's ecosystem—the business, its environment, and all its constituents are involved. The key is harnessing direction amongst human capital. One of the ongoing issues is that each perspective may have blind spots unless there is a sufficient understanding of what each constituent, including the owners, sees as risk and opportunity.

It is incumbent on business appraisers and advisors to identify and measure and address how these varying perceptions of risk impact business value. Part of their commitment to objectivity and independence is to ensure no professional bias creeps into the process of vetting others' perceptions or realities. Chapters 7 and 8 provide a lengthy discourse on many of these risks.

CASE IN POINT

Accountants may believe identifying tax deductions and credits means they're doing their job to lower risks and seeking opportunities to minimize companies from overpaying taxes. They may be focusing solely on income tax, failing to examine capital gains, estate, or gift taxes and how they may affect the business, other family members, and shareholder(s) down the line. They may see the additional taxable income where every dollar earned in new profits still means perhaps 60 cents held by the company. The point is most owners earning an extra $1 million in additional profits and possibly $10 million in additional value are likely to be okay with parting with $400,000. It's not all that unusual for accountants to file quarterly estimated taxes due to delayed accountings, which ties up millions of dollars of excess taxes paid (to be on the safe side), which have clear opportunity costs because these dollars aren't available to be deployed within the operating enterprise. Therefore, accountants may wish to see the big picture of the here and now as well as assisting in helping the client to arrive at the desired destination. This may not occur if the accountants' or clients' risk lenses are too narrow, which can unwittingly adversely impact a business's value.

Advisor neutrality can be difficult to implement, but it's important to try to see if a technical bias exists that may affect the business on a short- or long-term basis. If this exercise is done on an ad-hoc basis across several advisory disciplines, consider how it might impact the owner(s). Conversely, a cohesive viewpoint can exist to focus on a direction if not a certain course of action that could help exploit an opportunity or minimize risk—a win-win.

INEXPERIENCED BUSINESS APPRAISER LENSES

Neophyte business appraisers or real estate appraisers or accountants who dabble in business appraisal may complete just a handful of business and business interest appraisals a year. They often get bogged down when trying to determine the time and value of money, usually at the heart of the valuation thesis. Due to resource and time limitations some use nominal financial metrics that may provide skewed results or sometimes fall short—such as insufficient use of robust data for comparative analysis because too few engagements doesn't cost justify the data investment, which can be tens of thousands of dollars annually. It also explains why their fees may be lower.

They may over-rely on financial performance as value indicator without consideration of operational issues and human capital. As an example, seasoned valuation professionals may inquire the percentage of revenue of line-item expenses such as labor, repair/maintenance, and advertising expenses or the influence of human capital. Such items may give real insights into company-specific risk, which is at the heart of why "value is more than just a number."

Occasionally, CPA-trained business appraisers see and approach risk from their own lens, such as standards associated with financial reporting influenced by state and federal regulations. They don't necessarily adjust their orientation when they're placed in the role of business appraiser, which means they may have to share news their business owner client may not wish to hear. A low appraised value may dismay the client, which the CPA wants to avoid as the valued relationship and future accounting work could be at risk.

For example, the CPA appraiser may be unfamiliar with how a dissenting shareholder action may impact the standard of value (how equity is to be valued) or the impact of a CFO with inadequate private capital markets or treasury management experience despite having many years' tenure at the client company. The CFO may have started in the Accounts Payable department.

These issues often take time to gestate versus "learn as I go" for inexperienced business appraisers. The warning "buyer beware" (*caveat emptor*) would be appropriate here.

CPA LENSES

Some of the very best business advisors I know are accountants. Most, though, are trained to focus on tax and compliance issues. While it's certainly valuable for a business owner to know he is not paying unnecessary taxes, that's not the same thing as understanding operational risks that influence company and equity value. Many CPAs render value opinions without credential or formal training. They have seen sufficient reports cross their desk and think, "How difficult can this be?"

Risks that are associated with financial reporting and compliance with GAAP (generally accepted accounting principles) differ from far deeper and wider valuation considerations. Since the majority of CPAs that perform valuations only complete three or four valuation engagements annually according to industry association surveys, they seldom possess the requisite skill for more complex valuation issues. *(Consider this for a moment. If the theory of mastery dictates 10,000 hours and the average appraisal engagement takes 30 hours, this would suggest a part-time appraiser would need 100 years to achieve the mastery of a full-time business appraiser.)*

While occasionally assisting business owners who are contemplating the 6Ts of business—transitions, transfers, transactions, transformations, taxes, or trouble—the CPAs' abilities to measure, manage, and mitigate risk may be insufficient, as the level of due diligence and intellectual rigor performed is likely focused on revenues and profits which is inadequate to identify all company-specific risks without sufficient skills and experience.

A trained and designated CPA appraiser who has gone through a course of instruction by one of the national business valuation associations is provided basic training to apply the buildup method (BUM). BUM assumes that national investors first examine a risk-free rate based upon the likely period an investment is held and which presumes that repayment is guaranteed—a U.S. government obligation such as U.S.Treasury bonds, bills, and notes.

After determining that rate, the next level of valuing equity is examining the risks/returns found in larger public companies on an index like S&P's over a period of time. This indicator is for larger public stocks, which often represent stable, mature companies; and then there is the notion of volatility (or beta), which, depending on its level, may reflect more or less risk associated with companies within an industry sector and market (systemic risk).

Size premia is also at play here. In most cases, appraisers are valuing companies that are relatively small compared to larger S&P index companies. As such, over the long term, all things being equal, the smaller the company, the greater the perceived risk. What's important here is providing an apples-to-apples risk rate based on size.

Other elements, such as a company's tax status, will have an effect on value. This is because C corporations are double taxed. The public company proxies for risk are always C corporations; however, many go through machinations to report nominal or no taxable income with the effective rates paid nearer to half of the assumed 40 percent combined rate that are occasionally applied to pass-through private companies as part of the valuation exercise.

The overarching point here is that CPAs will value businesses based on the way they were taught to do it, and most are taught the same way. Theoretically, that means all CPA-produced values for a company should have the same result. This seldom occurs. (In fairness, this is also true for tax returns based upon the premise of certain assumptions and interpretations made.)

Part of the genesis for writing this book is arguably the most important step of BUM. The last step in determining value under the Income Approach is identifying ***company-specific risk***, and here is where there simply is insufficient experience, documentation, and intellectual rigor to support most risks cited. *(Weighted average cost of capital excluded from consideration.)*

This is where the issue, absent the knowledge, resources, and due diligence, often results in a significant spread of values with no credible explanation if one analyst expressed the company specific risk is 2 percent added to the BUM equity risk premium, and the other analyst expresses 6 percent (*further compounded based upon assumptions of growth rates*).

First, there are many full-time CPA business appraisers who do a fine job and adhere to the business valuation profession's standards. However, please understand business appraisers are retained and compensated to determine economic benefit (growth and income) and company-specific risk at the entity and equity levels. This means their opinions may influence millions and even billions of dollars. Therefore, adequately measuring company-specific risk puts a bright light on the issue of whether being a CPA in of itself is akin to being a qualified appraiser. The national association for which all CPAs are members is the American Institute of Certified Public Accountants. This issue is not limited to noncredentialed and credentialed CPAs. The AICPA has 400,000+ members, making them the most ubiquitous provider of these advisory services. The AICPA has provisions as part of their Code of Conduct that, absent intellectual rigor, CPA work product is "dabbling," which is a standards violation.

About a dozen years ago, several seasoned and credentialed business appraisers assisted the AICPA in drafting their valuation standards that became SSVS-1. Both accredited and non-accredited CPAs who are performing valuations *must* adhere to these standards. Yet, simply following prescribed steps may be inadequate due diligence to render a supported value.

How is this point demonstrated anecdotally? There should be pages in a business appraisal report that discuss company-specific risks—not simply financial metrics. Most reports have only about a paragraph or two addressing risks. Software-driven metrics may address some risks, but it's wholly inadequate to cover all legal, financial, and operational risks. You'll find many of these discussed in the lengthy Chapters 7 and 8, and that list is less than a tenth of risks—only some of the most common.

What often occurs is the claim "in my professional opinion," but there is often insufficient information provided to support the results provided. It is circular logic. This is because at some point the earliest report that the business appraiser performed was done the same way: which may have been and in all likelihood was not nearly as well supported (based upon most learning curves alone). If the original work product had not applied the appropriate due diligence, then any subsequent report on which third parties rely would be suspect. Unfortunately, the nature of this occurrence is often the rule versus the exception. Often, it's why there is such a difference in services fees and opined values. (*Further compounding this event perpetuating is those most often relying on this work product are attorneys and business owners, who may lack the education and experience in finance to identify work product issues.*)

Producing one work product using adequate due diligence, including time spent to generate company-specific risk, would take at least twice as long as another report where no effort has been made to support the risk and value conclusions. Because it's common that clients and most advisors have limited experience with valuations, they're unaware of the glaring limitations of the reports they receive. They occasionally perpetuate the somewhat flawed notion that valuation is as much an art as a science. The fact is with technology advances there is much more data available, so empirical support while occasionally imperfect is available. Further, in venues like a courtroom, a business appraiser would go through a meat grinder in the absence of providing adequate support of the level of risk at the enterprise and equity levels.

As a result, it's common some CPAs and others who offer valuation reports state they won't defend their valuation results in litigation. How good could the result be if the creator is not predisposed to defend it? Beware of valuations that are cleverly masked as a calculation. That would be akin to your physician eyeballing you and guessing the medication you require. You'll save money at the checkup—at what cost?

ATTORNEY LENSES

Attorney clients typically have represented 90 percent of my business. They offer an invaluable service that often goes unappreciated as it's nuanced. Attorneys' interests with respect to entity and equity value risks will often differ based on what discipline they practice. For example, transactional attorneys will be most interested in what due diligence is needed to ensure their clients' interests are best represented, while tax attorneys are likely to focus on how to minimize or defer tax liability.

Litigation attorneys will hone in on statutes and court cases to advocate for their clients' positions as plaintiff or defendant. Business, trust, and estate attorneys often work in the area of structure, agreement drafting, asset protection and preservation, becoming familiar with jurisdictional, statutory. and regulatory issues that drive how risk becomes codified and ensuring their proper representation in provisions.

Attorneys are in the business of risk identification, management, and mitigation as they're often tasked with anticipating issues and optimizing opportunities (risk shifting). It stands to reason that when two parties are involved and each has an attorney whose primary agenda is to best advocate client's interests, the outcome is often somewhere in the middle. What usually gets lost in these scenarios is what a professional valuation expert is advocating—not the client, which is the attorney's responsibility. While nuanced, this is the difference between a "hired gun" and a skilled valuation warrior-statesman who knows all the assumptions and biases the opposing side's analyst may use. As earlier stated, it's the rare attorneys who also have business, finance, economics, or accounting degrees. Many will express that their mastery of getting to the nuanced issues and use of experts offsets this knowledge gap.

If I memorized *Black's Law Dictionary*, this does not qualify me to render legal opinions. I have no qualms with not having mastered the practice of law, albeit I have reviewed thousands of legal documents and testified in court more than many attorneys will try their cases in a lifetime. It'd be reasonable to expect the same due.

A Juris Doctoral–level of intellect and a degree of humility suggests a degree of wisdom is earned when one knows what they do not know. The "secret" is knowing where to obtain the information and being able to apply and articulate its use. How is this evidenced? One way is in describing how legal documents' provisions may have an impact on a company's value. They may be elegantly drafted, but the attorneys who authored them don't always understand their impact on equity value. It has been my experience very few have sought appraiser counsel on how provisions on equity holder rights might impact value.

CASE IN POINT

A company with multiple shareholders has a document drafted based on voting stock (two shareholders hold 1% each and two hold 49% each of all outstanding stock) rights. If the two 1 percent interests hold all voting rights and disagree, there's no offset provision for this occurrence. And what if each interest held did have voting rights? The issue at hand is what the values of 1, 49, 50, and 51 percent are—an important distinction at the equity value level based upon the document's legal provisions and how interest holders have voted.

How about a provision providing the right of first refusal along with the timeframe within which it must be exercised before the next party gets its turn? From the beginning of a potential transaction, when considering due diligence and the time it takes to receive legal and tax opinions, over half a year may transpire before a third party can exercise its prerogative to purchase. What are the opportunity costs associated with a six-month time delay, which would be a financial consideration, where such an impact may have not been considered at the time of the provision's drafting?

Another example is the impact of an arrangement where the value is agreed on but the terms are such that by agreement, payment is not received until the end of the year at an interest rate that may be below the current market rate. What is the risk to the seller? As these last few paragraphs demonstrate, provisions authored by attorneys can have a great impact on value, so as they navigate clients' risks, the skilled valuator may be a worthwhile resource to call upon before the fact, not after.

INVESTMENT BANKER/BUSINESS BROKER/BUSINESS INTERMEDIARY LENSES

Much of the valuation work performed by investment bankers, business brokers, or business intermediaries operates on the notion of a specific buyer and seller—who's able and wishes to make such an investment. The difference between these professionals is often their licensing and credential to sell equities and enterprises as well as fund debt.

The very nature of these professionals means they are motivated either by the buy side or sell side in a transaction; their goal is to obtain the highest price on the sell side or pay the lowest price on the buy side as well as consideration of terms and conditions once an intended purchase price is agreed.

Arguably, the final transaction represents intrinsic value to the specific party or parties (if there was an auction with multiple offers)—the buyer and seller—and a single transaction data point. This is in conflict with the notion that value represents a pool of actual or probable transactions (multiple data points), regardless of whether the income or market approach to determining value is applied.

Couple that with another reality—these professionals receive compensation based on successful transactions, typically a percentage of the deal price or capital raised. Thus, there's a degree of potential bias based on those represented parties due to how they may be paid. Some deals may not even make sense or fail to achieve the synergies sought, but all involved usually want to see them closed.

Consider two examples. First, a company has beaten all the odds and is going to have an initial public offering (IPO). The value of the stock is set at $17 per share and by the end of the trading day it ends up at $25 a share—50 percent greater. Was the original value accurate and does the seller care? Now fast-forward a few months later and the shares are trading at $12.50—50 percent less than the $25 a share. Did the company performance change significantly during that month or two?

The other example is Company A acquires Company B for $20 per share; however, as is all too common, the synergies expected from the acquisition don't materialize. Is it due to the competency of Company A or their advisors or that a degree of irrationalism entered into the decision process, such as the acquiring CEO knowing his compensation would be boosted by the purchase or simply the love of the deal? The point is Company A overpaid as the synergies associated with paying a premium price were not realized (...of course it could have been a cultural mismatch which often occurs).

There's also a time element, since the typical period between listing, due diligence, negotiation, funding, and closing can be as few as several months, but a year or more is not unusual. In a strong market, the number of transactions investment bankers are able to complete is two to four annually. Nor is it unusual that 50 percent of retentions don't manifest in consummated deals. Does this mean the deal price and terms were unacceptable or the buyer or seller got cold feet?

Realistically, how much time is available to define the value of a business with a high degree of due diligence when at the same time investment bankers are looking to do deals? Spinning it another way, will an investment banker be more interested in a $30,000 valuation report fee or receiving a six- or seven-figure commission check from the funding or transaction of a business?

A large number of transactions result in a degree of buyer's or seller's remorse—human capital (knowledge and relationships as well as governance or cultural) differences may differ sufficiently that the value sought was not achieved. In these scenarios, financial trumped cultural and operational issues—which may have been uncovered if adequate due diligence was performed or post-merger integration had been funded.

If the previous issues are true, should the values opined by these professionals be given the same credence as a professional who performs 20, 30, or 40 independent engagements per annum? There is an argument by these professionals that they are involved in the transactions and therefore have a better feel for the actual issues governing what will sell, why, and for what price and terms. Is this the same as risk identification?

Where a strategic valuation architect comes into play is to offer independent opinion of value or to assist in value creation pre- and post-sale and/or merger by identifying, measuring, and managing risks. This is ideal when there are multiple shareholders and more than one class of shares where rights and fiduciary responsibilities may be required, such as funding liquidity using an employee stock option plan (ESOP).

COMMERCIAL BANKER LENSES

Commercial bankers look at risks from a creditworthiness standpoint. They determine the amount and cost of capital they're willing to extend usually based on the tangible assets of a business or its cash flow. (The bottom line is the ability to repay the loan.)

While it would serve a bank's purposes to assist business owners in identifying their operational risks and demonstrate how debt capital may assist in scaling the business, it seldom occurs. This is a shame as the commercial banker who knows business risks could have an important role to optimize client company performance and increase company equity value by leveraging tangible and intangible assets. Those who can look beyond rates, terms, and ratios to risks, growth rate, and profitability will be able to bring more value to business owners, literally and figuratively—differentiating themselves and their banks by having a keener understanding of operating, not simply credit risk.

If this was done, the weight given to primarily tangible asset based businesses due to their collateral (especially given what these assets sell for if bankruptcy occurs) may be shifted to cash flows generated by knowledge based companies, which is an ever-increasing segment of businesses in the United States. Failing to do so, creates a funding void that families of affluence and other investment groups are and will continue to fill after the 2009 financial crisis.

INSURANCE PROFESSIONAL LENSES

The insurance profession has an interesting backstory. Actuaries who determine appropriate premiums allow providers to make a profit between the premiums charged, and income generated on these premiums held net of claims paid. The core duty is deep data analytics to understand the probability, the payout, the premium, and the profit. They toil in the back office. Those in the front office, however, sell relationships and risk management capabilities, and their perspective is often more aligned with business value than most professions.

On a routine basis, insurance professionals deal with the impact of liability, loss, and life. They are aware of the impact when insurance is and isn't present. They see impact of disability, business interruption, and continuity. And their providers may find themselves in litigation with clients whose expectations of coverage were not met.

Insurance professionals understand that the amounts business owners pay in premiums reduces their companies' operational risks. There is a disservice when insurance companies choose to use software to produce a company's value (a subject discussed elsewhere in this book). This can result in instances of being over- or underinsured, and also creates a paradigm that underrepresents the extensive issues for which software alone simply cannot account. This was evidenced by the algorithms produced by PhDs in applied math and economics that failed to account for both debt and equity failing on a seismic scale during the 2008/2009 market crash. The perceived premium payment savings versus risk mitigation by having no or inadequate coverage is so nominal compared to coverage benefits of both the risk reduction and value creation. For example, if a $20,000 premium increased a company's value (by lowering risk) by $1,000,000, the 50:1 return on investment is evident and can be easily articulated.

These issues hold true for liability, property, and casualty insurance professionals as well as those who focus on life and disability insurance. Many in the latter group may also have the ability to assist clients by providing financial planning and management services that more seamlessly can tie liquidity and tax planning with asset protection and allocation.

WEALTH MANAGER/FINANCIAL ADVISOR/ FIDUCIARY/TRUST OFFICER LENSES

Professionals who operate as wealth managers, financial advisors, fiduciaries, and trust officers often have a great deal of knowledge and financial savvy, but it's often used to manage primarily passive investments like publicly-traded securities, which are historically considered lower risk (especially with hedging) and more liquid. Yet, assets such as real property and private company equities are also held by affluent families in trusts or holding companies. These interests are often difficult to manage and value. Most disputes tend to concern not as much the administration fiduciary duty, but the capacity to adequately manage alternative assets. Hence, this is why examining the role of a strategic value architect is prudent.

These aforementioned trusted advisors could reorient themselves and have a real impact on assets beyond preserving wealth. In part this is because part of their role is asset allocation, which attempts to minimize risk. Keep in mind, as earlier expressed, that this may be at cross purposes with the more risk-tolerant company owners and founders. This is because having accumulated wealth successfully even with concentration suggests they believe they can do so in the future, and may wish to do so (perhaps candidates with "caps" that limit too much capital to be invested in more risky endeavors).

Nothing makes this point better than attending family business events offered by organizations like the Family Business Network, Family Firm Institute, and Family Business Magazine's Transitions. These are attended by successful multigenerational family businesses, such as the Gallo family of wine fame or the Wiley family (the owner and publisher of this book). One family is five generations and the other is going on eight. One company is privately held and the other is public.

The wealth advisory opportunity may be missed to bring institutional knowledge that could assist owners in increasing the value of their assets (business and real estate). There is a gradual trend that the more affluent are gravitating toward direct investment and that level of institutional quality assistance is needed, but it's been at glacial speed.

As noted earlier, those whose fees are dependent on managed assets will see risk as anything that reduces the principal. While it's a worthy endeavor to maintain or grow clients' assets, that risk focus fails to answer a fundamental question: Whose risk is it? How risky are their investments? Over what period? Should they sell part or all or continue to grow their companies after they've mastered concentrated risk and outperformed most financial advisors? Does it serve their best interest to sell or invest in publicly traded stocks, bonds, and other assets?

Another important question for owners is in regard to fees charged by those who manage some or all of their assets. Are they tied to performance? What is the long-term performance? In addition, if assets are merely being preserved, are they protected adequately by insurance when they're illiquid? Is their growth keeping pace with inflation and market indices, and do they generate sufficient income for the payment of other obligations?

The answers to most of these questions usually come down to fees, ability to generate a consistent level of returns, as well as allocation. If the asset is bonds, fees are relatively low, but they get higher for less passive real estate, and higher still for direct investment equity, private equity funds, hedge funds, and funds of funds. Investing in ETFs or mutual fund indexes with lower loads (purchase and management fees) may make more sense, but the risk may be who manages the fund, how well, and for how long.

For owners who are sufficiently affluent and have adequate discretionary cash, allocation may already be a reality. This means they have sufficient liquidity that issues such as taxes, personal financial needs, and concentrated risk positions may have a smaller impact to their ability to weather market or industry level downturns. There are a sufficient number of successful multigenerational business-owning families who have mitigated the impact of concentrated risk through establishing family charters that have both a business strategy and family legacy component.

Modern portfolio theory suggests, all things being equal, the market will be efficient, its ups and downs will smooth, and the long-term performance of public markets will be favorable—however, that certainly wasn't true in the 1990s and for much of the 2000s.

In fact, the highest and lowest level of the NASDAQ was in March 2000 and March 2009, where it was 5,133 and 1,266, respectively. Current stock market performance may be arguably more a function of quantitative easing (the printing of more money flooding the markets, which may lead to inflation) versus the retail investors all returning to the otherwise frothy markets.

The point is that it has been 15 years since the low with current levels at north of 5,000. This means dollar values have yet to be restored due to inflation. This is the playing field dominated by institutional investors' algorithm-technology driven shorter-term best prognostications.

Many people believe market conditions have less to do with public company performance and more to do with speculation. This claim tends to be proven by the low percentage of investment firms and funds that match or exceed stock market indexes on a consistent basis despite presumably maintaining a balanced portfolio. As an example, if the resulting return of a small selection is X and after fees and loads it's below X as compared to an index, there's really no point in investing that narrowly; you may be better off investing in an index-based mutual fund.

The S&P 500 index has typically beaten nearly two-thirds of all actively managed large-cap mutual funds. Further, SPIVA (S&P Indices versus Active Funds) scorecard reported that 75 percent of actively managed mid-cap funds were bested by the S&P Mid Cap 400 index and that returns for 63 percent of small-cap funds were exceeded by the S&P Small Cap 600 index.

Here's a sobering statistic: 80 percent of pooled funds invested in private companies underperform the public indexes due to significant fees. This is a not-so-secret that is unknown to many investors.

In late 2014, Larry Swedoe of ETF.com wrote the following:

> *The private equity industry has changed substantially since the "Prudent Man" rule was modified in 1978 to give institutional investors the ability to allocate part of their portfolios to alternative assets.*
>
> *The industry has grown tremendously over the past 30 years, thanks largely to high returns on early investments. The vast majority of assets have come from institutional investors searching for alternatives that will help them meet their return objectives; however, despite the amount of funds raised has increased they're chasing fewer deals and more affluent families are now directly competing in active investments without the management fees.*
>
> *Before evaluating the performance of limited partners (LPs) that hold private companies, it's important to understand that private equity, a term used to describe various types of privately placed investments, is riskier than investing in a publicly traded S&P 500 Index fund. This should mean its returns should be higher for the level of volatility and risk.*[1]

For example, companies in the S&P 500 are typically among the largest and strongest, while venture capital typically invests in smaller and early-stage companies with far less financial strength. Investors in private equity tend to forgo the benefits of liquidity, transparency, broad diversification, daily pricing, and, for individuals, the ability to harvest losses for tax purposes.

The median return of private equity is much lower than the arithmetic average return. A relatively high average return, such as in the case of private equity, may reflect a small possibility of truly outstanding performance combined with the much larger probability of more modest or negative performance. In effect, private equity investments are like options (or lottery tickets). They provide a small chance of a huge payout, but a much larger chance of a below-average return. And it's difficult, especially for individual investors, to diversify this risk.

The standard deviation of private equity is in excess of 100 percent, which means swings of +/−50 percent in either direction. Compare that with a standard deviation of about 20 percent for the S&P 500 and about 35 percent for public small value stocks—a segment which I believe is underserved as most activist investors and institutional investors believe there is insufficient monetary upside for the level of effort and risk. I beg to differ with the application of GRRK balancing a strategy to leverage both the human and financial capital—something algorithms can't adequately capture.

RESEARCH ON RISK AND RETURNS

Berk A. Sensoy, Yingdi Wang, and Michael S. Weisbach—authors of the November 2013 study, "Limited Partner Performance and the Maturing of the Private Equity Industry"—evaluated the performance of limited partners' private equity investments over time. Their dataset included 14,380 investments by 1,852 LPs in 1,250 buyout and venture capital funds started between 1991 and 2006. They divided LPs into eight categories: public pension funds, corporate pension funds, endowments, advisors, insurance companies, banks/finance companies, investment firms, and others.

While only endowment LPs indeed performed higher than the 11.8 percent annualized return on the S&P 500 Index over that same time frame, it's also much lower (750 basis points to be exact) than the annualized return of 19.5 percent on publicly available and more similarly risky U.S. small value stocks as represented by the Fama-French small value index (making my point about the activist opportunity in private and small cap public companies). This finding, that private equity outperforms the S&P 500 but underperforms more similarly risky small value stocks, is consistent with prior research. Private equity overall returned 13.8 percent for the 20-year period ending June 30, 2005, outperforming the S&P 500 by 2.6 percentage points. That's according to Venture Economics, a provider of information and analysis on the venture capital industry. However, during the same period, small-cap value stocks returned 16.0 percent, outperforming venture capital by 2.2 percentage points and with less volatility.

The bottom line is this: The evidence clearly demonstrates that investors seeking higher returns than those provided by the S&P 500 index, and considering investing in private equity, would on average be better served by looking to small cap value stocks (both domestically and internationally) in the public markets via more liquid mutual funds and ETFs. Private equity and index performance is discussed further in this book. In order to understand smaller public companies as a value investor, one has to dig deeper into their operating performance and risk, which is much more than simple financial metrics. This supports the point that the same or greater degree of data analytics and due diligence is warranted for private companies.

While trusting a seasoned and well-designated financial planner or a fiduciary is prudent, the issue of their professional risk focus tends to be traditionally passive versus direct investments. Financial professionals can elevate themselves, if they can balance opportunity and risks with which clients with concentrated wealth wrestle.

Successful people may have figured out how to grow an entity, but they may not fully understand how their lifestyle is affected by concentrated wealth. They may need to rely on others with more financial savvy, and it can be tricky to figure out who is best suited to be of assistance. This is particularly true when a private asset has produced year-over-year double digit returns and, when sold, the client is expected to go on a somewhat crash fiscal diet with lower risk and lower return investments. The client might in turn tap into principal, which defeats the purpose of preserving wealth.

So who's trusted? One way is to look at the professional investment in obtaining designations that follow financial planners' names; a Certified Financial Planner® Professional (CFP) has invested 40 hours to achieve that status and a Chartered Financial Analyst® (CFA) has invested two years. Then there are the Certified Investment Management Analyst® (CIMA) and Certified Private Wealth Advisor® (CPWA) designations with more emphasis on alternative assets investments–blue ribbon education and three years of full-time experience. Compare this with an Accredited Senior Appraiser® (ASA) who has dedicated five full-time years before the requisite education, peer-reviewed demonstration report, and an examination with a rigorous pass rate.

Designation and education shouldn't be the only determinants, as the best financial planners are cognizant of the risks business owners wrestle with each day, and they also recognize the important role that other advisors play in the process of wealth accumulation, allocation, and management. The owner's goal is generally higher revenues, more profit, and easing the transition into a partial or full liquidity event that may include sourcing new human and financial capital. Too few focus on the value creation, leaving the client underserved and advisor possibly undeserving if not taking a holistic approach to serving the business owner client.

These advisors generally earn the trust of their clients; however, they can enhance their relationships by exploring the options afforded by better understanding private company dynamics and small-cap value options.

ECONOMIST LENSES

Some economists have obtained valuation credentials, but most have not—yet they still are comfortable opining on company-specific risk and rendering business valuation opinions. Even economists that hold PhDs who may have taken nominal formal training in business valuation will argue that by virtue of their education, they are qualified. This is a disconnect, since part of holding a PhD means acknowledging what you don't know. (I have heard the occasional owner and advisor jokingly express that PhD means "Piled High and Deep" keeping in mind the author holds a PhD.)

As was expressed when referencing CPAs and investment bankers, this does not mean many aren't capable and competent, but there is a sufficient dilution and confusion and absence of policing that any advisor or owner seeking to retain the professional should take a long, hard look at what services are predominantly being offered. As an example, economic damages and valuation can have similarities with one dealing with lost income and the other with lost value.

A fair number of economists who perform valuations rely on looking at market trends and base their findings on the theory fundamentals of supply and demand. Many start from a macroeconomic perspective, often looking at markets and publicly traded companies, and then making adjustment to come up with a risk rate (capitalization rate) or a present value rate of future earnings (discounted cash flow rate).

There is seldom any discussion within their work product of how the company-specific risks were determined. Like other trusted advisors, they preface their conclusions with the statement, "In my professional opinion. . . . " This occurs in part because many economists have no operational insights into the companies for which they're doing valuations. Unfortunately, reviewing financials alone has little to do with determining company-specific risk, which is a large premise of this book.

MBA/PHD/CFA LENSES

Let's start with MBAs. They may spend from half a day to a week over a semester discussing equity valuation. Even when they have a focus on finance, most of their training is aimed at determining price multiples and risk rates based primarily on public companies.

Most have no knowledge of comparative industry data to make adjustments to the comparable companies. Focus is almost exclusively on financial and not human capital. This book's treatise is that most intangible value influences will not be readily found on any financial statements or tax returns. Applying this approach is akin to knowing how to fire a gun but using the wrong caliber bullets.

Just because someone holds an MBA and performs financial modeling and forecasting doesn't mean that person has adequate knowledge to produce a well-substantiated value determination. That MBA holder would need to understand the correlation between certain variables and identify both qualitative and quantitative risks.

A good place to start with anyone offering valuation services is to ask for a sample report. My experience is that many read more like an academic paper and have some glaring omissions—most notably, how risks were isolated and determined in the context of the marketplace. If you choose to engage someone who doesn't have experience in the real world—knowing what's required to successfully operate a business—it's like buying a car without an engine. It looks great, but it's not going anywhere.

Similar issues may surround working with some PhDs, who may dabble in private company valuation. These highly educated individuals have expended significant time studying theories and practices, so they will offer a solid academic basis for their valuation conclusions.

However, if their focus has been mainly larger public companies, they may not be aware of the various resources for deeper data analytics available to examine private companies. They may not be aware of relevant court cases or legal and regulatory statute requirements that may influence methodology. They also may not be privy to nuanced issues in various market locations and industry-specific trends or how to quantify and substantiate equity-level risks.

While some of that data is readily available through research, many data sources are private and prohibitively expensive—which may limit a PhD's ability to provide robust support for entity- and equity-level risks and values. This may also be true for Chartered Financial Analysts (CFAs), who have mastery of financial analysis of multiple financial instruments, particularly in public markets. Many are or have been Wall Street analysts with nominal Main Street chops. Much of their focus is placed on data derived from publicly traded companies as many don't have access to the data sources previously mentioned.

As a result, valuation reports drafted by some CFAs (or PhDs and MBAs) may lack the perspective that comes from including private companies in their research.

For instance:

- They have no access to the size-related impact that distinguishes public and private companies, such as access to capital or liquidity.
- They may not be aware of how bylaws, shareholder agreements, operating agreements, buy–sell agreements provisions, and other legal and financial issues of private companies can have a significant effect on value.
- They often suffer from an absence of formal training on valuing private companies and the equity interests held in them.

This again falls into the category of not knowing what they don't know. While there is often significant academic rigor in reports performed by CFAs, PhDs, and MBAs, it's often insufficient without full-time experience, adequate data sources, and analytics relied upon by a full-time valuation professional.

No one wants to be on the wrong end of a *Daubert* competency challenge, in which the ruling indicates an opinion that may lack scientific support—by practice and theory within the profession. There are people who will attempt to demonstrate that a nontraditional method has validity even if it's somewhat rigorous, but if it can't be readily duplicated and it can't be proven, it will be excluded.

Under the *Daubert* standard, many factors must be addressed by a valuation expert. The previous *Frye* standard was actually a bit scary as it allowed that someone who learned a little about valuations—by reading this book, for instance—was no longer a layperson and could testify as an expert.

Almost all litigation matters involving value of an enterprise or its equity are settled out of court (98%), because there's too much risk associated with not being able to rely on the information provided and the unknowns of the judge and jury. When work product does become challenged, its author may lose future credibility as an expert witness, which can snuff a career. This is also true for the attorney and client who retained him as they may lose their case.

Understanding risk and relating it to a mid-market private company can challenge the best educated. Wall Street and Main Street and the hallowed halls of academia are not the same as the founder's idea that became the innovation. The innovation became the commercially used product and service and the unique role of owner's persistance, grit, and good fortune played to build a successful business.

OWNER/FAMILY LENSES

Effective business owners will occasionally take a 30,000-foot view of what they do. The family business founders often have a passion for innovation and a zealot's desire to do good. The most successful owners don't just want to take care of their businesses, staff, and family, but also to validate their own self-worth.

Most want to be well-rounded, be involved in giving back, invest in their families' lives, and understand how their business operates within a broader context of their community and marketplace. They want to know why and how clients and vendors operate and how advisors do what they do.

As a result of having an approach focused on abundance and awareness, these owners create value in its own right—which is very different than chasing business to top last year's revenues.

When clear differentiation, a story, and a benefit have been established, people seek out these companies. Their owners don't operate out of altruism, but they are clearly enlightened; they realize the business is more than a living organism, it is part of an ecosystem.

Owners can limit risk by seeing their staff and advisors as investments rather than cost centers. Through your strategic value architect's lens they are human capital.

It is helpful to see relationships as something to elevate—to offer an experience rather than just a commodity or a service. We all know these kind of companies when we see them—examples include Whole Foods, Tom's of Maine, Ben & Jerry's, Starbucks, Apple, Amazon, American Express, Southwest Air, and Nordstroms—because they exceed expectations and make us feel we receive value for the money we spent.

Making a difference motivates the owners of companies with "serve-first cultures." They expect no less from those who work for them where common is unacceptable and performance should be extraordinary.

Successful business owners know how to pace themselves to avoid the risk of burnout. They have the best intention with advisors and they know what good looks like. Consider this: Given all the accidents that occur on roadways across the United States, it's impossible that all drivers who rate themselves as being good really are. The same is true with advisors. Business owners know this, so they directly or through a trusted individual seek out best-in-class providers.

If ordinary is the goal, there's nominal harm in working with mediocre providers, but the harm comes from having an expectation of receiving more. The mindset of best-in-class owners who strive for excellence, and the people around them, is to build a culture that values those who have:

- A high degree of humility
- A desire to maintain enduring relationships
- A balanced personal life

That final point should not be overlooked, because having a personal life that crashes and burns is likely to affect an individual's business life. Family stability is definitely a form of risk, since its absence can dilute attention from operating a successful business. Another risk is personal health and well-being, since issues like alcoholism, diabetes, heart disease, or being obsessive-compulsive can impact business success internally and externally.

It's common to have individuals within an organization whose lives are out of balance and this can be the reason why they never reach their potential. Unfortunately, their issues usually won't be pointed out due to the fear of losing the relationship. This applies to family, staff, and advisors. Clients, on the other hand, may simply suspend doing business.

A very real risk that good owners will recognize is their relationship with their board. Do they have a board that tells them what they want to hear rather than what they need to hear? A strong board should be based on transparency and knowledge. (Think about having the chance to choose your parents or siblings.)

An owner should be thinking about how she can elevate employees so the owner's daily presence becomes preference versus priority. The need for an owner's presence is a form of risk that is quite common. Shouldn't the goal be a company's operation that isn't dependent upon the owner or key staff? It's important to understand the risks that stand in the way and develop a culture that supports the value of all staff.

CASE IN POINT

I recently spoke to 150 chief compliance officers on behalf of a global advisor, Thomson Reuters, presenting my thoughts on "Governance, Risk, and Compliance: Building Business Value." One of the examples I gave involved an organization not doing the right thing and thus causing systemic harm. The company had a complex environment and the culture was insufficient to allow it to do the right thing. I made the point that if organizations are just checking the boxes and operating within the letter of the law, it's not the same thing as operating within the spirit of the law.

As a result of some shortsighted thinking, most compliance officers and risk managers are perceived as cost centers. Owners who have this opinion are putting their companies at risk, as governance (from the board and the C-suite to the janitor) is missing the point that risk reduction enhances value.

CASE IN POINT

In one month during December 2013, Target, a department store, suffered an +$11 billion market value loss due to cyber-theft of +40 million users' credit cards. Had both staff and vendors been on alert to anomalous data breaches as part of the company's larger ecosystem, the loss might have been contained if not avoided.

A savvy owner should never forget that the intangible assets of a business (such as goodwill) include practices, policies, and processes (sometimes referred to as trade secrets). This includes relationships such as how clients and vendors are engaged in the company's path to growth and profitability. So, the corner office must find balance in its obligation to shareholders and the importance of maximizing its intangible asset value. Being tactical to achieve a quarterly result may impact overall strategic benefit.

Going back to our compliance officers, what if they could reduce risk, increasing the price multiplier and thus the value of the business? Expressed differently, if a company spent $5 million on compliance issues and achieved a $50 million increase in its valuation as a result, that's a 10× return.

Owners who want to increase the value of their businesses must think specifically about what they're doing to make that happen—rather than having focus on how much profit can be paid in compensation and distributions. Remember the point of Paul Thiel. The company's board and corner office have a fiduciary duty to maximize shareholder value. This requires long-term thinking and a strategy to support value growth versus gratification of more compensation due to higher profits. This is why executives are often provided stock options in lieu of higher salaries. For private companies not wishing to give up equity and/or control, they can offer phantom stock or nonvoting stock to key staff.

In order to instill the strategic framework that flows to every employee and externally from the company, companies must cultivate extraordinary cultures. Such cultures embrace innovation and being dynamic. This is because the market is not static, so serving it can't be, either.

CASE IN POINT

Walmart initially opened stores in second-tier locations and created disruption in the retail market by offering better pricing and selection. The market is littered with companies that didn't adapt, including Woolworth, Kmart, Sears, and JC Penney. In part it's because Walmart recognized it was a distributor and its secret was just-in-time inventory management; the moment product supply declined to a certain level, the vendor was contacted with a refill order—extraordinary supply chain management that allowed for enhanced capital management. However, Amazon has caused further disruption by letting consumers shop without leaving home, and the latest iteration is the game-changing Alibaba, which connects buyers and sellers on the retail and B2B side on a global basis.

When a company offers something game changing to a mature industry, it becomes a market maker introducing a competitive disruption that the dynamic company can control. It's nearly impossible to achieve this without involving clients, vendors, and advisors—having candid conversations with them about needs and challenges. While not every company can reach this level, by eliminating as many risks to long-term success as possible, owners can have viable businesses that have high price multipliers, and thus, high values.

Moving on to the family side of things, let's start with an anecdote. A panelist at an event for advisors who serves family businesses and family offices represented an affluent client in the sale of his business for billions of dollars. He shared that when one of his client's kids said, "We're rich," the dad said, "No, *I'm* rich." The point here is that unless you've walked in the shoes of that successful owner (or anyone else), it's difficult to appreciate what sacrifices he made to reach success.

Most owners wouldn't change the decision they made about going into business, but some would change the way they approached doing so, especially with respect to family. Many executives and owners lament all the time they spent away from their family, rationalizing it by saying they made a sacrifice so their families could have things that success allows. This can include everything from going to the best schools to having more options and not having to worry about the future. The other side of the coin is that family members are often frustrated that the executives and owners weren't around much. Both the founder and the family can feel somewhat slighted.

CEOs of most public companies know that to have attained this position, the company often has to come first. This heady sacrifice usually comes with significant costs that may not be looked at in favor of the economic benefits received. It's a delicate balance—plus a big risk—as the way time and resources are allocated can make the difference between being successful and happy, successful and miserable, or a failure and miserable.

The risk is the disruptive impact that family disharmony and dysfunction can have on the owners' and executives' business performance. A common behavior is to lose themselves in their businesses, because that is an environment they perceive they can control and where success can be measured. It gets very complicated very quickly when family members are also working in the business. The risk of the disruption to the business can be severe.

Many people are familiar with the abysmal statistics surrounding lottery winners. Those who are recipients of tens of millions of dollars in winnings discover who their friends are and how solid their family is—with most winnings squandered in just a few years. This is common with pro athletes and media celebrities. Hence, solid business managers and trusted advisors are needed. This "affluence equals love" paradigm illustrates what may be at the core of the family unit, which is not always rosy and loving. Many risks can remain unresolved when family members are involved in running and growing a company, and what may be perceived as petty slights take on a whole new meaning.

For instance, when times were good, the oldest child received nice clothes and a new car, and went to the best schools, but when times were not as good, siblings wore hand-me-downs, didn't get cars, and went to state schools. These kinds of slights lead to affluent family dysfunction, which may be manifested by amounts of tangible wealth being exchanged for affection, and often results in interfamily disputes/disruptions when wealth is transferred—and it's especially common when there are spouses and kids from multiple marriages. Add the unplanned event such as a death or a divorce and the pressure cooker can boil off the amassed wealth.

What about situations when siblings don't possess the technical or experiential skills or the temperament to hold company management functions, but they are given these roles anyway? When ill-suited family members have authority over staff, that is problematic, and their sense of entitlement may be adversely affecting the business in other ways, as well. These risks are concrete as they relate to a business. Therefore, while they are often based on emotion, they can translate into real risks.

Example inquiries that can unearth these risks during a valuation or strategic roadmap engagement include:

- Are family members involved in or shareholders of the business?
- What function(s) do they have and how many annual hours do they work?
- How are they compensated?
- How is the level of compensation determined?
- What experience and education do they have to hold a particular role and receive compensation for it?

CASE IN POINT

A family member earned her law degree and then spent six months in the branding and licensing department of her law firm before being given an executive position in the 1,000+ store family business, with responsibility for all market development and thousands of employees. Her technical education (unrelated to her current role) and the brevity of her work experience would tend to have a downward impact on the value of the company.

CASE IN POINT

The founder of a very successful mid-market company has his spouse—who has no formal financial or accounting background—act as CFO and COO during the times he's gone during the winter sports season. If the company had professional management in place, it could be worth 10 times its current value.

Those two examples illustrate how much impact family involvement has on a business's risk; therefore, while under-appreciated, the family ecosystem is irretraceable from the business and vice versa. The above disruptions have resulted in the value losses of hundreds of millions and even some billions of dollars in the space of a few years.

It's not all doom and gloom, as there are plenty of healthy companies that have thrived across multiple generations of family member involvement—as shareholders, board members, executives, and employees. Managing these complex risks and working hard to eliminate or overcome them is a challenge that cannot be overlooked and often requires the engagement of "soft side" advisors discussed ahead.

FAMILY BUSINESS ADVISOR LENSES

Like most trusted advisors, those who work with families understand human behaviors are not always rational. As an example, look no further than the irrational exuberance of the real estate and stock market that preceded the steep declines in 2008.

Enlightened advisors know a subtle truth. Most decisions are guided by emotion and then rationalized. Many gaps in the reasoning are filled by assumptions. This is the human condition. It's natural. It's flawed. This is of particular importance to family business advisors because they are often dealing with disruptions while trying to keep both a business and a family thriving.

They contend with the following disruptive *D*s:

- Disputes
- Dysfunction
- Divorce
- Death
- Disability
- Dilution

They are privy to why an 80-year-old business owner has not contemplated a transition from the business he founded or why at the eleventh hour the seller of a business disrupts the transaction and simply chooses not to go ahead with the business sale.

Family business advisors understand that family-borne situations, such as two brothers with significant business responsibilities not speaking, can affect the company's risk and its price multiplier. Unfortunately, they are seldom brought in unless a problem has occurred.

The more holistic families embrace the notion of retreats and councils that engage both the left and right side of their brains. This helps maintain a healthy environment and often allows for a multigenerational family business to flourish as they are able to articulate what wealth, legacy and liquidity means. These advisors could have a dramatic effect on family harmony and on company productivity and performance and should be called in earlier.

STAFF/VENDOR LENSES

Let's start with staff. Many entrepreneurial families experience an interesting paradox: In an effort to create a tight-knit extended family, they may create an imbalance between likability and profitability. It's an all-too-common challenge for owners and executives to be the nice guy.

Generally speaking, people understand that the ability to control all factors, including ebbs and flows in performance, is a Herculean effort. What do staff members want? They want feedback, opportunity, challenge, meaningfulness, and a square deal. They understand financial limitations may be at play, but there can be tradeoffs such as flex time, unpaid time off, and potluck Fridays.

A precautionary note regarding compensation as a reward for tenure or performance: Giving 5 or 6 percent annual wage/salary increases has a compounding effect, and overcompensation can result. In as little as a decade, the compensation of a single employee could more than double despite nominal changes in responsibilities—squeezing company profitability.

Alternatively, owners should recognize that well-compensated staff members who value their work are very difficult to lose. Thus, it's a balancing act; it makes no sense to have heavy investment in labor if net company performance doesn't correspond.

It's also worth examining whether labor costs are recalibrated based on significant increases or decreases in company performance and whether the absence of a deeper dive by departments or business units is masking specific operational or employee relations issues.

While it may appear at face value a happy workforce is ideal, that objective must be balanced against the level of compensation (labor cost) as a percentage of revenue—compared to industry peers. In addition, this is weighed against business development expense. This is because an engaged workforce may create extraordinary goodwill that is the catalyst for brand awareness and loyalty. This human capital should be captured in the company's intangible value. This is an example where financial ratios may not tell the entire story without adequate inquiry. It should be a priority when a company is determined to achieve equity value enhancement.

CASE IN POINT

A private equity group has a business with $5 million (13%) profit margin. The valuation examines territory and store-level performance and finds that one-third of the 100+ locations are either unprofitable or nearly so. Further examination suggests a store patronage demographic mismatch and underperformance of certain territory managers. Some units have an excess headcount based on the expectation of higher business that hasn't materialized, while others have issues related to bonuses; units with lower sales still received them, as did units that saw sales increases but had lower profitability. This is actually a good problem to have, as adjustments can be made to address them. The risk is whether management would have done so in the absence of due diligence.

One of the takeaways here is a deep understanding of how staff levels and responsibilities can influence company risk and performance. Creating untenable expectations can impact morale and business performance. Something else to be aware of is the risk of alienated employees. Never forget that staff is the company's eyes, ears, and soul of the organization, which is well beyond who's occupying the corner office. Disenfranchised staff members can undermine a company's success by taking trade secrets or client relationships and developing their own organizations using your resources.

Occasionally, good people will do bad things, with the most common transgression being embezzlement. This often occurs when employees who show up and do a decent job decide they want a lifestyle above their pay. They can end up siphoning millions of dollars from company profits.

Initiating checks and balances is one way to try to eliminate human and financial capital risks, but prevention usually goes back to a culture of relationships, when employees are empowered to go the extra mile—such as having discussions with potential clients that are unhappy with their current vendor—and incentivized to do so. They will likely be less disenfranchised and thus less likely to put the business at risk.

Another way to engender loyalty is to ensure that all employees know their input is critical to the overall success of the company. Respect and accessibility are important subtle ways to show all roles and insights are valued. As is mentioned elsewhere in this book, it's foolish to assume that due to title or function, an employee has less to offer than an executive. Observations from those in trenches are critical and can be invaluable.

CASE IN POINT

An employee designing a component for an auto manufacturer observed a functional problem but said nothing about it due to the fear he could risk losing his job. At that juncture, the correction would have been minor and the cost minimal. What happened were serious issues with the cars containing this flawed design that resulted in lawsuits and an expensive recall.

If the mindset at your company is "it's not my job—someone else will deal with it," that's an indicator of a greater problem. That kind of thinking can be circumvented when you realize that knowledge is not solely correlated with someone's education, tenure, or title.

Relationships are key to the success in every company, and how an organization defines its relationships with its staff speaks volumes as to whether the culture has esprit de corps or has more of a mob mentality where everyone is replaceable. When "we're all in this together" is the established company culture, it's a reflection of high-quality management and leadership.

There are ways to discover signs of whether the staff is part of an "all-in" culture:

- Responsiveness of key individuals to daily and critical issues.
- Employees are open and honest when talking about the company.
- Number of employees present at the end of the prescribed workday.
- Number of employees participating in company-sponsored activities.
- The number of big goals are no more than three at any given time to limit dilution and increase achievement.

This process is like watching a sports team. You can see when points are on the board as well as when the players are really in the zone.

Those in positions of influence will have a great deal of impact on whether employees are fearful about losing their jobs, are unwilling to share observations, or are motivated about being able to make a difference. The most successful companies see compensation and other employee-related expenses not merely as line items, but as opportunity costs.

What do employees want? They want feedback, to be paid fairly, to have a chance at upward mobility, and to have fair resolution—minus blame—when errors are made or accidents occur. One of the things companies don't want is to have staff's personal behavior reflect poorly on the organization, that is, DUIs or claims of harassment or prejudice or Facebooking or Tweets about internal company issues.

The line between what's politically correct and offensive may be somewhat unclear, but personal behavior that has the potential to negatively affect the company must be reviewed. Creating an environment that is too comfortable may actually put a company at risk—and remember that a little bit of discomfort can be a good thing, especially as it relates to innovation. The best case is when employees consider themselves stewards of the organization. Their positive energy and focus can counteract most business risks.

Moving on to vendors, most people understand that it is virtually impossible for one individual to know all things about every function. This should lead to the realization of the value of expending sufficient time to deepen and personalize relationships with vendors. How do vendors perceive risk? It usually boils down to not selling enough profitably or too much accounts payable (not being paid in a timely fashion). The latter instance can be especially telling, as it may be an indication the client company is having cash flow issues, has poor management, or has a philosophy of vendor indifference.

There's no better way to embrace a vendor than to pay within the billing period. It's also important to thank vendors and determine how you measure your companies' relationships: by price, referrals, golf games, tickets to shows, or serving as a best man or godparent. A vendor that is providing referrals or proactively exploring ways to improve their client's business reflects the healthiest possible relationship and should be a goal a company strives to achieve with vendor relationships. This is wholly different from a transactional mindset. One sees value; the other sees cost.

Getting to know a vendor in a more personal way can have a significant payoff. Consider a scenario where you know a vendor has a six-week lag time but you need an order filled next week. The response from someone you don't know well or treat poorly would likely be, "Sorry, can't do it," but from someone with whom you have a well-cultivated relationship, it might be, "For you? On it. We'll work two shifts and only charge you twenty percent more for the extra effort."

Since vendors are often fearful of having their clients stolen from them, they need to provide unique knowledge that makes them indispensable. For example, upon hearing that a client is frustrated about a certain process, they might design a better widget to help overcome the issue.

Vendors basically need to determine whether they want to merely be suppliers or valuable resources that can think out of the box. The first are order takers and the second are part of the client's ecosystem. The risk to the vendor should be not only lost revenues, but failing to cultivate enduring relationships where price alone is not the sole criterion. The risk to the company is evident. Loss of stability and reliability can clearly create imbalance in an ecosystem. Relationships just like courtships need nurturing.

Vendors can add value in a number of ways to solidify their client relationships and try to make them bulletproof. For instance, sharing competitive information—nothing proprietary, but best practices or market trends—and making suggestions like order on Tuesday, not Friday, are examples of relatively small things that can make a big impact.

While vendors often determine the nature of their relationships, owners must ask themselves a number of questions regarding their vendors, including:

- Do I have all my eggs in one basket?
- What are the ages and health of my vendor's decision makers?
- Can they grow as my company grows?
- Should I consider an acquisition or joint venture?
- What is the nature of my buyers' relationships with our vendors?

There's much more to it than just providing a product or service. A great example is our relationship with our FedEx guy. I have his cell phone number and have used it a number of times to request a pickup after hours. I also am sure to take care of him during the holidays. Think I could expect to receive that level of service without an existing relationship? It's unlikely.

CLIENT LENSES

One of the toughest things for companies to do is ingratiate themselves to clients. It's not as simple as it might first appear. Some organizations may accept unfavorable terms to get clients in the door, with the hope of renegotiating at a future date. This can be a flawed strategy; if clients don't respect what you do enough to pay a fair price and terms, that's self-inflicted.

It's quite common for advisors to be afraid to ask to be paid what they're worth. They fear that raising their fees may result in lost clients, but that may be indicative of failing to add value—a big risk—as is suggested throughout this book. It also reflects a relationship that has not been solidified—a transaction.

CASE IN POINT

As gas neared $5 a gallon, a company that produced and delivered products based on a fixed price saw that it was likely to lose millions of dollars due to increased fuel costs. The owner called the principals of every client, asking what they could do to come to a favorable resolution so the company wouldn't risk a major financial disruption. Due to the nature of the business and the relationships the owner had developed, he was able to reset client pricing or make other arrangements (like advance payments to offset cash flow issues) with almost every client.

One of the biggest risks a company faces with respect to clients is failure to deliver as promised, on time, or as described. It's important for organizations to be made aware of the impact of their miscue, which in some circumstances can be dire.

Other risks include failing to follow up when a client has provided you with a referral—which reflects taking the relationship for granted. Consider the following scenario:

I pay you. ➔ You do your job.

I appreciate you. ➔ I give you a referral.

I send you referrals. ➔ I put a premium on our relationship.

CASE IN POINT

There are a few real estate and machinery and equipment appraisal firms we send hundreds of thousands of dollars in business to each year. All do a fine job and their fees are fair. Who receives first shot for new business? Those who keep us in the loop, reciprocate with referrals, and ask how we can enhance the relationship.

Owners also have a hand in this process, and they can do themselves a favor by asking themselves the following questions:

- How do I measure the value of client relationships?
- Am I meeting with clients to explore other opportunities?
- Do I know the names of the client's key personnel?

With respect to the final point, it's of great value to have relationships with more than one person at any client. If the only person you know is the buyer, and that person changes companies, would you be up the creek without a paddle with respect to maintaining future business?

The purpose of this chapter is to ensure the reader understands and has appreciation for the many ecosystem risk perspectives that exist based upon human capital investment: that is, the unique roles and relationships of each constituent. The following four chapters challenge the reader to understand that GRRK is a tool for identifying and enhancing four significant influences to intangible value. Harnessed properly, the risks discussed earlier are not solely identified, but also are measured, managed, and mitigated.

But why just take my word for it that there is a need? Consider some of the following observations.

Richard Boulton in *Cracking the Value Code*[2] identifies four fundamental and integrated approaches similar to GRRK: (1) design business model for value creation; (2) master risk in an uncertain environment; (3) manage business as a portfolio of assets; and (4) use information to measure and report on all assets. The author recognizes that a company's assets interaction is its DNA to allow it to succeed or fail: These are often assets hidden below the company's financial statements that drive value.

In *Building Business Value: How to Command a Premium Price for Your Midsized Company*, Martin O'Neil recognizes there are value drivers that are both internal and external.[3] He also conducts risk impact studies and sees the need for alignment. He has an assessment tool that includes existing financial and banking advisors and focuses on value or revenues; degree of company reliance on key staff; a known strategy; and whether both capital and the will exists to scale growth.

Mr. Warren Miller in *Value Maps: Valuation Tools That Unlock Business Wealth* demonstrates a decided understanding of the need for the valuation profession to up its game and has led from the front in value creation using a SPARC (strategy, people, architecture, routines, culture) model.[4] These attributes tend to address human capital; however, he does examine financial and institutional capital as well. He similarly sees the need for strategic and risk management (SWOT analysis) and measurement; however, due to the multidisciplinary attributes it would be difficult for any single advisor to perform—it takes a village. He questions how typical valuation professionals are getting to their opinions without a deeper understanding and assessment of risk. GRRK delves deeper into governance, relationships, risk, and knowledge; however, the motivations to create value and improve our profession are complementary to Miller's perspective.

James Hangstefer, author of *Creating and Sustaining Company Growth*, states:[5]

> *The overriding aim for the CEO and the policy-management team has to be lasting company strength, achieved by creating value for the company's customers, employees, and shareholders.... Creating value is an eternal and unending quest. The Company culture has to be tolerant of mistakes, but intolerant of behavior that avoids acknowledging and correcting them. Learning is the most fundamental momentum driver. The growth of knowledge comes from purposeful learning activity that involves listening, reading, observing, experimenting, analyzing, synthesizing, and relating bits of information.*

A well-regarded business valuation thought-leader, James Hitchner, not surprisingly focuses on the financial side of the value creation equation of the need for improved profitability and use of capital. Common value drivers are stated as unique technology, customer relationships, cost advantages, access to capital, as well as trade names and trademarks. He does reference McKinsey's 7*S* model that assesses strategy, structure, systems, skills, staff, style, and superordinate goals.[6]

To his credit, Francisco Rosillo, the author of *Determination of Value*, does outline a few company-specific risks to be considered: SWOT, concentrations, controls reporting, management level, use of capital, contractual relationships, human capital, and growth strategy.[7] These very nicely overlap with GRRK.

Another considered business valuation luminary, George Hawkins, author of the voluminous *Business Valuation Guide*, makes references to shareholder value and value creation by other authors; however, he provides no further detail.[8] His treatise does provide a reasonably comprehensive list of factors to consider in determining company-specific risk, however, only nominal operational metrics. Like other valuation texts there tends to be some professional bias about risk being systematic ("market") and not company specific as value investors would hold diversified portfolios. Walking the floor of manufacturers and other businesses and interviewing hundreds of owners and advisors tells me a different story about measuring company-specific risk.

Known to all in the valuation profession, Shannon Pratt and Roger Grabowski dedicate an entire chapter of their *Cost of Capital* (CoC) treatise on company-specific risk and cite that a reasoned explanation is necessary.[9] Interestingly, there is no real reference to value creation/building, governance, strategy, culture, management, human capital, relationships, or knowledge. The CoC book does reference identifiable intangible assets such as customer relationships and assembled workforce with the latter associated with contributory assets.

Gene Pease, in *Human Capital Analytics: How to Harness the Potential of Your Organization's Greatest Asset*, recognizes the impact of human capital on intangible asset value and dedicates an entire chapter to the importance of "alignment" to ensure all stakeholders ("constituents") are involved in the process as well as the problem ("risks") or opportunity to be solved due to their varied perspectives and ideas ("knowledge").[10] By doing so, deeper partnerships ("relationships") are formed.

Further, he argues analysis should focus on root cause with issues that are core drivers associated with the organization's culture and values ("governance"). He goes on to emphasize the relevance of cross-functionality to create synergies ("value") and minimize resistance. Finally, he emphasizes the need to address resource gaps at every level from conception to final review and implementation.

The author of *Wealth Secrets of the Affluent: Keys to Fortune Building and Asset Protection*, Christopher Jarvis, expresses that an important element of plan selection is one where there is a commitment to execute on it.[11] It's akin to training for a marathon.

Day 1 is not completing 26.2 miles; it is to stretch and jog and walk a mile to break in your sneakers. But there are steps that make the process more easily embraced beginning with identifying challenges and opportunities that should not be addressed solely by the owner. These steps include: "The right advisory team is selected; the advisors will be paid for their wisdom; the plan will be implemented, monitored, and reviewed with new questions preceding new decisions; and that life is dynamic, so willingness to amend the plan or team may be wise."

Jarvis indicates it's ideal to minimize distractions, especially with important decisions where one or more days should be spent with family and advisors. Such sessions can often result in the most productive use of time and money through the families' lens.

Richard Jackim, known exit planning author of *The $10 Trillion Opportunity: Designing Successful Exit Strategies for Middle Market Business Owners,* stresses avoiding seat-of-the-pants management.[12] He notes not all benchmarks need to be financial, such as customer satisfaction and employee turnover, but they should be significant, relevant, and measureable; like other authors' and advisors' sentiment, he observes management teams should be stable and motivated. He provides other benchmarks such as a diversified customer base; a realistic growth strategy; ability to work on, not just in, the business; as well as various financial metrics.

According to Marilyn Kourilsky, the number-one (56% of respondents) reason people start their own business is to be their own boss.[13] They feel that their education, life experience, and working at another business prepares them to be a business owner.

Yet, interestingly, most business leaders feel education did not prepare them for: seeing opportunities others may not see; combining ideas and information in new ways; making smart use of time; budgeting wisely; managing and motivating others; coming up with solutions where everyone is better off; listening to others; the ability to distinguish between good and bad opportunities; preparing to start a business; and what prices to charge. Clearly, a disconnect exists between what CEOs see as the need and what the uninitiated believe. The burden is partially that of post–secondary education and advisory focus.

The use of GRRK may help with some degree of reorienting and aligning these disparate perspectives. In the following chapter we'll place relevance squarely at the feet of those tasked with ensuring equity value enhancement is central to the company ethos.

NOTES

1. http://www.etf.com/sections/index-investor-corner/23839-swedroe-a-close-look-at-private-equity.html?fullart=1.
2. Richard Boulton, *Cracking the Value Code: How Successful Businesses Are Creating Wealth in the New Economy* (Harper Business, 2000), 152.
3. Martin O'Neill, *Building Business Value: How to Command a Premium Price for Your Midsized Company* (Third Bridge Press, 2009), 35.
4. Warren Miller, *Value Maps: Valuation Tools That Unlock Business Wealth* (Hoboken: Wiley, 2010).
5. James Hangstefer, *Creating and Sustaining Company Growth* (Burton Merrill, 1997), 77, 81, 211.
6. James Hitchner, *Financial Valuation* (Hoboken: Wiley, 2003), 75–76, 946–947.
7. Francisco Rosillo, *Determination of Value* (Hoboken: Wiley, 2013), 66–68.
8. George Hawkins, *Business Valuation Guide* (CCH Incorporated, 2002), 913–914, 1703, 1719.
9. Shannon Pratt and Roger Grabowski, *Cost of Capital*, 5th ed. (Hoboken: Wiley, 2014), 372–399.
10. Gene Pease, *Human Capital Analytics: How to Harness the Potential of Your Organization's Greatest Asset* (Hoboken: Wiley, 2013), 33–60.
11. Christopher Jarvis, *Wealth Secrets of the Affluent: Keys to Fortune Building and Asset Protection* (Hoboken: Wiley, 2008), 54, 358.
12. Richard Jackim, *The $10 Trillion Opportunity: Designing Successful Exit Strategies for Middle Market Business Owners* (Exit Planning Institute, 2005), 130–133.
13. Marilyn Kourilsky, *The E-Generation* (Kendall Hunt, 2000), 23, 58.

CHAPTER 5

The Role of Governance

The concept of governance accentuates the board of directors' fundamental role of strategically directing, overseeing, and controlling the business, possibly the family, and its wealth. This must be done in a culture of trust and aligning all constituents' diverse interests in consensus and cohesion.

One of the main causes prompting an increased focus on corporate governance is the major loss of capital due to the global financial crisis, the loss of trust in the family's abilities to manage its wealth, and the loss of trust in family members that are involved in daily operations of the entities the family holds. The loss of capital and lack of trust has resulted in rising conflict, leading not only to family feuds but also to substantial financial losses.

Such disruptive events create ad-hoc crisis intervention. Yet, the board must keep its outlook more long-term where strategic goals are realized while being monitored in a short time frame, allowing for strategy assessment and adjustment. This vision not only shapes the family legacy, but its system of values will also guide every constituent.

Nothing can happen before the idea, the innovation, and the human and financial capital to turn passion into a viable, growing, and profitable enterprise.

The catalyst needed for this journey to begin is seldom the same as the factors that take an entrepreneurial endeavor into one that is professionally managed. All too often no strategy is developed to ensure an optimal exit or to go from a single location, product, or service to a regional, national, or global enterprise with a wide array of offerings.

There are exceptions like Michael Dell of Dell Computers. In almost all cases, the thesis of this book is that the board, founder, and/or leader knew how to harness the human capital factors of relationships and knowledge. That group or individual also looked at value creation, which understands that risks must be foreseen, reduced, or eliminated while opportunities are created. Also, shareholders were among the important constituents considered. This is not simply tactics, but a vision that is developed into a strategy that is articulated, planned, and executed. This requires stewardship and metrics.

Therefore, the first letter of GRRK stands for governance, which must be in place to ensure a culture exists to leverage the remaining factors of relationships, risks, and knowledge. This critically important element of valuation as well as value enhancement is embraced by enlightened companies and their constituents. For the remainder, it is often misunderstood or ignored by owners, investors, and even those tasked with preparing valuations.

While GRRK's focus is on mid-market, especially family enterprises, most of the items addressed in what follows are applicable to both public and private companies' boards and their C-suites.

What is governance? If you take the dictionary definition too literally, you might be confused about how the word relates to business valuation. According to *The American Heritage® Dictionary of the English Language*, *governance* is "the act, process or power of governing" or "the state of being governed."

I define it as a process for periodic review of what is done and how. More importantly, I believe effective governance extols the virtue of human capital in a social context. It's engagement. And with unique relationships and knowledge governance affords the environment where leverage can create value. In other words, governance is a zero-sum game if no shared benefits are achieved. That is when it is confused with control without limited or no support of constituents ("stakeholders").

Henry Cendrowski expresses, in *Private Equity: History, Governance and Operations*, that the private equity group (PEG) governance business model of using debt with a large equity upside ensures that management focuses on swift and deliberate actions to create value versus simply "growing the business."[1]

In *Valuation: Measuring and Managing the Value of Companies* (5th edition), Tim Koller recognizes that the best private equity firms don't just leverage financial capital, but improve governance as proven by a study of 11 private equity firms that examined 60 successful investments and found two-thirds of the new value created was from improved operating performance relative to their peers as a result of fruitful management between owners and executive management.[2]

Donald Kuratko's *Entrepreneurship: A Contemporary Approach* opines there is limited exposure by most business owners to strategic planning due to time scarcity, lack of knowledge, lack of expertise, lack of trust and openness, and the perception of high cost.[3] By far, fully 66 percent of even high-performing companies believe strategic planning is too expensive to do properly. Most claim it is a straightjacket that limits flexibility and implies change.

To support Kuratko's observation, in *Small Business Entrepreneurship and Beyond*, Timothy Hatten observes the number-one cause of business failure is ineffective or inefficient management, such as inexperience and neglect.[4]

GOVERNANCE

Stanley Feldman shares in *Principles of Private Firm Valuation* that there is a mechanism to develop a Measuring for Value Model (MVM).[5] MVM is a framework for which he dedicates a chapter to the use of optimal capital structure and employing a strategy for internal and external factors that creates value growth. He also recognized that the better ranked companies in stock performance had stronger corporate governance.

Dennis Jaffe, a renowned family business advisor in his own right, sees the need for professionals to have a deeper sense of how human capital can be harnessed and respected.[6] In *Stewardship in Your Family Enterprise* these advisors see the spiritual, family, structural, and societal elements along with human and financial. Each family member involved or impacted in the business as well as other constituents will have a different lens. To allow for mutual respect, a more formal process to codify purpose may be used.

While some refrain from the term *governance*, they may use *charter* or *constitution* where multiple generations and mixed families can create some complexity. Emerging families may wish to have a family council to help maintain cohesion while next-generation issues are being strategized. Such activities often begin with addressing the *how* from the *why* and the *what*. This is particularly important when there are one or more substantial businesses in which family members may be involved.

There's a common misperception that governance strangles innovation by attempting to codify things like vision and legacy, ultimately sapping any creativity in a quest for toeing the company line. That's a gross underestimation of the power of governance and its value to the success of any organization.

True governance does include codification and policy making, but it's much more. It encompasses many attributes that are measureable but seldom found in financial statements, bylaws, operating agreement, or any other document that's commonly used as part of a business valuation study. It is the essence of how the unique individuals; their relationships, and their knowledge are perceived and utilized by company decision makers, who also possess unique individual characteristics. It falls under the characteristic of "you know it when you see it." This might be the commanding presence of an unknown individual who walks into a room.

In a nutshell, governance reflects why a company exists beyond simply commercial reasons such as making money. While it's established to offer guidance and direction, it should and can be more. It provides differentiation from other companies through its amalgamation of unique talent and the reason for the company's existence—its story. Consider every U.S. professional football team performs the same functions; however, it is the team's assemblage of talent and what the fans, ownership, and coaching believe it stands for that differentiates it from its competitors. At the heart of it all is the company's or team's culture, something that is discrete as it is measurable—if you know where to look.

FOCUS ON CULTURE

Culture is often given short shrift during the valuation process, even though it can have a significant impact on a company's future value. "Between 60 and 80 percent of all mergers and acquisitions fail to meet their merger goals," according to Carol Koffinke, president and CEO of Beacon Associates, a performance improvement firm. She goes on to share, "It is the actual integration where most mergers fail to achieve their stated goals."

A primary reason is when merger decisions are made, they're typically based on financial rationale with the hope that 1 + 1 > 2. Unfortunately, what is not taken into account in most cases are the cultures that have been developed by each company—behaviors and expectations that may be decidedly at odds, and thus result in friction and often failure. This is witnessed when a company divests the acquisition within a few years of its purchase or applies a considerable goodwill impairment write-down as the value was not realized.

CASE IN POINT

Whole Foods began with a concept that's evolved into a following, a type of conscientious capitalism that's about more than just generating profits. Its purpose is to empower the lives of all stakeholders, including its competitors, by raising the bar in the health-food industry. The way success is measured goes far beyond financial results; thus, a merger of this organization with one that is geared on profits would likely be a disaster.

Culture is something that's dynamic; it consistently evolves but always adheres to some immutable core beliefs. I liken this to the difference between the number of changes to the Constitution over the past 250 years versus the number of laws during the same period. A culture at its most exuberant creates zealot followings—of customers, employees, and any number of relationships, including vendors. Some might argue that Google has achieved this despite its size, which usually causes more of a bureaucratic administration due to disparate business verticals. Clearly, culture will impact a company's equity value. This result is seldom attributed to financial documents, which is why many valuation practitioners fail to take it into account.

You're certainly familiar with the following companies, all of which have done a superlative job of building a culture that resonates internally and externally:

- Apple won't sell its products at a discount; it would rather discontinue items that are slow movers.
- Neiman Marcus empowers employees to make decisions on the floor and compensates them well; customers respond to its high level of service.
- Starbucks has created a desire among its customers to have an experience; do you think most people go there merely for the coffee?

As a valuator and analyst, it's important to look behind and beyond the numbers, so to speak—at the culture elements that can either support the big picture or identify potential cracks in a company's armor. For instance, most companies have written policy statements, visions, or reasons for being—but does the culture support them?

There are many things that can be studied with the goal of discovering potential red flags or confirming all is well from a culture perspective. As you dig, you may be quite surprised at what you uncover.

In most transaction-oriented businesses, "hitting your numbers" is frequently present, occasionally along with a lack of concern about how results come to be, but that type of focus will seldom be the case for organizations that have healthier cultures. One may ascribe that many Wall Street financial organizations that participated in the 2009 financial crash became dissociated with how financial capital built businesses by choosing bets over basics.

ABOUT BOARDS, GOVERNANCE, AND STRATEGY

Ever since Sarbanes-Oxley (SOX) regulations put boards and executives on notice as a result of a cozy relationship between Enron and its accounting firm, Arthur Andersen, financial controls have dominated business leadership focus.

However, doing the right thing because of fear of regulators creates a quarterly review mindset and stunts the strategic focus of the company's board and its CEO. Family offices and businesses recognize the benefit of a longer-term perspective, which is why direct investment in private companies, occasionally delisting public companies, or acquiring sufficient shares to influence performance have been common suggestions I have made, especially as memories are short and history repeats itself (that coupled by my general belief that institutional investment and high-speed trading that influence individual company shares prices has less to do with sustained company-specific performance and more to do with volatility and velocity or betting the spread).

Due to the 2008–2009 financial crisis and mismanagement of fortunes, interest in corporate governance has increased. Lack of good family office and business governance is regarded as one of the main reasons for the loss of many fortunes.

In times of good returns usually less family conflict occurs. Not surprisingly, in times of financial crisis discord with shareholders and family members can abound. Typically, intra-family disputes comprise 20 percent of my work. After 2008, it grew to almost 50 percent. Family business discord can quickly develop from a functional conflict into interpersonal conflict, creating a power struggles in the family that spills into the company or vice versa. At this crucial moment, if the family and/or business does not follow precepts of good governance for conflict resolution, the decision of some is to divest or destroy. The family, company, and their wealth ultimately will suffer from dilution of resources.

According to the Society of Trust & Estate Practitioner's Family Business Advisor of the Year (2013/2014) Martin Jenkins' empirical research there are four areas of wealth transition planning that tie directly to a lapse or absence of a governance strategy that leads to failure if not considered in time:

1. *Breakdown of trust and communication:* accounts for 35 percent of unsuccessful transitions.
2. *Failure to effectively prepare heirs:* accounts for 30 percent of failures.
3. *Ineffective governance with no cross-generational support for representative decision making:* accounts for 20 percent of failures.
4. *Lack of a family wealth mission statement/charter, and lack of consensus on the vision and mission of the family:* accounts for 10 percent of failures.

Fortunes are easily lost without consensus on strategy and risk tolerance, and without a structured communication system. Lack of governance leads to wealth atrophy. Therefore, implementation of good governance structures is crucial. Since strategic monitoring and management is a challenging task if there is a lack of expertise, especially at the board level, only a strategic roadmap can identify knowledge and relationship gaps and the significant risks and lost opportunities their absence has on the company and family.

Gregory Curtis, author of *The Stewardship of Wealth*, has an even more holistic perspective.[7] He states, "What keeps the moral balance of capitalism in the positive zone is this emphasis not on what capitalism does for successful capitalists, but what capitalism does for the rest of society—the greatest good for the greatest number." Curtis refers to this as creative capital: "capital that is earned and that is being stewarded." To share success is the epitome of American patriotism and free enterprise in a democratic society.

Curtis suggests a family must balance prudence of the speed in making an investment decision and that of achieving a desired return. Perhaps Warren Buffett said it best: "Price is what you pay. Value is what you get." The global economic recessions that followed collapsing financial markets also brought problems of illiquidity with minimal control function and neglected risk policies. The tendency of affluent families' portfolios being highly exposed to alternative investments, which in some cases in 2008 comprised as much as 50 percent of investments in private equity and other alternatives, hit even the very wealthy hard. However, the silver lining is it spurred discussions on direct investment, wealth transitions, education, and the importance of board governance and strategy.

HEALTHY BOARD GOVERNANCE AND STRATEGY CREATES VALUE

Dr. Vanessa Faktor, a preeminent authority of board governance, and Dr. David Teece, the founder of Berkeley Research Group and one of the most cited professionals/professors on strategic management, have helped shape my thinking on affluent entrepreneurial families and the board's and CEO's roles in determining strategic risk objectives and operational risk management practices. This can be achieved not only by the identification and effective implementation of entrepreneurial opportunities capture but also by detecting and preventing risks in a timely manner. This way, both the offense and defense risk/return objectives and the increased value of an enterprise can be realized. This requires governance that supports relationships that cultivate fresh knowledge.

The overall responsibility of dissemination of this information rests with leadership. Leaders should be in charge of managing the flow of information and communication among their constituencies as they have the most comprehensive overview of the organizational ecosystem. Family, staff, and advisory dynamics play a significant role, as conflicts can hamper the ability to maintain the sustainability of the concentrated wealth that is most family businesses.

In the worst-case scenario, a family member holds a leadership position he or she is not qualified to perform. The dynamics of the family can often cause difficulties for professionals hired to work on the family's and/or company's behalf. Rewarding or limiting of power in the most extreme case is seen as coercive power through the threat of termination of employment and lost family relevance. Conversely, the establishment of a leader–steward relationship is less affected by formal roles in the family-business organization.

Several servant-leader or steward-like traits sought for healthy board members are:

- Embracing change
- Creating win-win situations
- Being fearless
- Converting problems into opportunities
- Excelling at what you do
- Giving back to society
- Being humble

The stewardship theory (leader/manager):

- Is collective serving
- Is motivated by higher order needs
- Relies on personal power
- Is involvement oriented and uses trust in the leadership approach
- Embraces collectivism and embraces low power distance
- Takes a long-term view
- Emphasizes performance enhancement

The ownership strategy evolves out of the founder/family vision and then develops into the business's strategy. Both are dynamic and must transform.

The strengths of formal structures are:

- Long-term horizon for investments and strategies
- Uncomplicated and rather flexible structures
- Communication channels allowing for fast and uncomplicated decision making
- Leveraging of the human capital of the family

The weaknesses may be:

- Insufficient know-how, especially concerning strategic management/governance issues
- Missing incentives for attracting highly qualified staff
- Lack of liquidity patient capital and expansion
- Faulty or nonexistent succession planning

However, the business owners' strategy often defines the essence of the enterprise strategy and so presents the basic tools for the board activities:

- Set out the framework for the activities of the board of directors.
- Establish the details and implementation of guidelines.
- Identify the responsibilities of the board and senior management.
- Deviations from these guidelines must be submitted for the review and approval by the owner early on and in full transparency.
- The powers of the shareholders are determined by the law.
- Stakeholders alone are entitled to make decisions concerning the election and discharge of the board, auditors' appointment, final accounts approval, dividend payments, and equity policy.
- The shareholders determine the business areas and competencies of the entity; they are responsible for decisions on mergers, conversion of corporate entities, and any liquidation.
- Constituents such as advisors and staff should be consulted and engaged to ensure alignment between involved parties is achieved.

It is important to recognize there are many types of boards. Like personalities when grouped together create a culture, an early board is often tasked with operational issues, which it manages with nominal support from staff.

Collectives are common when boards are populated by family, staff, and friends known by the CEO, who is often the chair. Another similar example is when the CEO chairs the advisory board, which has nominal or no governance authority; however, this may not provide much-needed guidance in areas that may require two sets of eyes or a second arm's-length opinion.

Arguably, one of the more healthy types of boards is one that recognizes constituent interests as discussed elsewhere in this book. Such constituents often are beyond simply shareholders, and the board may protect constituents even if it may resist or replace company officers, but should refrain from daily operational issues.

A governance-focused board will have committees and relies upon the CEO to ensure the company vision and strategy to implement it is achieved. If results oriented, such as when the board is comprised of private equity or activist investors, the CEO may not have active voting rights but is provided leeway in the execution of goals. The CEO may report to the chair or the full board.

STRATEGY AND EQUITY VALUE

In an earlier chapter of my life I was responsible for planning as part of a strategy team in the military. Later, in corporate world I became responsible for corporate strategy and operational audits. Both functions require a fair amount of due diligence, intellectual rigor, objectivity, and big-picture thinking about the many what-ifs or alternative scenarios: "If this happens, what would I need to consider in response?"

To some extent, reacting to a market condition without a plan is like taking an aimless drive without knowing how far one is going and/or knowing whether one has the necessary resources—including time and capital—to get from point A to B. I refer to this simply as "knowing how to get from here to there" and looking for the resource gaps. Not surprisingly, these gaps tend to be addressed as GRRK and can reflect time and capital (human or financial).

Strategy requires that a company evolve, adapt, and remain proactive—that is, retain its focus as a market maker. The companies that should be proactive and strive to become or remain as a market maker are often the $100M+ companies out there; however, despite their size, even these companies lose their way.

Yet, this issue of governance and strategy should be at the heart of most company and equity valuations. "So, what's your strategy?" This broad question does not call for a mission statement or some general musings of desired outcomes.

If the industry statements are true—that most mergers seldom succeed in achieving the synergies sought—it bodes well to step back and consider this sobering fact. While there are a number of ways to talk about a distinguishing strategy from, say, tactics to improved efficiencies or customer satisfaction, for the purpose of this book, a successful strategy involves a series of plans and steps that increase shareholder value. This is a core financial premise for why most businesses are built or bought.

Consider the following: Few founders had a fully drafted strategic plan when they started their business. The number is something like 10 percent. Arguably, this 10 percent was influenced by funding sources like angel investors or venture capital or the bank wanting to obtain some assurance that the innovation translates into the ability to service borrowed capital.

Few founders maintain a plan during the conduct and growth of their businesses, simply reacting to the vagaries of the marketplace and sometimes just being lucky by offering the right products/services at the right price, place, and time. The next time the discussion on strategy arises, it's likely to be when it is a passing suggestion, or when the owner is contemplating some transition liquidity or legacy event like gifting to kids or key staff, an employee stock ownership plan (ESOP) or an outright sale.

Further, if there was no strategic plan at inception, what is the probability of having a plan somewhere down the proverbial road when the founder is contemplating a transition (such as a partial or full liquidity event)?

The previous comments about no plan then and now set the stage for more than a philosophical discussion. It opens up an opportunity to engage, that is, to provide objective concerns and identify opportunities.

First, can the existence of a strategy and its presence or absence be measured? Most assuredly. The analyst would want to determine whether the founder, board, and/or C-suite have an articulated strategy and how it was formed and tested. So, an examination of an ecosystem and constituencies would be a must. This means that staff, vendors, clients, and advisors, from bankers to accountants, should know the strategy and may have been involved in its formation.

The analyst would want to see whether the strategy is being followed and what rules exist for its execution, review, and revision. As an example, if the strategy is that annually the bottom 20 percent of clients will be divested and the top 20 percent will be given a clearly differentiated level of service/product than the remaining 60 percent, this is a part of a broader strategy. It's an ethos, and it finds itself within the culture of the organization. Paying lip service to a strategy when a quick buck might be made suggests it is not enduring, so a review where the above is not being done would require a revision to ensure it is being measured and managed.

Culture does matter, and it's the difference between Amazon versus Walmart, Apple versus IBM, or Starbucks and no-name café. The intangible asset of goodwill is born from the human capital of an organization—its culture, which reflects the vision, and the actions and behavior of its board, officers, and staff.

Consider Eastman Kodak. While the company was among the first to introduce digital photography, they believed that no amount of technological initiative would replace film. They must have not heard of Moore's Law (Intel), the premise of which is that with technology, every two years the capacity and speed double. Now, Eastman Kodak had a smart C-suite and board, but clearly the group-think bubble prevented management from sensing a shifting marketplace.

There was no demand to seize the opportunities in the evolving marketplace. In the absence of sensing and seizing, a company is unable to transform and leverage its dynamic capabilities in an ever-changing marketplace. Effectively, Kodak's management was concerned with doing things right and not with doing the right things. This is akin to digging a perfect hole that just happens to be in the wrong location.

These issues are unlikely to be found on a financial statement or uncovered during due diligence that's focused on accounting and legal issues. A strategy review or a postmerger integration strategy would have ensured the acquiring company had not overpaid (by retaining the low relative cost of strategy advisory services) to the tune of millions and sometimes billions of dollars for the acquired company.

Decision and selection entails finding an independent source that will not be an advocate for one or more board members (the business referral source). The folks with the funds and those advising them are not necessarily the smartest guys in the room.

The building of an organization that orchestrates its intangible assets into high-yielding capabilities is a market disrupter and game changer. A company with a clear strategy thrives in uncertainty. Developing a successful strategy is the differentiator that creates the competitive advantage. A valuation professional would have to be able to assess company-specific risk management as the subject company is clearly no longer part of the herd. Business owners' most common lament is that advisors don't use tools and language they can understand. The advisors claim the owner does not heed their counsel. If the advisors are the professionals, who is in the best position to address the gap? If cornered, accountants claim they don't make the owner's news; they report it. Safety from the sidelines. This is problematic as the family/founder has risk tolerance that has allowed it to own the company as a concentrated risk asset. Risk concentration, unabated, can be worth many times over the advisors' worth from the safety of their billable hours. It's a lost opportunity and may condemn the owner's future wealth if advisors are not more proactive in value creation, such as the aforementioned accountant.

So, what is the opportunity? Benchmarking a company's value is the easy part. The tough part is determining the existing gaps in resources (tangibles, time, and talent) to leverage the intangibles in order that the founder may realize a 50 percent or even a 300 percent increase in equity value in as few as two years. This requires the development of well-considered strategy where family, founder, company, and constituents are aligned. After all, the owner has his or her day job, and it's insufficient for advisors to simply express, "You must work *on* versus *in* the business."

The advisor's assessment of whether existing owners and staff are sufficient to bifurcate focus from the daily to the potential multiyear project often requires special skills in governance and strategy. It also requires the client's patience, aptitude, and funds to support what could be a 100 times or greater return on strategic initiative/business culture transformation investment.

There are many indices available to determine the presence of a viable strategy, which clearly will have an impact on equity value—especially if well executed. An analyst who doesn't perform the necessary due diligence to determine operational risks and strategy's presence and impact on a company's success is doing a disservice to the client and the advisory services community.

FAMILY HARMONY AND LEGACY AS A GOVERNANCE DRIVER

Ecosystems will function better if clear guidelines, direction, and key players are determined in the framework of establishing governance. In practice it has been observed that the linkages between the goal, mission, vision of the family, and their enterprise(s) are extremely important in order to maximize cohesion in the family, which creates added value. This might appear trivial, but with patchwork, multi-generational, and multicultural families living across multiple states and countries, building relationships can be extremely challenging.

A main aim of many affluent business-owning families is to establish a legacy. In order to establish a legacy, common values have to be in place and a historian may be required. This legacy can only emerge when these values are communicated and embraced by all constituents. This will create a feeling of fairness among the family members.

The assumption is that when family members understand why decisions are taken and feel that their voice is heard, they have the tendency to be more supportive. Understanding is necessary to create governance tools that will allow a fair and transparent decision-making process, with the aim that less conflict will arise in the family and in their enterprises.

BOARD STRATEGIC DIRECTION AND ACCOUNTABILITY

The concept of governance accentuates the board of directors' fundamental role of strategically directing, overseeing, and controlling the business, possibly the family, and its wealth. This must be done in a culture of trust and aligning all constituents' diverse interests in consensus and cohesion.

One of the main causes prompting an increased focus on corporate governance is the major loss of capital due to the global financial crisis, the loss of trust in the family's abilities to manage its wealth, and the loss of trust in family members that are involved in daily operations of the entities the family holds.

The loss of capital and lack of trust have resulted in rising conflict, leading not only to family feuds but also to substantial financial losses. Such disruptive events create ad-hoc crisis intervention. Yet, the board must keep its outlook more long term where strategic goals are realized while being monitored in a short time frame, allowing for strategy assessment and adjustment. This vision not only shapes the family legacy, but its system of values will also guide every constituent.

In determining the strategic direction, the board should precondition the following three components: strategic direction through leadership, strategic direction through education, and strategic direction through compensation. For successful governance, a well-structured representation of all three components constitutes the starting point for the strategic direction.

The Wharton Global Family Alliance Report (2008) indicates, "[Families] need explicit governance practices that hold professionals accountable, such as benchmarks, regular evaluations based on set criteria and clear reporting of outcomes," the premise of this chapter. Families and their entities need an integrated structure of governance that is holistic and can be put into instant practice and create net value to the entity. Such a governance framework should protect the three major objectives most families value: preservation and transmission of wealth, confidentiality, and catering to the needs of the individual.

This serves to support the enhancement of the family's authentic wealth—the intellectual, human, and social capacities of each family member—no more and no less than their actual net worth. When the family understands the importance of governance, there is more likely buy-in.

Boards are responsible for their companies' governance. They primarily focus on the safeguard incentive for shareholders investing in equity capital. However, the corporate governance framework should ensure the strategic guidance of the company, the effective monitoring of management by the board, and the board's accountability to the company and its constituents.

Together with guiding corporate strategy, the board is chiefly responsible for monitoring executive performance and achieving an adequate return for shareholders while preventing conflicts of interest and balancing competing demands. In addition, boards are expected to take due regard of, and deal fairly with, other constituents' interests, including those of employees, creditors, customers, suppliers, and local communities.

As an ecosystem steward, the board is expected to tailor governance and its strategies to the specific external and internal context of the entity while keeping in mind the family (as applicable).

In order to identify the appropriate governance framework, how it influences and is influenced by culture, requires reflection. Each entity and family has distinctive values while creating their governance structures. The following principles contribute to operational success as well as positive interpersonal relations to:

- Grow in a sustainable and healthy way.
- Finance this growth with its own operational earnings.
- Achieve leadership through constant improvement and innovation.
- Grow both as people and as an organization.
- Be vigilant, client-centric, dynamic, and profitable.
- Carefully identify, measure, manage, and mitigate risks.
- Be aware of the family members: their needs and desires.
- Control the level of involvement and transparency.

The reasons for creating governance vary according to the specific family's source of wealth, history, location, and family structure. Apart from the desire for confidentiality, the goal of wealth preservation leads to the establishment of a family governance strategy for the following three most cited reasons:

1. To obtain a professional wealth management operation for the family
2. To manage the proceeds from the sale of the family business(es)
3. To separate family and commercial affairs in order to create confidentiality

BOARD STRUCTURE AND MEMBER TRAITS

With a well-structured, independent, and expert board, families and businesses can operate more successfully through the implementation of strategic direction, management, and control. Such governance serves to establish a high amount of satisfaction by aligning individual interests and agendas. The core challenge of affluent entrepreneurial families is to optimize the safekeeping of assets and provide freedom of wealth for family members.

Therefore, the founder/family plans the vision, mission, and purpose of the entity and designs their ownership strategy. The decision-making process follows this scheme. Another significant difference to other economic entities is often the absolute autonomy of who is accountable—apart from legal and tax obligations—to the family beneficiaries and other stakeholders.

There is no one-size-fits-all model of governance to safeguard a family's own legacy. Over generations families should employ multiple quantitative and, more importantly, qualitative techniques to enable them to make more positive decisions regarding the employment of their human, spiritual, intellectual, and financial capital.

There are four key distinctions for a successful governance system: freedom, flexibility, horizontal perspective, and history in decision making. The advantage of such a system is its speed, which also allows conditions where family members can work together.

However, with an increasing number of family members and growing assets, those dinner-table meetings ("kitchen cabinets") can no longer guarantee good governance for communication, information aggregation, strategy, and risk management.

Each individual board member should demonstrate, apart from professional expertise, the capacity to apply a combination of relevant competencies to direct and control the business entity. At the board team level, this combination describes the evolution from a group of stars to a star team.

The development of directors of the board at an individual level will depend primarily on each director's personality, expertise, interest, and intellectual curiosity. The individual development will also be influenced by the culture and the atmosphere that influences individual relationships.

Boards often consist of family members, lawyers, and financial advisors. In order to gain a competitive advantage by establishing a board of directors, it is important to define the function, role, and concepts with which the board is charged. It is equally important to determine the values, functions, and mission as well as ensure that the directors understand and adopt them.

These functions include providing coaching and direction for the next generation and their successors. Due to the complex business dealings and often immense wealth involved, confusion without adequate structures for information aggregation can occur. The following questions need to be asked:

- Where are we today?
- Where do we want to be tomorrow?
- How do we get there?

A core set of guiding ideologies should be established in order to support a family and its entities when faced with its toughest challenges. Identifying a family's collective vision, values, mission, roles, and responsibilities is essential in helping manage a codified family governance system that can also be understood and adopted. This is often referred to as the *constitution* or *charter*.

GOVERNANCE AND RISK MANAGEMENT

The board should first propose well-defined goals, including a detailed risk policy. From 2000 on, integrated risk management encompasses not only financial and operation risks but also strategic risks and extends to risks inherent in corporate governance. No surprise its inclusion reduces risks and enhances equity value.

Risk management has to be integrated in the family office and business management and strategy. It should not become a parallel organization by itself. Together with company officers, it is advisable to acknowledge through risk analysis the type and level of risk acceptable. Risk analysis should be reviewed at least on an annual basis and, as part of governance and risk management, be incorporated into the due diligence agenda.

Governance must:

- Develop strategic goals that are executed.
- Determine the resources required to reach strategic goals.
- Ensure an appropriate allocation of resources for achieving goals.
- Create guidelines for management on how resources are to be applied in achieving goals.

Boards should be reviewed on the following risk management and governance topics:

- Board guidelines (where?)
- Board culture (how?)
- Board structure (with what?)
- Board meeting management (why?)
- Board diversity (from where?)
- Board champions (who?)
- Board stakeholders (for whom?)
- Board feedback (with what success?)

Reputation and relationships are inherent focal points in the execution of the business and cannot be delegated away from the board, which should monitor these human capital factors with ongoing due diligence; whereas custodian risk, often concerning third outside parties, can eventually be hedged and insured against. The board's ability to provide this level of accountability depends on having independent nonfamily members.

The board should consider the following topics:

- Family legacy
- Family governance and decision making
- Family relationship
- Investment performance
- Family business leadership
- Fiduciary exposure
- Family dynamics in business
- Family reputation
- Personal ownership responsibility
- Legal exposure

Morten Ahlström, a member of a family with the experience of 160 years of industrial operations, spoke clearly and precisely about his view on what it takes to achieve a successful governance model:

- Manage/control your destiny.
- **Steer the whole value creation chain.**
- Always improve/simplify.
- Choose the right people with the right attitude, agility, energy, competence.
- Focus on what to *stop* doing.
- Focus on what you do best; **outsource the rest.**

QUALITATIVE VALUE MEASURES

The creation of a culture that adds value rather than detracts from it is a long-term activity. Here are some things to review as part of every company valuation:

- Who's on the board of directors, and why. Is it made up of family and friends who provide rubberstamp approval or is it a more objective panel that offers sincere feedback and expert professional guidance? (The former equates to greater risk.)

- Is one individual both the chairman and CEO? (This can be a red flag if too much responsibility has been given to one person, with minimal oversight.)
- Is the charter and bylaws adhered to by family and firm? (It can be an issue if they don't.)
- Are legal documents up-to-date and accurate? (Companies that have access to current legal documentation should be valued higher than those that don't.)
- Who is providing advice? (This is similar to the board issue; it's better from a valuation perspective to be getting professional guidance rather than relying on old friends or family members.)
- Does the company actively participate in industry organizations and associations? (This demonstrates taking a leadership role.)
- Are key employees publishing or presenting on a regular basis? (This is a good indicator that a company is considered a thought leader.)
- How well informed are line-level employees? (It can be problematic if they don't know what's happening outside their own departments.)

This is just a sampling; you'll find a longer list of governance measurements later in this chapter. It is worth mentioning here that of the many things that can affect a valuation, some are "I didn't know" issues—a reality that underscores the importance of having a quality board and advisors as does the running of companies in a professional manner.

Can management pinpoint the causes of the company's success? Perhaps prices were raised, new territories were opened, or new products were introduced. Along those same lines, failing to have a well-defined plan for the future—an endgame—is not going to enhance a company's valuation. A company is not being run professionally if it doesn't have a long-term vision and hasn't outlined the actions that will lead to its equity value enhancement realization.

TAKING CONTROL

Control is an important facet of governance, and while that word alone can evoke fears of micromanagement and a loss of innovation, it's important to differentiate between healthy and unhealthy control. Bestowing too much power on one person or creating an organization filled with yes-men has the potential to negatively affect a company's value. It is true that there are times when absent any dire need, consensus is nice; and during more time critical issues, a decision can be centralized.

Team decision making is always a good idea, but if "the buck stops here" is the mantra of a sole decision maker, then ensuring that person has access to objective counsel—whether from board members or top management—is going to positively affect company risk prospects and equity value.

CASE IN POINT

A steel company that's grown from being a small player to an industry leader has had the same CPA since its inception. While having such a loyal advisor is certainly a good thing, it can also be a problem if the client has outgrown the CPA firm's capabilities. More specifically, long-term advisors may not disclose key operational issues given their vested interest in maintaining their business and billable relationships. A better, value-friendly alternative—one the steel company did opt for—was forming an advisory board that partnered their CPA with an external one from a larger firm. The advisory board CPA was comfortable asking hard questions about issues like inventory management, private capital markets, aging reports, and related issues not previously addressed.

This is a good illustration of taking control as a way to minimize risk, an action both healthy and necessary for a professionally run company. Other examples of healthy control include:

- Limiting crisis management mode to actual crises
- Cross-training to bolster redundancy of key positions
- Embracing alternative ideas and having a process in place to encourage and vet them
- Encouraging upward communication of feedback without threatening the source

In the best-run companies, a long-term vision is present. In addition, team members are purposeful about doing their jobs and they understand the role they play with respect to the success of the whole company. Control is not considered as something negative, since they're driving the car; it's not driving them.

Bottom line, those who are accountable must have answers to most *why* questions, such as: Why didn't we hit our numbers? Why do we have so much excess inventory? Why did we have so many products on backorder? However, they must have access to information and the authority to address those same issues. When healthy controls are in place and companies evolve into being professionally managed, this reflects less risk to most valuation advisors.

CASE IN POINT

A multigenerational container business worked hard to build a great reputation in the industry, with both customers and the competition. As a result, when it sought to grow its business via acquisition (taking control), the target company didn't feel assaulted, but complimented instead.

And unhealthy control? It can be somewhat of a fallacy that more control minimizes risk. On the contrary, it can be stifling to have the wrong kinds of controls in place if it negatively affects culture and results. This can lead to higher risks and lower valuations. A few examples of unhealthy control are:

- Turning entrepreneurial innovation into institutionalized thinking
- Controlling access to information that eliminates the culture of creating alternative ideas
- Using an contentious style outside of a crisis
- Rewarding tenure and loyalty over capability
- Saying "we've always done it this way" whenever challenged

The use of these approaches, and those like it, can quickly sap a team's energy and have a decidedly negative effect on a company's overall performance. The result of unhealthy control won't always be evident on financial statements—just like culture issues won't—but a savvy valuator will discover it and realize it doesn't bode well for the organization's value.

THE SECRET SAUCE

It should come as no surprise that the less risk associated with any organization, the higher its value is apt to be. A few things often overlooked by valuators can have either a positive or negative effect on the work product (the valuation report). On the plus-side are attributes such as:

- Successful onboarding
- Ongoing upward mobility
- Consistent flow of communication, up and down
- Thoughtful oversight
- Nimble decision making when called for

On the flipside, attributes that can be troubling signs of future issues include:

- High turnover
- Nepotism claims
- Short-lived business relationships
- Significant litigation
- Too many chiefs

Another potential source of trouble is a company's inability to change with the times. As previously noted, flexibility needs to be part of any culture; yet, it is rare for most organizations to operate proactively. Not doing so can have absolutely dire results as evidenced by firms like Sears, Barnes & Noble, Quicksilver, American Apparel, Blockbuster, and Eastman Kodak.

CASE IN POINT

Two successful organizations ignored the advent of technology and thus allowed their more savvy competitors to dominate emerging markets. AT&T had a telecommunications monopoly from the 1960s to the 1980s, but it failed to respond to the emergence of fiber-optic technology, thus its competitors carved up the once fledgling but now robust wireless market.

During the valuation process, it's important to gauge how willing a company is to act in a dynamic way: reviewing, revising, and repeating. Even as the challenges of today are being addressed, the possibilities of the future must be on the radar screen. To assist in that process, an in-depth analysis of company strengths as well as the potential to grow vertically and horizontally is a prudent exercise. A candid conversation will determine whether the company has the staff and advisors to implement and execute a strategy while still working on the daily navigation of the company. If they do not, then does the company have the desire and resources sufficient to retain outside experts to team with staff and advisors?

It's also invaluable to take a hard look at the actual work environment to uncover governance issues that have the possibility to impact the long-term success of the organization. A good deal can be learned about a company by seeing if:

- Employees are reading the newspaper or playing computer games in the middle of the day (perhaps a sign personnel cuts are warranted).
- The phone rings four or five times before it's answered (possibly reflecting less than gung-ho customer service).
- Meetings are vibrant and offer opportunities for contrary opinions to be expressed (the alternative "check-the-box" scenario does not bode well for innovation or employee loyalty).
- Does there seem to be too many employees for the work capacity needs?
- Do the people at each hierarchical level have the appropriate skillsets?

If the company is overstaffed and/or some of its team members are ill-suited for the responsibilities they've been given, such shortcomings can be masked in the short term; but it presents a significant risk that can have an adverse effect on equity value down the road.

CASE IN POINT

Three executives decided to form a company and gave themselves no-show jobs as the company grew and prospered. Eventually, many layers of management were created, resulting in abnormally high labor costs. Since the company was still making a profit, no one worried about the long-term impact of such top-heavy spending—but a valuator would identify insufficient capital was allocated for company growth that reduced its market value by $20 million.

GOVERNANCE MEASUREMENTS

Looking past financial statements to determine a company's value is not always an easy. Following are a dozen ways to measure the influence of governance and strategy, some of which have already been mentioned:

1. **Turnover at the staff, management, executive, and board levels.** It's not necessarily a bad thing when people choose to move on to other opportunities—especially if they weren't significant producers—but it can be an obvious sign of trouble when turnover is excessive and/or a number of key people leave around the same time, and join competitors. Losing valuable knowledge is one negative result of turnover; another is the cost of training replacements.
2. **Management of advisory board and other knowledge relationships.** Where advice is coming from is very important to know. Merely having an advisory board is positive—reflecting the understanding that multiple heads are often better than one—but both the board members' composition and the way its input is responded to either buoys or blunts its impact. The same goes for relationships with professionals like CPAs, attorneys, bankers, financial planners, and so on.
3. **Backgrounds of those who serve in executive and governance positions.** Have individuals been groomed for leadership roles or promoted due to determinants like technical skills, tenure or familial relationships? Ensuring that those charged with oversight have the experience and expertise is a critical part of planning for long-term success.
4. **Compensation's connection to performance and the marketplace.** What determines executive compensation? Is it connected to specific results? When salaries aren't based on performance, it can lead to complacency and stagnation. Additionally, if salary levels aren't competitive based on industry norms, that can negatively affect morale and increase turnover.
5. **Time spent annually in the C-suite function.** Believe it or not, CEOs who spend an abundance of time focusing on day-to-day business can represent a red flag to a valuator. The question that needs to be asked is whether the company would be able to operate in that person's absence. CEOs are expected to be visionaries; if the knowledge they have isn't transferred, value is lost. Too little time is invested in the future.
6. **Tenure.** This is related to turnover, as companies with lower turnover are going to have more employees with significant tenure. As long as those seasoned employees are still around because of the significant contributions they make—not because management is fearful to rock the status quo—having an experienced team is a valuation plus. Long-term

employees demonstrate loyalty to the organization, and their knowledge of its history can be invaluable in making plans for the future.

7. **Tools and talent that have been augmented based on growth.** Is the company able to raise the "A" game of its personnel as it grows? Has it had any successful mergers? As any company grows, it's going to face issues whose resolution can make or break its long-term success. It's really a question of having the ability to perform at a high level despite the various daily uncertainties confronting management.
8. **Improved capability to adapt in the company or marketplace.** This is related to the item above, as it also has to do with being nimble and able to respond to both internal and external changes. One thing is certain in the business world: Change will be a constant. Companies that are culturally flexible and open to the "research, revise, repeat" strategy are going to curry greater valuations.
9. **Leadership within the industry.** Exhibiting leadership skills at a company is a big positive, but being an industry leader as well is even more powerful. Those who serve on local, regional, and national boards related to their industry of expertise have the chance to showcase their skills and develop a reputation as a thought leader. This is beneficial on a personal level, but it can also pay significant dividends for the company with which the individual is associated.
10. **Receptivity to outside advisors.** This goes hand-in-hand with the second item on this list. When management is not receptive to outside advice from a formal advisory board or a professional banker, attorney, CPA, and so forth, that is a source of concern. And, if advisors are in place, how were they selected and evaluated? Do they have a vested interest in not being disruptive or are they truly objective and willing to tell it like it is, regardless of the business consequences? One way to gauge this is by looking at how frequently the CFO or CPA firm is changed, and whether meeting minutes are boilerplate; are meaningful discussions occurring and/or are suggestions to management weighed and implemented?
11. **Centralization of relationships with key people in the industry.** It's never a good thing to operate in a bubble. It will be looked upon with favor when company management can demonstrate its ongoing efforts to stay in close contact with those considered to be key industry leaders.
12. **Degree of family member involvement and qualification/training.** Family businesses, even publicly traded ones, which are more prevalent than one might think, must deal with a unique set of dynamics that were addressed earlier. The most important thing to determine from a governance perspective is what qualifications company leaders bring to their responsibilities. Is Cousin Joe really qualified to be the CFO, and what about your sister, Fran? Is she management material? Too often,

family members are gifted with positions for which they have little or no training or experience, and that's a problem from a valuation standpoint. When a family business is a lifestyle business—such that it exists to support the family and its personal expenditures—this will cause a reduction in value as well as the potential for litigation if it's thought management has breached its fiduciary duty to either family or nonfamily shareholders.

GOVERNANCE TAKEAWAYS

Organizations that give little heed to governance issues may have little interest in how strategic results are attained. They will typically present higher risks for investors. Valuators who look beyond the standard financial documents are likely to vet a few things: a company that's dynamically oriented toward strategy, or a transactional company that's reactive in nature. In most cases, companies that fall into the former group are going to receive higher values, and when harnessed, have the dual benefits of driving healthy growth and happier and more empowered personnel. All hope is not lost on the latter. It simply has to be a source of sufficient economic pain to choose to evolve before value declines.

NOTES

1. Henry Cendrowski, *Private Equity: History, Governance and Operations*, 2nd ed. (Hoboken: Wiley Finance, 2012), 174.
2. Tim Koller, *Valuation: Measuring and Managing the Value of Companies*, 5th ed. (Hoboken: Wiley, 2010), 403.
3. Donald Kuratko, *Entrepreneurship: A Contemporary Approach*, 5th ed. (New York, NY: Harcourt College, 2001), 471.
4. Timothy Hatten, *Small Business Entrepreneurship and Beyond* (Upper Saddle River, NJ: Prentice Hall, 1997), 26.
5. Stanley Feldman, *Principles of Private Firm Valuation* (Hoboken: Wiley, 2005), 9–32.
6. Dennis Jaffe, *Stewardship in Your Family Enterprise* (Winchester, MA: Pioneer Imprints, 2010), 10, 35–60.
7. Gregory Curtis, *The Stewardship of Wealth: Successful Private Wealth Management for Investors and Their Advisors* (Hoboken: Wiley, 2013).

CHAPTER 6

The Role of Relationships

While I refer to this as optics, the perception of the decision maker is paramount, which can often be demonstrated by his or her fee aversion. What is the correlation with the fees charged and the solution or opportunity found? That's the calculus of the owner who writes the check.

Do you want to create an awkward moment for an advisor paid an hourly rate or a commission who is seeking a business relationship? Simply inquire whether the amount paid is for services or products rendered. That is referred to as "price" paid. That then sets up the second issue of "worth." Since the price is established, the natural orientation is to seek a lower rate.

This is wholly different from the notion of "value" received. Value requires one to articulate that the outcome will be far more favorable than amount paid. Otherwise, why would examination of relationships versus transactions and technical or tactical advice differ?

In Chapter 5, "The Role of Governance," leadership and strategy along with other issues are discussed. The premise of Chapter 5 is the need to harness both financial *and* human capital. The challenge of obtaining such leverage of human capital is to identify resource gaps: often ones of skills, temperament, time, and funds. Then there are the dual issues of prioritizing the filling and managing of these constituency gaps.

Because there are multiple perspectives, the time and ability to achieve constituent alignment require a more considered approach than "I'm the owner and I pay them (staff, advisors, and vendors), so they should do what I ask." Or the founder's lament about family: "Don't they realize the sacrifices I have made? Why don't they show this achievement the respect it deserves?"

Because priorities and perspectives differ, wanting and obtaining their alignment can be a full-time endeavor in its own right. Then there are the additional perspectives of the family, board, clients, and others, where influence may be somewhat limited.

The term *relationships*, one of the two *R*s in GRRK, may be one of the most overused and misapplied in the business world. This doesn't negate the importance a variety of relationships has with respect to investor risk and opportunity that impact company value.

In this chapter, we discuss a number of different types of relationships: those internal and external to an organization.

Keep in mind organizations are ecosystems that can be distilled down to people (human capital). Human capital can be thought of as relationships and knowledge. Human capital alliances and coalitions that are healthy bring enormous dynamic capabilities and differentiation to an organization. The premise in most endeavors is that coordination, cooperation, communication, and cohesion often trump control (with the possible exception of a crisis).

Further, the ideas and innovation brought to the fore can increase focus on new opportunities as well as reduce risk and create new knowledge that is often unique to the organization. Think Apple and how it from top-down has led its innovations with nominal price concessions while dedicated patrons wait hours on line even before the product has been released.

As the chapter is read, consider how governance overlaps with relationships. For instance, an organization's culture influences relationships and relationships influence its culture for better or for worse.

Misaligned cultures such as the postmerger of two companies tends to produce conflicts. This is why a deeper understanding of the nature of staff and with whom they do business should have a complementary fit. If a CFO or outside consultant were charged with company rightsizing, would they know who within the organization has deep relationships with outside vendors and clients? So, viewing staff as a business line item expense versus a valued resource could result in some tragic terminations.

Prior to addressing specific relationships, let's reflect on what relationships truly mean in the world of business. Think about what makes up an organization: the infrastructure that supports people and ideas. These people include entrepreneurs, key employees, and trusted advisors—all of whom are likely motivated by creating leverage: a better way or outcome.

The combined skillsets of these individuals, if judicious selection and hiring has occurred, can result in something that's truly unique—and is fueled by ongoing collaboration and relationship development. Consider the role that relationships have in the following three examples:

CASE IN POINT

Many years ago, the board of Apple Inc. made the decision to fire Steve Jobs, architect of its most innovative products, because they saw him not fitting the corporate mold. Sometime later, realizing they'd lost more than just an executive, but rather a visionary with unusual imaginative powers, they patched up the frayed relationship and hired Jobs back—and the rest, of course, is history.

CASE IN POINT

Nike decided to add a rainbow-colored sneaker to its very successful product line, knowing full well that some potential customers (primarily those prejudiced against gay people) would reject it. What has happened? Nike couldn't keep these shoes on the shelves. Its potentially risky business decision demonstrates both its innovation and the fact that it has developed a special relationship with its customers.

CASE IN POINT

My wife bought a $255 shirt at a Saks Outlet and after wearing it tossed it in with our other clothes destined for the cleaners. It was returned with stains on the collar and sleeve, so I encouraged her to call Saks and let them know what had happened. The Saks employee asked just one question: Would you like your money back or a new shirt? The store reimbursed half the price of the shirt and also sent a replacement.

This level of customer service—provided by empowered employees—is what solidifies customers' relationships with stores like Saks, Neiman Marcus, and Nordstrom, and keeps them successful even though their merchandise is priced higher.

Specific circumstances may vary, but successful relationships are often at the heart of successful business: between boards and top executives, between management and employees, and between organizations and customers. Successful businesses have tremendous upside that results from prioritizing relationships rather than simply measuring transactions. That means nuanced issues are amplified, and customers receive greater value than what's reflected on a price tag or invoice.

Focusing on relationships as a means to success is not for the faint of heart, and it's not always intuitive for the many that have leadership responsibilities. Most managers and supervisors administer and most executives manage—but few actually lead and fewer still are stewards who build leaders. They confuse hierarchal control and reporting with leadership. True leaders find their authority not from their title, but from loyalty and relationships. They tend to seek and listen to insights from others before making decisions. They tend to influence corporate culture judiciously and are able to maintain strong relationships throughout an organizational hierarchy as well as external constituencies ranging from shareholders to regulatory bodies. They often embrace teams over individuals and have mastered communication and transparency.

The overall responsibility of effective dissemination of information rests with leadership. The leader is in charge of managing the flow of information and communication among the stakeholders as he has the most comprehensive overview of the organization and its direction.

The challenge presented, apart from value judgments, is that communication in a larger organization and marketplace (*ecosystem*) can be confusing unless a structured form is in place. As a rule, communication should be complete, objective, understandable, timely, concise, and logically arranged. It is perceived as cogent and from a trusted source.

While I refer to this as optics, the perception of the decision maker is paramount, which can be demonstrated by his or her fee aversion when one seeks a business relationship. *What is the correlation between the fees charged and the solution or opportunity found?* That's the calculus of the owner who writes the check.

Do you want to create an awkward moment for an advisor paid an hourly rate or a commission who is seeking a business relationship? Simply inquire whether the amount paid is for services or products rendered. That is referred to as "price" paid. That sets up the second issue of "worth." Since the price is established, the natural orientation is to seek a lower rate. This is wholly different from the notion of "value" received. This requires one to articulate that the outcomes will be far more favorable than amount paid.

Otherwise, why would examination of relationships versus transactions and technical or tactical advice differ?

If you don't believe relationships are important, consider how most relationship-centric wealth advisors are well-schooled in the art of putting clients and prospects at ease so they'll trust their firm with their assets. From my perspective, a good advisor provides good answers. A great advisor has the humility to know she doesn't have all the answers, but knows the right questions that must be answered. The advisor then earns the right to offer advice after she shows interest in persons and organizations she's seeking to serve.

The measure of an organization is often how it embraces good leadership and relationships when failures occur. Is it a learning, a denial, or a reprisal organization? Not surprisingly, many mature companies are burdened with a bureaucratic philosophy that hinders relationships to the detriment of new ideas and innovation. Sameness reinforces risk minimization, not innovation.

In such organizations, management and those seeking upward mobility will often find ways to maintain the status quo and are often risk averse. Blaming and hiding trumps fixing, which may have contributed to the bad press General Motors experienced with defective ignition switches and airbags.

The irony is key staff in such organizations may be social animals who master the unwritten rules of the game, but don't necessarily make strong contributions to the company's future. Private equity groups often recognize this and flush out those obstacles that hinder growth and profitability. Organizational innovators, on the other hand, often focus on overcoming challenges by taking advantage of the relationships they've cultivated to develop strategies that may be considered out-of-the-box; however, it can be game-changing, say Google versus Eastman Kodak.

CASE IN POINT

You might not be surprised to learn that companies that are first to market are usually innovators—but what about those that are second to market? For many years, Avis has centered its marketing efforts on the tagline "We try harder," embracing its position as #2 behind Hertz. It took an innovative leader to green light that initial campaign, since we're not hardwired to trumpet anything less than being #1.

CASE IN POINT

Internal to the way General Electric operates is that if the product or service line will not become the market leader or no less than second in market share, it is divested or shuttered. That drives innovation.

The most successful innovators find a way to keep relationships relevant while maintaining the highest professional standards. That balance is well illustrated at Google, a company well known for offering great employee perks but expecting superlative work in return. It has managed to develop and maintain reasonably healthy employee–employer relationships without compromising on its expectations.

CLIENT RELATIONSHIPS

Now that you know a bit more about the importance of relationships, let's start reviewing the different types of relationships found at every company. We'll begin with client relationships, which at the surface would seem to be the bread-and-butter of any successful organization.

All businesses will have clients, of course, but savvy valuators will take a look at the client mix to determine whether any red flags exist. For instance, no client should typically represent more than 10 percent of a business's revenues or accounts receivable. Companies don't want to put too many eggs in one basket, as that can indicate an untenable risk. The value of having strong client relationships can't be overstated, since that can lead to word-of-mouth advertising and minimize or even eliminate business development costs.

Businesses with growth rates that don't exceed inflation might consider ramping up their client-centric activities with the goal of growing sales to or above their industry while keeping business development expenditures at or below industry norms. This can be done by both broadening and deepening existing client relationships as well as seeking referrals from loyal customers.

What constitutes a good client? Most people would mention three things: They pay on time, they have a good rapport with key individuals, and they're loyal to the business. Owners should put special focus on the third item, for there's no substitute for clients that become immune to pitches from competitors. In a perfect world, those immune clients are the ones in a company's "A" group—they may generate the most revenue as well as the highest profit. But that begs the question: What are you doing to differentiate those "A" clients from those who are considered "B"s and "C"s? If the answer is nothing, that shows you're taking relationships for granted, which makes them vulnerable to poaching.

To solidify relationships, are clients asked what else the company can do to help the client improve their business? Supporting them in gaining new revenue streams is going to pay much greater dividends over the long term than treating them to a round of golf.

When you become a trusted resource, more than merely a vendor, that's when you've been successful in creating a special client relationship—and there's great value in that. Your objective is to ensure clients have ways other than transactions to gauge why they should keep doing business with you. Some examples of upping your game in this way include providing project timelines that are regularly updated, making introductions to potential clients and suppliers, providing industry information, and even sitting on their board.

You might wonder why I haven't talked about pricing as a means of differentiation and gaining client loyalty. It was a deliberate omission. Let's say you choose to reward a loyal client by decreasing their price. What message does that send? Unfortunately, it might be that you've been overcharging them—and that's not going to make them loyal. In fact, what it does is turn a relationship into a transaction, not a good recipe for generating long-term profitable business.

When the use of this best practice becomes embedded in your business, you give clients a very important message: "Your success is my success."

If you want to become a go-to resource or problem solver, you need to provide services that are above and beyond what anyone else provides; that makes it difficult for your competitors to come in and undercut you on the value you provide. You become a concierge—a connector—a repository for solutions.

CASE IN POINT

Airlines must rely on service differentiation to attract and maintain customers, since in essence they all do the same thing: getting people from here to there. The airlines that do the best job in providing platinum service to Group A customers while making those in Group B and Group C feel they're getting special treatment as well are going to be less susceptible to losing customers to competitors—this is apparent on airlines like Virgin.

Something else to think about with respect to client relationships is making sure you're focusing on the right clients. Keeping in mind that it's always less expensive to maintain current clients than obtain new ones, you still need to ensure that company resources are dedicated toward the clients that provide you with the most in return. You shouldn't be afraid to jettison your lowest-tier clients if that means you have greater bandwidth to expand relationships with higher-tier clients that can add more to your bottom line.

How can you ensure you maintain relationships with valued clients and even persuade them to give you more business? It all starts with who's tasked with relationship development. If it's just one person, even the company principal, you have an exposure risk. Each significant client should have at least two people assigned as liaisons. And preferably, the same is true for the client in case one of the two leaves.

A by-product of establishing strong client relationships is protecting your firm from losing business when something goes awry—as it invariably will. Clients who see you as simply a vendor obviously don't put much stock in the value of the business relationship, so they'll be apt to ask for things like cost concessions to make up for whatever went wrong. On the other hand, clients who value you as more than a supplier of goods or services will be likely to give you the benefit of the doubt—at least the first time while seeking shared solutions so the problem can be fixed and not repeated.

ADVISOR RELATIONSHIPS

We've focused on internal business and client relationships to this point, but they are just the most obvious when it comes to adding or subtracting value from a company. Let's now move on to advisor relationships, which can have a significant impact on both a company's success and its valuation.

Among business owners' fears is if they ask questions, they appear they don't know what they're doing. Nothing could be further from the truth, since the most successful leaders focus on their strengths while harnessing the expertise of others to fill knowledge gaps.

Another sore spot for business owners is paying to receive advice where it is not apparent it provided the value sought. As you'll see later, quite a bit of business advice is available at no or nominal cost. And much of it is commonly offered for free on the Internet. If the knowledge that is readily found is "common," so is its perceived value. This makes me wonder about the stock market when all advisors say "hold", "buy," or "sell." Being in the majority or herd does not make the action correct, but it's often followed as it's familiar.

Making decisions in a vacuum while making assumptions on what is unknown can be detrimental to any business. Savvy owners will understand that trusted advisors can be invaluable when dealing with any number of situations, including bringing on a #2, buying out a partner, realizing things aren't working out with your son-in-law, thinking your CFO may be leaving, realizing that your chief estimator is integral to 75 percent of the company's relationships—and he's 63, acquiring a competitor, or seeing revenues flatten or decline.

The common denominator in all these situations is that they require actions that are best identified by a group of talented collaborators that may very well include advisors in relevant disciplines.

CASE IN POINT

To use a medical analogy, when you visit a general practitioner, you're paying for intake that allows the doctor to identify your health needs—and one possible outcome may be a referral to a specialist who can provide the relief you seek. Businesses are really no different; advisors should be solution providers who identify issues before they become urgent or result in a crisis. Think of it this way: Would you rather see a cardiologist before or after a heart attack? Prevention makes more sense than reacting to what's already happened. Knowing what you don't know limits the amount of guesses on which most assumptions are usually built. This is not exactly the best foundation on which to build a successful enterprise. This is what is meant by *filling resource gaps*, which can refer to time and human and/or financial capital.

The fact is, it's not an effective business model to always be working on the critical issues—especially if they've been looming for some time. The value of relying on advisors, who may be in a position to anticipate and stop such issues from becoming critical, can't be overstated.

We'll start with reviewing the value of guidance from advisors whose counsel is usually free or often so—commercial bankers, investment bankers, insurance agents, and wealth advisors, as well as your own board of directors, clients, and vendors. Many owners pass up the opportunity to add value to their operations by developing strong relationships with these constituents, who often can provide invaluable business insights.

COMMERCIAL BANKERS

During the research part of any valuation, one of the questions asked is whether the business has a relationship with its banker. An answer other than "yes" constitutes a red flag. I'm downright flabbergasted when company owners can name just the bank and not their banker.

A bank is not merely a place to park money. A solid banker can provide a great deal of advice that can result in significant top- and bottom-line benefits like increased sales and higher profits. Bankers can be invaluable sources of information when you contemplate acquiring real estate, making significant equipment purchases, or contemplating a merger. They will also likely know the optimum debt to equity a company in a given industry has as well as industry norms for return on assets and equity. If they don't, any good business appraiser will have multiple comparative industry sources to include similarly sized (based upon assets and/or revenues) and profitable versus unprofitable.

Savvy bankers should be very familiar with the inner workings of your business, and based on what they learn, should ask you questions like these (as appropriate):

- Why do you keep a significant amount of cash on hand?
- Why do you have little to no debt?
- Why are accounts receivable and inventory at their current levels?
- Why haven't you made a significant investment in your capital assets in some time, a course of action that's led to high repair and maintenance costs?
- How would your business growth change using increased capital?

Your banker can get you thinking about funds and cash flow in ways that may have never occurred to you. For instance, she can explain that debt in the form of a bank loan is often a sound strategy, since it splits the risk between the company and the bank. It usually comes down to cash flow needs of the business and the interest rate (cost of capital).

Bankers who understand the importance of adding value to their relationship with you—transcending a transaction-based association of rates and terms—will also be able to assist you with forecasting, an important task of any business. If your banker can't or won't do this, it might be time to look for another banker.

INVESTMENT BANKERS

Investment bankers tend to specialize in recapitalizations (better rates/terms or allocation of debt to equity) or the combination of equity- and debt-based funding. Do you know what debt-to-equity ratio is best to get the highest performance? Good commercial bankers should know, but may not; investment bankers must be able to answer questions like this.

Both investment and commercial bankers may be able to examine partial liquidity options. The commercial bank may suggest the tax benefits of shares held by employees through an employee stock ownership (ESOP) plan holding 30 percent or more of the company's equity. The investment banker may be able to arrange a minority interest holder who may not require control, but wants to support a well-run company with the potential of further investment. This may be a private equity group, a wealthy investor, a family office, and occasionally a friendly competitor who may one day be an excellent candidate to acquire the remaining equity in the company.

Investment bankers have the knowhow and connections with traditional lending institutions and private parties who may be willing to fund assets like real estate, machinery, and equipment; however, they often excel in funding sources for companies that don't have a great deal of tangible assets like technology, financial, and business services companies. In short, they are plugged into the world of business financing, so they know what investors and buyers are looking for. When you develop a relationship with a licensed investment banker, you are raising your game. You'll be working with someone who thinks strategically, not just tactically, and has access to private capital markets and deeper and broader financial networks. They know what investors and corporate buyers are looking for in a company and when and why they'll pay a premium.

A good investment banker knows what will move the value meter, so to speak, and is an excellent resource to have in place when a liquidity event is contemplated, and especially one that's unplanned. You don't know when your personal expiration date (your passing) will be; so to ensure a fire-sale doesn't ensue after you die or become disabled, you need to have all your ducks in a row before such a catastrophic event takes place.

CASE IN POINT

Many people in their thirties don't think about health issues derailing their family and company futures, but anyone who owns a business needs to consider that possibility and make contingency plans for the "what if" event. A young entrepreneur who owned several businesses had a stroke, and didn't have an existing investment banker relationship in place, nor did he have advisors to help make his businesses more saleable in a timely fashion. How much do you think these businesses were worth?

In most cases, banking knowledge is free; you just have to know how to ask for it. Developing relationships with commercial and investment bankers can result in some very tangible benefits, even enhancing your company's performance and value.

INSURANCE AGENTS

Insurance is a resource that's often misunderstood and underutilized. Few owners like to pay a premium for an event that may never happen, but most are very glad to have the coverage when they do have a claim. However, when looking at insurance from a valuation perspective, it's more important to consider its role in risk management rather than focusing on premiums. Your insurance agent can be your new best friend.

As a business owner, you need to think about insurance as a risk elimination or mitigation tool, much like you probably see your savings and retirement accounts as a buffer against unforeseen financial adversity. Good insurance professionals will look at many issues—things a business could or should be doing differently to keep premiums down and coverage adequate. Your broker-agent can serve as an ad-hoc risk manager, getting you to secure coverage for risks you may or may not have considered, such as:

- Business interruption
- Information technology theft
- Wrongful acts by your landlord
- Employee accidents while representing the company

The best agents will make sure your policies cover what you think they do, and they'll also go the extra mile to uncover risks. For example, if your office is in a multistory building, would you be covered if water damage from the floor above you affected your computer room?

Premium cost is always going to be a consideration, but rather than concentrating solely on the expense, it's more important to think about the potential for lost business and value if risk isn't appropriately managed and the right coverage isn't in place. A good insurance agent will review your existing coverage and identify areas where gaps are present or your level of coverage is insufficient. The goal is to ensure that any loss you incur is an inconvenience rather than debilitating—and you might be surprised to learn that when the proper protections are in place, it reduces both your risk and the amount of your premiums while increasing equity value.

If the founder was to pass away unexpectedly, would she want the legacy of a business or real estate to be sold just so the tax implications were adequately covered? The combination of a high-end life insurance professional who may offer premium financing for a $25, $50, or $100 million policy and a skilled trust and estate attorney with a viable zero-tax strategy may be family heroes if deployed well in advance of such an unfortunate event.

If a business brings in two new partners, it's important to ensure they have death and disability coverage, and at an appropriate level. At many good-sized businesses, this type of coverage is surprisingly nonexistent or inadequate. While you may be happy to be controlling the cost of your premium, a valuator looks at that situation and sees increased risk (thus less value).

It's also beneficial to receive an assessment of your complete operational risks—everything from IT security and work-related injuries to the identification of possible errors and omissions exposure to key individuals whose loss would be most strongly felt. The best insurance agents will use a holistic approach to working with the business owner.

In addition to mitigating risk, labor-related coverage like health and dental insurance can be leveraged to allow for better relationships with employees and thus lower turnover of critical staff members. Recommendations on lowering workers' compensation premiums may also save hundreds of thousands of dollars and increase value by millions of dollars.

CASE IN POINT

Let's say you run a company that provides two primary services, lawn and tree maintenance. The risks are much higher for the latter than the former, but that won't be reflected in what you pay for workers' comp insurance. If you bifurcate the company, however, with lawn maintenance and tree maintenance considered on their own merits, you may be able to save hundreds of thousands in premiums. This is the type of advice a savvy insurance agent will provide.

Certain types of insurance coverage may elevate a value multiple, something that adds significant value, since at the end of the day the owner's foremost duty is to optimize the return realized by stakeholders. D&O (directors and officers) coverage is one such example. Many owners use insiders—family or key staff members—as board members; and they assume significant liability by serving in that role, especially when there are outside shareholders. It can be more beneficial to have outsiders on your board, people more likely to provide you with an honest perspective since their livelihoods aren't tied to you, but it's hard to attract talent without liability-insulating D&O coverage in place.

An insurance professional who's focused on strengthening his relationship with you will always be thinking about how he can positively affect your bottom line. If you operate a transportation company, for instance, and always allowed employees to take company cars home at night, an agent who's on the ball might suggest altering that policy so the cars remain at your office parking lot overnight—significantly reducing your premiums.

Some insurance professionals will also explain the tax advantages and cost benefits of re-insurance or self-insuring through programs such as Captive Insurance. These are products that are especially popular for blue collar labor intensive businesses that are profitable.

A savvy insurance agent will do more than contact you annually to renew your policy. Someone who really wants to add value will ensure he's aware of any changes to your business that might affect your insurance needs, anything from the addition of new employees and purchase of valuable assets to the creation of intellectual property.

It's a good idea to meet quarterly with your insurance agent to discuss where your business has been, where it is, and where it's going. What comes up during that meeting may help you run a more profitable and less risky business—and it comes at no real cost to you while driving up your company's value.

When you begin looking at insurance as more than just a necessary evil and a line-item cost, you may be surprised at the savings you can achieve without compromising coverage—with a little advice from an insurance professional who understands how to add value to client relationships.

WEALTH ADVISORS

The goal of a wealth advisor is to help you invest your discretionary earnings and assets. While these individuals are compensated for working with you—on a percentage or fee basis, depending on your preference—they can also be a great "free" source of financial advice.

Your wealth advisor should be intimately familiar with your business to ensure she can provide the most appropriate advice. For example, she may question why you keep $1 million in cash on hand when you only need half that amount as working capital, and suggest investing the other $500,000 so you're earning a higher return while maintaining liquidity if needed. Instead of getting a paltry interest rate from a bank, she may steer you toward a safe liquid investment that offers a 3 percent risk-free rate, earning you $15,000–$30,000 per year.

Good wealth advisors will also be able to provide value with respect to retirement plans and other types of employee benefits. They have the potential to save and/or generate hundreds of thousands (if not millions) of dollars, depending on the size of your business. Wealth advisors can be great sources of market intelligence, which makes it important to choose someone who understands your business and may have a number of other clients in the same industry. They can be excellent conduits to professional referrals such as bankers, insurance professionals, trust officers, transaction, tax and trust attorneys, and CPAs.

Like the other advisors we discussed, you want to be working with someone who's interested in adding value to your business as opposed to merely making investment suggestions.

BOARD OF DIRECTORS

If your goal is to create a larger enterprise, you should never forget how important it is to have an alter ego that helps you think strategically. You should consider your board of directors to be like the sage elders of yesteryear who were counted on to provide counsel to villagers.

As noted earlier, many boards consist of people who rely on you: family members, key employees, or paid advisors. This is not a good strategy if you truly want objective advice; instead, you may want to reach out to other founders or CEOs, who, like you, are in search of guidance to lead their businesses.

You have two options when it comes to structuring a board of directors:

1. *A governance board*—This type of group will work on the business proactively rather than reactively, and consist of people with diverse perspectives. It's a challenge to maintain balance while giving up control, so many owners may not prefer this organization style.
2. *An advisory board*—This type of group operates as a sounding board, providing perspectives with the sole intent of giving decision makers more options. It's a necessity that members have relevant industry expertise.

Whichever structure you choose (or both), you may be surprised how valuable you find the counsel you receive from your board. It's often lonely to lead a business, and it can occasionally even be unrewarding, so getting different opinions from people you trust can be quite rewarding. If for no other reason, the presence of independent board members with gravitas and expertise will elevate a company's value.

The board's focus between management accountability and its ability to strategically execute on vision is what enhances shareholder equity. Historical focus is on top- and bottom-line growth. This book posits that emphasis must be on a strategy of value building and creation and leveraging human capital to reduce risk and seize opportunities.

THE BOTTOM LINE ON "FREE" ADVISORS

It's important to realize that free advice can provide you with million-dollar ideas and open doors other than being a technician serving a specific tactical or transactional need. And, when you work with advisors who are at the top of their game, they'll know other advisors who are top-tier and may make good additions to your advisory team.

Even in the absence of problems, it's a good idea to review your advisors on a regular basis. Familiarity doesn't necessarily make a good marriage; your relationship must be an ongoing courtship that can't be taken for granted by either party. That being said, reciprocity should always be on your mind; are there introductions you can make or speaking opportunities you can provide that will benefit your advisor? True relationships versus those that are merely transaction based are preferred.

Let's move on to discussing advisor relationships that aren't always free: accountants, attorneys, and fractional CFOs. Many of the same things noted as being important with respect to free advisors are applicable for working with paid advisors; of greatest importance is ensuring that the people you choose should be adding value to your business rather than serving solely in a transactional capacity.

ACCOUNTANTS

Many owners assume that all accountants are the same, and nothing could be further from the truth. Some focus on taxes, others on audits, and still others on administration of trusts and estates. Thus, in seeking to form a relationship with an accountant, the first thing you need to determine is where your needs exist, so you can pursue the type of accountant that will provide the most value.

When meeting with accountant candidates, you want to listen for individuals who frame the conversation based on value creation. That, in a nutshell, is the difference between a good accountant and one who's worth his or her weight in gold. Many accountants provide limited or no business advisory services other than anecdotal experiences with a particular industry, so it's wise to learn their specialized knowledge in your industry and the relationships they maintain with other professionals so subject matter expertise may be handy if needed.

While you will be usually be charged when you ask accountants to perform specific tasks, you may be able to get valuable advice nearly or completely free from accounting professionals who understand the value of differentiating themselves from their transaction-focused colleagues. For instance, you may have discussions about the following topics that relate to tax benefits and tax reduction:

- Is your company a good candidate for cost segregation?
- Would accelerating depreciation be a good strategy?
- Is operating as a C-corporation right for you, or would you be better served as an S-corp or LLC?

A "gold" accountant will also get you to consider strategies that can help you minimize taxes, reduce your liability exposure, and save money, such as:

- For manufacturers, moving significant assets to a new entity that leases the use of those assets to the original company
- For C-corps, pulling real estate out of the company and leasing it back
- For any company, using outsourced labor for a variety of tasks, like:
  - *HR administration and reporting*—it may be more cost-effective to have these personnel matters handled by external specialists.
  - *IT*—It might not make sense to have an entire department, but rather to have access to the knowledge you need.
  - *Marketing services*—It might make sense to create a separate entity for these projects that charges as work is needed.

Significant benefits can be realized by having a straightforward conversation to explore actions that can have tax advantages—but it's important to not let the tax-tail wag the dog.

CASE IN POINT

Let's say your company reports $10 million in net income, but it has the opportunity to raise that to $15 million. Instead of dwelling on the fact that you'll have more tax liability, you should be focusing on what will cause the profit increase. Your thought process may depend on your age and wisdom, your company, and your accountant, as well as whether you live in a high-tax state like California, New York, or Illinois.

Some accountants will tell you it's wiser to focus on income tax than estate tax, but many of the tax-associated decisions you make will hinge on your future transfer plan for the business. In particular, if you're passively involved (i.e., only drawing income), how you choose to proceed may be significantly different than if you're very involved in day-to-day operations. This issue in fact is frequently at the heart of what makes a business thrive or fail within three generations (or sooner).

Having a holistic accountant who asks the right questions is critical to making appropriate financial plans. He may also suggest having an accounting team with various specializations such as real property and tax credits.

He should want to know how the business is operated and while he may begin with the company's financial statements, it should only be a starting point for his due diligence.

Some of your accountant's questions will be focused on cash balance and debt, as he seeks to determine what's contributing to performance and how risk is concentrated. He may ask some of the same questions a good banker will, something that underscores their importance:

- Where is your cash?
- Who's managing it?
- Is it generating much income, and why or why not?
- Would it make sense to incur debt?

In addition, head count and compensation will be two areas on which a strong accountant will focus. As it pertains to accounts receivable and inventory, she may have other inquiries. With respect to the former, do you have net repayment terms and are they enforced? Do slow-paying clients affect cash flow and by how much? How would you benefit from receiving more timely payments, and how are you damaged if payments are too delayed? How do you determine pricing? Is revenue growth from increased clients, higher pricing, increased sales per client, new markets, increases in specific products or services, or two or more of the above?

Moving on to inventory, does your inventory level make sense given the size of the company as well as its cost of sales and revenue? What is your inventory turnover? What percentage of your inventory is obsolete? How is your inventory tracked and managed? What pricing concessions do you receive and how many suppliers do you use and why?

CASE IN POINT

If you keep a large inventory and sit on it until orders come in, you're tying up capital that could be used for more valuable purposes. A more effective strategy—one used by online retailers like Amazon—is to arrange to get items on an almost-real-time basis reducing the need for space and use of capital.

Your accountant should understand that inventory may be an important indicator of company performance, and it's fundamentally tied to your expenditures on net fixed assets and repair and maintenance. The first expense line item a good accountant looks at will be repair and maintenance, comparing your expense with the industry norm.

For example, if you spend 3 percent of annual sales each year to repair and maintain equipment and the industry norm is 0.2 percent, you're going to lose money every year. The 2.8 percent difference (which would otherwise be an increase in profitability) may reflect the fact that older machinery is being utilized, while competitors are using newer models that don't break down and produce double the finished goods in half the time. This would impact labor expenses as well.

Another expense/cost your accountant should be zeroing in on is labor. If you have a higher employee headcount than other companies in your industry, you're simply not going to be as competitive as they are because your labor costs will likely be higher as well.

CASE IN POINT

General Motors lost a significant share of the car market to Japanese competitors that had a lower production cost due to controlled labor expenses. GM's labor cost was 60 percent greater, something that enabled the Japanese to sell their cars for less.

When it comes to developing a relationship with an accountant, you really have two options: work with someone who will report the news, or someone who will help you make the news. Three or four isolated line items taken independently may not mean a lot, but in aggregate as demonstrated above can scale a company's growth and raise its value.

Working closely with a talented accountant to identify issues that affect company value as well as the bottom line will make companies become better managed. When an accountant is permitted to provide significant value, fees charged becomes almost irrelevant. For instance, if you paid 20 percent more to an accountant who could help you generate more profit, would this be money well spent?

I always am cautious of the notion of "my accountant saved me 'X' dollars in taxes." My reply would be, why were you overpaying your quarterly withholdings and not reinvesting that amount instead?

ATTORNEYS

Attorneys have historically been among my top clients from transformation- to trouble-related engagements. Like most insurance professionals, their role is to minimize, mitigate, or eliminate risk. As the complexity of a dynamic organization grows, so does the need for sage advice—and thus the importance of legal counsel.

Most entrepreneurs shy away from anything that smacks of rules and bureaucratic red tape. Yet, attorneys, particularly those with extensive business and tax backgrounds, can often provide invaluable advice to navigate through or around any potential roadblocks. They can also ensure that buy–sell agreements between partners or shareholders are codified to protect against making shortsighted decisions that can lead to conflict.

A good attorney will serve as a dispassionate professional who understands how a rash decision can be a multimillion-dollar mistake. Attorneys can help moderate the exuberance to enter into agreements that may be less than favorable or even catastrophic to your business's future. They can also extricate once an imprudent decision has been made such as the firing of an employee without proper documentation.

While attorneys operating in the business world are most widely known for drafting agreements, bylaws, and contracts, they may also provide a healthy dose of realism that can protect valuable assets like human capital, intellectual property, and trade secrets. They can also provide labor-related advice such as:

- Whether you are giving too much equity too soon to a prized employee
- The merits of bringing family members into positions without adequate experience

- Whether employee compensation is too high/low
- The merits of a relationship with another company

As your business grows, the issues you face become more sophisticated and your exposure is greater; thus your need to have good legal counsel is magnified.

That brings up the issue of how you select an attorney. It's always a good idea to be careful of institutional bias, such as ignoring boutique firms because you believe a larger firm will somehow do a better job for you. Remember that your relationship will be with an individual attorney, not the firm, so you should start your due diligence by learning candidates':

- Age
- Health
- Years of experience and discipline education (including undergraduate education)
- Allocation of time across what disciplines
- Percent of time they've served business owners

You'll need to decide whether a generalist is ideal or specialization may be wise. You also want to ask questions about what value they will bring to your business. If replies to queries seem general or the attorney won't commit to specifics—buyer beware. Additionally, if you are considering a large firm and speaking with a senior partner, ask if the partner will be actively involved on your account, or if a junior associate will handle the work. You want to ensure you get what you're paying for, but with that in mind, the worst yardstick you can use when vetting attorneys is their hourly rate. This is because sage advice while appearing expensive based upon the hourly rate can be worth multiples of 10×, 100× or more in savings, safety, and sleep (as well as enhanced company value).

FRACTIONAL CFO

It's not unusual as businesses grow to find that there is no CFO in place, or the person who now has that title was moved up the ladder—starting as an accounts payable or receivable clerk before becoming controller—so he may not have the knowledge or sophistication the job requires. This may be evidenced by no experience working in the private capital markets or preparing businesses plans or shepherding firm strategy.

In any of those situations, bringing in a fractional (outsourced) CFO on a full-time interim or part-time basis may be an invaluable move. A good fractional CFO will help you think strategically so you don't have to react to every daily operational issue that arises, but can keep your eye on the longer term.

This professional should have a strong accounting, HR/IT, or operational background, and in a perfect world, all of the above. It's also important to work with someone who has experience working at rapidly growing emerging businesses or more mature operations that may be growing more slowly but are profitable and may be contemplating a merger, a divesture, or an ESOP.

In short, the role of your fractional CFO is to make sure as much funds as possible flows in and as little as possible flows out of the company while risks are controlled. Some of the ways that can be done include:

- Streamlining the use of information technology
- Focusing on metrics that mean the most
- Renegotiating or obtaining lines of credit, loans, and leases
- Helping front office/sales oriented firms become more grounded
- Implementing checks and balances to optimize cash flow
- Determining the amount and type of square footage to invest in

From a bottom-line perspective, it's the CFO's responsibility to ensure that a philosophy of "win at any cost" doesn't cripple the business. Identifying obsolete inventory, future capital needs, and adequate cash reserves are three ways these CFO's can be of assistance. They may also bring an increased understanding of what other activities need to be monitored and reviewed. In the best situation, your fractional CFO will provide you with an alternative view, a fresh perspective that may have you saying, "Wow, I can't do things the same way anymore as it detracts from value building activities"

In addition to time savings, the owner should also realize a significant ROI from having a fractional CFO on board—5, 10, or 20 times what the owner is paying. And, this individual will be able to suggest when it's time for you to hire someone on a full-time basis (usually when your annual sales are +$25 million depending upon industry).

FAMILY RELATIONSHIPS

As clearly reflected elsewhere in this book, families are inextricably involved in many mid-market businesses as shareholders, board members, enterprise officers, and staff. They are occasionally related parties doing commerce between family enterprises where some relationships are by marriage, blood, and/or business. Such relationships tend to seek an obligation to be accountable for one's actions and to hold others as such.

This requires leaders to be thinking, listening, and sharing in terms of mentoring and modeling as stewards. Such responsibilities tend to require expressed expectations and a commitment to common goals. As is the theme throughout this book, metrics should be established to provide continuous feedback and provide actionable solutions based upon favorable or unfavorable outcomes. Because neither families nor business endeavors are static, metrics may require review and revision. Because these interactions require communication, interpersonal skills should not be taken for granted whether founder or friend.

Cohesion is created when all constituents are engaged, which requires some balance of emotional and financial understanding as to how *success* will be defined and measured. Future generations of leadership and ownership can be groomed by being engaged as the bridge to the future. They do so by bringing new energy and fresh ideas. They and the enterprise can share the benefits of business transformation.

SHAREHOLDER RELATIONSHIPS

As a pragmatic matter, private business owners and investors tend to think in terms of income or distributions (i.e., amounts and frequency of funds shared). It's often an afterthought about equity valuations, agreement and trust instrument provisions, and tax consequences (income, gains, gift, trust, and estate).

When shareholders are family members and the business may be central to the families' respect and relevance, emotions can become central to thinking. This is sometimes as relevant as financial issues. As such the means and message of communication can be key.

VENDOR RELATIONSHIPS

Often overlooked as a simple cost or expense, the nature and depth of vendor relationships can be critical in a business. This may be true depending upon the lead time for supplying product or services. It may be the benefit of the perspective of a vendor who works with competitors to share what best practices they may apply that are not presently used by the company.

If nothing else, a vendor could be a future acquisition or a source of intelligence, so respect and not solely price and terms should be how such relationships are preserved. Consider the client who needs a product or service yesterday. If you will need to rely on your vendor and your relationship is purely transactional, what's the likelihood their management or ownership will bend over backwards for a matter you believe is critical?

Which type of relationship is likely to bring higher value?

COMMUNITY/LEGISLATIVE/PHILANTHROPIC RELATIONSHIPS

There are those successful family businesses and mid-market companies that wish to be known for something greater than making good on their commercial promise. They want to be a community steward. John Mackay, CEO of Whole Foods, refers to this as "conscientious capitalism."

Some companies allow staff to contribute as much as a month annually of their paid time to helping a cause. Some families create a foundation to harness the spirit of giving and business savvy to make the world a better place and engage family members in doing good beyond making donations. This is becoming increasingly popular among Millennials. Most know Paul Newman's efforts with Newman's Own Foundation, which has contributed over $400 million of total company profits to charities that help military families and support volunteers as an example. Hedge fund billionaire conservationist Louis Bacon and billionaire environmentalist Tom Steyer have committed hundreds of thousands of dollars supporting lobbies that support green initiatives.

The point is family and business are but vehicles that may make a genuine impact and offer a transition from transforming a company to transforming an industry to transforming the world as Bill and Melinda Gates of Microsoft fame have done with health and education initiatives.

If nothing else, relationships are the human capital glue that should be based on trust, something that doesn't come with a price tag, but is built. Advisors who focus on transactions rather than adding value are doing nothing to enhance the trust factor—or help make a more positive impact on business owners. And nothing says "your success is my success" like directly or indirectly assisting a business by enhancing its value.

Nurtured relationships are always a two-way street where to gain one must give. Not doing so can be costly. Two quick examples come to mind. The technology provider for Target Stores was aware of the significant uptick of data flow coming from Target and is indicated as having notified store executives in December. The reaction was slow. As a result, after the cyber-security breach made media headlines, in less than a month the company's share value had declined by $11.2 billion. This is a clear example of how relationships and risks truly intersect, as our next two chapters reflect.

CHAPTER 7

The Role of Risk

Financial- and Legal-Oriented Risk

Founders, CEOs, boards, and trusted advisors tend to gravitate toward financial control, examining and reviewing figures, percentages, and ratios for current performance metrics. This is not strategy, which requires a well-considered overarching perspective that drives governance/culture, relationships, and the use of knowledge to provide a means to identify, measure, manage, and mitigate risks. In short, an owner's strategy should tap into human capital in order to enhance shareholder value in the most efficient and effective way possible.

This is one of two chapters that delve into company specific risks. They comprise the majority of this book, which is partially the point of writing it. That is advisors and appraisers of all stripes can best assist stakeholders by identifying, measuring, managing, and mitigating risk, which in turn increases value. This is why I state, "Values are more than just a number."

For full disclosure, these chapters and this book are the author's own viewpoints and not necessarily that of the associations of which I am a member or the companies in which I am employed or a shareholder.

Further, there are limitations to this book. It is hoped that discussions ensue on how to take specific indicators and develop quantifiable measures to support enterprise and equity level risks. This would entail both selecting which risks are applicable, what degree they individually and collectively have an impact and which may be more heavily weighted based upon the risk, the company, the industry, the market, and economy as of specific points in and durations of time.

After all, as expressed earlier, risk perceptions differ among investors, which is true when there are buyers and sellers involved in any transaction.

What can be culled from this book is the following understandings; especially amongst my business appraisal peers. There is comparative data in which we may use to indicate whether the subject company is performing at, below, or above the median. Data sources have limitations and do not always agree with each other's results. The breakdown of data by asset and revenue size can be somewhat arbitrary and may skew results with reporting influenced by the number and accuracy of inputs.

That said, we know that under the Market Approach that given sufficient transactions, we can create quartiles to isolate performance and while interviewing parties of prior transactions is often beyond the scope of most engagements, such an endeavor might allow more qualitative and quantitative data to filter and isolate risks to better quantify pricing multiples as well as discount and capitalization rates. While I use internal methods to demonstrate how much weight given risks have for a specific engagement, because the purpose and some subjectivity may arise, I would not at this writing dare to suggest an infallible methodology exists to capture what can be hundreds, if not thousands of variables, influencing risk and value.

Lavern Urlacher, author of *Small Business Entrepreneurship: An Ethics and Human Relations Perspective*, underscores that risks are usually addressed after the fact and that a risk assessment for more than insurance coverage should be conducted.[1] She prioritizes causes as lost income, fiduciary breach, personnel issues, and acknowledges a mistake—the oversight of an unforeseen event—can "put you out of business." Constant review in the form of risk management is advised. She suggests risk transfer, risk avoidance, and risk minimization. She further suggests including processes, procedures, and outsourcing.

In *A Random Walk Down Wall Street: The Time Tested Strategy for Successful Investing*, Dr. Burton Malkiel suggests considering investment in a small-cap index.[2] My read of his pronouncements is to understand company-specific risk and find securities that are occasionally undervalued with low P/E multiples, but otherwise healthy for the longer term. Dr. Malkiel also warns about the conflicts of interest between researchers and investment banking services within the same firms. I share his belief to invest in companies with growth at a reasonable price (GARP); therefore, occasionally, stocks with low price–earnings multiples may be better selections as earnings' forecasts are historically hard to predict. In many ways, his influence on not only measuring, but managing and mitigating risks has been significant. This is as true in the private capital markets as it is in the small public company space.

"No risk, no reward" is a phrase we've all heard—and it's true that taking thoughtful risks in business can result in significant rewards. The ultimate risk management is to achieve the highest return with the lowest level of risk associated with that activity. However, the unfortunate reality is that many companies are operating in an unnecessarily risky fashion and they don't even know it. Even more tragic is that most valuators limit their discussion of risk in valuation reports to three or four sentences—when it's often the most critical determinant of a company's price multiple and capitalization/discount rates.

Executives and entrepreneurs commonly understand that their most valuable asset is the business itself, which is an amalgam of tangible and intangible components with much of the latter associated with human capital referenced in this book as *governance*, *relationships*, and *knowledge*.

Executive risk stewards/managers and strategic value architects are often painfully aware that their ultimate responsibility is to increase shareholder value—seeing how much value they can create above book value of tangible assets—and that often results in sleepless nights as they wrestle with how to best concentrate risk in the living, breathing entity that is their businesses.

Sadly, the uncertainty associated with company risk is that it is typically examined tactically and reactively—and this fundamental flaw is often the difference between leading a $10 million versus a $100 million or $1 billion+ company. Why does this happen? It's a matter of strategy, which is addressed in the governance chapter of this GRRK book. To underscore, an owner must treat a business as if it is a private investment where return on invested capital is among the top indicators that are being tracked. This brings us back to the importance of first benchmarking value to know where the investor is at and managing and mitigating risk and seeking opportunities to enhance value.

Founders, CEOs, boards, and trusted advisors tend to gravitate toward financial control, examining and reviewing figures, percentages, and ratios for current performance metrics. This is not strategy, which requires a well-considered overarching perspective that drives governance/culture, relationships, and the use of knowledge to provide a means to identify, measure, manage, and mitigate risks. In short, strategy should tap into human capital in order to enhance shareholder value in the most efficient and effective way possible.

How do any of these financial metrics identify the existence of founder, board, executive, family, staff, and advisor alignment? In order to maximize the client relationship experience and outcome, wouldn't this be an overarching priority?

Any strategy intended to address risk must start with identifying the vision that makes the business different from its competitors. Arguably, this is referred to as *dynamic capability* whereby actions are proactive. This perspective is something that allows a business to sense, seize, and transform during internal and external disruptions regardless of the velocity of those issues.

CASE IN POINT

Think about the companies that went on the offensive, looking to make acquisitions during the financial turmoil that marked 2007 through 2010. Their long-term strategy was enduring and more focused on results years from the present. Those companies on the offensive didn't consider their behavior to be risky, but it might be said that risk is often in the eye of the beholder.

From a valuator's perspective, individual and market risks are just the beginning. Any company-specific risks, which include those affecting the entity, equity, and/or assets, drive the pricing multiplier as well as the equity discounts and premiums that reflect investor concessions. Thus, by addressing those risks, owners and advisors have an extraordinary opportunity to align and integrate activities that are matched to overall company strategy.

As we discussed in the relationships chapter, the ability to leverage staff, vendor, client, and advisor knowledge and relationships (human capital) can be important to mitigating or eliminating risk. Once that process becomes organic and continuous, it provides a broad and deep ecosystem that's a differentiator in and of itself. It's really not an earth-shattering concept—it actually seems self-evident—but it's often uncommon based on the more than 1,200 engagements I've participated in over the past several decades. This is despite the fact that addressing risk can be the difference between a price multiple of 5× versus 10×. If the economic benefit is $10 million, that would be a $50 million difference and possibly more.

This chapter will address a litany (by no means all) of potentially risky behaviors, but here are some examples to jumpstart thinking:

- How do you consider and measure human capital investment?
- What is the impact of company information technology (IT) capabilities and vulnerabilities?

Let's start with human capital, which is often a company's most valuable intangible asset. Many professionals and laypersons refer to this as goodwill. Goodwill is simply a subset of human capital as the focus is on relationships and not necessarily knowledge. As stated earlier, human capital doesn't show up on a financial statement other than as a labor expense. It's quite common to discover that very few companies are monitoring, managing, or mitigating efforts employed to leverage personnel. The answers to the following questions can be quite telling (and uncover areas of potential risk):

- Does a human resources handbook exist?
- What's the rate of company turnover at both the staff and middle/senior management levels?
- How often are law and accounting firm relationships terminated?
- Do most of the ideas come from the company founder and C-suite, or are they created and communicated from the staff?
- Is the staff cross-trained?
- How often are performance reviews given?
- Can staff members self-assess as well as assess their direct reports without fear of reprisal?

More about this short warm up later, but for now let's just say that a healthy HR function with governance, compliance, and risk management needs to be part of the growth plan for most companies.

Moving on to IT, there are countless ways the technology function can elevate a company's value—or degrade it. If you think of an organization as a human body, the IT function is its central nervous system, so it's certainly critical to its overall health.

Is there a mechanism in place that eliminates redundant activity between the front and back office? Is there a system to track progress and monitor the more significant risks common in an operating business? How can IT be leveraged to minimize what can be adverse outcomes that inhibit growth?

CASE IN POINT

Ebbs and flows in the delivery of raw materials or in receiving customer payments can significantly affect cash flow. Putting technology to work to limit or eliminate cash flow unevenness can have astounding results, ultimately ensuring that performance expectations are not just met, but exceeded, without affecting existing headcount, equipment, and inventory—and that leads to a more robust bottom line (and business value).

The use of IT, ranging from computer-assisted design and manufacture (CAD/CAM) in manufacturing to customer relationship management (CRM) tools, is highly relevant to any business. Any company that limits its use of technology to Excel spreadsheet financial reports is probably underutilizing it. The investment in IT systems and personnel may be considerable, but failing to do so can mean the difference between remaining stagnant or growth by enhancing your technological capabilities. During a site inspection, there are ways to see how technology is or isn't being used, but this is something that's usually missed as part of a valuation, as it's not required to be examined. More about IT later.

Common internal risks to a company's long-term fiscal success include management depth as well as levels of profitability, growth, and debt. Externally, there are market-related issues such as competition and interest rates. Oftentimes, this is as far as a review of risks goes—and that means a great deal is being left out. For instance, I've occasionally seen a valuation report that does not discuss provisions such as buy–sell and partner agreements—yet these may shape a company's performance and rights of equity holders. Additionally, functional areas like operations and finance are seldom examined.

Simplicity often rules the process, which means a check-the-box result that likely does not reveal the company's full risk profile and thus the result is at best thin and at worse inaccurate. Despite the fact important risks are not discussed by professional valuators, legal and accounting professionals, industry associations, and academics, that doesn't mean they don't exist.

And, it leads to a rather interesting question: "How are business owners supposed to enhance their companies' value if they don't know what they don't know?"

CASE IN POINT

A company has no capable alternative to its founder, a 65-year-old man who hasn't taken a vacation in the past 10 years. He believes he has mastered the management of company risk—but from an investment perspective, what would happen if the founder became disabled or died?

After working with entrepreneurs for 25+ years, I genuinely understand their frustrations as well as their desire to unlock value. I equate it to purchasing a home and being told that every room has a collection of precious gems—but they're in vaults that can't be accessed without the combination. There's no value there if you can't get to it.

Fueling entrepreneurs' dismay is that they often seek to enhance value without much assistance from their trusted advisors. This may be why they frequently see the fees for technical abilities of professionals as expenses versus investments.

A paradigm shift needs to occur for entrepreneurs to overcome risks in an effort to build value by spending more time pursuing opportunities and not simply daily blocking and tackling. Owners and their advisors need to move from being transactional, technical, and tactical to being strategic and holistic. Those owners and officers who take this path—and enlist advisors willing to be stewards to assist them—will be better aligned to unlock value and thrive in uncertainty.

COMMONLY MISSED RISKS

As promised, what follows is information about common risks that are often missed during the due diligence process. The 27 items noted in this section sometimes also contribute to acrimony among family members and equity holders and may contribute to advisor misalignment.

When company-specific risks are not considered during the process of determining entity- and equity-level values, it is virtually impossible to arrive at a supported rate of return. The frequency of occurrence of this risk being present during due diligence is indicated after each item as a percentage (%). The upside is many of these items can be relatively easy to address with nominal expenditure of time and capital.

When these risks are identified and managed, the pricing multiples can increase by 40 percent and sometimes more. So, as an example, if the cash flow was $5 million and price multiple was 5×, the value would be $25 million. A 40 percent increase would be $10 million or a new value of $35 million. How much would advisors recommend an owner invest if it's known the value would increase $10 million or more?

1. No Documented or Articulated Strategy or Business Plan (90%)

Bankers and investors require companies they support to have a business plan, but most entrepreneurs don't go this route to fund their operations—so it's probably not surprising that those who bootstrap (friends and family funding) to get started have no business plan going in (fewer still have a transition plan to address new leadership over the long term or when they transition out).

Why don't advisors require a business plan? Frankly, most advisors have worked for someone else and know when and for how much their next check is coming. Anyone who's ever started a business or acquired one knows it's like giving birth to a child and then raising it—pouring in a huge dose of sweat equity along the way.

While seemingly self-evident, the planning, caring, and feeding is somewhat of a foreign concept to many. Yet, business owners will find themselves dealing with a variety of situations, everything from negotiating leases to figuring out how to fix the copier. And most will be expected to be a jack-of-all-trades and a master of some. They will typically perform one or both of front- or back-office tasks.

The takeaway from this is that entrepreneurs seldom do both front- and back-office tasks well—and without a solid business plan to guide their way as to how to fill resource gaps, some important things may not get addressed. Having a plan can be the difference between operating a robust, growing company or one that's stagnant and underperforming—and has a lower price multiple.

Do you have a plan or strategy that drives your culture and the decisions made by not only the board and C-suite, but line personnel as well? This critical component is seldom present, and even when the desire is there to have a plan, both entrepreneurs and advisors often confuse strategy and tactics. The former is the program and the latter is the process.

Your business plan may also determine whether your company impacts its market—or reacts to it. There are many examples of business planning leading to great success, or to abject failure in its absence, and no one wants to be noted for the latter.

CASE IN POINT

Apple went sideways when it competed solely with PCs. The iPod was a game changer, and they planned for what would come next: the iPhone and iPad. They knew well in advance where they were going to go; thus they drove the market.

CASE IN POINT

Tesla knows there will be economies of scale as it seeks to add market share, but it seeks to remain at the cutting edge of the electric car market. Its brain trust realized that the common element in all electric cars is batteries, so the company is expected to invest $5 billion in that arena—a truly brilliant move that will have long-term ramifications while its competitors who need these batteries are just trying to carve out electric car market share today, which is why Tesla made most of its intellectual property publicly available to hasten competitors to produce more electric vehicles.

CASE IN POINT

The once-dominant cell phone provider Sprint failed to stay current with the innovations that its competitors saw coming, focusing instead on sales and financial control. This lack of vision made it a target for acquisition after faltering performance.

If your organization does not have a strategy that guides it, reflected in the time and tenacity to draft a business plan, it makes it more difficult to move the multiplier meter. For example, companies with plans may earn a 5.6× multiplier, while those without may have a 4.0×. That's an example of the 40 percent greater referenced earlier. Not every poor decision can be eliminated by having a business plan, but the odds are better a company will prosper over the long term and earn a high multiplier during the valuation process because more effort is placed in understanding one's market and opportunity and capital needs when planning is done.

2. Bylaws, Articles of Incorporation, and Agreements May Require Updating (70%)

It's quite common to find many important provisions were drafted years if not decades ago. Laws and regulations change. What the company does and who its officers or directors are may have changed significantly since then. This can be problematic because the existing leadership can be bound by legal provisions—even if they are unaware of their existence.

Provision discrepancies can be exposed any time, such as when funds have been disproportionately distributed, potentially breaking the company's own rules. Let's say a company's three founders have made agreements that are inconsistent with the language in an existing buy–sell agreement. This situation may void the original agreement or allow it to be used as leverage in a disagreement or dispute among officers or directors, whose duty it is to look after shareholders' and employees' interests.

Let's say your partner and you choose not to fund your buy–sell agreement with insurance that would allow the surviving partner, upon the other's death/disability, to buy her shares. That means you (the survivor) now have a new partner—your partner's spouse or heirs—folks with whom you may not wish to be in business.

Any number of things can be incorrect on documents that haven't been updated in a while, including how the company is valued and who has rights of first refusal, or documents may simply have been created from boilerplate text. Regardless of why it has happened, outdated documents can have a significant impact on valuing equity.

Like it or not, a valuator during due diligence may discover a lot of inconsistencies; some of these may be minor and easily correctible, but others can present a potential liability. Is it a problem if your bylaws call for three board members and you have four?

What about if the equity ownership percentages have been incorrect on tax filings? Some owners may consider reviewing company documentation to be a dreaded exercise, but when made aware of the value of ensuring consistency and accuracy, they are often glad they did.

3. No (or Poorly Written) Agreements, or Agreement Provisions Not Being Adhered (60%)

This is along the same lines as #2, except it may be the case that no agreements exist, or those that do are poorly written and/or not being adhered to. Missing agreements should be drafted while existing agreements should be updated, restated, and/or cleaned up and their provisions followed.

What about preferred shareholders who may have had rights to unpaid, but accrued distributions and then a decision is made to convert all shares to common?

Does this mean there is a contingent liability to preferred shareholders or additional shares were issued to them when only common shares were decided? Will this dilute the value of other shareholders' equity?

Another example is, does your company have non-compete and trade secrets agreements? This agreement should be in place to protect the business by ensuring that key personnel don't leave and take trade secrets or client lists, solicit or induce current employees to leave, or take valuable data with them to a competitor.

What's the carrot for employees? How about "golden handcuffs," which may be in the form of stock options vested over time or that may be forfeited. Think about the thousands of new millionaires who emerged from companies like UPS, Microsoft, Google, and Apple; they were rewarded for staying with the organization as it grew from an idea to a successful public company.

Business owners may be asked whether they have considered putting an employee stock ownership plan (ESOP) in place. ESOPs offer tax benefits, and also provide a way to reward employees when the company does well, giving them the chance to vest ownership as their tenure lengthens and the company prospers. These are examples of missing agreements that could add value to a business by protecting its proprietary information/ideas/innovation and acknowledging how important employees/human capital are to its overall success.

4. Related-Party Agreements Not Complied With or Not at Market Rates (50%)

These documents are crafted with a focus on limiting taxes, asset protection, providing outsized control and income. They may become "out of sight, out of mind," as circumstances change.

CASE IN POINT

A company rents space at twice the market rate to a related party. While the landlord may be thrilled, the economic benefit to company investors may be impaired; they may claim the company has breached its fiduciary duty to them.

CASE IN POINT

A company is paying $300,000 in rent from the common owner of the building. It should only be paying the market rate of $150,000. This is considered unfair enrichment and funds that could have flowed to shareholders in the form of distributions.

CASE IN POINT

A company has its rent reduced from the market rate of $150,000 to $75,000. However, a future company buyer may not be so fortunate and could be charged market rents, reducing company profits.

CASE IN POINT

A company decides to hire a marketing firm and must choose between two options: an outside firm ($100,000) or a firm founded by the owner's spouse ($500,000). Opting for the latter option may be akin to making a distribution unless it can be demonstrated the 5× amount paid provided five times the result (value received). That arrangement may be okay for operating purposes—but not if the owner plans to sell the business.

5. Shares/Units Held Do Not Reconcile between Certificates and Tax Returns or the Number of Shares Authorized and Outstanding Doesn't Reconcile (10%)

This is often an issue of math. Let's say a company has been given the authority to issue 1,000 shares. That means at no time should more than 1,000 shares be issued unless there has been a recapitalization, say 5 to 1 shares. For simplicity's sake, each share is worth $100. Thus, an investor who holds a 10 percent interest in your company (100 shares) can assume that equates to $10,000. However, if more shares have been issued—2,000 instead of 1,000 for instance—that results in dilution and the investor's per-share value has been cut in half.

These issues may exist when there are numerous classes of shares or stock-splits or if shares were acquired by the company. The amount of control is based upon agreement provisions as well as the number and type of shares held and the amount of distributions received. This is something that can go unnoticed for some time until a milestone event—like a transfer, sale, or merger.

6. Common, Preferred, Warrants, and Options Are All Treated the Same (20%) or Accrued Dividends for Preferred Are Not Reflected (50%)

When companies are formed, a myriad of thoughts about structure are considered, with the final decision usually driven by tax and voting right considerations; some may choose to operate as a C-corporation while others prefer a pass-through structure like a partnership or subchapter-S-corporation.

Another consideration at the onset of a company's life is what equity will be held and by whom. This is often determined by how the company is funded; that is, collateral may be used to secure debt financing or owners may prefer to bootstrap using unsecured financing vehicles like credit cards. In addition, there are more complex forms of debt, including convertible debt, which means at the election of either or both parties, debt can convert to equity.

Another funding may involve various classes of shares, units, equity, or interests. Having just one class is most common, but the issue of how many shareholders can own what stock may ultimately become relevant.

Most companies are not going to have an initial public offering (IPO), but they still must adhere to state and federal rules regarding the number of shares and interest holders. Also at issue can be various classes having differing rights.

CASE IN POINT

Let's say a company has Class A preferred shareholders who have a right to a 10 percent per annum dividend that may accrue if unpaid and may be compounded. This becomes relevant if the company has an inadequate cash flow to pay these shareholders earlier during formation. The accrued liability ensues to these people since the preferred amount was never paid so this may be treated as a liability to the company.

More trouble can occur when classes of equity holders have been given voting rights, a provision that may not be relevant initially but can become highly relevant as time goes on. Over time, this provision can be forgotten—but it's still recorded.

Provisions influencing voting rights can also be quite problematic. For instance, each unit holder, regardless of the percentage held, may have a single vote; this is uncommon, but does occur. Voting rights provisions may also require varying vote levels, from majority to supermajority to unanimous, so depending on the number and type of equity holders, making changes to or within the entity and how it operates may be difficult or impossible.

Some share classes have economic rights but no voting rights. So, it's possible for someone to own a majority of shares but have no influence in common business decisions, including but not limited to:

- The future of the business
- How the business operates
- Who the CEO is
- How much the CEO is paid
- The amount and frequency of distributions to equity holders

As time goes on, equity-related components of certain bylaws, articles of incorporation, certificates of organization, operating agreements, shareholder agreements, employee agreements, and buy–sell agreements can either be absent, contradictory, or no longer followed. When this ensues, under the best circumstances the company is guilty of inaccurate reporting with the worst-case scenario being the potential of litigation that can involve board members, the CEO, and even trusted advisors.

Equity reporting issues can be under an even greater microscope if the company has elected to create an ESOP, meaning it will be subject to regulatory oversight as it is considered a retirement plan.

So much can change from the time a company was formed and started to raise capital, including new management, new advisors, and new equity holders. If the initial provisions regarding equity aren't reviewed as subsequent decisions are made, countless risks can result. It's critical to engage in ongoing due diligence to ensure that company documents jibe with the equity reported.

The takeaway from all of this is that whether a company is young or more mature, maintaining current records and ensuring the company is operating as intended is critical. Absent that, the risk can be tremendous and result in significant reduction in equity value.

7. Property Is Not Properly Titled or Assigned (10%)

How could something like this happen? Here's one way: The equity holder of a family business, founded by his parents, was diagnosed with cancer and sadly passed away. His wife was also involved in the business, and her mother-in-law decided to unilaterally remove real estate assets from the company and arrange a leaseback. This intentionally reduced the company's profits, but it gets worse. The mother-in-law then sold the real estate, something she could do because the title never changed to being a legal asset of the company. It was reported as company property, but her title prevailed.

You might think this is an unusual situation, but the point is this: When equity ownership changes, a close eye should be paid to title issues—ensuring that transfers and transactions are completed and are at arm's length. Failure to report a change in title can have legal and tax implications as a seasoned valuator's due diligence will note.

When a company holds real estate or most any valuable asset, it's important to be able to answer the question of who owns title and how held. It's not sufficient to just look at the appraised value as many do. The extra step of ensuring accurate title needs to be taken—and this is even more important when a business has multiple assets and locations.

This issue of ownership may not be limited to real property; it can also apply to intellectual property (IP). Think there's much risk involved if IP rights have never been assigned to a company, but are still held by the creator of the IP?

CASE IN POINT

I was recently involved in litigation that involved two shareholders suing the founder of a company because he failed to grow the shareholders' value as was implied. That might seem absurd, but due diligence determined the company's secret sauce—its IP—had never been assigned by the founder to the company, and that IP represented the majority of the company's value. As a result of the owner's inaction, the company had no value and the shareholders had a good case. Who owned the rights to the IP made all the difference.

It's also a good idea to be aware of who owns the rights to tangible property that is used by a company. A good example of this can be found in the landscaping industry.

CASE IN POINT

Let's say company A provides landscaping services and company B leases assets to company A, such as trucks, lawnmowers, and blowers. If the owner of company A seeks to sell it, there are no tangible assets, only relationships, to sell. This would lower the company's value unless the two companies are sold together.

8. Meeting Minutes Are Boilerplate (90%)

It's quite common for CEOs to fail to differentiate between the duality of their roles—operational and fiduciary. When they're also a 100 percent shareholder, that usually presents no real issue, but when other equity holders are present or if there is debt, it can begin to be problematic.

When a meeting takes place, it may take a long time to draft the minutes and file them—assuming this occurs. Meeting minutes should include much more than which board members were present (although that should be noted), but also record things such as: critical events that occurred since the last meeting and what is anticipated in the upcoming time period; significant decisions made and actions taken and the rationale behind them; and who guided the process. This historic perspective can tell a compelling story and add value to a company.

Absent this documentation, equity holders and possible acquirers become increasingly vulnerable, especially if they're not board members and the board is made up of family, friends, or inside directors (officers). Where is governance oversight to ensure short-term thinking does not rule the day?

Since a key purpose of operating a company is to enhance shareholder value, there should be an accurate recording of the decisions such as distributions are equitable after consideration of reasonable officer compensation and company reserves.

CASE IN POINT

If the board votes to give the CEO a salary increase or bonus that's twice the industry norm for someone of similar experience, the rationale should be found in the minutes. This gives rise to the question of what's the priority for the board and the company's officers. Well-kept minutes will provide a complete story as to how the company is operated and managed. They will cover reasonable and significant decisions that impacted the company and thus its equity holders, including when it:

- Hired the first CFO
- Took on additional debt
- Paid bonuses
- Invested in a significant asset
- Rightsized headcount

It's also important to document instances of internal and external factors that influenced company behavior, such as why all those activities noted earlier took place when they did. This transparency provides insight into the decision-making process and demonstrates that the actions taken were made on behalf of the best interests of equity holders. Frankly, it's less of an issue when decisions prove to be good ones, but when something has gone awry, shareholders will want to be able to learn who was responsible for making bad decisions, including what their rationale was.

If the company or market has changed and the meeting minutes don't reflect this milestone, then the reader may assume that management inadequately oversees or plans for unique events.

When it comes to gauging a company's value, having thorough minutes in place will enhance a company's value, whereas not having them available will diminish it.

9. Indicated Number of Board Members Is Not Correct (25%)

A company's legal documents usually include a provision noting the minimum and maximum number of directors allowed and indicating actions needed to change those numbers. As the company evolves, changes can occur in key staff or family involvement that may not be recorded in the legal documents, opening the door to risk.

If your legal documents don't reflect changes that have occurred at the board level, that goes to the issue of adequate due diligence. It is the role of the board, as well as officers and advisors, to ensure the company adheres to the provisions of all legal documents.

With respect to board members, the fact a discrepancy exists between the established and actual number is usually not an issue unless it's discovered during a dispute.

CASE IN POINT

A company's documents call for three board members but the company actually has four. When they reach a stalemate on an important issue (stalemate at 2–2), someone discovers the discrepancy and says the last board member seated needs to go, and his side thus loses the vote.

The moral of this story and those previously mentioned is to complete an annual review of legal documents to eliminate any possible issues that could put the company at risk and lower its value. In one recent matter, a sister of two siblings was terminated without cause. She was an officer of the company and her sibling did not have the unilateral authority without board approval. The "fired" sister was also a board member and was then removed despite the provisions being unclear as to authority to do so. Further compounding matters of no longer receiving a salary as an employee-officer, her benefits as a director had been suspended. The bad acts included no distributions paid because the two other siblings increased their compensation. Clearly, the reading and interpretation of these provisions may have headed off the need for six-figure litigation and expert fees.

10. No Effort to Track Research and Development (R&D) Investment (60%)

When a company is trying to increase its revenues organically, it has a few options:

- Test price elasticity (raising prices to a level where overall sales increase even if more price-sensitive customers are lost).
- Open new markets.
- Offer new or updated products or services.

For the latter, there is often a considerable investment in resources required to produce a viable new offering, including staff hours; knowledge; and expenses for overhead, new software and equipment, prototypes, outside evaluations, and more.

CASE IN POINT

A pharmaceutical company may spend hundreds of millions or billions of dollars prior to ever bringing a product to market. It often reports that outlay as a capital investment that can be amortized (a tax write-off) or as an expense that may entitle it to tax credits. This information provides a baseline that shows how committed the company is to a particular product as well as a window into its potential pricing and market position.

When this categorization is absent (i.e., no R&D documentation is available), a review of documents will likely provide only nominal insight as to how a company is refreshing itself and its offerings. In many cases, companies that lack these records may be considered one-trick ponies.

I've seen plenty of instances when companies were buried under labor expenses and other capital outlays with no information that suggests they're spending for future revenues and profits. If their investment in R&D is not evident or is lower than the industry average, that's a red flag. It's important that companies document what's coming down the pipeline, probability of success, and forecast for expenditures and when commercially profitable.

It should be no surprise that companies that are nimble and adaptive are often seen as innovative and market leaders by disrupting their competition. When it comes to the process of establishing value, a company that's innovative will always command a higher value multiple than one that just transacts business. How can you prove innovation? Documenting R&D is a good starting point.

11. No Lines of Credit (60%)

It's almost universal for company founders and homeowners to celebrate when debt has been paid in full, but the former often overlook an important financial consideration. Certain industries have cycles as to when and how they receive payment and product/service demand. This can become critical if there's a prolonged delay by a key client or a number of larger clients. It can have a detrimental impact on cash flow and a disastrous or debilitating impact on the company's ability to move forward.

CASE IN POINT

A company in the nautical space was contracted to build several specially outfitted vessels, but then the general economic downturn occurred as well as for their industry. With the contractor being unable to fund the ongoing building process, the company needed interim financing to keep the work going. At the same time, it was losing top-line revenue from customers that were cutting back.

Because of its long-term relationship with its bank and personal guarantees made by several shareholders, a loan was made to fund the completion of the vessels. End of story? Unfortunately, no. The client owes the company and may not be able to pay—so those shareholders who stuck out their necks to help fund completion may find themselves in a very precarious position, perhaps even losing their homes.

What would have helped the company through this situation? Having an outstanding line of credit to draw might have saved the day. Surely you've heard this before: The best time to ask for funds is when the need doesn't exist. It's true! Also true is that the best time to leverage a financial relationship is when the risk is shared between equity and note holders. This is also referred to as risk shifting. Some folks wiser than I indicate the typical debt to equity should be 1:1, or stated another way, for every $1 of debt there should be $1 of equity.

Now certainly there are optimal levels of debt as well as appropriate uses for a line of credit (one of which is *not* paying employee bonuses). It never ceases to amaze when companies take on debt without considering whether the company has the growth and profitability to sustain the debt service. Some owners are simply unaware that if their profits are too low, then there is a limited business rationale unless the return on investment for which the borrowed funds are used exceeds that of the tangible assets held. Stated another way, the company must create sufficient earnings from tangible *and* intangible assets. Otherwise, the company has little more than an assemblage of tangible assets such as inventory, accounts receivable, and depreciable assets with little to no intangibles like goodwill from loyal clients. This is why we also have chapters on governance, relationships, and knowledge. Successful companies have leadership that surrounds itself with solid people who inspire and executed on innovation. This includes staff and external constituents. This is the leveraged human capital needed to support growth.

The takeaway from this is a line of credit should be established before it's needed, but make sure you're only drawing from it for legitimate reasons, for example, to fulfill your largest order to date ($3–$4 million), which necessitates an investment in additional people and equipment, and only if future higher volumes may be expected. A valuator will be concerned if a company has a limited banking relationship or doesn't have a line of credit or borrowing is used in an inappropriate way.

12. Loan Interest Rates Well Above Market Rate (50%)

In the last several years, it was common to see entrepreneurs using revolving debt and sometimes factors (at egregious interest rates) as part of their operations, usually when cash flow was low or to take advantage of historic low interest rates. CFOs, controllers, and CEOs may not have the requisite understanding of their company risk profiles. If a favorable rate can be close to "free capital" when considering the deduction of interest expense against taxes paid on profits, this is ideal. Sometimes rates paid are 800 or even 1000 basis points above prime during a period when the bankability of a company may have been in question. If the company has turned that corner and has not sought to recapitalize the debt, it could be costing the company tens and sometimes hundreds of thousands in unnecessary interest payments. So, not only is there less profit, but the absence of this management oversight will adversely weigh against the business risk.

Stated another way, it's not uncommon to see rates of 8 to 10 percent on a 10- or 15-year loan, for instance, when a rate of 3 or 5 percent may be possible. That can make a significant difference to a company's cash flow.

When I review an income statement I look for interest and principal payments and its proportion to profits. If there is a loan agreement in place, I ask to examine it to determine if the rate or term is less than favorable and, if so, I ask the question: Why not refinance/recapitalize?

13. Transfers of Equity and Loans with No Supporting Documents (70%)

Poor recordkeeping and no documentation of any loan transaction—including those made with no intention of repayment (perhaps from family)—can make even legitimate funding appear suspect. If business is routinely conducted in that manner, with no or nominal documents, it creates a taint—a lifestyle business—and a valuator will see this right away as a sign that inadequate financial controls and measures are in place.

When the owner is the only shareholder, his fiduciary duty extends only to himself, so absence of documentation won't create many red flags. The minute there is more than one shareholder or a likely sale in the future, however, if that weak financial management practice continues, the company has exposed itself to significant risk based on the duty-of-care responsibility the majority owner/officer/director has to the other shareholders. Having control alone does not afford these protections.

It's worth noting that even in the absence of additional shareholders, failing to have financial documentation at the time of a transition—such as a sale—will be exposed during the due diligence process and will have an adverse effect on the price multiplier.

CASE IN POINT

Let's say buyer and seller have agreed on a sales price, pending the completion of a review of the company's finances. The review reveals undocumented liabilities, such as accrued preferred dividends due to a former shareholder that significantly reduce the company's value. Thus the sales price plummets $10 million from the original agreed-upon figure.

The solution is ensuring that when you have an agreement, such as the previous case, to or from the business, it's documented and the terms adhered. In addition, such documents need to be amended and updated as necessary. Failure to do this may cause the veracity of provided financial information to come into question.

14. No Budget or Forecasts (80%)

It's fairly common for businesses with $50 million in annual sales to not have a budget or make forecasts. This tends to suggest a company that reacts to its market. It's typically expected that larger businesses will be proactive and recognize how they influence their market and what forces influence them. Budgets and forecasts are needed as they provide a barometer of cash flow and an indication of the difference between informed estimates and actual revenues and expenses. Then quarter to quarter, month to month, and year over year trends can be determined that will further improve forecasting. Stated another way, they're needed to demonstrate that management has a clear understanding of the company's sources of revenue and expenses and how their decisions influence bottom-line profits and whether value creation is considered. An example might be sales and marketing expenses reduced by 25%, but revenues growth remains steady, which suggests higher profits and more goodwill; hence, higher value.

Many entrepreneurs loathe the idea of having to draft a budget. They tend to focus on cash flow and not as much on what produced it. Having a deep understanding of how things like staffing and marketing affect sales, profitability and value can be reflected in a budget. Then one may see the difference between forecast and actual results. The closer the actual results come to the budget estimates, the better management and company prospects are trusted (and the lower the risk and higher the company value).

You can equate this to public company CEO/CFO quarterly investor and analyst calls. Their shares tend to go up when estimates are met or exceeded and down when they are not. Why this is so important is when growth is not a stable single digit per year, so future forecasts for growth may be more heavily relied upon based upon historic sales in determining value. The more accurate past forecasts have been, the greater the efficacy placed on management's estimates.

CASE IN POINT

If a company discovers that sales per headcount have declined, management could come to the conclusion that overstaffing is to blame if it has no other information (such as what's driving revenue) to review. What if it is poor performance from order fulfillment or customer service?

Valuators cannot gain insight into what's propelling a business when they see no budget exists. It's usually not management's vision, but the marketplace—and this is somewhat like taking a car trip without knowing how fast you're traveling, in what direction, or how much fuel remains.

Entrepreneurs like to point to the amount of cash they have in the bank as being an indicator of success and what the future will bring, but that really is an inadequate measure of performance. Forecasting is closely tied to strategy, and strategy can only exist and be successful when the resources needed to get from here to there are considered and executed. It's also necessary to make adjustments based on assumptions as more information becomes known to which there can be a response. Yes, it's imperfect, but that doesn't mean it shouldn't exist.

Returning to the car analogy, there are some things one may be unable to plan for like getting a flat tire, but a functional spare tire in the trunk, the lug wrench, and the jack can certainly be on hand. Then there are other things that demand planning, such as knowing you'll be traveling 500 miles and a full tank of gas will take you 250 miles—necessitating at least two fill-ups, or you'll arrive with zero gas in the tank.

When it comes to budgeting and forecasting, remember that it is always important to measure what you manage and manage what you measure.

15. Failure to Address Lower Gross Margins or Profits (65%)

Growth that exceeds industry norms almost always contributes to higher price multiples; however, growth in revenues without growth in profits may be a yellow flag of underperformance and/or tracking the wrong metrics.

Owners often focus on topline revenues, but without tracking line-items, it's easy to miss significant operational expense issues. The combination of increased material costs and labor expenses—which may have been brewing year over year in double digits while sales growth may be single digit—may have potential cash flow issues as well as reduced gross and profit margins. A way to circumvent this situation is to look at what's driving growth on the top line, particularly if the business has multiple locations or offers multiple products or services to varying markets. This level of deep-dive due diligence is seldom done.

Also, consolidated financial information may often fail to disclose operating strengths and inefficiencies. For example, it's not sufficient to simply have one figure that represents percentage of sales; the percentage of sales for each line item year against year is needed as is identifying the level(s) of increase or decrease and why they happened.

CASE IN POINT

An owner with multiple franchise locations may only be interested in the value of the holding company, a consolidated entity. Without looking at each location's performance, it's difficult to determine things like underperforming management, staff, location, product, or services, which can contribute to lower profits and reduced equity value.

The nature of these metrics will often allow owners and advisors to leverage strengths and shore up weaknesses. Failing to do this type of data analytics is risky—it's like driving a car with a smeared windshield and no rearview mirror. You can still drive, but you're significantly more prone to having an accident or missing a turn because your visibility is hampered.

16. Advisors and Labor Seen as Costs versus Investments (70%)

There are two ways of looking at human capital: as a budget line item that must be contained as much as possible to enjoy higher profit margins or as an investment in the company's present and future. We've talked about the value of engaging strong advisors elsewhere, so our focus here will be on staff.

With the line-item expense approach to employees, you may not feel you need to recognize or reward them for their efforts; after all, they're doing their job and receiving a fair compensation. When this mindset occurs, employees are less likely to feel any purpose or passion for what they're doing. Reinforcing process with policy can further reduce personnel value. The result is staff may consider the work a job that pays their bills—and they may be anxious for their next opportunity elsewhere. Examining the rate of turnover on a department-by-department basis can pinpoint issues such as problematic managers, whose removal can demonstrate the company values employees and their contributions.

CASE IN POINT

Starbucks pays for healthcare for its part-time employees. What does it get in return? The quality of its baristas is arguably above that of employees of other food and beverage purveyors. The additional investment hasn't stopped the company's growth or its increased market value.

When labor is considered an investment, management must temper its desire to be too patriarchal (process driven) or matriarchal (people driven), as that can be detrimental to both the bottom line and the company's long-term prospects. For example, legacy employees who have been performing the same function year over year and receive compensation that far exceeds what a comparable hire in the marketplace would be paid aren't fruitful if they put the company out of business with too high labor expenses. Consider ways to minimize the compounding of annual salary increases, such as bonuses and extra paid vacation days.

Putting the needs of employees first may be admirable, but this altruistic practice can significantly cut into the profits of the organization and may even place the livelihoods of the owner and those employees at risk. Embrace being a benefactor but remember the company officers' responsibilities are to safeguard the company's fiscal health and elevate shareholder value.

17. No or Minimal Correlation between Executive Pay and Performance (60%)

Early on in a business, the owner undoubtedly works long hours and makes many personal sacrifices to get the company running profitably. Because of what this person has given up to see to the care and feeding of the concentrated risk lovingly referred to as the "beast," there comes a point in time when the founder seeks a financial reward—certainly a reasonable expectation.

Few owners enjoy paying state and federal taxes, so compensation may initially come in the form of "loans" from the company (untaxed) and the "kitchen sink" being buried within various line-item expenses. This should be curtailed to prevent such actions from being considered as "effective distributions" from taxing authorities.

At some point, with the help of internal HR staff or external firms, executive compensation should be formalized. This is even more true if members of family are paid staff, especially if they may not have the requisite skills or responsibilities to justify their compensation.

Prior to doing so, the owner may wish to consult with legal and tax advisors to ascertain the value of their past services performed for the company that were not paid or paid below market rate. Occasionally, it makes sense to report this figure as deferred compensation while embarking on a survey to get a legitimate feel for what other leaders and executives are being paid at companies of a similar size in the same market with consideration for seasoning and skills that may allow for a company operating above its peer group.

If compensation is too low, a qualified expert is likely to note that means there will be less money to pay a replacement as a result of a planned or unplanned transition like retirement or disability. If it's too high—say, when profits decline by 30 percent, yet compensation is the same or it increases—that suggests to a valuator that the owner is more interested in pocketing every last penny than reinvesting in the company.

Determining the right level of compensation involves criteria like how many hours the owner works (60 versus 40 per week), whether she wears multiple hats, and whether the company is operating in the top quartile of its industry. It also should be noted that compensation is not a single line item, like salary. This becomes especially true when a clever owner personally owns the real property where the business is located and charges either above or below market rent. This may minimize the amount of taxes paid, but can paint an inaccurate picture of the company's true profitability.

The fact that compensation is not tied to value creation poses a significant risk, and indeed, it is a major reason why company growth often stalls or declines. Thus, it's always good to consider paying for performance.

Owners must also remember that a profitability decline as a percentage of revenues in and of itself may not be a bad thing—depending on how it compares with what's going on in the market and with competitors and investment in future growth. From 2008 to 2010, for example, many companies saw a 30 percent decline or more in revenues; the smart ones responded rapidly on both the top and bottom lines to control their profitability decline. Companies that took action like that were successfully able to navigate choppy seas—while other organizations drowned.

18. Lifestyle Business and Lowest-Taxes Mindset (75%)

Don't starve the beast. Owners should make a concerted effort to determine the amount of cash reserves to keep in the business to ensure growth and reduce the odds of having to use credit during lean times—but this is not always foremost on their minds. The personal struggle many owners go through to achieve success often results in their desire for gratification that reflects the fruits of their labor. This can cause them to take financial draws in the form of compensation, distributions, or loans that increase in proportion to the appetite they have to purchase the finer things in life. It's akin to being on a strict diet and then gorging at a Las Vegas buffet; it may feel good for a while, but there will be consequences if not kept in check.

Owners can use financial metrics as well as the assistance of accountants, financial advisors, and bankers to ensure that draws are more incremental—and make sure they're not spending money they can ill afford to lose. This is referred to as "starving the beast."

How critical is it for owners to understand their personal spending limitations? A simple analysis can be applied to identify the continuum of a lifestyle business operating for the next few years. If the company is growing year over year at or above the rate of industry growth, then value is unlikely to be as adversely impacted. But that would require the owner to know what that growth rate has and will be. This is something a business value analyst can access. However, if growth is below the industry growth rate after compounding year over year, it can be significant. Let's say that $1 million should have been reinvested each year instead of buying an enhanced lifestyle, which over five years would have provided $30 million in additional organic growth and the price multiple of revenues was 80%. If the growth was only $10 million during that period without the reinvestment, then the "lost" value would be $30 million × .80 or $24 million less the $5 million taken by the owner at $1 million a year for five years (no adjustments for inflation or alternative). So, the owner effectively lost $19 million in five years. What would have occurred if this behavior continued for a decade or two? If the more frugal owner had a business that grew at 8 percent per year, it would have more than quadrupled in size in two decades compared to the 4 percent growth of doubling. That is some serious cash left behind.

From 2008 to 2010, most banks would not accept the risk involved in lending to companies with annual sales below $10 million because revenues had been or were declining due to the weak economy. Many of the companies that suffered during this time frame (and perhaps eventually closed their doors) did so because the last thing their owners did was reduce their own economic benefits; they still wanted luxury cars, annual vacations abroad, to dine out three or more times a week, and to send their kids to private school as well as pay for their college education.

Some of those expenses are fine, but when the income source begins to fail, the excesses become readily evident. Unfortunately, most accountants merely report the results and owners also can't count on intervention from their advisors, as they might not perceive their role to be a financial gatekeeper. The company's banker will care about the out-of-line spending if loan covenants are breached as the bank's first priority is debt repayment.

It should be clear that the significant risk associated with this owner's behavior is that during periods of significant decreases in revenues and profits, there is insufficient funds kept in reserves to get the business through those (often inevitable) downtimes.

The value of cash management and having a disciplined approach to growth cannot be overstated. It's invaluable to engage trusted advisors—those already providing counsel or hiring new people with specialized skills—to assist in these critical areas. This is why although it may sound self-serving paying for a comprehensive business appraisal to benchmark where an owner is at and could be going with annual or at least bi-annual updates is a prudent investment and a useful tool for the other advisors to plan around versus a best guesstimate.

Moving on to the issue of taxes, few owners enjoy paying them, but don't let the tax-tail wag the dog. For instance, in a very simplified example, if the tax bite is 35 percent on the first $100 you make, is that justification for not pursuing the second $100? The net gain will still be 100 percent. Business owners should wholly embrace the notion of being tax-efficient, but that should not be a top priority if it affects enhancing shareholder value. That said, an accountant will be able to navigate income, capital gains, and gift taxes to maximize the best overall result, not just now, but during the future.

19. Limited or No Tracking of Margins/Profits across Services/Products (60%)

A deeper dive into understanding what works and what doesn't work—what to discard versus what and where to invest—is central to most businesses. A classic example is taking on new work because of the increased revenue it provides, but expending so much resources that the margins are razor thin. A simple benchmark is return on invested capital. Say, for the industry the norm for the company size is 8 percent and capital is $50 million. This would mean .08 × $50 million or $4 million. If the company has $200 million in revenues and a 2 percent margin, this would provide $4 million. This is simply breakeven and would suggest the company has not mastered its bottom line or has too much capital producing too little results to reflect the influence of any intangible assets. Stated in a cold and direct way, what point is running this business if the value is nothing more than book value of assembled assets when a passive investment could generate higher returns and at lower level of risk? You want a job, sell the business and form a philanthropy you can support.

To be more succinct, the $50 million would likely perform better if invested in real estate, which is likely to offer higher yields and returns.

Even businesses that have been operating for some time often lose the ability to track line item by line item whether certain offerings continue to make sense—or it would make more sense to allocate resources elsewhere.

> **CASE IN POINT**
>
> If a company's business development expenditure doubles, and the resultant increase in revenue is 5 or 10 percent, is the net benefit justified? Can management identify whether the increase in sales was even due to the business development spend?

Tangential to this examination is to understand how much each product or service is contributing to the bottom line (sales less costs of sales and operating expenses). It is evident that deeper understanding of what generates sales and of what generates profits is equally important.

20. Banking Relationship Is Solely Transactional (80%)

Bankers and owners each lament they don't have a deeper relationship with the other, but it's all too frequent the reason is both parties see banking as a transaction. Many bankers say that customer relationships are paramount, but nothing says "I care" more than helping an owner in some way with their business.

For that to occur, the banker needs to look past the deposit amounts, interest rates, and loan terms to gain a deeper understanding of how the company's cash flow and operations work not only from the bank's credit risk perspective. Rather, what risks does the client or prospect business face in which the banker's experience with similar industry clients or similar situations may provide solutions and opportunities?

It's a rare banker who genuinely has an understanding of the flows and risks of customers' businesses going beyond the risk black box that's used to determine a company's creditworthiness. Bankers often use metrics produced by Risk Management Associates' (RMA) comparative financial ratio database. While the data provides some useful ratios, there are inherent weaknesses in the data. The RMA data uses a relatively small sample size, plus it doesn't take into account expense line items like labor. The data also fails to include figures on common industry growth or growth expected over the next five years and some sample companies may skew the results based upon age or how financial data is reported. Frankly, the banks have an overreliance on software products that provide average results.

If nothing else, this chapter and others in the book illustrate the myriad key performance indicators that are often overlooked. Bankers have some financial background and commonly reference tax returns, financial statements, and forecast P&Ls; reading their figures and making recommendations for improvement should be a natural action—but it is a rare differentiator.

CASE IN POINT

A banker reviewing the file of a manufacturing client notes that the acquisition of newer equipment improves the company's odds for growth and increased profitability. How would the owner respond? The discussion that would ensue reflects having a relationship that transcends transactions.

Bankers who sit on the same side of the table as owners can be a significant resource. It really doesn't take long to determine the pulse of a company. Therefore, there can and should be a natural affinity between commercial and investment bankers and other trusted advisors, such as attorneys, insurance professionals, accountants, and appraisers. While banks always tend to rely on real estate appraisers, the same is not necessarily true for business appraisers. This may be because more real estate and tangible assets like equipment are funded than going concerns due to collateral and the natural risk of operating companies. Yet, as demonstrated in the previous examples, the valuation expert will be able to demonstrate reasonableness of line items and return on invested capital that RMA data is loath to provide. The "real" question is will new funding create growth in company value above tangible assets.

21. Little or No Cash Management or Understanding of Cash Flow (70%)

Although this issue was somewhat touched upon earlier, it bears repeating. Anyone with a personal bank account has heard stories of people who consider an ATM to be like a money tree—providing an endless supply of cash. When withdrawals exceed deposits, the resultant insufficient funds notification can come as a surprise and be quite distressing.

The same issue, on a larger scale, confronts some businesses that aren't aware they can't usually write checks against account receivables. It's critical that the inflows and outflows of cash are managed and understood. Absent that, it shouldn't be a surprise to have a cash flow crunch when a big purchase is made and no corresponding increase in sales occurs or sales decline and no corresponding cost controls are put in place. It's the difference of considering principal and interest payments versus interest payments alone as reported on a tax return.

Owners must know their clients and understand if it will be necessary for the company to plan for longer payment cycles. For instance, a construction company that's performing work for a municipality may have to wait 60+ days to get paid.

Another issue with respect to cash management and understanding cash flow may seem like a good problem to have: a company that has significant capital on hand that's well in excess of its working capital needs. All things being equal, if there's significant cash on a company's accounts and some level of debt, it may behoove the owner to revisit the terms of the debt to secure a better rate based on its healthy cash position and flow situation.

Conversely, investing in safe, short-term financial instruments may be an opportunity for a business to earn well in excess of a 10- to 100-basis-point

(0.1–1%) yield. And, a skilled financial advisor may recommend investments that provide 3 to 5 percent in the low-yield environment present at the time this book was written.

If a business is well operated and indicators show its cash is being well managed, that will impact the company's price multiplier and its value in a positive way. All it takes is demonstrating a nominal understanding of treasury management. Absent that, all a valuator will see is excess capital not being deployed to scale company growth.

22. No Knowledge of Balance Sheet, P&L, and Growth Norms for the Industry (75%)

Many owners have similar characteristics whereby they operate within a bubble. They may have some awareness of what's going on in their business, but they may not compare today's results against prior performance other than higher sales and possibly more income. They may have limited curiosity to study how similar their actions are to the results reported for various line items within their industry.

CASE IN POINT

A company has a significant number of vehicles: trucks and riding mowers. Comparing two recent periods may show a similar level of sales but differing profit. Additional due diligence shows that fuel costs might have been high during the period, creating a lower profit, or that acquiring new, more fuel-efficient vehicles had a positive effect on the company's bottom line.

As mentioned earlier, it's important that owners remain active in industry associations, as they often provide good-quality information regarding common performance measures found in financial statements. Barring that or in addition to it, owners need to take advantage of the expertise of their accountant, banker, or life insurance professional, each of whom may be familiar with similar industry metrics, but if not asked for input, are unlikely to volunteer it without knowing the interest is there and a need exists.

The Internet is also often a good source of data. At the risk of making a plug for the business appraisal community, its cornerstone is comparative analysis, so most full-time business appraisers should have several data sources to perform this function. Higher-cost, higher-quality firms may use six or more data sources—providing a robust indication of low and high performance on most balance sheet and profit-and-loss line items.

For example, when looking at cash on a balance sheet, a company's percentage of cash to total assets may be 7 percent, but the industry norm is double that. The first thing most analysts will do is look at whether the company's account receivables is higher than industry norms, one of many explanations as to why the 7 percent cash may be a reporting period aberration. It's important to remember that financial metrics taken out of context are less meaningful. A company's year-over-year growth may mirror how its competitors are doing, but if the owner doesn't have access to that industry data, he or she is operating in a vacuum and may feel the company is under- or over-performing in the absence of supporting data. Similarly, to get a true picture of what all the numbers mean, it's necessary to have a deeper understanding of each line item.

CASE IN POINT

A company's advertising spend is 5 percent, while the industry average is 1 percent. Questions will arise as to whether this level of spending is excessive, but those numbers alone won't answer the inquiry. Is management knowingly making this expenditure because the company is young and they're trying to accelerate growth by raising market awareness? Or, a formula may be developed that shows the investment is well worth it due to the corresponding increase in sales and profits. The 5 percent in and of itself isn't a bad thing, but if only a nominal correlation can be made between it and any rise in sales (and profits), this may be an area where spending can be reduced.

This same line of thinking can be used when spending is less than the industry norm. For instance, a company that spends just 0.5 percent on advertising (half the industry norm in our example) but has growth comparable with industry norms may indicate that the company has particularly strong goodwill or brand recognition and thus doesn't need to spend as much on advertising. Does that mean it shouldn't experiment with a higher ad spend?

It can be a worthy exercise to determine what would transpire if that second company increased its advertising spend to the industry norm.

If there was only nominal change, that would confirm that 0.5 percent is adequate—or even indicate that a further reduction may not be harmful.

Having information without adequate data or insightful analysis is somewhat empty reporting—as there is no evidence of the actions that influenced the numbers or the perceived risks. Seeing this on a consistent basis may suggest a company has management and staff with limitations and it's not using advisors adequately. The net result is perceived greater risk that can be mitigated to raise company value.

23. No Review to Optimize Debt/Capital Structure (90%)

Similar to item #11, no lines of credit, and #12, loan interest rates above market, understanding capital structure and risk as well as access to debt and equity from other than traditional funding sources is fairly uncommon. Many owners, rightfully so, are pleased that at some juncture in their company's growth, they have paid off all their long-term obligations. Arguably, this is a good thing, but if the goal is to grow the business and optimize performance, in most cases using debt capital is often prudent.

Unless the company is generating significant profits or has significant cash on hand that can be reinvested into the business to accelerate its ability to scale, debt may make sense. The issue isn't really whether to have debt, but what the optimal debt level should be.

CASE IN POINT

Regardless of the way a company is structured and taxed, interest expenses reduce a company's tax liability. Thus, if the interest rate is 5 percent and aggregate tax is 40 percent, the effective after-tax rate is 3 percent (0.5(1 – .40) = 0.3 or 3%). With consideration for inflation, that's almost "free" money.

It's also important to remember that loans lever the business, and they're paid off in depreciated dollars, which favors the borrower. Thus, borrowing makes sense, especially when the money is judiciously used to allow for higher growth. Some owners choose to fund with a hybrid, using a bank loan funding an employee stock ownership plan where *both* the principal and interest are tax deductible, which has the impact of a sales price with net proceeds as much as 60 percent greater due to tax considerations.

A simplistic example of the value of borrowing can be found in the world of auto racing. Let's say a racecar with a 400-horsepower engine that cost $50,000 wins 1 of 10 races, offsetting the maintenance costs for the engine. The owner decides he wants a 600-horsepower engine that costs $70,000, and he borrows $20,000 to be able to purchase it. If his car now wins half the races, did borrowing make sense? Absolutely.

It's common to find a balance of company level of debt with equity. If there is a 1:1 ratio with 50 percent as debt and 50 percent as equity and the investor-owner obtains an optimal result from that blended mix, this is ideal. However, anything more than optimal debt where growth and profitability must be at certain levels can cause a cash flow shortfall that can place the company at greater risk.

The second consideration is if the sale of a minority (or majority) interest might make sense. Let's say you'd like two race cars, but the cost is prohibitive and debt is not the best way to go; there are private equity groups and family offices (very affluent families worth +$300M) who may lend in certain industries and may have longer-term expectations for obtaining the return on their investment. They may also enjoy relationships that could increase the business's revenues and market exposure. As the book title suggests, leveraging *both* human and financial capital can provide equity value enhancement. In fact, the infusion of equity capital can often allow the borrowing of debt capital in larger amounts and better rates.

24. No Review of Optimized Labor and Occupancy (70%)

Depending on the type of business, these issues may be intertwined. With respect to occupancy, you should determine, based on current operations, what the capacity for growth is before it may outstrip physical facility. Turning to labor, the impact of adding more staff to a current location needs to be considered.

In the past, there were certain square footage calculations based upon function and level of staff importance; however, based upon technology and staff preferences, record storage and data transfer require less, not more space. This may be less true for asset-intensive businesses such as ones with significant inventory or manufacturing; however, the number of labor shifts (7 to 4 o'clock, 4 to 12 o'clock, etc.) may be a consideration.

The overarching point of a review is to determine what needs may exist in the years to come and options include adding/reducing square footage (at an existing or new location). Other considerations may be vanity versus value. If more expensive Class A space is occupied, but customers don't come to the location, consider moving to Class B space, which carries a lower per square foot cost, or when much of office space is based upon storage needs.

Simple items like this can have impacts of hundreds of thousands of dollars annually, but are often overlooked.

If a company operates in a space it owns, that has the potential of a series of capital efficiency, tax, and liability issues. Many if not most advisors suggest real estate shouldn't be held within a business, but in a separate holding company to mitigate those tax and liability issues. When contemplating the sale of the company, this arrangement offers the seller the opportunity to bifurcate—leasing the space to the buyer at market rate or selling both the business and the real estate.

This issue of space may appear straightforward, but it can be complicated, especially when it comes to manufacturing and warehousing. For instance, an efficient manufacturer may not need as many square feet if its vendors keep supplies until they're needed, using the just-in-time (JIT) production strategy.

All businesses, but especially manufacturers, don't want to have underutilized space, so the best-case scenario is to configure it to maximize current needs—and also consider size years from now based on the forecasted sales trajectory. In some cases, the same location may be better utilized by running two shifts, since much of occupancy expense is the same whether people are working one or two shifts.

Like the space issue, it may be the case that fewer people will be needed in the future to do the same (or more) work. As computer-assisted design and manufacturing (CAD/CAM) and artificial intelligence become more common, the need for personnel typically declines, sometimes dramatically. Consideration also should be made as to whether it makes more sense to outsource some functions to save money and space.

It's always worth determining if operations are efficient by looking at both sales per square foot and sales per headcount; if those figures are below the industry norms, there are probably too many employees or ineffective store and product layout.

Having a good handle of optimal performance will impact equity value favorably.

25. No Independent and Regular Independent and Qualified Valuation (95%)

God bless attorneys, accountants, and other advisors for looking after their clients. No good business appraiser would deign to offer legal or accounting advice unless he or she was suitably educated and licensed to do so.

Interestingly, it's all too common for trusted advisors who aren't trained, certified appraisers to provide their two cents regarding the worth of the business. One of the reasons this might occur is due to the fact that particularly when a business first formalizes its operations, it incurs greater professional fee expenses.

It's not uncommon that a company's attorney and CPA are each expecting to be paid for professional services. Because attorneys and accountants have the most trusted advisor relationships, and the owner may have already written two sizeable checks to each, she may be loath to write a third check to a business appraiser. This behavior is often penny-wise and pound-foolish.

What happens when a business appraiser is not engaged is that the attorney or accountant, singularly or collectively, occasionally suggests some multiple of revenues or earnings based on previous experience. They may also affix the book value of the business as the company's prescribed value (which may be risky). Unfortunately, this sets up a series of unanticipated issues that frequently don't rear their ugly heads until later.

Some may rely on the rule of thumb (ROT) that says a company's value is 40 percent of its revenues, but any good business appraiser can provide plenty of examples to dispel that myth. For instance:

- If two companies have the same revenue, but one has debt and the other does not, their equity values would be different and thus their company values would be different as well.
- If two companies have the same revenue but one is twice as profitable as the other, using only the revenue figure to determine value would be failing to acknowledge the benefit of achieving higher profits.

And, how do years in business operation affect value? It might surprise that it's not necessarily a plus to have been operating for a long time, due to the stasis that can set in that produces nominal year-over-year increase in sales. Recently, a client was pleased over its past five years that its sales had grown an average of 10 percent each year. This was prior to learning that the sales growth for the industry for the same period ranged from 12 to 39 percent per annum. Operating in a vacuum without metrics is not going to help make wise choices.

If two companies have the same revenues and earnings, and one has been operating for 20 years and the other for just 5, the younger company actually has the larger growth rate and thus more value to the notional investor. It should be clear that determining a price multiple solely based on revenue is not the way to go, as that type of analysis does not capture what investors want—bankable cash flow and strong growth.

Some trusted advisors understand that revenues alone shouldn't determine company value, so they use the ROT to gauge multiples based on earnings or earnings before interest, taxes, depreciation, and amortization.

This creates its own set of problems, as advisors who are not trained as business appraisers may lack the skills needed to make accurate earnings determinations; for example, they may not understand the nuances that go into determining an owner's compensation—or working capital needs to fund growth or pending needed capital expenditures.

Similar to the previous examples, if two companies have the same earnings but one has twice the revenues, would their value be the same? Using the ROT that only takes earnings into account, the answer would be "yes," when clearly it is seldom so. The potential upside for the higher revenue company if better managed may afford it a higher price paid; or, conversely, the lower profit percentage of revenues may suggest higher risk to the investor.

Remember that risk appetite is closely aligned with perceived opportunity, which is demonstrated in publicly traded stock every time shares change hands. The buyer sees upside compared to alternatives and so does the seller.

How does it happen that advisors like CPAs have established a perceived monopoly on valuation engagements sometimes done on the cheap? The reason is simple: Owners often believe CPAs should know what their businesses are worth since they're preparing their taxes and are familiar with their financial reporting. But reporting the news is not the same as mastery of what makes the news. This has not stopped some enterprising accountants who after several years have seen the appraisal work product of other providers and decide, "Why not me? It looks easy enough." And then the oversimplification finds its way into buy–sell agreement formulas and other documents that may influence decisions.

The reality is a bit different, and one way the agreement can be pierced is if the interest holder can demonstrate that the formula used to determine the company's value has no bearing on the actual market value. Like marriages, some business relationships are not happily ever after; so sometimes it depends on whether the formula used to draft an agreement is found to be beneficial to one or more parties and binding on the other(s)—and the impact of such provisions on value is something that can be determined by retaining the services of a valuation expert. If this professional finds the formula used has no bearing on the arm's-length market realities, an attorney, legal or regulatory authority will argue that the agreement should be rendered invalid.

Timing can also be an issue, as valuations only reflect a stated value based on the particular point in time. Just recently an IRS examiner stated the value should be higher because the industry norms for profitability were higher when determining the control value. Two examples were used to dispel this flawed logic. First, if an activist investor buys publicly traded stock, it is being purchased because after exerting influence on performance the investor expects a value increase. More simplistically, if a neighborhood of million-dollar homes has a home listed for $1 million and during the home inspection after the asking price was accepted it was determined the roof needed to be replaced and the cost would be $100,000, the seller would have to make a concession of at least $100,000 as the home is acquired as-is.

Because businesses are not static, values aren't static as well, and unfortunately, the person most sparsely armed to rectify that situation and avoid failure is the owner. Agreements dictating equity value should include a provision that mandates a valuation be done annually or if there is a significant internal or external event that could impact value then more frequently.

CASE IN POINT

A company's last valuation was performed five years ago, and it's reporting $25 million more in revenues since then; however, profit margins have declined; therefore, an update would be warranted.

This situation can become compounded and standards go by the wayside (bringing in the issues of intellectual rigor and independence), especially in cases of family businesses, when the company's accountants will provide valuations to clients. In the best of circumstances, this may bruise the perception of independence; in the worst, it's often a conflict waiting to happen as some parties with sway may wish the value to be higher or lower such as when the tax basis differs between two parties.

A fair number of CPAs performing valuations aren't credentialed. They have a general idea of the format required, but they usually don't have adequate data—so in essence they're guesstimating—and this can have an adverse impact of thousands or millions of dollars. When a value is disputed, one of the first questions to be asked of the CPA or other trusted advisor that produced the result is whether he or she was operating independently. Any conflict will disqualify the work product and sets up the possibility of litigation.

Intellectual rigor will also come into play as valuations must be compliant with industry standards, and a non-appraiser trusted advisor often performs just three or four a year—and may not be certified in the valuation discipline. What research has taken place? Where's the data? Is the value more than just an opinion or is there empirical support?

While inaccurate valuations can have big consequences for owners, advisors who overstep their abilities to provide them usually receive nothing more than a slap on the wrist when lacking competence is discovered. It harkens back to the savings & loan crisis of the late 1980s and early 1990s where many loans went into default as a result of poor skills or fraud of real estate appraisers or the lending institutions and the advisors who exploited the lack of investment due diligence.

Independence suffers if the same party that is performing the business valuation is also one that has been engaged in the discussion or guidance addressing how to relieve the company's tax burden, whether the owner should take a company loan or change officers' compensation—and would any of these things change the value? It should be clear that an advisor should not wear two hats.

There has been a significant increase in the standards of practice within the valuation industry, so owners and their trusted advisors would be well served to adhere to these higher standards by hiring a full-time professional to perform valuations—at an adequate compensation level. Remember that while attorneys and accountants are advocates for their clients, a valuator is an advocate for the opined value of the business, and that difference is significant to ensure credibility.

26. Little or No Training Budget (80%)

Many different types of education exist, including technical education—how to do the job better; education by doing—often seen in those entering leadership positions; and education on soft skills—such as understanding human interaction, and dynamics between departments, business units, and functions. The most successful companies will provide opportunities for employees to gain new skills, rather than sink or swim, expecting them to figure it out.

Staff training should be an ongoing concern and involve everyone in the company, even those at the top level, who may benefit from enhancing their negotiation skills, learning ERISA standards, and understanding how to better counsel wayward employees. Adding new skills to an already rich skillset makes managers more well-rounded and may reduce the human capital risk presented by disenfranchised employees while leveraging relationships within and external to the organization.

It raises a flag when valuators don't see an education line item or the amount expensed compared to revenue is low. Perhaps the best way to encourage employees to take advantage of programs and training is to set aside funds for each based upon their compensation in an account earmarked for education. This speaks volumes, as employees will see the company is investing in them—and that may motivate them to complete an AA, BA, MBA, trade school, or GED.

The return on investment isn't just in hard dollars, but how the company culture evolves because a relatively important asset—human capital—has significantly upped its game. The flipside is the increased risk that better trained staff will seek more responsibility and compensation and the company may not be able to provide the opportunity when it is sought, losing the human capital investment.

27. No Tracking and Revision of the Business Development Budget and Results (70%)

When businesses set out to develop their brand and customer loyalty, it's not unusual for them to spend 5 percent or more of revenue on activities to establish the business in their market. As the company grows, the question becomes: "Is 5 percent too much for business development, or is it not enough?" The answer is: It depends.

The percent of revenue that should be designated to business development efforts will differ considerably from industry to industry. For example, if a company receives most of its work through contract bidding, advertising is not likely to be a great expense, but networking with key contract officers may be necessary. Conversely, in the retail and services sectors, expenses may be much greater than the 1 percent.

"It depends" really comes down to how the brand is messaged and positioned. Are end users the target, or is it more important to get in front of influencers? As an example, an insurance company may market to the wealth advisors who sell its products—and it would also be well served to reach out to influential accountants, attorneys, business owners, and commercial bankers. Being well networked is more important to this firm than paying for advertising. Then there are pharmaceutical companies that both call on physicians that advise patients as well as earmark millions of dollars on media buys to influence the public.

The fundamental question is still how much should a company spend on business development, and why. If 5 percent is spent annually, is there a correlation between that expenditure and the purchase of new products or services? If after two years there appears to be no distinct correlation or just a nominal one, it may make sense to either increase or decrease the budget to determine the impact of the spend.

If a company's growth is organic, understanding why customers buy is key. Is it the price, the message, or special sales? Maybe it's a unique differentiator like a clever tagline: "Where's the beef?" or "Got milk?"

The most frustrating thing to see is heavy investment into any new advertising without existing measurement of preexisting advertising. If what causes revenue isn't fully known, it's hard to discern why customers are buying. There can be any number of reasons why a company attracts new customers. Maybe it's an improved presence on the Internet, but it could also be better articulating of the company's differentiators to create clarity and adequate change that generates new business. Remember this: "You can only manage what you can measure."

If a 5 percent spend causes a 20 percent increase in revenues, the owner needs to know, "What are profit margins from this investment and will the clients repeat their buying behavior?" If your margins are small and the client spend is one-time, a 20 percent revenue increase may not be adequate to cover the additional business development expense.

Retention and new business measures become very important—as does any allowance for discounting products or services. A 20 percent increase in revenues that causes loss of income will grow a company into bankruptcy. This is where the adage of "losing money, but will make it up in volume" is derived.

The takeaway here is an owner must identify what's causing growth and then track what is working and why. Therefore, not knowing why, or an underinvestment or overinvestment, will lead to a reduction in a company's value.

FINAL THOUGHTS

There is a good equation to remember when weighing build-versus-buy and the ability to plan and execute while also challenged by the daily rigors of life and work (i.e., blocking and tackling):

The more efficient > the better the cash flow > the lower the risk > the higher the price multiple = the higher the value of the company.

For instance, if you know a client is contemplating a business transformation, wouldn't it make sense to have the timeline and understand the role each constituent (key staff, advisors, bankers, vendors, and clients, as well as possibly family members) plays in it?

Actions that are communicated, prioritized, aligned, and coordinated should provide the business owner with the best and most timely options. Perhaps it is understated, but owners to build value must think like investors who are seeking the highest possible return, which means not only above-industry average growth and profitability, but reduction of risks that will in turn increase equity value.

In many ways, those who provide professional services are supposed to be the best educated, but they often handle planning and coordination haphazardly. A simple example is a call or a meeting without adequate preparation of others to be able to address whatever agenda items the time expenditure requires. And in most occasions milestones are not agreed upon. How is it possible to advise someone on taxes or asset protection or wealth management or insurance or general business operations without having any metrics upfront?

Using another example involving cars, if you know you want to drive to Poughkeepsie, but you don't know your starting point, getting there is unlikely. Knowing you must travel east is simply not enough. Unfortunately, in the world of advisors, it's not uncommon to be oblivious to the current state of the businesses to which they're providing direction. At the very minimum, it's necessary to know where a business is at, where it's going, when it wants to get there, and what needs to happen to ensure its plans come to fruition.

Staying with our car analogy, if a trip is 500 miles and average fuel consumption is known, one has a sense of how many tanks are needed to reach the final destination, how much cash is needed for fill-ups, and how long it will take to arrive at the destination based on a specific average speed. Often in business, these types of details are taken for granted; rather than road mapping a company's future, everything is often done ad hoc. The answers to these questions allow for certain assumptions and they must be fine-tuned as outcomes occur. Owners are expected to scrutinize their businesses in this way, and so, too, should their advisors, since they chose to enter into collaborative professions.

After reading this long chapter, the phrase "risky business" will likely mean more to you than an old Tom Cruise movie. As shared before value is derived when the level of risk is lowered and economic benefit is known. Way too much emphasis is applied to the more simple to identify—economic benefit—and, arguably, not enough on risk measurement. It's critical to consider the influence of both tangible and intangible assets. The owner and advisor must understand the dynamic nature of risk to allow for the planned and unplanned events that otherwise could be disruptive, if not disastrous, to the business and its industry, such as availability and cost of fossil fuels.

There is definitely a cost benefit involved to mitigate risks, but controlling them will require less of an investment than dealing with the higher festering costs stemming from disruptions and disputes. The intent of this chapter has been to provide numerous examples of items that influence risk, and representative risks, but this is not intended to be a complete list. It will be more exhaustive depending on the business or the industry's complexity as the next chapter will show.

NOTES

1. Lavern Urlacher, *Small Business Entrepreneurship: An Ethics and Human Relations Perspective* (Upper Saddle River, NJ: Prentice Hall, 1999), 348–356.
2. Burton Malkiel, *A Random Walk Down Wall Street: The Time Tested Strategy for Successful Investing* (New York City, NY: W. W. Norton, 2012), 262–266.

CHAPTER 8

The Role of Risk

Operational-Related Risks

Performing due diligence as protection from threats must occur both internally and externally. Those who can't anticipate what the marketplace may be like three or five years out with some degree of certainty may suffer the consequences of having threats at the doorstep of their business. Being reactive rather than proactive may be the difference between exploiting the market while others are failing and ducking for cover. The threat associated with human capital and succession of key staff hangs over every business, since no one knows his or her exact expiration date. Without proper threat mitigation processes in place, the untimely demise, disability, departure, or dispute with key officers or staff can have dire consequences.

As was discussed in the introduction of Chapter 7 concerning legal and financial risks, the author wishes to illustrate a common issue before addressing the below operational risks: one of optics through the lens of owners and investors when holding direct ownership in assets, enterprises, and equity. Through my own lens is the impact of trusted advisors, who collaborate have when assisting a common business owner. It is an extraordinary thing. Time and time again, I have found this to be a key factor in a company that levels off at about $25 million in sales and one that may have 10 times or greater revenues.

This is among the reasons I needed to write this book. Initially, it was intended to be a text with perspectives from both owners and individual trusted advisors. I solicited hundreds with whom I have worked and ended up with 72 who said they would like to co author. Once we agreed to the book's theme, we then had a tentative schedule of submissions and edits. This was two years ago.

Two months prior to the first draft being due, the number of contributors had already been halved mostly due to expressed competing commitments and other such explanations.

By the first deadline only three submissions were received. One needed to be flushed out, but was solid. The remaining two were "infomercials," meaning their chapter's orientation was how the contributor could be utilized if his services were retained and not from the perspective of the profession or that of the client.

The deadline was extended to obtain the remaining 30 or so contributors' submissions.

This effort to get colleagues and clients to stick to a commitment is no small feat. By this time, the half remaining halved again and indicated they just had not gotten around to completing their drafts, so the deadline was extended again. One of the original drafts was received corrected and another was the proper length and content. Three additional drafts were received. A full-year had come and gone with five accepted submissions. I had to make the decision to write the book on my own or herd cats. You're a smart cookie. You know the rest.

The point of this segue is to demonstrate that even well-meaning trusted advisors get bogged down in doing their work. The additional step in engaging peers from related professionals is more along the lines of "have to" versus "will do." This is why the owner is confronted with the challenge of getting her own advisors to coordinate and communicate in a more cohesive manner. Then she also has her own daily obstacles to confront, so this desire gives way to the familiar operational issues needed to keep the doors open and lights on.

More extraordinary is the owner who understands and applies this observation to corralling not only her advisors, but has the rare ability to expect that they and key staff will work in a more integrated fashion.

These issues are very, very common. Yet they are rarely part of any operational due diligence when businesses are being prepared for sale. Even rarer are their consideration and weighting when pondering company-specific risk as part of the process of determining how a company will be valued.

This is why governance, relationships, and knowledge become so key, as the governance is needed for the strategy to exist that when executed must include trusted advisors' active involvement. Only then can their own knowledge and relationships be harnessed. The interesting thing is the owner in her own right influences how some of these advisors will approach other client relationships in a more holistic and integrated fashion.

For the balance of owners and professionals, this is why I refer to myself as a ***strategic value architect***, as it's insufficient to simply provide a value if it's to be used more than solely as a benchmark.

Such a role also requires the relationships, knowledge, and influence to effect the transformation of the way the owner, advisors, key staff, and others interact, internally and externally, with the company's constituents.

Conversations are more like, "So at a cost ("investment") of *X* how much will expending this effort or resource or using this service or product impact my client's business's *Y* value?"

Therefore, this chapter endeavors to challenge the reader to consider operational impacts. While, occasionally, operations have visible financial metrics, they are the result of one or more activities or absence of actions making analytics more difficult, yet necessary. A common theme in what follows is data analytics and human capital leverage.

1. No Performance Metrics and Nominal Knowledge of Market or Competitors (80%)

It's common for successful companies to enjoy growth occasionally without knowing what caused it. For instance, you might be delighted to have your third year of double-digit growth, but can you point to why it's occurring? Is it due to new clients, more business from existing clients, or a change in pricing?

Many companies can't answer that question, which can hide a significant problem. Let's say 85 percent of clients are repeat business, which means after taking into account retention more than 15 percent of business has to be derived from new clients, assuming pricing and consumption patterns are the same. This would result in similar sales from last year. What if operating expenses increased during the same period? Depending upon the market area, in about seven years, unless new products are offered, new markets pursued, or old clients purchase again, the top line may suffer.

It's important to know the players in your industry—locally, regionally, and globally—and discover competitive information such as their pricing or leadership or product strengths or weaknesses. In addition, it can be invaluable to know which clients, past and present, are dealing with key competitors, and if so, why. It's very common to place metrics on gross margin, EBITDA, or units of production, but there are myriad intangibles and risks that can be identified and measured from sales from how new advertising increased cash flow to better inventory, receivables, payables, and cash management to new advisor referrals to new external client recommendations or what caused lower staff turnover.

CASE IN POINT

If a company chief estimator bids on and is awarded 60 percent of revenue based on his estimates, what level of management assessment has taken place to learn the skills of the estimator, the financial rewards he's earned, the margins when awards are made, and what the impact would be if his absence caused a disruption (via death, disability, divorce, etc.)?

It's usually the unseen and unexpected that can cause catastrophic loss, thus the importance of metrics cannot be overstated. For example, if you operate two manufacturing plants, one in San Diego and one in Boston, could you determine why there is a significant difference in revenue per headcount between the plants? Is it a function of price differential, market saturation, plant management, or something else? You can't make important decisions without adequate metrics to study.

The key is to select and religiously track the five or six most important metrics at each business level. These metrics (preferably factors that reflect an increase in value) might not always be the same throughout the company, but what's important is to gain assurance that things are occurring as expected within each business unit—as this will influence enterprise-level performance.

Metrics are deeply embedded into strategy implementation and company culture. It's often not just one indicator that tells the whole story, but it begets the investigation of a number of other indicators.

CASE IN POINT

A manufacturing company hasn't made recent investments in capital equipment, so it would be valuable to review a variety of line items to determine the effect of that decision: net fixed assets (the cost of new equipment versus fixed asset depreciation), work in progress, raw goods versus finished goods, inventory, repair and maintenance, labor, cost of sales, and profitability. If this company reports a 4 percent profit and the industry average is 7 percent, then answering why and the corrective action(s) should be a foremost thought. It is all too common to blame. This is an opportunity to engage staff for creative thought and ideas. Many ideas may originate from other than the C-suite. A collective and holistic look at the items noted above may reveal a number of disturbing things:

- The older equipment is making half the widgets in twice the time.
- An increased headcount (the process is more labor-intensive).
- The increased scrap and energy waste produced increases costs.
- More equipment downtime and repairs.
- Staff to identify errors and take corrective action.

It doesn't take long to make the connection that failing to make capital purchases (new equipment) has led to higher manufacturing costs due to labor and repair expenditures.

When you see the entire story, looking through the lens via metrics, you can get to the heart of the matter and fix it. Let's say you have twice the industry profits—congratulations—but you don't know why. Is this temporary? Is it an accounting anomaly? The message here is that a snapshot of what's occurring is not always causation. No business operates in a vacuum, so understanding both external and internal influences are key.

2. No Annual Review of Insurance (90%)

It's important to look at insurance through a critical lens every year to address coverage, amount of deductibles, whether the best price for premiums is being paid, and whether anything has changed since the last review that would necessitate amendments. It's not unusual to find that several areas are overlooked with respect to insurance, and this can result in significant risk to the company.

Does your company have directors and officers (D&O) insurance? Without it, the potential liability may be so great to directors and officers that the caliber of those you attract won't be too high. It's your responsibility to mitigate directors' and officers' exposure via D&O insurance to ensure the "best and brightest" want to serve.

What about insurance that covers business interruptions with clear riders so coverage is adequate? This can come in handy if occurrences are beyond your control, such as a building failure that prevented staff from coming to the office. A day is bad and a month could be fatal due to the significant financial loss and lost new business.

It may also be worthwhile to investigate IT insurance to cover events resulting from lost data from a cyberattack. The unfortunate events of 9/11 caught many large and small companies by surprise, and companies without information redundancy (offsite backed-up systems) or protection via insurance often folded.

What about life insurance? Owners insulate the company from risk when officers and key employees whose death or disability would have a dramatic impact on operations are covered by adequate life insurance. It's common to see buy–sell agreements that remain unfunded after a decade, underfunded, or funded by life insurance, with the amount of coverage being determined by a back-of-the-napkin value. Not surprisingly, that figure can be woefully outdated if annual reviews don't occur.

CASE IN POINT

Life insurance for four partners was secured five years ago based on the value of the company at that time, $20 million. Since then, the company's value has increased to $50 million, but the amount of life insurance has remained the same. If a partner dies, this can present a quandary because the proceeds from the life insurance won't be enough to allow the purchase of the deceased's share of equity based on the current value of the company.

Underfunded buy–sell agreements are just one of the issues that are problematic with respect to insurance. Another is when entrepreneurs are penny-wise and pound-foolish by either not securing insurance at all or failing to secure it at the proper level—and that can have a significant effect on the company's price multiplier. Let's say the value impact of having adequate insurance is $1 million, while the premium is $10,000 a year. Most people would sign up for something that would provide a 100-to-1 benefit, right? There is premium finance life product that may offer some wonderful investment and tax benefits, so consult with a professional.

Speaking of premiums, there are myriad good firms that can either recommend an increase in deductibles to lower premiums or find lower premiums for the same or even higher levels of coverage with a different carrier. Verifying the track record of carriers is wise as well. The insurance business is highly competitive, so you should use that advantage to ensure obtaining the highest benefits at the lowest cost.

If a company has a high number of employees or is in a trade with a higher accident risk, the owner may want to investigate the benefits of captive insurance, a mechanism through which the entire company is self-insured. This entails deducting funds from the company profits and placing them in a separate entity, where, after reserves, they are accessible for reinvestment. Captive insurance isn't right for every company, but it can have significant tax benefits when it is.

By isolating higher-risk functions like manufacturing from those with lower claims, such as accounting, an entire company is not affected by the higher insurance premium. The company can create a "new co" that may have consequential tax and premium benefits depending upon structure selected. Also previously discussed was how making subtle policy changes—such as not allowing employees to take company cars home at night—can have a positive effect on insurance rates and mitigate risk to the company.

It's worth remembering that insurance provides a metric to the way a company sees risk and how to mitigate it. A good valuator can tell right away if strong risk management policies are in place—written or unwritten—and the answer is often they are not.

3. No Understanding of the Leverage of IT/HR Functions (80%)

The human body is a complex mechanism that we often think of as a conglomeration of muscles, skin, and bones—forgetting that what really drives it is the nervous system and blood flow, both of which must communicate and work well to ensure growth.

Contrasting the body with a business, you can replace nervous system and blood flow with IT and HR, two functions that must be working well to ensure long-term company health. If the phrase "knowledge is power" is true, it's certainly in evidence with respect to these two disciplines.

Focusing first on IT, you can think of it as a way to store, access, analyze, and leverage the vast amounts of knowledge collected by any business (aka data analytics). Given low costs and high computing power, not tapping into this knowledge nugget is fool hardy. When you have an integrated system, rather than disparate functions, many redundancies are culled. Data analytics is an emerging field that allows organizations to respond to internal and external stimuli—information gained through people and processes. This supports real-time responsiveness when the phone rings; computers are populated with caller information to enable rapport to be established right away, as opposed to beginning with a series of redundant questions.

What does this have to do with risk? Companies that are not embracing the latest IT innovations put themselves at risk of falling behind competitors that do.

Moving on to HR, if the owner recognizes tangible assets of a company include its building, machinery, and equipment, as well as its reason for existing (which often drives the culture), they should quickly come to the conclusion that HR isn't just tasked with making sure people get paid and reporting sick days and vacation time. At its finest, the HR function can be leveraged by ensuring people are motivated and provided skills to perform at a high level—reflecting an environment of care—*understanding that human capital is the most important intangible asset a business possesses.*

Some companies are so well regarded as places to work that their turnover is a fraction of their industry average. Their employees are often more educated, dedicated, loyal, and often well compensated—and innovation is allowed to come from anyone. They understand how to leverage their people.

HR should ensure the organization is refreshed and dynamic, operating with clarity and transparency. The healthiest businesses will realize that everyone on the team—from the janitors to executives in the C-suite—are part of the company's ecosystem. All have important roles. Great things can happen when the traditional pyramid, with management on top, is turned upside down so leadership becomes stewards tasked with supporting staff and their interactions with clients and vendors.

The correlation with risk should be evident. A nonexistent or underperforming HR function may contribute to employee dissatisfaction and high turnover—two things that will certainly have a negative effect on productivity and innovation and company value.

4. No Business, Marketing, or Succession Plan (90%)

Employees who decide they no longer want to be part of an organization and/or those who have an idea they are really passionate about who form businesses are a mixture of risks and opportunities.

As was noted earlier, with the exception of those who seek funding from venture capitalists and angels, few other business owners create a business or marketing plan upon formation, and even fewer have a plan for transition events, like having their children sufficiently qualified to run the company upon retirement or death. (Yes, there is always crowd funding or the television series *Shark Tank*. Good luck.)

Why does this happen? A common reason is owners don't want to feel constrained by a strategy or a written plan. Other than the requisite effort, this is a shame. Think about the first car you purchased new. You notice the model more on the road afterward. When a plan is crystallized, you can sense and seize opportunities, as they are larger than the next sale of product or service. The owner is more prone to seek and see ideas. By having a plan, the business adapts to pursue the objectives born from its strategy. But a plan without execution is like having a meeting without an advanced agenda. Lots of time, lots of ruminating, and not much action. You can't transform a company by continuing to do what's familiar.

In the absence of the clarity of what makes a good company great, erroneous thinking can be further compounded by interactions with advisors who have a minimal understanding of the company's plan, so their alignment or integration falls short, and thus may offer advice that's either of nominal use or conflicting—making planning difficult for even the most receptive owners.

Business owners are typically focused full-time on operating the business, dealing with the here and now. Yet boards and CEOs are generally tasked with the vision of where the company will be not just next quarter, but in 5, 10, or 20 years. They may be told that they need a plan moving forward, but what's more helpful than that vague advice is actually being introduced to people who can assist with developing a plan and executing it so it becomes organic rather than a distraction—after all, most owners' daily blocking and tackling leaves little time to ensure that strategy drives their decisions. Most advisors are technical, tactical, and transactional, so the result is often mediocrity, as this is the rule versus the exception.

Pushback often occurs when planning is seen as amorphous, so the writer of the check for payment of such services if unconvinced considers the process only as a cost. Likely its investment benefit and time to effectuate change have been inadequately articulated.

Not having a business or marketing plan in place can cause any number of issues both in the short and long term. Seldom will a commercial bank provide a loan without being able to review a document demonstrating how the debt will be repaid. At a minimum, that means outlining the market, the piece of the market the business has attained (X), how the business plans to get from X to Y, and its projected profitability for repayment. A business that is seen as robust and following a plan will likely receive better funding, rates, and terms than one with inadequate or no planning documents.

Owners must realize that passion alone doesn't equate to business success. Lack of planning and preparation are significant reasons for funds running out and high failure rates.

CASE IN POINT

A man decides to open a donut shop after seeing long lines at his local Dunkin' Donuts. He focuses solely on perceived demand and doesn't think about how much money he'll need to open the shop, pay the staff, put toward marketing, and allocate to debt repayment—much less how many 99-cent donuts he'll need to sell to break even.

A common reason more business plans do not exist is the perceived soft and hard cost to produce them. No doubt a well-conceived plan is difficult. It takes a good deal of time. A plan forces one to consider myriad what-ifs as well as timelines and metrics of performance and pushes tough questions around assumptions. It certainly is not a sprint; it's more like a marathon. Nobody expects to run 26.2 miles on day 1. They do expect that months of training will be necessary.

A solid plan will include, but not be limited to, the following:

- What is the ecosystem? (the environment, the need, and the constituents)
- Who are the constituents? (decision makers and influencers)
- What is the unique, dynamic capability?
- What are the resource needs of time, treasure, talent, and temperament?

This process may start with vetting key advisors to see who will proactively assist in company growth and considering an independent board or an advisory board. It would require discussions with prospects, clients, and vendors. It would determine whether there is a clearly articulated message understood and agreed to by constituents to harness alignment of aims and actions. It would assess the landscape and the path selections. The meeting with constituents and filtering innovation and achieving alignment can take weeks and often months to cement.

Then a framework and roadmap is needed that outlines each role and activity as well as agreed-upon metrics. A final activity is to report, review, and revise. This is an undertaking that finds gaps and exploits opportunities while constantly reducing risks. By doing so, focus is not solely on top and bottom line metrics, but on value creation. This is why most successful business owners indicate that the best time to plan for a business exit is when the business starts its strategy.

If the capital outlay is not in the budget, take advantage of the services offered by counselors from Service Corps of Retired Executives (SCORE).

Also, many universities have business school students available to assist business owners while the students also gain insights. Their MBA programs often have students perform this advisory work under the watchful eye of their professor for a nominal cost.

This reality to scale and grow value is as challenging as it is to start a business from scratch—and why many owners turn to franchising. Much of the hard work has already been done, so if the script is followed, franchise owners may become successful, especially as they expand to large markets and even regions. (However, there's never a guarantee of success.)

Getting back to planning, a robust marketing plan should be a part of any good business plan. Key elements to a successful marketing plan are how marketing dollars will be used, why those choices were made, and what is the intended result and metrics to measure success.

The more specific a plan, the better the roadmap and metrics will be—and that means adjustments can be made to assumptions based on outcomes that provide more data points. Those organizations without marketing plans may, through sheer doggedness and luck, get to the point where the business sustains itself and the owner, but that is often a lifestyle business sufficient to pay a salary but not to build value, as growth is sacrificed for gratification. Most founders have loftier goals, but they won't get there without solid planning.

Think about how difficult it is to lose weight. Many people try to diet on their own without much direction, but those who follow a specific regime of a pound loss at a time are likely to be more successful and see ongoing results than to think "I must lose 35 pounds." In a business, the goal should be to realize controlled incremental growth, but that doesn't happen by osmosis. It's a by-product of investing in the people, processes, and property that make it happen.

CASE IN POINT

Businesses that see nominal growth and merely provide a nice paycheck for the owner are likely to garner a nominal sales price, as buyers will realize they're acquiring jobs rather than a company. They have no guarantee that the benefits they receive will offset the risk that the relationships remain with the seller.

How can having a marketing plan lessen risk and increase the value of a business? Quite simply, it acts as a driver, supporting the ability to track referrals, repeat business, and sales levels from new and existing customers. Having this information allows setting price points with a healthy equilibrium to maximize the elasticity between the highest numbers of buyers at the highest possible price.

For instance, if your tracking efforts show you've lost 3 percent of your customers but those you've retained are paying 10 percent higher prices, you have no cause to panic. It's a solid strategy to attract and retain better customers who want to pay more while ensuring you have fewer customers who want to pay less. Some say pick two: fast, cheap, and good.

With a marketing plan in place, you have the ability to determine how you've spent your marketing dollars and where those investments have paid off. You can go deeper into why people are doing business with you.

There are also creative marketing alternatives (e.g., guerrilla marketing), which may include getting customers and other ecosystem members, like advisors and vendors, involved in sharing the company's unique story.

Any good marketing plan will answer the question of how you plan to differentiate from the competition. Remember that the marketplace is dynamic, so static means death.

By reviewing results within the context of a marketing lens, new product and service offerings can be considered as can expansion into other markets. The build-versus-buy metric may also suggest that acquiring a business—either verticals (part of the chain of services) or horizontals (natural extensions of core competency)—is a solid strategy for growth.

CASE IN POINT

Valuators like to see evidence that companies are not one-trick ponies with one offering or high client concentration.

Examples abound to mitigate this risk, such as the plumber who decides to open a plumbing parts store that offers supplies near cost (vertical growth) or a company that specializes in water damage restoration services (horizontal growth).

Many owners are unable to accomplish this type of innovative growth because their day job is working in the business and they perceive the notion of strategy with a greater-purpose vision as a luxury. The fact is, seeking new ideas that can transform a company is important, and the existence of a marketing plan provides a mechanism for creative thinking as well as successful implementation.

Now we come to the most seldom created plan, the succession plan. Many people refer to this as having an exit strategy, but I prefer the concept of transition. Regardless of what it's called, it's a rare owner who's put a lot of time and effort into determining what will happen to the business once he decides to reduce involvement. Arguably, the genesis of the discussion is an external event like an advisor inquiry or a family friend suffering a terrible injury that is life altering whereby she is not able to return to work

Many owners assume their accountant—the person who has the most intimate knowledge of their finances—will help with creating a transition plan. On occasion, that can be true. Usually accountants may assist in the tax considerations and ensure robust financial documentation that affirms operational results. While very important, that is the tip of the iceberg.

Without the counsel of other trusted advisors, owners are left in a quandary—because they don't know what they don't know. This is referred to as having "resource gaps." The resources are commonly time and capital (human and financial). Owners all too often rely on metrics that are akin to counting on developing strategy based on what they want, but not necessarily on what they need or are willing to do. The need is to fill these gaps so decisions aren't solely based upon weak assumptions and hope.

Either owners have no earthly idea or think they have some idea about what their business is worth. In all my years as a valuator, only twice did I run across owners who thought their company was worth less than what it was. Most times, owners place a higher value on their "baby" because over and over again they see this investment through their lens.

Think about the car enthusiast who spends tens of thousands of dollars beautifying classic cars. When they broker a sale, they seldom recoup their investment because the value is intrinsic to them—seldom to potential buyers. Its value is the potential as is, where it is, not under new management or ownership.

Another good analogy involves selling a home. Is it best to sell a property as is or add value by replacing the aging roof or upgrading an outdated kitchen, with the aim of more than recouping the home improvement investment in the form of a significantly higher sales price? A real estate professional can provide counsel, and the same type of guidance is relevant when it comes to business owners needing transition advice. It takes time, as was articulated by the training for a marathon analogy.

It can take months and often years to get a business (and its owners) in shape for a transition (even with a plan in place). Among other things, there's a need to secure tax and legal advice; properly position the company; qualify potential buyers (which can be a very lengthy process); and for consideration of the use and application of net proceeds whether philanthropic, entrepreneurial, or recreational. Woe to the owner who on a whim or due to unforeseen events must sell and transition in six months or less. It's difficult to realize the full value of a company without filling the resource gaps.

Failing to have a succession plan in place might be at the top of the list, but also high up is not making an investment in advisory services. Among the first questions that should be asked of a potential advisor are how she gets paid and the nature of promised results. It may be wise that the advisors have some skin in the game—that the greater your success, the greater their compensation—where regulatory requirements and conflicts are not an issue.

The advisors must be capable of thinking and acting strategically—and that could be a tall order, since most provide tactical assistance, leaving their clients to think ahead. Evidence of high levels of seller's remorse is almost exclusively the result of failing to think through the transition and resolve issues early in the process. Here are a couple other sobering thoughts: One out of two pending sales fails to close, and 80 percent of merged businesses don't succeed in getting the synergistic value of their assets.

Having a succession plan provides direction that is invaluable for owners and their families, company stakeholders, and employees. The goal may be to obtain the highest possible price for the business—which may mean losing key personnel after a sale. Perhaps the intent is to keep the legacy by rewarding loyal staff through the use of an ESOP or turning the business over to key personnel, a family member, or a minority buyer (such as a private equity group or family office) who eventually may subsequently acquire the remainder at an even greater price. And, in the cases when a sale is the desired way to go, will it involve assets, equity, or both?

The plan should also spell out the role the owner wishes to have post-transition: serving as chairperson; working five hours a week; having nothing further to do with the business; or securing an MBA candidate or professional management as a #2, which allows the owner to receive equity benefits without a sale and long hours at the business.

Looking at succession as a transition rather than an exit supports planning to write another chapter rather than the end of the book. A succession plan is one of the vehicles that can ensure an owner's wishes are carried out; operating without one is like walking a tightrope without a net. Now that's risky.

5. Little or No Effort to Cull Clients (80%)

Some of the best professional services firms pride themselves on retaining the most select clients instead of the largest number of clients. Why is this relevant with respect to risk? If you believe the Pareto Principle (that 20% of something is responsible for 80% of the results), it's not a stretch to see that a handful of top clients may be responsible for a large percentage of annual sales.

It's ill-advised to have any one client represent more than 10 percent of your business—due to the inherent risk of client concentration, which can significantly impact revenues, profits, and accounts receivable. Review the bottom quintile of clients on an annual basis to determine which ones will likely scale in growth and which are draining limited resources versus the top quintile, which could almost always use additional dedicated service.

There are a few ways to divest those clients that seem to provide a disproportionate expenditure of resources for the value (or lack of same) they provide:

- Propose the addition of new services.
- Raise rates.
- Sell book of business to a competitor better suited for this type of client.

Once divested of lower-performing clients, review the top 20 percent. It's important to determine how to differentiate products and services to add value by providing additional customized solutions—with the aim being to make it easier for clients to consider their business relationship as a top resource.

CASE IN POINT

A boutique law firm has made it clear to clients that due to the breadth and depth of its relationships, it can address the majority of needs a business might have, even those that are outside the scope of its legal expertise. Thus, it's common for the firm to become a go-to resource that receives calls from clients who need professional input on all matters, such as an investment banker, insurer, and, yes, a strategic value architect.

All professional services providers should strive to become a most trusted advisor, or as I refer to it, a connector, concierge, or consigliore. When do you know you have a consigliore relationship? That occurs when clients ask for both professional and personal advice; the nature of the relationship is not just technical—it's priceless.

Thus, it can be a valuable exercise to consider the amount of available staff-hours that are used to serve 100 clients versus the top 10. It will quickly become evident that it doesn't take 10 times the effort to serve the top 10 percent—so if time and talent are freed up by divesting the bottom 10 or 20 percent as noted earlier, that will provide more time to become embedded with top clients with the aim of achieving consigliore status.

On the more tangible side of the business spectrum (i.e., manufacturing and construction), when a company has a concentration in intellectual property or assets like machinery and equipment, the focus becomes, What are the ways to leverage hard and soft assets to ensure the highest possible benefit to clients while ensuring the highest level of profitability? This is often an issue of market and client selection.

CASE IN POINT

Some family members were displeased a multigenerational business went from high eight-figure sales to half in a few years. They failed to recognize the prior business model was suffering from lost demand, product commoditization, and declining margins. Although the revenues did decline, offering customized services more than doubled profits, providing higher shareholder dividends and a greater company value despite much lower revenues.

A residential builder may choose to build fewer luxury homes with higher margins, while another homebuilder wants to construct 300 or more modestly priced single-family homes. They're both in the same industry, but they have had to determine whether they want to provide upmarket or down-market offerings. Part of a company's purpose and process is deciding how to differentiate itself from other players in the marketplace, thus choosing the relationships it wishes to leverage.

Manufacturers often have to decide whether to be a mass-market provider or a producer of custom one-off products for which precision and speed are client priorities. The latter, as you would assume, usually generates margins well above industry average with a greater barrier to entry. This also presents lower risk and higher value.

It's also important to have a cultural understanding of your clients. Nimble firms with better margins often have cultures that include the process of reviewing clients every year. While it may be difficult to perceive giving up the bottom 20 percent of your clients and the revenues they generate (consider profits, too), to keep weak clients or to make too many concessions may dilute the company's message of quality and service. The risk is commoditizing product or service where price is the primary factor instead of value. If the first inquiry concerns price (cost to patron) versus worth (value paid), be concerned.

This way of operating turns some people off and does require some retraining. However, leading with price reflects a person's inability to differentiate valuable knowledge and relationships from a transaction—a price tag on the former is difficult.

CASE IN POINT

A call from a client of an attorney who represents one of the largest landholders in the Midwest was seeking options about a potential deal. Our firm's due diligence blew them away in about an hour. We never discussed price. I was planning to comp them for my time, but they said to invoice them and prepare a retainer agreement for future services. That is respect.

How is your business at risk if you fail to cull clients? You don't have to worry about those top clients who seek your expertise and are more than willing to pay for it; they seldom cause problems. Be wary of clients with disproportionate expectations—those who want Cadillac service but are only willing to pay for a Chevy. This situation exposes advisors and owners to disenchanted clients and all that may mean. No turnover may mean too low pricing; whereas, high turnover may mean disenchanted clients. Not knowing the "why" and "how" increases risks associated with maintaining and managing client expectations. This is a real risk that will impair business value.

6. No Clear Communications Up, Down, or Across Staff and Management (65%)

In the effort to maintain control at the enterprise or department level, communication is often in one direction, from the top down. Work environments like these, either wittingly or not, suggest that individual ideas, observations, and problems often go unheard or unheeded. At a minimum, this will negatively affect morale, and at its worst, it can be destructive to the company.

Earlier in the book, I told the story of a GM quality control team that seemingly had its concerns about ignition switches ignored—a situation that resulted in loss of life, significant litigation, a huge recall, and an ugly black eye for the car giant. This is an example of failing to listen and respond appropriately impacting GM's profits – in the short term.

Ideally, committees representing departments or a cross-section of the employees should be established to allow the business to sense opportunities and hurdles—to seize the former and mitigate the latter. These gatherings can also be invaluable sources of ideas that transform the company to remain competitive in a dynamic marketplace.

The gatekeeper at the front desk, assistants, line workers, and field reps often see things management does not; thus, they're in a prime position to contribute to opportunity seizing and obstacle mitigation. However, a cultural shift often needs to take place so this valuable information as well as appropriate and timely action can be taken. This requires a degree of transparency while relevant data is managed at the appropriate organizational levels.

In this same vein, as part of the strategic planning effort, no company can truly and effectively serve its markets as well as when it solicits and encourages input from its ecosystem: staff, attorneys, accountants, bankers, insurance professionals, clients, vendors, board members, and even sometimes competitors at natural venues such as association meetings and tradeshows.

This flow of information is often taken for granted and yet if acted upon suitably, it can provide uncommon knowledge and performance enhancements. Having the fortitude to be transparent can significantly mitigate the risk that comes from operating in a silo.

7. Little or No Employee Review or Turnover Monitoring (70%)

As children and adults, most of us seek approval and validation; we endeavor to do the best job we know how under any given circumstances. Sometimes we know we've exceeded expectations and other times we realize we have failed to deliver.

Given the individual makeup of the collective known as "the village" or the company ecosystem with owners, officers, and staff as stakeholders, each employee has earned the right to constructive feedback, preferably written. Employees have also earned the opportunity to evaluate their own performance as well as that of their immediate direct reports, their departments, and their company as a whole without fear of recriminations and reprisals.

When this happens, each employee can compare his or her perspective to that of management and management can determine if certain direct reports are placing similar weight on performance (think of the grade school teacher or professor who never gave an A+ because there is always room for improvement and the other who never provided less than a C+ so no one felt too poorly about their evaluation). Keep in mind that an evaluation is what an employee earns, not what is given.

If the reviewed and reviewer have performance aligned perspectives, that's ideal. If not, it opens up a discussion of roles, responsibilities, and possible obstacles and opportunities through the lens of both the employee and the direct report. Clearly, if the perspectives are wildly dissimilar, with the direct report unaware of his or her suboptimal performance, that may warrant a transfer into a better-suited department or the provision of alternative employment options (i.e., being let go).

Documentation is important to both provide a trajectory of improvement and cover the company's exposure in cases of disenfranchised employees. It also provides a somewhat tangible means to evaluate cross-training, additional education, or promotion potential. As leaders can see, one single line item (human capital) presents the full spectrum of issues that can affect employee performance. It tends to prove the point that a broader and deeper holistic approach to human capital is a worthy investment of time and resources.

The bottom line is that employers have the chance to inspire their staffs, professionally and personally, by conducting regularly scheduled employee reviews. And occasionally unofficial feedback is also a mechanism to do that. Inexperienced management tends to find items to correct, whereas seasoned management will reinforce positive behaviors by praising in public. In private, they will counsel staff that needs guidance. Letting employees know where they stand as well as setting goals for future performance are additional ways to inspire while creating enduring loyalty and a deeper level of trust.

Turnover monitoring can be somewhat aligned with providing employee reviews. For instance, if you see a trend that suggests lower evaluations are being given in certain departments (something that can result in employees leaving), it may require recalibration by discussing with management what is considered outstanding, at par, or below par. As shared above, "good" to one manager may be "great" to another, so consistency matters.

In situations like this, the best outcome is to identify what's going on and attempt to rectify it if that is the required action or the worst is to realize a difficult manager (family member perhaps) is in charge. This may be someone who is threatened by superior subordinates. Managers like this may attempt to torpedo their best employees with subpar evaluations, so offending staff members ultimately vote with their feet and leave. It's important to determine whether these evaluations are accurate or if there is a systemic issue with a manager who's failing to mentor employees and instead is trying to "keep them in their place" in an attempt to ensure his or her position isn't endangered.

Those who are threatened by the success of key employees are a real problem. Their behavior is risky not only because they can cause good people to leave along with the company's investment in them, but if it can be proven that their actions are based on gender, race, or other protected-group biases, the business owner can end up in court.

When turnover is higher than the industry average, the future of the company is at risk because knowledge is lost. Such terminations of good people can negatively affect staff morale and incur higher training costs due to the constant stream of new employees.

8. Family with Inadequate Skills in Critical Roles (60%)

It's the rare owner who doesn't dream of one or more of his or her children taking over the family business. It's also the rare owner who can remain objective regarding the skills, merits, and impact of having family (including spouse and siblings) involved in the daily operation of the business. This holds true for any size business, whether it records annual sales of 6 or 11 figures.

Families must decide if they can make a distinction of the inherent dynamics that separate the business of family from the family in business. It's human nature to have favorites, and while that may create some awkward friction, if not acknowledged and properly managed it can be destructive to both the family and the business.

Early identification and involvement of a trusted family advisor is often the key to ensuring decision making occurs through an objective lens. This professional can help articulate passion and purpose and establish protocols, policies, councils, and constitutions, particularly in multigenerational family businesses where dozens if not hundreds of family members and business staff may be impacted.

CASE IN POINT

The husband of the owner's favorite daughter is hired into the company as VP of Sales, when there was a very qualified sales manager in line for that role—who now feels slighted. Also feeling out of sorts is another sibling whose spouse was not considered for that or another executive role in the company. What will become of the sales manager's business relationships and family business revenues based upon these slights?

It's also critical to make determinations with respect to equity ownership and the distinction between egalitarian and equal. Do all family need or should they have equity in the business? Should allocation of financial transfers to family be the same? What drives the considerations and consequences of "who has it and who might get it," particularly as a result of blended families, divorce, or death? And policies, processes, and procedures have to be carefully considered, such as how to deal with the child who's graduated from college and may wish to hone his business skills elsewhere before applying for a position within the family business.

Then, there is the issue of the relationship the owner or other managers may have with outside advisors. For instance, if the CFO has a unique and personal relationship with the outside accountant, should this be disclosed and transparent? Should the company's buyer of supplies be permitted to acquire products and services from another family member who has his or her own business? Should a new division be established for the sole purpose of not disappointing family members if the division is hemorrhaging cash?

What of the family business and the no-show job, which involves appointing a spouse as the company CFO when that person at best may have a little bookkeeping knowledge, and no tax, treasury, or private capital markets experience. Situations may also occur when the owner draws more funds from the company than may be prudent. How does that impact essential outside investors, family members with equity, and nonfamily employees? Individually, these issues may be minimal for a healthy family, but suffice it to say, healthy families are often in the minority.

As noted earlier, having a trusted family advisor, attorney, or CPA in place to provide guidance and transparency with regard to mitigating issues that often occur within family businesses is wise. Advisors are cautioned, however, that if they only interact with and solicit the person who writes their checks, they may risk the continuity of the relationship when those in charge transfer the responsibilities to the next generation.

It's always important to consider a clear distinction between the roles of owner, chairperson, CEO, employee, and shareholder—even at a nonfamily business. Given the family dynamic, these businesses can experience unique difficulties during the 6Ts: transfer, tax, transition, transaction, transformation, and/or trouble.

These are often partial or full liquidity events (the sale of the company or its shares) even when this activity is planned that can cause disruption. Unplanned transitions—due to death, disability, divorce, substance abuse, gambling, sexual addiction, and so on—are guaranteed to create dysfunction/disputes, so mitigating these risks is a prudent human capital investment.

9. Culture Is Control, Silos, and Tactical (80%)

While understanding that outcomes are important to every owner, if control becomes an obstacle to growth, the results are often counterproductive. A common issue seen in companies with stunted growth is the failure to entrust and delegate.

Plenty of anecdotal evidence exists regarding the overwhelming majority of business owners who lament not having someone to whom they turn over key responsibilities. For example, a general manager may have no business development experience and a VP of marketing may have no prowess in the area of operations. When "gaps" appear in management's ability to address areas that are key to the company's success, it begs the question: Who is responsible for developing future leaders within the organization? Owners with control issues will often not have an answer; they say they want to delegate, but they're also afraid to let go of the reins, which often leads to mediocre results.

The issue of silos differs from control in that it often involves conflict. Consider the case of the owner who allows superstars to run roughshod over staff, bottleneck information, or take credit for others' achievements. Such behaviors are counterproductive to the company's long-term success—and who, but the owner, is responsible for these behaviors?

With regard to tactical cultures, it's understandable they exist when owners serve as CEOs and are dealing with day-to-day firefighting to keep the business on course. However, being tactical is a reactive behavior. It means responding to internal and external events or receiving advice from advisors who address the problem but not its root cause.

Compounding that issue is the fact that it's quite common for owners to receive disparate advice from those they trust most—as each sees the world filtered through their own technical lens, experiences, and personalities. To combat this, it's necessary to have a strategy that allows for a longer-term perspective (preferably aligned), so when day-to-day issues arise, their importance is prioritized against the backdrop of how they affect the company on a long-term basis.

It's certainly true that a CEO often wears multiple hats, but responsibilities can be boiled down to just one: charting where the company is headed and determining how to best get there. Resource gaps and culture shifts need to be addressed to ensure success.

For example, daily blocking and tackling should be delegated so it's off the CEO's plate—as it's nearly impossible to do a good job in both an operational and a strategic role for any sustained period of time. The second best option is to task the company's CFO with this duty. However, as previously discussed, an inventory of on-hand management, staff, and advisors is necessary to determine the time, human, and financial capital needed to ensure a robust and cohesive strategy is both planned and executed. This is often where tapping into trusted advisor relationships and their knowledge is wise should they not have applicable talent to assist in certain areas, such as facilitating the strategy itself or developing nonfinancial performance metrics. This is an area in which a ***strategic value architect*** is ideal.

Again, I cannot stress enough that the risks of failing to cede control, break down silos, and solely operating tactically are too numerous to mention but are also fairly obvious.

10. Board Comprised of Family, Inside Directors, and/or Friends (95%)

Just like #8 above, *familiarity creates trust, while competency creates capital*. Undoubtedly, and in the course of all relationships, developing trust is paramount. But it's not unusual for people to be well trusted yet mediocre at what they do. Ideally, you become well trusted as a result of having high character as well as technical capabilities; one without the other doesn't provide an ideal result.

Many private companies have family, sometimes staff, and occasionally trusted advisors, as members of their board. Let's deconstruct why and also uncover the risks inherent to opting for familiar over ideal criteria for board selection.

When you have directors who are also company employees or officers, what ability does the CEO, likely the controlling interest holder, have to influence outcomes? This type of influence on others, which might not be in the best interest of the company, does not reflect true governance or leadership. The same holds true for family members who serve on boards and may have emotional or familial reasons to toe the line when asked and occasionally just the opposite by impeding progress due to a real or imagined familial slight.

As for advisors, when a company pays them for services, can they truly be independent, when they may refrain from sharing their opinions due to the risk of having their business relationship terminated? Clarity also is needed about whether opinions are representing the founder's interests or those of the company, which, understandably, are often seen as the same thing even though, as demonstrated throughout this book, delayed gratification is hard when larger reward is delayed.

This doesn't mean a board can't include some of these constituencies, but the benefits of having outside directors should be weighed when considering their unique ability to shore up weaknesses or blind spots the company, or its human capital, may have. For instance, owners who are operationally adept but weak on strategy or business development may be well served to have directors who possess those skillsets.

A good board will challenge management to consider, what does the company stand for (its purpose, or "Why are we in business together?"); it'll seek balance between risk and resiliency, and that of fear of metrics versus good feedback.

For a manufacturer, having directors who are Lean Six Sigma subject matter experts may make sense as may having directors with private capital markets and/or international business experience. And for any organization, having an accountant who's not preparing the company's taxes on the board may provide a valuable second set of eyes—someone who will tell it like it is without fear of losing his or her livelihood.

Why do many owners want to stack the deck when it comes to the makeup of their boards? For private companies, it's likely they don't want anyone standing in the way of what they set out to do.

Occasionally, there is merit to the concern where "velocity of capital" requires timely decisions. For public companies, it's often more about CEO controlling compensation, shareholder influence, financial controls, and regulatory management that may suffocate the strategic ingenuity.

As a minimum, form an advisory board that suggests, but may not act on, governance issues, but might ask management to consider longer-range questions of what's being done currently to consider what the company will be doing three and five (sometimes 20) years from the present. They may ask deeper questions such as How does the company create conditions with which others are self-motivated and hold themselves accountable? They will usually encourage listening and research before decisions and actions are delivered. They can balance making bad decisions with encouraging taking reasonable risks.

Absent the deeper wisdom that such a group can provide, an owner may not be leveraging knowledge because her need for control trumps the collection of broader inputs. In the context of a family business, she may wrestle with the tension of the individual versus that of the family and decisions that are pluralistic versus singular.

If a company is of adequate size, it can be a good idea to create cross-functional teams or communication across different staff levels, as that can create newly expressed perspectives that, when harnessed, have the dual benefits of driving healthy growth and happier and more empowered personnel.

Overall when there is communication, there is cohesion. A strong leader will offer encouragement and respect others' ideas and identity. They will seek counsel and align divergent views. This can make for a healthy family and a healthy business. The risks to owners of failing to secure advice and counsel from a variety of sources far outweigh any perceived loss of control. Failing to do so will often have a measurable impact on value and reduce viable buyers should the controlling interest holders and/or founder wish to sell most or all of the company.

11. Limited or No Involvement in Own or Client Industry Associations (80%)

Most advisors seek continuing education and networking opportunities within their own industry. Some will consider attending complementary events to generate both relationships and business while gaining a better understanding of issues that can have a direct or indirect impact on their area of expertise.

Put it another way: Would you rather work with an advisor who understands your industry space and is conversant on its issues—or someone who's not? A small percentage of those who attend industry events are thought leaders who are often tapped as presenters. The pinnacle of education is to question if there's a better way to do something, and more importantly, to pursue the answer. There are those who create new concepts we take for granted—like family limited partnerships; such individuals are skipping happily to the bank. For owners, the same issues apply. Some join practice area, industry, or trade association groups or exhibit at complementary events—and what should always be in the minds of the C-suite is the pursuit of best industry practices.

While trite, the axiom "Knowledge is power" holds true. Owners who religiously attend local, national, and sometimes global industry meetings are likely going to be more competitive than those who don't. Those who become thought leaders and industry board members shape the future of not only their company, but also their sector as a whole.

At the time of this writing, I serve or have served on multiple boards and committees of legal, finance, family business, family office, valuation, academic, nonprofit, and business organizations. I've worked hard to gain respect within the valuation industry and the industries that complement it, authoring whitepapers, presenting at professional events, and getting involved in projects that can benefit from my experience and expertise as I can from others. This gives me panache that not only helps secure new clients but also provides credibility in litigation.

CASE IN POINT

The owner of a successful manufacturing company was pleased to have built a fine organization, but part of his strategy was to grow by acquisition. He sought to fill board openings in his industry and those tangential to it with the aim of broadening his perspective and gaining access to information that will benefit both his company and the industry. By doing these things, competitors come to him without listing their company for sale in the open market because they know he will offer a square deal—a win-win.

It's important to have a broad perspective when thinking about with which organizations to become affiliated and that includes considering all parts of the product/services chain, which can include end users and suppliers. In addition, every so often, business owners will realize their own knowledge gaps and attend executive management programs offered by a local or nationally renowned university. They benefit from new and finely honed knowledge as well as the development of new peer relationships that may become monetized.

The activities I've described, including my own, are not the norm, even though they can mean a significant difference in a company's value. The risk of sitting on the sidelines is seeing other companies in your space get it, gaining a competitive advantage.

12. No Risk Assessments/SWOT Analysis (80%)

In examining risk, there are those risks associated with, but not limited to, governance, relationships, and knowledge. A SWOT analysis, which looks at strengths, weaknesses, opportunities, and threats, is a key tool to thoroughly understand the landscape of a business prior to developing strategies to address what has been learned.

Strengths, the *S* in SWOT, is an inventory of the amalgamation of all the attributes of a company that allow it to be competitive in the marketplace. Interestingly, this review can unearth differences in what management perceives to be strengths and what actually are. As an example, a company whose leadership believes in conscientious capital, being socially responsible, or embracing impact investing may have a story of how it serves the community besides the benefits of its product and service lines.

Organizations that consider their strengths to be competitive pricing, quality, timeliness, and their customer service aren't differentiating themselves—because there are few competitors that don't believe the same. It's not a strength if everyone else claims the same. A deeper examination—after eliminating the previously noted attributes—often results in silence.

The fact is, strengths are often perceived externally, so it's valuable to determine how advisors, vendors, and clients perceive the company, and then what has been done to quantify those results. For instance, if a company has a 95 percent retention level, what would happen if prices were raised as a way to determine how much elasticity is present in its relationships?

If the price is raised 5 percent and retention drops to 80 percent, then price is a strength and the offering is a commodity requiring increases in volume of sales. If the same price increase results in a client loss of less than 5 percent, that may indicate the company is not placing adequate value on its offering(s) and may wish to reconsider its pricing. A company's strength is often reflected in the way its employees have been empowered to make decisions free of management intervention up to certain parameters—as this gives them ownership of outcomes. Often a telltale sign is a flat organization without the occasional bureaucratic bloat of middle management.

Companies that are consistently ranked among the best by chambers of commerce, professional organizations, or trade associations may have demonstrated clear and definitive strengths. Many companies will feel they should fall into the best category—that's human nature—but not everyone can be in the top 1 percent or even 10 percent. One of the most obvious strengths of a company is striving to be better instead of just *being (existing)*. One way to determine whether the latter is the case is to determine the company's return on invested capital. If the industry norm is 15% and the specific company is 10%, then the assemblage of assets (and possibly debt) doesn't generate sufficient profit to justify the company's sustained operations. Put in less financial terms, the company is providing jobs but inadequate investment incentive for a buyer to pay much more than book value – a sad, but quite common reality.

Weaknesses, the *W* in SWOT, are the flipside of strengths. Let's start our discussion by asking what metrics are in place to evaluate a company's intangibles—much of it human capital such as its governance, relationships, and knowledge. The real issue, and the most common weakness, is having no ongoing calibration that allows for reviewing and revising the manner in which a company senses, seizes, and transforms to develop and/or pursue opportunities and eliminate or minimize risks.

It's not enough to see what top companies are doing; however, a competitive analysis *will* provide valuable data. Absent this, you're just working *in* the business, and not *on* it within a vacuum. If you have no clearly articulated strategies, your "business plan" is tactical and based on reacting to the marketplace—part of the herd rather than a leader of the pack. Another good question to ask is why a company's marketing budget is what it is. If the answer is, "It's always been done that way," that's a weakness.

Debt can also be an indicator of weakness. If a company has no long-term debt, it can signal that the owner doesn't understand how it can actually shift risk and significantly change the return on its capital investment, depending on debt level and how debt is used.

CASE IN POINT

An example of bad debt would be an owner who regularly withdraws too much capital from his business for his own purposes and has created a self-induced cash flow problem—so he needs to tap into his line of credit. Conversely, good debt would be borrowing from a funding source to replace old with new equipment that produces twice the widgets in half the time, as new equipment reduces waste (scrap) and improves raw material inventory usage. It may lower labor costs and allows the company to become more competitive to provide more timely delivery to clients requiring tighter turnaround.

Opportunities is the O in SWOT. The market is dynamic rather than static. Doing the same thing on a different day even though the market is evolving is not a sustainable recipe for growth or increased value. Having an overarching strategy drives opportunities by bringing focus to where and when to look. This includes seeing adverse economic trends such as higher interest rates and higher material and labor costs due to a more robust market. This might allow the company to hedge from the impact of such changes. When a company seizes the opportunities presented by economic realities and other relevant activities rather than reacting to them, it becomes a market leader rather than a follower. Volumes have been written about this topic as it pertains to the marketplace.

Leading is deliberate while following is not. Some may ask whether it's wiser to let the leader take risks and thus avoid opportunity costs. However, the company that takes a leadership position has the opportunity to change the terms of the game as long as it stays in the forefront in the marketplace. Companies that are primed to take advantage of emerging opportunities will have a firm strategy in place. They seldom have to wonder what their competitors and they will be doing next week, next month, or next year because they are already planning the next three steps ahead.

Threats is the *T* in SWOT. Risks to the business—known or unknown—can be considered as a threat. For instance, if a company has one client that represents a substantial volume of annual revenue and/or accounts receivable, it faces a huge potential threat. What would happen if the client's new CEO or someone in the C-suite has a preferred relationship with a competitor? A significant source of revenue could disappear. The same bad outcome can occur if that client hires a new buyer who prefers to do business with a vendor he already knows. Overreliance on one client—putting too many eggs in one basket—can threaten a company's very existence.

Another threat can be failing to look far enough into the future to see if a decline in demand may affect revenues. As an example, a golf club manufacturer needs to be aware that a downturn in the economy can result in the number of people playing golf declining precipitously. In addition, it needs to know that the number of Millennials who play golf doesn't come close to the number of Baby Boomers who do or did.

Think about the significant threat faced by those who sold horses at the time the horseless carriage came into the marketplace. Even those with the finest carriages weren't immune to extinction when demand for four-legged transportation plummeted.

Performing due diligence as protection from threats must occur both internally and externally. Those who can't anticipate what the marketplace may be like three or five years out with some degree of certainty may suffer the consequences of having threats at the doorstep of their business. Being reactive rather than proactive may be the difference between exploiting the market while others are failing and ducking for cover.

The threat associated with human capital and succession of key staff hangs over every business, since no one knows his or her exact expiration date. Without proper threat mitigation processes in place, the untimely demise, disability, departure, or dispute with key officers or staff can have dire consequences.

CASE IN POINT

A fire restoration business expected its insurance company to pay the cost of a significant claim, but that did not happen. As a result, the company's owner of 30 years had to sell, receiving pennies on the dollar in what is known as a distressed sale.

The moral here is that numbers only tell part of the story of every business; real threats don't always reveal themselves so readily, so the ability to mitigate and anticipate them is a legitimate skillset. Failing to anticipate occurrences that can threaten a business is like reading only the first few pages of a book—you only get part of the story and make too many assumptions to make an informed decision and response.

13. No Review of Education, Experience, Age, and Health of Key Personnel (80%)

When owners lament that there's no one at their company with the adequate ability to replace them, they are unwittingly indicting themselves—in particular, their inability to groom future managers. When this occurs, the price multiple and business value decline because this is a significant risk.

It's critical to develop people who can lead the company down the road, replacing the members of the current management team after they have accepted another opportunity, retired, become disabled, or die. To ensure these future leaders have what it takes to be successful, a number of components must be taken into account, including their age, health, education, and experience for the position in question.

What happens when proper due diligence doesn't occur? It's easy to end up putting people in positions for which they're not really qualified, which creates turmoil for the direct reports and personal friction with the new hire, who either digs in or succumbs to the problem and leaves or is fired.

CASE IN POINT

A CFO has been with the company for 20 years, starting as a billing clerk and being promoted to controller before taking on his current role. This person has no formal finance or accounting expertise, so questions about taxes are forwarded to the accountant and questions about investments go to the wealth manager and banker. This CFO doesn't have the depth of knowledge the position warrants to ensure future growth and may be too reliant on others' competence.

As that example illustrates, it's not enough to say a person has *X* years of experience without drilling down further to determine his or her true skillset. Poor decisions can emanate from someone who's underqualified;

for example, a purchasing manager may choose to use a vendor's product bundling, which allows for the purchase of multiple materials at a discount—and the result may create a cash flow problem, because cash has been expended to purchase materials that aren't currently needed.

In family businesses, the practice of overlooking due diligence in making leadership decisions can be highly detrimental. How will staff react when owners choose to entrust their newly college-graduated sons or daughters in management roles despite having no experience, no people or leadership skills, or the necessary competence? The risk of losing good and more qualified people can be staggering, and the company's professionalism can also be adversely affected.

It can't be overstated how important it is to uncover potential biases and shortcomings that could be exposed in the instance of an unplanned transition. For instance, who's getting paid more than they should? This might involve family members or legacy employees. An example is the CFO-wife who's not qualified for the role; thus, perhaps another staff member is required to shore up the functions the wife is unable to handle.

Another red flag for a valuator will be if no life or disability insurance is in place—especially when a site visit reveals the level of health such as an obvious smoker or a morbidly obese person.

The basic question becomes whether the business is being run as a lifestyle enterprise or the owner is really intent on optimizing the company's success over the long term. The answer, to a large degree, can be found by seeing who has been entrusted with key positions.

While this section has focused on negatives—not having the right people in the right roles—there can be an upside to how human capital is tracked and managed. Take the case of a seasoned owner who's effective in his job and only comes in 10 hours a week, entrusting two key people to lead the team, with no adverse effects. A company like this is commonly saleable and at a greater multiple and value because the risk of their absence has been mitigated.

14. High Concentration of Vendors (80%)

While the issue of having too much business tied to one customer has already been discussed, it's worth visiting vendor concentration as well. For instance, if a manufacturer relies on a certain component that requires a six-month lead time, a valuator might ask for a list of suppliers. If there's just one, with no redundancy, that can be perceived as a significant risk, as can selection of a vendor because of lower prices. Consider that the scrap rate of lower standard material may more than exceed the higher-priced competitor in waste, utilities, and additional labor.

Companies often become comfortable working with a particular vendor or professional due to familiarity. If no refreshing to see what else is out there occurs, the business might end up paying an unnecessary premium or a better process or product may now exist that didn't when the relationship was first begun. When it's business as usual, alternatives go unexamined even when they may result in cost savings or improved performance.

Think of it like a tenant asking for options at the time of real estate lease renewal. The landlord may be willing to lower the rent or add new perks, such as tenant improvements—but those things are usually not offered up front; it's up to the tenant to ask for them.

It's a good idea to refresh vendors and advisors annually (that does not mean they should be replaced, but rather that they are still providing the best available service compared to their peers based on more than just familiarity)—which includes most relationships—and minimally every three years. The results of these meetings can greatly benefit the business on the bottom line as well as identify products and services that may no longer be needed or, conversely, should be additions to what is already provided.

15. Little or No Leverage of Trusted Advisors (90%)

Before discussing how to leverage trusted advisors, it's important to think about how they are selected. When a specific advisor is needed, how is she selected? If the response starts with how much does the advisor charge, it might be beneficial to review your relationship with current advisors. The adage "you get what you pay for" may be true here.

When an owner thinks about advisors, don't forget those whose services are not directly paid like commercial bankers and insurance professionals. While you may not be writing a check to their firms, you are paying indirectly through premiums and interest rates.

How can the best trusted advisor for your business be selected? It can be difficult, but it's not impossible, and sometimes it starts with chemistry. Every owner must decide how much likeability figures into the equation: If one advisor is a skilled technician while a second is average but likeable, what's the cost of getting quality advice? (*Hint:* It should be greater than the cost for mediocre advice.)

In a perfect world, the top 10 percent of advisors are those who have strong technical skills and strong rapport-building abilities. What does this look like? Top-tier advisors will be able to provide top-tier recommendations. Most firms can be defined by those with whom they choose to do business.

All things being equal, if you pay 30 percent higher fees to work with someone who has three times more experience and a cadre of top-tier trusted advisors with whom she works, would this equate to receiving your money's worth? That said, experience alone is an insufficient gauge as to an advisor's worth. In addition to judging advisors by the company they keep, you should consider the following barometers of ability:

- Are they known within their industry as an expert or a thought leader?
- Do they author articles reflecting they know what they're talking about and not rehashing what others already know?
- What do they do for continuing education per annum to remain current?
- What certifications, designations, and licenses do they have?
- How active are they in diverse and industry-specific organizations?

Many advisors do just enough to satisfy compliance requirements. Those who do more than that are demonstrating their enhanced professionalism. Think of it: the more experiences, the more knowledge (assuming these are good lessons learned). Receiving good advice can be priceless.

To get the most leverage from advisors and vendors, it's best to do business with those who have a deeper understanding of your business and industry, such as where the company is in its growth curve and what influences operating profits.

CASE IN POINT

A publishing company looking for a CPA should ask potential candidates how many clients they have in the publishing industry. If the answer is two or three (or none), that may not be adequate. A good advisor knows what he's good at and doesn't try to be all things to all people.

A generalist can come in handy for smaller businesses, but true leverage for owners wishing to scale comes from those with specialized knowledge. Going back to that publishing company, how valuable would it be for the owner to be able to leverage the skills of an attorney who has experience with copyright law and other industry-specific issues, versus being a generalist who doesn't have that depth of knowledge?

Working with advisors who are perceived as the best also has its benefits. What does it say about a business when a third party sees that its attorney is one of the top practitioners in the field? That will be positively reflected in management's decision making and in the price multiplier of a business.

16. No Independent Advisory Board (95%)

Like #10, even competency isn't sufficient if board members rubberstamp the decisions of the CEO without challenging alignment of compensation with shareholders obtaining the highest return on their investment through value creation. Think of the somewhat lackluster performance of Bank of America and the dissent by shareholders to have the CEO have the dual role of chairman. Nothing says "I want to be the best in the industry" like someone who seeks to be challenged by other people's perceptions and knowledge. Unfortunately, this is a rare occurrence.

For instance, as a strategic value architect and business appraiser, it's one thing to provide professional advisory services incident to the 6Ts (transfer, tax, trouble, transition, transaction, and transformation). Nothing ups your game more than the prospect of having another advisor or an attorney question your work product.

The function of an advisory board is not to be adversarial or tell an owner how to run the business. Instead, based on the specialties of the board members, this group should be asking insightful questions that may or may not receive adequate consideration by the owner and her existing board (as it may be).

As noted earlier, owners don't know what they don't know—and their advisors, especially those who are paid, should be able to fill the void (if asked and preferably comfortable enough to volunteer). An advisory board can provide an extra security blanket, guidance from individuals who have no direct skin in the game and thus can be candid. Barring that, at a minimum, companies should have an independent committee made up of staff to provide summary inputs so no one individual can be singled out for recrimination.

While gaining perspective from insiders can be valuable, it doesn't take the place of a well-formed advisory board that has the aim of ensuring the optimal performance of the company and optimal return for the company's shareholders. As mentioned before, some owners choose to stack the deck, selecting key, trusted employees and/or family members to sit on their board—but will that really result in getting objective input?

A better way to form an advisory board is to see where operational overlap would be valuable. Companies that deal with lots of contracts may benefit from choosing someone with a legal background, while an accountant may fit the bill if nuanced accounting and some finance issues are common.

Owners who know they're weak in business development may want to include a marketing/PR professional, as an advisory board member, and those who are interested in gaining a 360-degree perspective on their industry might add someone with specialized knowledge of its pulse, like a vendor, client.

It's important to remember that an advisory board is quite different from a board of directors, which is a governance board. Those who serve on an advisory board will often be focusing on strategy, vision, and financial controls (compliance and risk), providing recommendations that may or may not be acted on. They're insulated from the exposure that directors can face since they serve solely in an advisory capacity.

A company's price multiplier can be significantly affected—positively—when both a board of directors and an advisory board are in place. This goes a long way to demonstrate that the owner is interested in having experts weigh in on important decisions as well as long-term strategy that serves to harness human and financial capital while managing risk.

17. Little or No Leverage of Knowledge and Relationships (90%)

The advisory board's cousin, this issue often rears its ugly head when owners are loathe to rely on others who can provide valuable counsel for fear of either losing a measure of control or seeming to be deficient in some area. Let's take a look at the groups that may be ignored—usually to the owner's detriment.

Staff. Some owners operate under the belief that if their employees were smart, they'd have their own companies rather than working for someone else. Yes, there's a certain amount of arrogance in that statement.

Not everyone is cut out to be an entrepreneur. Many may choose to be employees who prefer a steady paycheck, but they can possess significant expertise and experience that when tapped may mean the difference between having a good or a great company. Whether employee input is sought and appreciated is a function of a company's culture. Almost inevitably, that starts with the owner or the executives in the C-suite.

Management. Some people won't offer advice except when asked. This is true of managers who may not want to be perceived as challenging the current wisdom. Management that has the ability to foster ideas and implement them with the requisite approval and consensus will provide more leverage than those who seek safety. Management is the eyes and ears in a company, like staff, but with a broader perspective. Managers may have experiences that should be tapped into on a regular basis. Owners would be wise to ask themselves two questions: Do I ask staff and management for recommendations? Do they feel safe providing responses?

Vendors. Your vendors are obviously selling to more than just one company, so they may have insight into the practices of others in your industry that may not be perceived as a conflict for them to share. If you look at vendors from the perspective of "how much?" instead of "what do you think?" you are missing an opportunity to leverage their industry expertise and contacts.

CASE IN POINT

A seasoned travel agent may book a certain destination, and that's all that person will do. The really good travel agents will want more information: When are you going? What is your budget? What are your ideal activities? What are the ages of the people who will be traveling with you? They want to understand individual preferences so they can customize solutions for the client.

Looking at this good-versus-great situation from a vendor's perspective, would you rather work with a vendor who merely provides you with requested goods or services, or one that suggests ways to improve your business by selecting what they understand what's needed? For instance, a great vendor may recommend you not use service C, when A and B make more sense—and the result of following that advice can be a dramatic improvement in productivity or savings—or both.

When you look at your vendors this way, it becomes easy to differentiate those that are mediocre from those that seek to deliver something unique and specific to their clients' needs. Vendors can be worth their weight in gold, since they often have their ear to the ground—and thus can provide valuable intelligence. Consider the pipe supplier who believes due to a pending embargo that metal used in the pipe may be hard to come by so a larger purchase to cover the disruption may be wise.

It's a common practice for vendors to take clients to lunch, but it can be a good strategy to turn that around and invite valued vendors as a lunch guest. This demonstrates that you see the vendor as an equal and their relationship is valued. By changing the dynamic from servant–master, you may gain significant leverage from your vendors. Failing to do this leaves your vendors wondering why they should do more than just sell—and you've commoditized their offering. What would you do on behalf of this extra treatment by one of your own clients?

Client. How often do you pick the brains of your clients? It can be invaluable to ask if there is something your company can be doing differently—and not just when indicators show you may be losing them. You might be surprised at the return on investment (ROI) you receive when you let clients know you seek a deeper relationship with them—you really want to understand what they're doing and why they're doing it so you can provide assistance in unique ways that might not have previously been considered. This requires a willingness to learn they need another advisor's help.

CASE IN POINT

When a real estate agent or attorney learns a client is selling the commercial building it operates from, rather than just brokering the sale, they should be asking some questions: Does the company need capital? Is this the first indication that the business is winding down? Is there some other liability or opportunity it's considering? When these professionals understand why the sale is occurring, they can help with the transaction at a deeper level.

If you request information from clients, especially what their short- or long-term plans are, you can provide greater value to them than what they pay. Put another way, your fees are the price somebody pays-not your "worth". This is not the same thing as what your product's or service's value might be. The greater the value your clients place on what is delivered, the deeper the relationship can be. Interestingly, a premium is often associated with getting what they need and certainly more than what was expected.

In addition, what you learn from clients can have far-reaching effects on your own business; you may change your strategy or how you deal with other prospect and client companies. It's somewhat rare that a client acknowledges he's not the smartest person in the room. Clients that realize the value of having different perspectives of information—not operating from within a bubble—are going to realize the greatest returns and the lowest risks.

18. Limited or No Tracking of Client Buying Patterns (70%)

We can all stand to learn from giants like Google, Amazon, and Facebook about the power of accumulating significant information from the public based on online behavior. For instance, if you like antique cars, you're probably going online to look at sites featuring them and/or attending events that are related to them. Odds are you will find a banner ad popping up on sites that track the cookies from your computer that relate to antique cars.

As a business owner, would it be helpful to know how much your customers are spending, what they're purchasing, when they make purchases, and in what quantity? This type of information (data analytics) can provide critical real-time insights that influence your growth, especially as it relates to other products and services you may wish to offer, or whether it may be time to change the relationships you have with some customers.

Data analytics can be invaluable for learning about customers' preferences. If someone buys from your company once a year, it will likely provide insufficient information to make any predictions of their future needs or wants, but looking at a larger quantity of buying behavior may suggest some seasonality or opportunities to reach others or trends among groups or locations, as examples.

Companies that don't keep and examine information about their clients won't be able to tell if they're growing, facing hard times, or even experimenting with another vendor. This puts you in a reactionary mode, whereas being proactive—doing something in response to the information you learn—can be a great segue to enhanced customer interaction. You can demonstrate that you're deeply engaged in that relationship.

CASE IN POINT

Five years ago, a metal fabricator added electroplating to its menu of services. If the company was not aware that a longtime metal fabrication customer had a need for electroplating, that would represent a huge missed opportunity. A simple exchange might determine that it would be cost-effective to bundle the two and offer one-stop shopping.

Intelligence gathered that relates to customer buying patterns can be invaluable to any business, but especially one that is intent on making decisions that will support both the owner's and the owner's clients' ongoing growth. It certainly will flag trends that present opportunities and may pose risks if not addressed early on.

19. No Effort to Identify, Protect, and/or Leverage Intangible Assets (80%)

This discussion begins with human capital—the understanding that combining the knowledge and relationships of all employees can provide synergies where 1 + 1 equals much more than 2. Further leverage might be achieved by integrating processes, procedures, technology, and data analysis to result in a combination that provides unique insights and innovation, and more still when the owner's purpose is articulated and passion is pervasive.

Think of a company like Tesla. It's selling a technology platform that happens to be in a car. Some say this is disruptive to the industry; it's never been done before. While tangible assets were certainly involved in the development process, it's the company's intangible assets that conceived of the idea and made it possible to implement. From that came the understanding that batteries were an important resource both for cars as well as to store surplus electricity for homes with solar power generation.

You also must tip your cap to innovators like Apple, which have been able to create a buying cycle that includes demand occurring before a product is even available. Millions of people who purchased an iPhone 6 were eagerly anticipating its delivery. Sure, the phone is a tangible asset for Apple, but the marketing savvy and creativity that give it market-leader status clearly fall in the intangibles bucket.

When it comes to knowledge and secret sauce, you must understand if you have it, and if not, that you need it. Otherwise, your company is destined to be a follower that reacts to the marketplace rather than being dynamic enough to lead by being transformative.

When you've identified your sources of knowledge, it's critical to know how to protect the intellectual property like patents, trade secrets, processes, policies, and procedures with noncompete agreements and golden handcuffs. The protection methods selected will have a measurable impact on risk and the value of the company. Since tangible assets can be seen, that's where most of a company's focus usually is, but it can be argued that the true worth of an organization is going to be found in things that can't be seen: in its intangible assets.

Metrics like finances are easily seen and measured, but an effort to understand what creates value beyond tangible assets is a very worthwhile exercise. Intangibles can be a company's location, its combination of personnel, its standing within the industry or the community, how and why it innovates, and how it sees its role in the broader market ecosystem.

CASE IN POINT

A college student sought to earn extra money beyond the funds his parents provided him, so he and friends bought nuts in bulk and sold them in small packets at local events, making a decent profit. This particular student was a second-generation entrepreneur, so he understood how important it was to innovate to be successful over the long term. He learned that the bits of the nuts that break off during production aren't sold to the public, and a company in France was taking those bits and adding nutrients to them to make a paste that was sent to Third World countries. One pouch of this paste provided the same nutrients and caloric intake as a day's worth of meals.

This intrigued the young entrepreneur, so his company started doing the same thing on a smaller scale. Thus he had a story to tell, and ultimately he placed his company's nuts into Costco, overcoming the product's high commodity factor. Then he had a meeting with Starbucks, which has an expansive vetting process that's almost impossible to pass the first time through—but his company was one of the few that did. Over a five-year period, this young man went from having a nut stand to a 40,000-square-foot facility and a company earning in the mid-eight figures, which he sold before he was 30. This entrepreneur wasn't selling nuts; he was selling a story to which immense intangible value could be affixed. Many young professionals have similar success stories and form the group Young Presidents Organization (YPO).

As you step back and look over an organization with a more studied eye and deeper insights, you can see what creates value. It's not just bricks and mortar, what's on a financial statement, or the assemblage of fixtures and equipment. It's the leverage when these things are a combination—when something much more than just the sum of the parts is created—and almost always includes human capital of relationships and knowledge as well as the purpose and the passion to be something more than simply a company that sells its products and services.

What about the value of giving back, which is certainly an intangible? At many companies the focus is solely on expansion, increasing sales, and making more money, while some organizations seek to make a significant social impact.

It raises eyebrows when valuators look at the financial statement of a company that generates millions of dollars in profits—and little or nothing is going toward educating staff. Conversely, when funds in the range of 1 to 5 percent are earmarked for this purpose, it's clear that ownership recognizes that the company's role is not just to produce products or sell services.

A company has a reason for being when its ROI is substantial enough that it's evident it comes from more than tangible assets. There's even a valuation method—the excess earnings method (ARM-34 in the tax code)—that was put into law in 1934, when the U.S. Treasury sought to collect on value exceeding tangible assets (i.e., the result of speakeasies' ill-gotten gains during the Prohibition era).

The idea was to demonstrate that if earnings return was above and beyond the book value (based on tangible assets), it must be the by-product of something that wasn't tangible, such as distribution channels and relationships. As an example, if you invest in the raw materials that make alcohol and you receive a return higher than your investment, say an 8 percent yield, but the business generates 15 percent, what is the source for the other 7 percent?

You'll generally see a higher yield when intangibles are combined with other assets, and the dollar value of those intangibles directly correlates to the level of risk such as ease of losing goodwill, company trade secrets, or the knowledge or relationship of key staff.

CASE IN POINT

Let's say a company has $3 million in annual revenues, and after expenses its profit is $300,000. Its tangible assets are $400,000 and the yield for its industry is 10 percent ($40,000 in this case), which when deducted from the profits leaves $260,000. If the value of the intangible assets is 4X, adding that figure plus the tangible assets would leave an enterprise value of $1,440,000—of which $1,040,000 (~72-percent) is due to intangible assets. Hence, clearly focusing on intangible assets and risk to them is very important.

The underlying point is that companies that only focus on their tangible assets may be missing out on the significant value resulting from intangible assets—and that is a problem as well as an opportunity, as the correction is not too difficult.

20. Owner, Management, and/or Advisors Have Reached Growth Capacity (80%)

One of the most aggravating things for an owner or a company's management team is to reach a plateau where they experience burnout or frustration such that they're unable to continue to scale the business. This is often a by-product of knowledge and relationship (human capital) limitations, but it doesn't have to be permanent. Overcoming it does require the contemplation of equal parts of humility, desire, and preference and not solely believing the solution is more financial capital.

The first question owners may wish to consider asking themselves is if the reason they entered into business is the same now and what they want it to look like in 5, 10, or 20 years. Many owners have successfully scaled their businesses to $50 million, $100 million, or more, working through the headaches associated with a complex organization. Others have intentionally limited growth, seeking a work–life balance by putting their families first and embracing the idea of having a more intimate staff and operation so the business is not all-consuming.

While some owners may be satisfied operating a business that produces $5 million in annual sales, by and large many want their companies to become 8-, 9-, and 10-figure organizations—but to achieve that growth requires a degree of sophistication where doing so single-handedly is seldom an option.

The owner who walks into a company conference room and prides himself on not being the smartest person in the room is apt to find great success due to that attitude. This type of leader surrounds himself with people who have specialized abilities and competencies, and as the business scales and hits various plateaus, understands a healthy reexamination is necessary to determine who can enhance their abilities through education and when external hires make sense. This same process is also valuable for trusted advisors. The best ones will acknowledge that a client may benefit from a specialization they don't have and might advise a broader, deeper bench at a midsized firm.

CASE IN POINT

A community bank may be an ideal fit for a small metal fabrication shop, but that may not be the case for a $50 million plastics injection molding business with global clients. It may make more sense for the latter organization to be banking with a regional or national institution with overseas relationships.

While passion and purpose can be one explanation of what creates value, along with relationships and knowledge, it's also what limits value creation if it's single-minded and too narrow. Kitty litter was originally a solution for oil spills.

It's common to see owners of $10 million companies being frustrated because their competitors are growing larger and they can't figure out why their own success has plateaued. They often fail to look in the mirror (to realize they control everything, even areas outside their core competency) or see that they're working with B- or C-caliber staff and advisors because they're trying to control costs. They often don't know how to get to the next level, when they need to be working with A-caliber human capital.

It's not possible to climb a ladder that lacks rungs, but that's exactly what many owners try to do. It is possible for most businesses to scale with the right assistance and leverage of human and financial capital, but as these chapters illustrate, it is purposeful and requires a commitment to a different approach to conducting business. Most folks understandably don't want change and are frustrated with untold expenditure of time and resources, realizing they were going down the wrong path or, worse yet, have no idea where they are much less how to get to where they want to go. Answers may be available from groups like Vistage and SCORE or from advisors who have a skillset not found within a company's C-suite.

There really is no limitation with innovation, desire, and leveraging resources as long as there is willingness to sometimes allow others to perform the roles for which they are best suited, which may mean the owner is not always the leader.

21. Absent or Inadequate Insurance (70%)

While similar to #2, no annual review of insurance, this risk is not the same. The #2 risk is whether such reviews by management were done to determine optimal coverage at the best price. This category's focus is to determine how management seeks to evaluate its risk management and exposure and obtain adequate coverage and have policies in place to mitigate risk.

Owners should evaluate every day and long-term risks in a business, as there is an insurance product available for almost every type. Savvy owners and advisors may endeavor to eliminate or minimize some risks, but it's almost impossible to eradicate many of them, so coverage must be prioritized for those that remain. Some of what follows has been mentioned elsewhere, but it bears repeating.

If a business has key staff members whose absence would have a significant impact on company performance, life and disability insurance might make sense. If employees are out in public using equipment or vehicles owned by the company, it's important to ensure adequate coverage is in place not just for loss of or damage to the asset, such as a company vehicle, but for liability as well if the employee ran a red light and caused harm.

If owners wish to attract the highest-caliber people to serve on their board or as company officers, directors and officers insurance is a worthwhile investment, especially if there are multiple shareholders, even when most are related to the founder.

Valuators will take a close look at a company's insurance coverage because if some of the risks that have been identified are not addressed, the price multiple will be negatively affected. This becomes even more germane as a company grows larger and thus faces more exposure to risks with greater financial implications.

22. No Price, Distribution, or Demographics Analysis (80%)

An ongoing issue, and a plight of most trusted advisors, is the ability to make distinctions between price, worth, cost, and value. Clearly, there are those who recognize that their services should command a premium, so they have pricing that allows prospects to self-vet. That old saying is true: "If you have to ask how much, you probably can't afford it."

While my economist friends may feel I'm oversimplifying, the intention is to provide a layperson explanation. *Cost* is that which is considered and the benefit that a best alternative would have given. *Price* is the amount paid in return for goods or services, whereas *value* is the measure of the benefit believed to be provided by a good or service and the amount one is willing to pay, which may or may not be its *worth*.

If users of services don't understand the distinction between precision and technical mastery, average consumers will first look at cost. The burden is on business owners and advisors to provide an admonition that price alone is an inadequate measure of something's or someone's value.

As shared earlier, if the hourly rate or percent of assets under management is the common benchmark, then no value may be perceived beyond that which is paid.

CASE IN POINT

If two individuals offer professional services and one charges $200 an hour while the other charges $300, at a minimum curiosity dictates what distinguishes the $300 from the $200 level of services. It very well might be that the higher-priced professional has considerably greater wisdom and may take only a quarter of the time it would take the lower-cost provider to complete the same project. Thus, if the lower-priced individual would bill 40 hours, while the higher-priced person would only bill for 10, the actually amount paid for the $200 per hour is $5,000 greater ($8,000 versus $3,000).

Unfortunately, few owners and advisors do a good job articulating their value proposition.

The best practice when dealing with clients or prospects is to prepare people to distinguish you from competitors because of your abilities—so the first line of questioning doesn't involve cost, but whether you have the solution to their problem. You must change the conversation from "how much" to "how good," and understand that most people will be able to discern whether you have the wisdom they need. Perhaps an inquiry like this might help: "Before we discuss your investment in our services, may I ask you a few questions to have a better sense of the issues you have and how best to serve you?"

If a client needed heart surgery, would the prospective patient ask the surgeon first how much it's going to cost before querying the success rate for doing the procedure? Would the patient rather have someone operate with an 85 percent success rate over hundreds of cases (one-third above the industry norm), many of which are quite difficult, or someone who has a 100 percent success rate but has only performed one similar surgery?

Unless true differentiation is achieved, the owner and advisors are doing a disservice to their true worth with a significant risk of becoming commoditized in the market. That's right—an owner's actions, or lack of action, may put the thing he values the most at risk.

It is important for owners to review price, worth, cost, and value on an ongoing basis. Their knowledge of price elasticity and equilibrium—known to laypeople as supply and demand—will go a long way toward ensuring the success of the business. Consider the value of water. Wouldn't it be more sought after in an area experiencing a drought, as opposed to an area experiencing a typhoon? The savvy owner knows prices may be raised in the former instance, while they may need to lower them in the latter case.

In simple terms, think about needing to fill a car with fuel. Would it be worth it to drive several miles to save 5 cents a gallon or 20 cents a gallon? Metrics in this example are relevant when it comes to balancing price with issues like time and distance. It also helps to understand what market is being pursued. For instance, the market share Kia pursues is unlikely to be the same as Ferrari—they clearly have different price points. Kia's focus is on economy and value, and it seeks to attract many buyers, while Ferrari will have fewer buyers, but offers a perceived value based on appearance and performance.

On a more micro-level, if you're selling something for $100 and have a certain number of customers making purchases at that price, what percentage would stop buying if the price were raised to $110? If that 10 percent increase results in the loss of just 5 percent of customers, that increase might makes sense—assuming the same quantity of purchases are made and no fewer than 9 percent less. Conversely, if sales growth has been limited or flat, it may be the result of price point sensitivity. If the price were reduced from

$100 per unit to $90 and profits declined from 12 to 10 percent (17% decline [1 – (10/12)]) but volume increased as a result of 30 percent higher sales, that drop also might make sense, as overall sales and profits grew.

Without market testing, there is seldom any consideration as to who the client is and whether multiple clients exist who would pay a different price point based on real or perceived value. If this type of analysis is not routinely done, then pricing may be based upon what the competition is charging—and that can be a recipe for disaster if it has lower operating overhead or deep pockets whereby it can temporarily lower prices with the aim of forcing a competitor's financial ruin in the short term, while generating more profits in the long run.

CASE IN POINT

Many valuators choose to perform early-stage company appraisal reports (409A) when the company's low-paid staff incentive is high upside if stock values in their companies have a meteoric rise. This appraisal sector has lowered its prices from $5,000 to below $2,000 to attract clients from low-priced competitors. What they've failed to consider is that they need to complete 2.5 more engagements just to get to the same level of revenues they were at a year or two ago. They are dead men walking as would be any business that does not think through the short and long term of increased competition. So why would they continue to undercut their fees? They may have not found an alternative to replace the service and hope that subsequent engagements from these fee-for-service clients will have a higher fee based upon complexity of the companies when reappraised. Hope is not a strategy.

Those valuators, and many other business owners, could benefit from relying on the thrive (versus survive) method of pricing. Starbucks does; its direct cost per unit of coffee is—wait for it—may only be 20 cents a cup, but it's certainly charging much more and customers are gladly paying for the opportunity to enjoy the Starbucks coffee experience. There's little doubt that significant market research went into determining its price points, and an ongoing analysis occurs as well to ensure the prices set remain palatable to the market. Is this being done with your business?

Now let's turn to the cousin of price, which is distribution. When finished goods are sold to customers, margins are affected by shipping costs and returns that may vastly impact gross margin. For instance, a company that sells a lightweight item like feather down vests is going to face a different shipping issue than one that sells steel pipe.

Regardless of what is sold, when one considers overall market penetration and physical market size, margins can be significantly impacted the farther away clients may be. Thus, the question becomes one of whether to compete with geographically remote businesses after shipping costs are added to the equation. This is as true for hamburger chains as it is for providers of asphalt.

The issue of distance is also relevant when it comes to businesses that attract customers their location. For instance, a yoga studio needs to know most clientele is going to come from within a three-mile radius. As a result, the owner needs to understand the demographics of the area: ages, incomes, whether the population growth is going up or down, whether it is local residents or office workers nearby, and so forth. This type of analysis is a necessity, because location can have a real important impact on the viability of a business—and the market is not static. Also, if a local area is working well, it may make sense to open a second location elsewhere with similar characteristics.

Most owners are aware they have two options available to achieve significant growth: offering new products or penetrating new markets. It's something owners who want viable long-term business growth must consider and act upon.

Businesses that understand how significantly such issues influence margins may choose to deal with that reality in different ways. Manufacturers and distributors may decide to have multiple locations so they can ship to customers from the closest facility. Construction companies usually operate close to an aggregate source (a quarry), because while the cost of materials is low, the shipping cost is high. They can ensure their competitiveness by being close to quarries or establishing locked-in contracts to hedge price fluctuations.

In the absence of these types of analyses, businesses risk seeing a reduction in their profits even when there is an increase in sales. Both owners and advisors share the burden to examine these very real issues, but unfortunately learning the hard way tends to occur. When there are clear and detailed responses to this type of inquiry to address opportunities and risks, the value is likely to be greater.

23. No Supply Chain Analysis (90%)

The cousin of the above considerations of price, market, and distribution is supply chain analysis. Many businesses rely on outside sources. It's not as simple as purchasing X as a finished good or raw material, preparing it for sale, and then selling it by a certain date. In any business, cash flow is king, and the amount of cash on hand is even more critical for businesses that must carry some degree of inventory, which is why quantity on hand and timing are crucial elements.

Many businesses have failed after receiving a big order because the time between purchasing the materials and paying for the labor and delivery far outstripped their ability to keep up with costs before being paid by the customer. They didn't have enough capital to offset late or uneven customer payments. This ties in nicely with the admonitions of having lines of credit or the often high costs to use factor financing by collateralizing accounts receivable and receiving immediate cash for a percentage of the amount believed by the funding source to be collectable at interest rates that can easily be double digit.

There are things a company can do to minimize its financial exposure, including analysis to manage, commonly known as cash management, which was discussed earlier. This can be a sophisticated issue that may be beyond some, especially those who've moved up the ladder to a controller position to their current responsibilities without mastering cash flow. For instance, it's critical to know the quick ratio—have an idea of the number of days it takes for accounts receivable to become cash plus the number of days allowed for accounts payable and contrast that to the money that's tied up in inventory.

It's not enough to know that an order is coming in; savvy owners will think about how they can tweak performance to their financial advantage. One way of doing this is depending on relationships with suppliers, requesting that they carry materials until the last minute—a measure known as JIT (just in time). Other ways are really zeroing in on particular projects, not tying up capacity by ensuring the production line is ready to go, shifting gears or double shifts if necessary to provide quicker delivery, or batching items to get incremental improvements. Lean management, as reflected by Six Sigma practices, can provide significant benefits.

Technology evolves rapidly, so it's necessary to make critical decisions regarding lead times when producing a specialty item like processors. Significant coordination is required within and between organizations and throughout the ecosystem from vendor to shipper to warehousing to shipper to client. The more relationships with suppliers and bankers are managed, for example, so they really understand your business and your exposure, the better off the company, such as when securing a letter of credit.

For projects that include a variety of disciplines, such as construction, it's important that all the parties be well sequenced. It can be an art to ensure the most efficient allocation of time between securing permits, bulldozing, installing electrical and plumbing components, pouring concrete, and so on. When done well, it emulates an orchestra producing music from various instruments, with each instrument played how and when required. The reverse can be a horrible racket from bad timing, resulting in inefficiency that will be reflected in the bottom and top line. While clearly there is a financial metric, the risk metric is the ability to manage the supply chain.

24. No or Minimal Processes or Procedures (65%)

It may have occurred to the reader that many of the risks and certainly governance, relationships, and knowledge are very central to harnessing human capital that will create additional equity value.

However, nothing says a broken culture like continually hearing, "How or why do we do this?" from employees. This usually happens due to turnover or existing preferences that may or may not make sense or differ between parties performing the same or similar functions. And just because it's always been done a certain way in the past doesn't mean that's the best way now or in all circumstances.

A healthy dose of occasionally asking, "What if we did it this way?" is important, because, as already mentioned, companies and the environments in which they operate are not static. It's beneficial to most organizations to have an ongoing review of processes and procedures that may be outdated or redundant. For example, when customers place orders or request services, what process ensues? Is it dependent on the type of customer or the type of request? If there are elements common to most requests, how can they be standardized, creating greater efficiencies and less redundancy?

CASE IN POINT

Redundancy is rampant in the healthcare industry, since patients may need to provide their medical history, insurance information, and purpose for a visit repeatedly—at patient intake, with the billing department, to the nurse and then the doctor, to the specialist, to the insurance company, and so on. This is highly inefficient and prone to entry error (not to mention frustrating for the patient).

Whether a professional services firm or a manufacturing company, understanding how to facilitate configuration and efficiency without a loss of service or quality is paramount. Using a manufacturer as an example, if raw materials are being received on one side of the facility, but they're placed into machinery that's all the way on the other side, doesn't it make sense to move the receiving area closer to where materials are needed? You'd lessen the time and resources required to move the materials from point A to point B.

Configuration done successfully involves seeing what parts of any process can be replicated by equipment (which never gets fatigued and may lessen errors) and where people are needed. Constant review leads to thinking to determine whether this is as good as it gets; however, the owner may wish to consult an efficiency or expense expert to find more efficient, effective and cheaper ways.

When companies report and record how and why things are done in a certain way, they sometimes discover they've created a trade secret—a more effective way that is disruptive to the market. This occurred with Amazon, which started as an online bookseller and now offers close to one-stop shopping and has more in common with eBay than with brick-and-mortar retail operations.

Amazon minimizes what it warehouses, and often realizes that it makes more sense to have items drop-shipped by sellers, so it merely serves as the middleman. Its distribution channel is more efficient than Walmart's, for example, because it doesn't have any stores to worry about. And, because it has warehouses in strategic locations, it's even disruptive to FedEx; depending on when an order is placed, it may be delivered that same day.

You're risking quite a bit if you're not constantly reviewing your processes and procedures—or there is no prescribed way of doing things. The "same old, same old" often creates inconsistency and is often very inefficient, especially as staff turnover occurs. These human capital issues, when addressed, lower risk and increase company value.

25. No Stated Performance Standards (70%)

One of the most common laments of personnel is that they receive infrequent feedback about how they're doing and it's more common to be "caught" doing something the wrong way than to be praised for doing something in an imaginative or efficient way. This is as true for those in management as it is for people who work on the line in a manufacturing plant. It's not a good idea to live by the philosophy "If you're not doing well enough, we'll let you know."

The more an organization can communicate when good is not good enough and great is rewarded—and by what metrics—the more it will impact a firm's culture, the motivation of its staff, and the desire to take well-reasoned risks.

Metrics are not designed for the sole purpose of a bureaucracy that finds value in standardization, but for departments, business units, divisions, and enterprises to determine how people are doing as individuals and as part of a collective.

Since human capital often provides the greatest ROI and the highest intangible asset value, lacking measures makes it almost imperative to leverage innovation and performance.

Understanding individuals and what motivates them is highly relevant. There are hundreds of stories that involve top sales performers being promoted to sales manager and the result is both the newly anointed managers and those who report to them being wholly dissatisfied. In cases like that, it was assumed that the salesperson would want to move into management to remain upwardly mobile—but it was never considered that the individual was ill-equipped for the new responsibility or not interested in having a more administrative, hierarchical role that provides more direct reports, more headaches, and often less compensation they can control.

Any good owner will understand that different things motivate people differently. For example, a professional who's married with no kids may want higher compensation even if it requires more travel, while a single parent may desire flextime.

Although this risk is about measuring, reviewing, reporting, and revising performance standards, it's worth remembering that there are few examples other than perhaps the military and some specialized functions where standardization is always preferred. As such, that leaves owners with plenty of things to contemplate with respect to handling their human capital, including:

- What happens when someone comes up with new ideas?
- How are cost center departments evaluated versus revenue-generating departments?
- Are bonuses only paid to the sales team?
- How can employees be incentivized to perform at the top of their game?

Organizations that are oriented toward being entrepreneurial can realize significant value from rewarding their employees for innovation or when they find and reduce risk.

26. No Consideration of Synergistic Growth Opportunities and Challenges (80%)

Through the prism of starting and growing a business, first for work income and then for wealth income (owner, then investor value creation), organic growth tends to be the principal consideration. As each year goes by, owners should have in the back of their mind: build (more organic growth because it is at acceptable levels and duration) or buy (a new market that may be ready to go on day 1 and a smart investment if the company didn't pay too much and terms were advantageous). Despite the availability of bankers and of market opportunities, very few owners consider, much less actually acquire, a complementary company or divest a noncore business unit.

Yet some of the most successful businesses are those that look at opportunistic enterprises for acquisition. Owners of these companies understand that a successful post merger integration can allow company size to be scaled quite rapidly—with the operative word being *successful*.

Since most every business has tangible and intangible assets—one of the major focuses of this book—as cultures and operations are combined, the foremost thought should be achieving the optimal results through the nexus of human and financial capital. This requires metrics; it's not enough to pencil out the deal and examine where cost and expense reductions and new revenues will be derived. Undoubtedly, this is among the motives of the acquirer—recognizing that two CFOs and many administrative personnel will be redundant, as may be occupancy, legal services, accounting services, and so forth.

It's understandable that this is where most of the conversation goes—as the measures to be taken are often self-evident—but as has been mentioned previously, the greatest leverage (highest return) for a company is almost always achieved through its intangible assets. Realizing this may be the difference between additional successful acquisitions and having paid too much when the synergy anticipated unravels and occasionally ends up in litigation between buyer and seller and/or with one or more advisors.

The flipside is not only should the captain of the ship (the owner) be navigating to safe harbors, but the company may also benefit from first considering revocable strategic relationships and joint ventures where revenues, expenses, risks, and opportunities are shared—but each organization remains independent. If successful, the relationship can be more formalized and larger enduring engagements can be pursued.

In the same vein, owners may wish to contemplate private equity group (PEG) or the patient capital of family office (FO) funding—debt or equity capital in which they acquire a noncontrolling or controlling interest. The difference between the two options of a PEG versus an FO is holding period and the degree of involvement by the funding source. Their involvement can be a great thing, as they often have access to the knowledge and relationships the business owner may not. An infusion of financial and human capital can certainly accelerate growth—and the value of the company—establishing additional options to remove some chips from the table (i.e., a partial liquidity event) while maintaining a leadership function.

Companies can put themselves at risk by failing to consider options other than operating as a standalone entity simply because they are unfamiliar with the opportunities that often abound. An equation of 1 + 1 = a result that's greater than 2 should be a given.

Knowledge and relationship intangibles have significant value to a company looking for opportunities beyond simply relying on organic growth. A-class trusted advisors may be the best source of counsel when considering a divesture, merger, or acquisition, since they have more concern about client success than fear of losing relationships, and thus may be as proactive as you need them to be. Companies that have had experience with successful mergers and acquisitions integration or divestures will tend to have higher price multiples.

27. No or Minimal Cross-Training of Personnel/ Redundancy of Key Functions (80%)

Remember: the more efficient > the better the cash flow > the lower the risk > the higher the price multiple = the higher the value of the company.

If an owner is contemplating a business transformation, wouldn't it make sense to have the timeline and understand the role each constituent (key staff, advisors, bankers, vendors, and clients as well as possibly family members) plays?

Actions that are communicated, prioritized, aligned, and coordinated among staff should provide the business owner with the best and most timely options. Perhaps understated, but *in order for owners to build value they must think like investors who are seeking the highest possible return, which means not only above industry average growth and profitability, but reduction of risks that will in turn increase equity value*. This also includes leverage of staff to pursue seen and unseen opportunities.

If success or failure often hinges on staff caliber, perceiving any function as mundane is a disservice to both employees and the value of the company. For example, what happens when "the girl" who's on vacation is the only one who knows where the keys to the cabinet are or what documents are needed for a meeting? While a bit humorous, this type of situation often indicates something greater is at play.

In professional services, such as a law firm, how are executive assistants, paralegals, legal secretaries, administrative aides, and even first-year attorneys exposed to different practice areas? How are they treated? How are they able to show the potential for being promoted?

While specialization has its merits, the value of having a diverse and broadened perspective, as well as an understanding of how a particular role affects the department, business unit, and organization, should not be understated. This issue is found in many industries, including construction, where tradespeople who pour and form concrete are also trained in bricklaying, doubling their ability to add value, as does the plumber who is also trained in Heating, Ventalation and Air-Conditioning ("HVAC").

For manufacturing plant employees, broadening their skills and having a better understanding of how functions relate to one another may motivate staff to perform at a higher level and offer insights and suggestions on ways to improve their slice of the operation—which may result in them being groomed for supervisory roles. Think about the benefits of switching people on a line every six months; this often increases operational efficiency and can lead to bumps in salary for those who demonstrate mastery of multiple functions.

CASE IN POINT

A company decides to have its plant supervisor shadow the company general manager. The goal is for each of these individuals to gain a better idea of what the other does and the challenges and bottlenecks they confront. When key staff are able to swap roles or cover for each other, this type of redundancy reduces risk.

When companies cross-train employees and groom them for new roles, it can identify education gaps that may be filled with courses such as finance for nonfinancial professionals. These types of organizations are often more dynamic, while in the absence of such activity, organizations become robotic—employees know that getting raises is a function of tenure rather than anything they do to improve their standing. The former behavior raises company value. The latter reinforces taking limited person risk.

28. No Shareholder/Key Person/Buy–Sell Agreements, They're Not Followed, or They're Underfunded or Unfunded (80%)

When businesses are just starting out, owners, rightfully, focus on saving money and only spending on items that are necessary to keep the business stable and growing. At times, it's not easy to understand the business world or the owners' roles within it—so some rely on seeing things through the eyes of an experienced attorney or accountant. Why is this relevant to the topic at hand?

Let's take a simple example: A founder makes an initial investment of $100,000 in his start-up business. He decides not to treat that investment as a loan, but instead receives equity (shares in the company) in exchange for the funds. The owner usually assumes she'll be able to convert the initial investment back to cash quickly and without cost—but that is seldom the case.

As the owner's efforts and funds go toward both working capital and to develop brand awareness as well as pay for operating expenses, the owner's hope is that a reasonable level of return on this active investment is the result, which is understandably in most cases more risky than investing in a seasoned public company; hence, the expectation of a higher return (above just paying a salary at market rate for the CEO function). He is an owner-investor, officer, and employee. This seems evident, but as will be explained shortly, add a few additional investors who are not officers or employees or officers who are not investors or employees who are investors and who has what rights can get convoluted right quick. If allowed to fester, great litigations ensue.

So it's time to revisit tangible and intangible asset investment.

Tangible assets (inventory, equipment, etc.) are acquired. Income they generate ***must exceed*** the risk associated with converting cash into these assets; otherwise, the investment (even if profits are generated) makes no sense, as it could have been deployed to a less risky endeavor with the same level of return such as real estate or a portfolio of public companies (mutual fund/ETF, etc.).

As more intangible assets (developed and evolving client relationships and knowhow) are created, the return on the nature of these investments should make sense, which, if all goes as desired, will exceed the level of tangible asset level returns ***and*** the level of return of public companies. This is because the level of risk of many private companies tends to be perceived as greater (ye ole risk-versus-reward equation) than that of public companies. The desired result when combined with time and talent should make the initial $100,000 worth much more. If the yield is $30,000 after working capital, capital expenditures, and debt service and before taxes, it is 30 percent. If growth is 6 percent, then total return is 36 percent, which implies that the business, if operating the same way, will double the investment in two years' time, which isn't too shabby.

What's often missing from this scenario is an understanding of the real value of the owner's time and knowledge (sweat-equity investment). This becomes even more convoluted when more founders or equal owners are involved, especially when some aren't involved in the business and others are.

The author has been involved in litigation when a CEO can't seem to understand as the 40 percent shareholder why he was removed by the "outside" investor who held the 60 percent interest because the agreement or bylaws provided the 60 percent holder the right to do so. Conversely, why the 5 percent interest held by the employee sues the founder because he is paying himself an excessive salary and making no distributions to the 5 percent owner of equity, not just the employee.

Add family to this powder keg and really see the fireworks.

In addition, a review of the relative merits of debt versus equity funding or doing a combination of the two is usually overlooked as a business gets going—but down the line that can become relevant as the company gets its legs and strives to scale. There are also legal and tax considerations, such as fiduciary duty of controlling equity to others without control (minority interest holders).

When transferring equity to a partner or key employee(s) is contemplated, in a perfect world, a handshake understanding is made and everyone agrees on the percentage to be received. The issue should be the size, the rights, and the value of these interests. The author has written numerous chapters and white papers on governance and valuing of equity interests as well as reviewed thousands of agreements and bylaws to know that the most elegant documents are loved by the authors and seldom read by those whose actions it governs.

Many agreements oversimplify how equity value will be determined, and while it may seem potentially advantageous to take a percentage of book value or use some rule of thumb as a proxy for an arm's length equity sale. It's just not a very good idea to save fees on the intellectual rigor an equity valuation provides. The reality is that in most jurisdictions, the legal standard of value prevails, often beyond any legal agreements. If an independent and qualified third party wasn't retained to opine market value based on sound valuation principles, at some point in the future this can come back and be a significant problem that was preventable.

An example of what not to do in this instance may be to establish an ESOP for the wrong reasons. Let's say an accountant is attempting to help a long-standing client owner realize some of the cash value of his company—partial liquidity. As such, the accountant has opined a value that may be very favorable to the business owner. The owner's duty of care (especially if also the ESOP trustee) is to the participants who are now the new shareholders represented by the ESOP trustee as well as his being the likely controlling shareholder and company officer.

This can manifest as follows: The value may have been overstated, which is beneficial to the owner when the liability (debt) was incurred to fund his equity stake. However, subsequently the value is reduced, which may more accurately reflect market value to the detriment of the ESOP participants-investors-employees. This could be construed as self-dealing, with the aid of a trusted advisor—unwittingly or not—and is a ticking time bomb of litigation, as the participants are immediately underwater on debt for equity that they will not fully realize until they become vested five years later.

The overarching point is any buy–sell or shareholder agreement should always be in place to memorialize the equity holders' intents, especially if an unplanned event occurs, such as disability, death, divorce, and even more frequently, a dispute among partners or shareholders.

A big difference in equity value may be based on how the agreement provisions are drafted between determining the fair market value of the operating business (usually referred to as 100% of equity) and the equity held in the business. It is often thought that it is simply applying the percent of interest held as the numerator, such as What is 10 percent of a $10 million valuation? It's $1,000,000, referred to as fair value in the valuation community—a pro rata amount without applying a premium or discounts that may be attributable to the equity held based upon its rights and economic benefits and the rights and economic benefits of other equity holders.

Historically, it's almost always the value to a notional third party, not what one or more specific parties believe. This is wholly different than determining the fair market value of equity held by a specific partner or shareholder, which will usually be adjusted by the premium if control and impairments associated with a private company equity having limited liquidity and possibly little or no control.

Unfortunately, as mentioned previously, it's commonplace that a trusted advisor, like an attorney, accountant, wealth advisor, or life insurance provider, will establish the value of equity despite having no formal expertise in valuation. This was done with the use of software with limited inputs and all kinds of disclosures that it should not be relied upon solely by the user. When this occurs, an owner will likely infer that the process is uncomplicated and not worthy of a financial investment in an experienced valuation professional. The cost for the service in a subsequent dispute is far greater.

This all is further proven by two compelling facts:

1. A great majority of buy–sell agreements remain unfunded, meaning there has been no cross-purchase of insurance policies to cover the value of the equity held. For instance, if a company has two equal shareholders and the equity is valued at $20 million, it stands to reason that each would insure the other for $10 million.
2. Noncompliance with buy–sell agreement provisions is rampant, including failing to adhere to the provision that provides for annual value updates. Further, if two parties can't agree on a value, agreement provisions usually dictate they may each retain an appraiser—and should the value of those two reports differ by more than 10 percent, a third

appraiser would be selected, and whichever figure comes closest establishes the value. Wouldn't it have made more sense that both parties agree to a single business appraiser in a joint retention to mitigate against the claim of bias?

Looking at the financial and market realities of public companies, if it's accepted that over even one month's time, an actively traded stock could result in a company's value changing by more than 15 percent, then what is the practical reality of a provision where a 10 percent spread of a private company equates to +/–5 percent? The 10 percent spread provision suggests a degree of precision that is seldom found in private capital markets.

CASE IN POINT

A company owner wants $22 million for his business, while the buyer wants to pay $18 million. That represents a $4,000,000 (plus or minus 10%), which equates to a 20 percent spread. Given larger public companies can have value changes due to market volatility routinely of plus or minus 15 percent, it stands to reason the drafters of such agreements may require a better understanding of the vagaries of company and market-level influences that could cause company values to be at similar or greater amounts.

Often law addresses advocacy issues where whether one party loses is not germane as long as it is not the client retaining counsel. However, the optics of an investor is that at any given time, based upon the current and anticipated risk and liquidity calculus, is there an alternative that presents itself that is more favorable? This type of investment decision occurs daily in the millions of buy–sell trades in the public securities market.

What makes the private company somewhat different is that in private capital markets it is generally understood that the company is less liquid, so the benefits of buying and holding for a sufficient period to realize a certain beneficial return become paramount. However, this investor lens often devolves into the owner of today wanting yield (income) and/or compensation for the work of the officer. The three hats of investor, owner, and officer/employee become blurred and with the machinations of an agreement making what is supposed to look like a duck (walks and quacks) end up looking like a platypus. Hence, the agreement often confuses causation and correlation with the intention of highlighting what is supposedly concurrence by parties entering into the agreement.

It's very common through the eyes of an investor that one party believes an opportunity is greater than the other party does. It's critical to revisit such agreements, since, when they were drafted, the company may have been in the mode of conserving capital and had nominal value—but if 5 or 10 years have passed, the situation may be quite different.

It's the responsibility of the parties involved in the agreement and their trusted advisors to ensure three things:

1. The agreement is funded.
2. The equity valuation is accurate.
3. The agreement is periodically updated since the market and company are dynamic.

Many things can have a significant effect on equity valuation, including a significant uptick in profits, the loss of a key client, a dramatic change in interest rates, or another type of market disruption. If any of those things hold true, then using the last valuation and price multiple despite circumstances having changed is neither desirable nor fair.

As previously noted, issues like value are always exacerbated when an unplanned event occurs—disability, death, divorce, or dispute—so when determining the level of risk a company faces, the presence and provisions of and adherence to an agreement may have a significant impact on equity value.

29. Lack of Advisor/Staff Alignment (80%)

One of the reasons this book was written is the frequency with which business owners and their families fall victim to the disconnect between their wants and needs and the advice or lack thereof from trusted advisors.

Think of a human dilemma—where an individual making a significant life-changing decision seeks counsel from 10 people he trusts. Invariably, he'll receive up to 10 different opinions, which, in a perfect world, he overlays, reconciles, and then acts accordingly, based on emotional and factual input. And, what if the luxury of ruminating does not exist due to a crisis?

Contrast this to the plight of the business owner who's overwhelmed by information and endeavoring to get ahead. He's mistrustful of advice that may at first blush be perceived as self-serving to the advisor giving it—but he may not fully understand the context or language that's technical in nature, concepts that come naturally to the advisor.

Then, amplify that by advice received from advisors from different disciplines. It's the proverbial scenario where the owner can't tell if it's an elephant because one advisor describes the tusk, another describes the tail, and a third the trunk. A common reaction to this is to either ignore the advice or defer the decision—neither of which may be optimal or preferable.

The problem is compounded when the owner understands the advice he's receiving, but what he's hearing from different advisors may differ with respect to the direction suggested. Why is this so common? Advice is usually sought as a reaction to some event, so some context might be lost. In addition, many owners have a disdain to pay for advice—especially when they may not know if it's good or poor advice, particularly when the result or consequence may have a lag time of years (or if ever). For instance, how can an owner tell how good an insurance policy is if he's never made a claim?

Why is advisor alignment so relevant? Imagine the efficiency and effectiveness created if all of a company's trusted advisors sat around a table with the owner, addressing a clear agenda of items on which guidance was sought. Everyone would be weighing in on the same issues, and any misunderstandings or clarifications could be addressed right there. That kind of alignment creates leverage—everyone is rowing in the same direction at the same time. And, its up-front cost is a lot less than the cost associated with doing business as usual—in other words, ad hoc (different speeds and directions).

One of the primary reasons why ultra-affluent family businesses establish family offices is so they receive and leverage dedicated tax, legal, and financial advice in real time from people they hire full-time. When this doesn't occur, many issues that began as technical concerns exacerbate latent human conflicts that are best resolved by family business advisors.

It's not the intention of any trusted advisor to be unclear or disruptive; nevertheless, serving multiple clients or having multiple practice priorities creates greater risk (that of many masters and dilution as well as timeliness of attention) to the owner—which will be considered when valuing his company and advising on how to be more opportunistic and leverage human capital.

30. No Risk Identification, Measurement, Management, and Mitigation (90%)

Consider the process of an experienced business investor. She is often looking for the best value based on risk appetite over the short, middle, and long term. The fundamental premise of business investing—buy low, sell high—really comes down to risk considerations of which there can be hundreds of factors and assumptions.

Due diligence is a process that commonly occurs when businesses change hands. While it's quite effective in uncovering some financial, tax, and legal issues, operational and cultural risks are two examples that can be quantified and are clearly observable, yet are often not part of the due diligence equation: an example of which is personalities and skills of key officers, executives, and midlevel managers as well as the culture they have created.

In addition, it's insufficient to just identify risk; both the degree to which it can be measured and its impact are highly relevant—as evidenced by the pages of this chapter alone. More importantly, because it can be identified and measured, it stands to reason that it should be managed and prioritized to allow for the most effective operations. Value is enhanced and risk is lowered when ownership and officers select the right indices to measure and manage.

The fact that this chapter is lengthy in comparison to the balance of this book is not by accident. Also, note the number of risk items that concern human capital, which will seldom be found on financial statements. Hence, consider just how relevant governance, relationships, and knowledge are to the constituents of every business's ecosystem. This chapter's intent is to provide insights to risk identification.

However, measurement is why most business valuation professionals or others are retained. It's hoped this chapter dispels the notion that all practitioners are the same and there are limitations on software-driven value-in-a-box alternatives.

While the opinions expressed in this book are my own and may not reflect those of the organizations with which I am affiliated, I believe them to be factual and accurate. As this chapter was written, finding an eloquent and elegant way to express observations born of 25+ years of full-time experience seemed elusive.

Most are familiar with the notion of 10,000 hours—the duration it takes most to achieve a degree of mastery. In large part, this is why the American Society of Appraisers is often considered the valuation industry gold standard because of their requirement of five years of full-time appraisal work plus a log of each engagement; coursework and associated competency and standards exams; and a demonstration report reviewed by two seasoned ASA credentialed business appraisers to be considered for the Accredited Senior Appraiser (ASA) designation. It could be argued that this is a floor and not a ceiling.

For almost every business industry, there are numerous data sources that provide norms based upon company revenue and/or asset size. The fact the various sources don't always report the same results indicates the need for more rigorous scrutiny or requisite intellectual rigor to address the reasons why for each resource's limitations and strengths. In part, these differences are the result of the sources from which the information is received, ranging from business intermediaries to banks to tax returns reported to the IRS.

Each data source has its limitations and is subject to some skewing based upon the quality of data and how it is grouped, averaged, and reported. So, reconciling a company being compared to the data requires some professional seasoning. Here is the thing: There is nominal discussion by any of the national business appraisal bodies as to the use and reporting of such data. Given the heavy reliance to compare and reconcile, this can artificially set the bar too low for practitioners who are performing engagements part-time.

Past industry surveys suggest that most practitioners performing valuation reports complete two to four annually with most reports taking between 20 and 40 hours to prepare. Assuming the midpoint of each metric, this means an average of 90 hours spent per annum by the majority of business valuation practitioners. This is also the reason that certain professions that dabble in valuation are challenged in this book. It's not because the professions or individuals are bad, but "buyer beware" is not a message that adequately gets to the end users of work product.

There is good reason to pause as the aforementioned annual expenditure would suggest it would take a part-timer a lifetime (and then some) for the level of mastery, assuming the 10,000-hour floor. How can this be? Few part-time valuators have their work product challenged; yet, nothing fine-tunes work like having it challenged in litigation or audit and examined for any flaws or leaps of faith (opinions borne on layers of assumptions or none at all).

The point is that risk measurement requires a significant investment in and deep understanding of comparative data and the weighting of relevance of each data point. So, while software-driven results can generate some stellar illustrations, it is hard to conceive the thousands of permutations of algorithms needed for each industry for the nuanced issues of each company that define the levels of risks associated within its ecosystem.

A very simple example is the "advertising" expense line item. It seems innocuous enough, but how is it reported by a company? Does the company group business development as part of its advertising expense? Is printing of sales material treated as advertising? What about lunch with prospects or attendance of tradeshows? What about different year-to-year reporting of expenses? Is there any correlation with revenue growth? What is the lag time between prospect brand awareness and the first client-billable event, especially if it exceeds a year? How does this expense as a percentage of revenues differ for the number of years in business? Do low advertising expenses compared to the norm mean strong company or individual staff goodwill or owner bias not wishing to spend the money? Do market areas differ and how much does local competition impact the annual amount expensed?

So, if a company generates $100 million in sales and lists $1 million in advertising, can the 1 percent of sales investment be understood and weighed against the relevance of a 0.8 percent industry norm for the company's size? What happened with sales growth when the amount expensed by the company was 0.6 percent or 1.2 percent of revenues? While counterintuitive, most companies cut back on advertising when the market and sales soften as it is treated as a variable expense. Does this mean management-ownership really does not have a handle on this expense? Is this an indicator of other issues, or that its relatively small size has nominal bearing on economic benefit and risk of the overall company?

Consider all the line items reported on financial documents versus all the other nonreported items addressed previously (and hundreds more not discussed). Any one item (or a series of small items) may be highly relevant. If any or all are improperly examined or omitted from consideration, the result may be a skewed risk and performance profile.

The point is that the more complex the company and the situation, the more relevant the ability of the professional, like a physician, to locate, distinguish, and diagnose the cause and effect of one or more indices. It would be absurd to tell a physician, just limit your examination to one possible symptom, when a broader examination may be needed to identify the reason for the patient visit. This includes the confirmation that everything appears okay and sleep and rest is all that is required.

Then there is risk management. There are many business advisors who rely on either "proven systems" or professional opinions to serve clients. In the medical example provided earlier, in the absence of benchmarks, it is hard to trust the results and the cause(s) leading to them. Was weight loss due to diet or exercise or a combination of the two? If the combination, how much did one activity influence the other? Some may suggest, if the weight loss occurred, why does it matter? The reply, not meant to be snarky, is, What was learned from the past experience should weight gain return?

From a strategic value architect perspective, this is where a blend of skills in business operations, strategy, and finance may be most useful. By identifying resource gaps and leveraging time as well as human and financial capital to address areas of misalignment, management can be the steward toward significant value building and creation. Having the benchmarks and the playbook is the beginning. Crafting the strategic plan and executing on it once metrics are in place is Nirvana to owners who have struggled not being able to get from "here" to "there."

Risk management execution is key, which requires intake and reasonable concurrence from all constituents to ensure that all are rowing in the same direction at the same time and at similar speeds. This requires many advisors and the vision of owners willing to loosen the reins and have a degree of humility where others' contributions can really transform a business.

Finally, risk mitigation is not simply minimizing or eliminating conditions that elevate the level and presence of risk. Sometimes the unexpected occurs. Being able to address unplanned events, when a window of opportunity exists or a risk looms, requires a dynamic and nimble organization that is comfortable with transparency and change. It stands to reason the organization would have to be prepared for contingencies when things don't go as planned. An entire insurance industry is built on this premise.

So, stopping doing things that are making messes for the company is as important as being able to respond to threats from others who may place the business at risk due to a dispute (unhappy labor or shareholder uprising) or action by nature (fire causing business interruption) or third party (i.e., vendor/client contract dispute, new competitor).

31. Little or No Investment in Innovation (85%)

The concept of gain sharing (sharing profits and/or savings by company, business unit, department, and/or individual) is not new. However, the value of having staff and other members of a company's ecosystem with a vested interest in the success of the company should never be understated. This is especially true when fresh ideas through innovation are sought.

Input that is highly relevant to the overall performance of the company—such as ideas that create cost savings or increases sales—is likely to be more frequent when an allocation of monetary or other beneficial rewards is given and public recognition ensues.

CASE IN POINT

A department recommends the installation of a CRM system that may cost $500,000 up front, but eliminates tens of thousands of staff-hours spent on a duplication of efforts, tracking, reviewing, and revising. This results in savings of millions of dollars. The department's reward is a long weekend in Cabo that costs the company about $50,000—and they come back with a "let's do it again" mentality.

Exotic travel may not be in the cards at smaller organizations, but perks like an extra week of vacation or the chance to have lunch with the CEO (reinforcing an open-door policy) are fine rewards for significant contributors. Management can earn goodwill and loyalty by doing things like catering dinner when its team has to work late—conveying their efforts matter and the company is invested in supporting them.

A way to share the wealth is by tangibly thanking those who send new business. Telling a banker who teed up a new client "thank you" is nice, but, if permissible, sending him two tickets to a game featuring his favorite sports team is nicer; and nicer still is reciprocity of a new business referral in the other direction.

This abundance mindset tends to feed upon itself; yet, it's pretty uncommon. When permissible, I allocate 1 to 3 percent of paid advisory billings to sources who make engagements happen (even the client), and I research their likes to send an appropriate thank-you—a Mont Blanc pen, wine, round of golf, dinner at a local steakhouse, and so on.

When people are reminded how important their referrals are, they will work harder to continue sending them. The flipside is true as well: Companies and individuals that receive many referrals and take them for granted don't receive them any more.

The sad thing is explaining the concept of gain sharing to that unappreciative someone is unlikely to change the way he operates. And what's the risk of failing to be magnanimous when the opportunity arises to give back? You'll likely have fewer referral sources—which may lead to a company's overall performance and value suffering.

This chapter as well as this book strives to emphasize just how important human capital of owners and advisors can be to the success of a business. The purpose, the principles, and the passion differ greatly from policy and procedure.

The antithesis of innovation is bureaucracy. The risk is failure to be dynamic or applying a shotgun approach that dilutes the creative process. Some good ideas are cut short—not given enough time to take hold—and a double whammy occurs when it's never examined why something that was approved didn't work.

Innovation translates into degrees of change. Some people are comfortable in environments that evolve while others are not. A balance is needed between these two constituencies, or it must be clear from the vetting and hiring process that the hire must be suited to the business's culture. However, when business as usual doesn't work anymore, it often means an organization has an imbalance—it's not seeking to adapt and is unable to sense opportunities with little direction.

Dynamic organizations have a sense of mission. While innovation is a double-edged sword—since many ideas don't pan out—it's invaluable to have strategic leadership in place that allocates a good deal of focus to new business opportunities.

Think about VCR manufacturers and VCR tape providers like Blockbuster, which failed to respond in a timely fashion to the advent of the DVD. And then there's the timeline of developments in DVD delivery, starting with Red Box, which offered the first disruption in providing consumers with kiosks at which to rent DVDs, and then Netflix, which said, we'll do that one better and send DVDs directly to consumers. Netflix saw its place in the market undercut by live streaming, which allows consumers to bypass DVDs and watch content on their electronic device of choice. So, not only did Netflix adapt to this new change, but it is offering its own programming and content as is Amazon.

A good valuator will look at the percentage of current profits held in reserve for R&D and ask the following questions:

- Is the company having meetings to brainstorm new ideas?
- If so, who's participating and how are they rewarded?
- Is an idea considered bad if it doesn't work?

It's never a bad thing to constantly think about how to do something better or how to streamline an existing product, service, or process. Remember, innovation is about what can be, anticipating needs not yet known. Clear examples are drones primarily used for Homeland Security and the defense industry, which may have many commercial applications; however, loss of public privacy may be an unintended consequence.

The point is the risk is not thinking strategically enough, and failing to invest in *better* by being satisfied with *good enough*. One only has to look at when Google and Yahoo had parody and the significant difference in size and markets of the two now.

***

It is not accidentally that the last two items on the list are risk and innovation. Opportunity is the flipside of the risk coin. The purpose of Chapters 7 and 8 is to demonstrate to the reader there are many metrics of risk and opportunities to enhance value—some metrics are easily identified and others require research and analytics. However, all share something in common. Value is created when both financial and human capital are leveraged and risk is managed and mitigated. Doing so creates knowledge that is unique and uncommon. This is addressed in Chapter 9.

CHAPTER 9

The Role of Knowledge

Arguably, the core issue of knowledge is the following fact: With technology and access to information, a well-conceived plan can be disruptive to any industry. If the knowledge offered is common and easily accessed, it will become commoditized and have nominal value to end users.

The concept of knowledge might seem fairly straightforward. Most would suggest it is having information. Arguably, analysis of information to cull out the relevant from the minutia and the ability to act in order to provide something uncommon may be a more appropriate statement. In the military, the distinction between information and "intelligence" is to have sufficient collaboration by two or more distinct sources that makes the result actionable. Otherwise, most decisions would be made almost purely on assumptions. Many see entrepreneurs as "seat of the pants" types willing to take risks against the long odds; however, those who have created a sustainable business are usually quite risk adverse.

Think of it as gambling at the blackjack table. Starting with a $100 bet and winning against the house three times results in $800. The initial stake may have been small, and if lost, the gambler might just walk away thinking no harm, no foul. If a start-up has nominal costs and ease of entry, this could be likened to the first $100 with many betting and as much losing (if not more) than those winning.

However, if the first bet was $800, the stakes are higher and so is the desire to ensure the success of the venture: especially, if the cash is from a credit card advance (debt needs to be repaid, so essentially the bet can lose twice). There are fewer staking this bet as the fear of loss usually outweighs the desire to win. Now add some zeroes to the $800 and call it a business.

Each incremental "win" usually makes the owner more cautious because both years of time and serious financial investment are now at stake.

It would stand to reason, the owner wants to be more informed; however, wanting and becoming more informed is often the challenge. As sheer volume of business grows, the same skills to start the business differ from those to sustain it.

Simply put, no matter the good intention, desire, and hard work to do more with less, at some point an owner must acknowledge she is at capacity and must augment with other's involvement. Often it's a spouse or child, but that too will quickly reach the need for additional insights from advisors and staff.

Knowing something and acting on it becomes more critical as decisions become more incremental as the risks grow. The point of this introduction is to have the reader reflect that successful owners recognize making too many assumptions to justify actions is akin to building a foundation on sand.

Therefore, the greater the access and speed to relevant and actionable information, the more decisive and nimble an owner and her organization can be.

When one considers human capital, it's what we uniquely know as a collective that allows for differentiation in the marketplace. It is having the structures and culture in place under governance to allow information to flow and be acted upon that allows a company to be dynamic. It is having the executed strategy for internal and external relationships in place to reduce risks and pursue opportunities.

Gareth Jones states, "Knowledge must be transparent, complete, accurate, reliable, relevant and timely."[1] Donald Kuratko points out as part of knowledge management, "Strategic Leaders must enable their organizations to develop, exploit and protect the intellectual capital contained in their citizens' knowledge bases."[2] Dr. Kuratko emphasizes the importance of collaboration.

According to Marc Dollinger, knowledge is difficult to copy when it is tacit, nonteachable, nonobservable in use, complex, and multidimensional, or requires interdependent skills. He also categorized this as the unique relationships of human capital. Emphasis is also placed upon its protection by establishing barriers to its imitation.[3] Often-cited and well-regarded valuation expert Robert Reilly dedicates an entire chapter of *Valuing Intangible Assets* to the importance of human capital as an intangible asset.[4]

His chapter's focus is on a trained and assembled workforce orienting to knowledge and less so to relationships. There is consideration for tenure and cost to recruit, hire, and train; however, governance is not referenced.

The 2006 Nobel Laureate in Economics, Edmund Phelps, of Duff-Phelps fame, recognizes the impact of knowledge:

> *Even the worker of ordinary education can be engaged in or can gain intellectual development from the formation of skills—a type of knowledge—arising from problems that are put to him or her in the workplace—or could be put to him or her if the workplace were desirably organized.*[5]

This quote speaks volumes and lends credence to the importance of having governance and a corporate culture that embrace human capital as being something of a "wisdom" differentiator if well-harnessed.

Arguably, the core of the issue of knowledge is the following fact: With technology and access to information, a well-conceived plan can be disruptive to any industry. If the knowledge offered is common and easily accessed, it will become commoditized and have nominal value to end users. This last statement rattles a good deal of advisors. This is because most are trained the same way to achieve the same result. Law and code dictate what the usual actions should be by an attorney and accountant. Investment theory tends to drive allocation and wealth advice. Rates and terms are comparable as the cost of capital for most banks is near the same. So, meaningful differentiation becomes increasingly more difficult because so much of what is generally needed may be accessed from the Internet.

This is why a good portion of this book is geared towards fellow advisors and how owners can best utilize the skills of those who are differentiated or wish to become so.

Further, it's important to realize that knowledge is quite broadly defined; it can be associated with patents, logos, trademarks, trade secrets, copyrights, and so on.

Thinking about knowledge from the perspective of an owner, an advisor, or an entire business justifies deep contemplation and potential revisions to the other three areas of GRRK: governance, relationships, and risks. All three elements are indivisible and influence the relevance and focus on knowledge.

Knowledge is often a company's "secret sauce," something difficult to replicate and worthy of protecting by all means possible. It's what should differentiate one organization from another. This may also be a challenge of articulating the difference as I have endeavored to do by coining the term *strategic value architect* as being much more than a run-of-the-mill business appraiser. It is that important to find a way to express that difference as most clients will not invest the time in researching what good enough, good, and great ought to be like. So, think very, very carefully and ask "Why you? Why your company?" Now be honest, how much difference do you think your response is from that of your professional peers (competitors)? Try again ad nausea until you have found your own unique response. More likely than not, it's your story, that of your company, or both: "We know how to make good coffee." "We excel in banking relationships." "We are current on tax law." All are fine claims—but would the competition say anything different? What if a banker said, "We know more about your specific industry and how to use debt to grow a more profitable business." That is knowledge that most owners could distinguish, differentiate, pursue, and embrace.

Using the example of a CPA, being current on tax code and regulations is expected; therefore, differentiation would be where a firm recognizes that the tax-tail should not wag the business-dog. The firm's expertise should ensure a more profitable and successful business client. That kind of thinking acknowledges that company issues may be operational, structural, or regulatory in nature. It also is couched in terms of what the business owner needs, instead of what the accounting firm has to sell.

A similar type of thinking holds true to the business itself. What solutions are being provided sufficiently that are difficult to replicate, ever improving, and that address current market needs that may contribute to changing the way an industry operates?

CASE IN POINT

Wells Fargo's trade secrets—a subset of knowledge or intellectual property—include its approach to the market and rejection of certain risks, which has allowed it to be a big bank standard. Contrast that to Bank of America and its troubles with various regulatory bodies—resulting in billions of dollars in fines and an exodus of customers and investors that's reduced its stock price dramatically.

A MATTER OF CULTURE

A company's culture can and should harness knowledge. Most relevant is understanding the business is comprised of tangible and intangible assets. The human capital of knowledge deals primarily with the latter, but influences the former.

Here are two examples of million-dollar ideas based predominantly on knowledge:

1. Consider the manufacturing process for shoelaces. Anyone who's worn laced shoes has experienced the laces coming undone, even when they're

double-knotted, requiring them to be retied. Along comes a shoelace that provides a twist in the lace so upon tying the laces, friction keeps them from becoming untied.

2. A similar disruption occurred when barbed wire was invented. By inserting occasional spikes and twisting the wire, a relatively low-cost but strong means of keeping cattle in or out was created.

These seemingly innocuous inventions made their founders wealthy. Of course, not every new concept will be a million-dollar idea, as the television series *Shark Tank* demonstrates. But following existing methods certainly isn't going to shake up the market; it's why most midsize sedans, regardless of manufacturer, all look about the same.

When it comes to ensuring the unique distinction provided by company knowledge is maintained, some organizations believe everything—ideas, processes, policies, unique relationships, key staff, and so on—should be protected through all legal means. The late Steve Jobs ran Apple, Inc., that way, akin to the Fort Knox of protecting its intellectual property, with a culture that was secretive by design.

That philosophy is often found in sectors where the majority of revenue is derived from knowhow. A simplistic example would be Microsoft, which has expended billions on its operating suite, resulting in a competitive advantage even though many users love Corel's WordPerfect.

In the case of Microsoft, its system is closed source, so it relies on consumers to beta test it, identify and report flaws, and wait for those errors to be fixed. That is very different from open source, where any qualified code writer can make fixes and patches.

A big proponent of open source is Elon Musk, founder of Space X and Tesla, two successful companies. He recently took his proprietary methodology and elected to make it open source—available to the market—with the logic being to accelerate the change from petroleum-based fuels to alternative energy, mostly electric. The business reason behind this decision is brilliant. The secret sauce to Tesla's genius isn't just the fact that it produces a cutting-edge electronic vehicle; the mass production of batteries lowers their cost, and guess what? As mentioned earlier, Tesla invests in battery production and storage.

Musk's strategy and vision are game changers, and this includes what's happening at Space X, which is among the first commercial companies to produce rockets NASA uses at a fraction of the cost. The takeaway here is that knowledge is valuable when it pushes the envelope from current practice—it's disruptive and even when replicated in time, the next iteration leaves competitors catching up. For this innovation to occur, it's important to have a culture that permits mistakes so as not to exclude groundbreaking ideas that are too costly or too far ahead of the curve. A good example of that failing to occur is found at AT&T, which produced one of the first video phones, 20 years ahead of its time. It also produced the first tablets (two decades ago), but the combination of cost to market, lack of infrastructure to support and strengthen demand, and inability to articulate its value caused the products to fail.

Conversely, Domino's Pizza adhered to its early success by cracking the 30-minutes-or-less delivery code—success it believed would continue. Sales then flattened as competitors matched the delivery times with better quality alternatives. Instead of ignoring the market, it went back to strategy, giving customers a voice as to what was needed to be the predominant player in a saturated market of me-too products. This novel approach is part of Domino's trade secret, part of its knowledge.

There is a significant people (human capital) component to knowledge, so companies must consider that disgruntled employees may share their knowhow with clients as well as new employers. Every company must consider to what lengths it's willing to go to protect this knowledge, perhaps requiring non-competes or pursuing legal remedies for breaches of intellectual property.

Mary Kay Cosmetics, a 50-year-old direct-selling organization, certainly understands the value of its multilevel marketing. Its three million beauty consultants worldwide are independent contractors. Their agreements make it quite clear that the company will use all means available, including legal remedies, to prevent the sale of its products in any other ways than what's permitted by their contractor agreements.

For example, consultants can't arbitrarily discount products without written approval. In addition, if they sever the relationship, they may not sell Mary Kay products, or solicit existing customers or current or past consultants for cosmetics or any other business opportunity—including after they retire. The penalties for breaching the agreement include having Mary Kay terminate any retirement compensation that's directly related to their prior performance as a consultant (goodbye to that pink Cadillac).

In this example, Mary Kay has clearly assigned and protected its rights, but it's not always so clear. For instance, when an employee develops a better mousetrap, do those rights belong to the individual or the company that employs him?

Along the same lines, there are a number of industries that are primarily driven by knowledge of the client list, like professional services. In a perfect world, an individual's relationship with these clients may remain the company's property, but as banks, insurance companies, wealth advisors, and even attorneys and CPAs know all too well, when that individual either chooses to form a practice or leaves for another organization, oftentimes those clients follow. That is where relationships and perceived knowhow overlap. Arguably, the most valued advisor is one who not only knows his technical areas cold, but is capable of vetting other trusted advisors from the "herd" to provide clients value-add services across a broad spectrum.

HEALTHY KNOWLEDGE

What is healthy knowledge? It's an intangible that allows companies to differentiate themselves and owners to leverage in-house knowledge by taking a holistic approach to their businesses, ensuring that constituent relationships translate into an ecosystem where legitimate benefits can be derived. These benefits more often than not exceed just monetary gain, but allow businesses to be community stewards. Owners who do this best have the ability to acknowledge that not knowing isn't a weakness, while not acting on not knowing is.

As was noted earlier, it's certainly not necessary to be the smartest person in the room, but it is important to be surrounded by those who should be. The ability to wield knowledge in a timely, efficient, and effective manner can create extraordinary success.

Think back to high school, when some people knew where the best parties were; they had knowledge that was beneficial to those interested in the party scene. As it pertains to business, being plugged into industry, vendor, or client associations or tangential organizations like those dealing with leadership, negotiation, executive learning, and more—all are examples of developing an interconnected web of knowledge where early adoption often becomes a competitive advantage.

"Sensing" is another kind of knowledge that will set a company apart. If a company's tentacles are spread far and wide, the result is access to disparate information that with analysis can recognize trends and opportunities as they unfold. Conversely, a degree of isolation or operating in a bubble can severely limit growth as new knowledge is untimely and/or limited.

Mark Cuban of *Shark Tank*, Broadcom, Mavericks, and other holdings fame has expressed he reads three hours daily (as do I, but I don't have a $B after the last zero of my bank account, not for the lack of trying and doing). His reason is simple. If there is just one knowledge nugget derived from a periodical, newspaper, or the Internet, the investment is well worth it. (I wonder if the television network hosting *Shark Tank* has considered engaging the audience by having them text their preferences to the value proposition and offer some kind of crowd-funding, so even "losers" might have access to capital and winners may be able to decide that they want the human capital that Mark and his fellow successful peers offer along with their funds or opt for the capital offered by the television viewers. Undoubtedly, there is some SEC regulations that may need to be overcome.)

Owners and sometimes advisors lament there's just not enough time for them to know everything. This type of thinking is considered adverse and could lower a company's value because it's indicative of an owner who fails to realize the importance of delegating information gathering to others.

By far, the primary reason companies tend to have flat or declining growth is that in the absence of evolving—which means transforming from new knowledge and to leverage the nimbleness in order to pursue dynamic capabilities—they are reacting to the market instead of seizing new opportunities.

BE TRANSPARENT

One of the most important characteristics of healthy knowledge is transparency. The more clearly investors, customers, and employees understand roles, relationships, and the benefits derived, the better they can see opportunities and share them. A simple example that may seem trite occurs after the purchase of a new car, when a buyer becomes aware of all the other identical models on the road.

Whether reading an article, listening to the radio, or attending an industry meeting, the more one is attuned to one's purpose, the greater the likelihood that an advantage may be identified as new information is filtered and acted upon.

For instance, some investment companies are using data analytics to look for global, geopolitical, social, and financial disruptions—and what they might mean to an investment. They are looking for opportunities even before the trends fully evolve.

What would be the advantage to a company that became aware of the issues between Greece and its banks—a precursor to the fact that the country was expected to default on its obligations? Having early knowledge creates a distinctive advantage, in the same way that Facebook tracking applies sophisticated algorithms to determine users' likes. This is done so user preferences can be reflected on their screens.

While some people are concerned with sharing too much information, it's necessary to weigh the benefits against the risks. The more knowledge is accepted and shared, the greater all the eyes and ears within and outside of a company can be leveraged. This is why great pains are made to express the need for owners to ensure all their advisors are looking for those knowledge-adding opportunities. The knowledge they provide must transcend the knowledge available from other professionals in the same sector; otherwise it is at risk of being commoditized.

ENCOURAGE TWO-WAY COMMUNICATION

In the best situations, knowledge is bidirectional. In many companies, the organization chart looks like a pyramid that narrows toward the top (the board and CEO) and widens as different layers are added: others in the C-suite, executives and senior management, middle management, supervisors, and line workers.

Those in the ivory tower express needs that occasionally trickle down in a timely and accurate manner, but there should also be solicitation of the impact and needed resources of those requested actions. Often there are bottlenecks or misunderstood or corrupted communications that lead to incorrect, incomplete, or no action at all.

All constituencies should be encouraged to express ideas and concerns that flow as quickly back up the chain of command. Otherwise, it's an organization where everyone follows orders because of the adverse risk of standing out. Among the worst thing that can happen is for individuals to be aware of a problem but remain silent because they're not encouraged to express themselves. When this manifests into a crisis, at whose feet does the blame go? If it's the workers—clearly, a systemic issue is present within the company.

In an ideal (or should I say idea) organization, information flows in both directions and the pyramid may even be turned upside down, based on the notion that the leaders' function is to empower and support those with the greatest amount of external contacts in the company's ecosystem. This two-way flow is an important part of healthy knowledge.

With respect and consideration, assuming no crisis is occurring, processes, procedures, and policies—"If it ain't broke, don't fix it"—should be challenged, reviewed, and updated on a regular basis. Clearly, there must be a distinct mechanism, committees, or open-door policies that encourage improvement through new knowledge that transforms.

KNOWLEDGE AND HUMAN CAPITAL

Neal Beaton, ASA, CFA, is the National Partner in Charge of Grant Thornton's valuation services. Several of the knowledge factors[6] he examines are:

- Assessment of management team
- Compelling nature of the value proposition
- Evaluation of the intellectual property

In *Human Capital Analytics: How to Harness the Potential of Your Organization's Greatest Asset*, Gene Pease recognizes the impact of human capital on intangible asset value and dedicates an entire chapter to the importance of "alignment" to ensure all stakeholders ("constituents") are involved in the process as well as the problem ("risks") or opportunity to be solved due to their varied perspectives and ideas ("knowledge").

By doing so, deeper partnerships ("relationships") are formed. Further, the analysis should focus on root cause with issues that are core value drivers associated with the organization's culture and values ("governance"). Pease goes on to emphasize the relevance of cross-functionality to create synergies ("value") and minimize resistance. Finally, he emphasizes the need to address resource gaps at every level from conception to final review and implementation.[7]

What is evident is these authors identify intangibles which are primarily human capital. Most venture-backed companies assess the human capital from application of knowledge to commercially viable product and service lines as part of their go–no go investment criteria.

The same risk/opportunity criteria would apply to more mature companies when contemplating future growth. Given that management's history and ability to forecast is often relied upon to develop equity/enterprise values, the risk identification to develop the discount rate of future cash flows is paramount. This is especially true as the terminal value that requires sustained growth estimates can often reflect a large portion of the present value + terminal value equation.

Thus, the elements of GRRK are certainly interconnected, and one of the most direct ways that knowledge ties back to governance is in how companies use knowledge—strategically or tactically. With regard to customers, would it make sense to know what they perceive as growing trends that might affect business? Getting in front of those trends may provide new business opportunities as a solutions provider—rather than merely a vendor that provides a product or service. Thinking is strategic when this becomes ingrained into the culture of an organization. It's particularly necessary in industries where trends change rapidly, such as in outerwear and accessories.

With respect to personnel, the issue may be identifying a better approach of interaction and delivery to customers. The approach would be tactical, but the empowerment is clearly strategic, ergo, "In this company, we value all staff opinions that allow us to better serve our constituents."

To have healthy knowledge, particularly in the corner office, requires a degree of humility and is expressed in the concept of servant leadership or stewardship. When leaders recognize their own limitations, it allows for the elevation of others, should they feel their contribution is validated.

There are those who believe that true wisdom is knowing what needs to be known and where to find answers. By reverse engineering from the destination where a company wishes to be headed and awareness of where the company currently stands, a strategic roadmap is crafted. The gaps in resources and information will be identified and can then be filled, which is a wholly different approach from "learn as you go." These gaps will sometimes occur because dealing with everyday operational issues can be all-consuming regardless of someone's level on an organization chart. A healthy organization will allocate certain internal and/or external "knowledge workers" to ensure strategy receives adequate time and resources so knowledge can be leveraged.

Looking over the horizon is what differentiates companies that have 8-, 9- and 10-figure revenues and double-digit growth rates. Either wittingly or not, they all have strategies—they keep their eye on the prize and aren't distracted by daily issues. They almost always tap the knowledge of those within and outside the organization and solicit advisors with special skills in developing and executing on strategic roadmaps. An exceptional advisor not only provides maps (or playbooks), but can also partner with and augment staff and other advisors to ensure alignment and execution of the strategic plan. In large part, this is what I do as a strategic value architect.

One of the best indicators of a knowledge-based organization is one that seeks to answer questions like "what if?" or "why not?"

Perhaps Marilyn Kourilsky, author of *The E-Generation*, summarizes knowledge and/or its absence best. The number-one (56% of respondents) reason people start their own business is to be their own boss. They feel the knowledge gained from education, life experience, and working at another business prepares them to be a business owner. Yet, actual business leaders feel education did not prepare them for: seeing opportunities others may not see; combining ideas and information in new ways; making smart use of time; budgeting wisely; managing and motivating others; coming up with solutions where everyone is better off; listening to others; the ability to distinguish between good and bad opportunities; preparing to start a business; and what prices to charge.[8]

Confucius said: "When we see men of virtue, we should think of equaling them; when we see men of contrary character, we should examine ourselves." Hubris is a terrible thing if it causes an owner or advisor to be blind, refuse to see, or lack the humility to see that thinking they know and knowing they know are not the same thing.

KNOWLEDGE MEASURES

The overarching message with respect to knowledge is that the more unique, timely, transparent, and encouraged it is, the better. We've talked about it in esoteric terms, but its presence or absence can be measured. Some examples include:

- Are processes, procedures, and policies documented, and is there evidence that they are regularly reviewed and updated?
- Is there an allocation and active management of intellectual property?
- Is there an understanding of where revenue comes from (perhaps intangible assets), so there can be an adequate allocation of future resources?
- Is there a methodology to the development of new intellectual property, its acquisition, or divestiture?
- How robust are efforts to brand and license as appropriate?
- If the company is in the knowledge business (i.e., professional services and many business services), are there whitepapers or articles that it posts on its website or shares in the media or within the industry?
- How much is invested in R&D and how is the investment determined and tracked?
- How does the company go about protecting its knowledge assets and the transition—planned (retirement) or unplanned (death or disability)—of key personnel?
- How often are agreements checked and updated based on internal and external factors such as new-to-market products and ideas to ensure adequate protections and optimal receipt of revenues?
- How often are there meetings away from the day-to-day distractions to challenge current methods and encourage brainstorming and thought leadership?
- How much of the company's annual expenses are invested in professional services such as tax and legal advice and best practices for operations, market development, and leadership?
- How much money is allocated annually to better educate staff, regardless of white or blue collar?
- If there are key performance indicators, how are they developed, shared, and assessed, and how often are they revised?

I assert that while there are numerous books written on intangible assets and intellectual property, the largest contributor to company value above tangible assets is how much the company is worth based on its human capital.

Knowledge is part of human capital as is governance and relationships.

A considerable amount of time was expended on risks. Combining that information with what's found in this chapter demonstrates that the more uncommon knowledge is, and the more it's protected and leveraged—lessening risk—the higher the value of the business. With refreshed knowledge, there can be dynamic capability where governance and strategy can be leveraged by sensing and seizing opportunities, minimizing risks, and transforming an organization to pursue opportunities.

It is important to remember, particularly for companies that provide services that clients are apt to have fee bias, so one of the greatest challenges is being able to articulate and differentiate the investment in uncommon knowledge to create the very real benefit of being a steward and receiving a premium as a result.

NOTES

1. Gareth Jones, *Introduction to Business: How Companies Create Value for People* (New York, NY: McGraw Hill Irwin, 2007), 276–278.
2. Donald Kuratko, *Strategic Entrepreneurial Growth* (San Diego, CA: Harcourt College, 2001), 132.
3. Marc Dollinger, *Entrepreneurship: Strategies & Resources*, 2nd ed. (Upper Saddle River, NJ: Prentice Hall, 1999), 37, 100.
4. Robert Reilly, *Valuing Intangible Assets* (New York, NY: McGraw Hill, 1999), 399–409.
5. Edmund Phelps, *Mass Flourishing* (Princeton, NJ: Princeton University Press, 2013), 276.
6. Neal Beaton, *Valuing Early Stage and Venture-Backed Companies* (Hoboken: Wiley Finance, 2010), 46.
7. Gene Pease, *Human Capital Analytics: How to Harness the Potential of Your Organization's Greatest Asset* (Hoboken: Wiley, 2013), 33–60.
8. Marilyn Kourilsky, *The E-Generation* (Dubuque, IA: Kendall Hunt, 2000), 23, 58.

CHAPTER 10

Valuation versus Value Creation (GRRK)

Stated another way, due to perceived risks, equity investors often expect total returns of 30 to 40 percent compounded, especially for lower middle market companies. The main point is that existing corporate finance tends to focus on modern portfolio theory of efficient markets. Most midmarket companies and their competitive environment are anything but efficient, which is part of the premise of this book. Slee examines cost of capital across a spectrum starting from traditional debt to venture capital and factoring, which is reflective of risks.

Where Slee leaves off on company-specific risks, this book hopes to triangulate with the premise that the goal should be to measure the change (absolute gains) in value such as return on invested capital as a key metric of performance improvement.

—Slee, 2011.

Not even sports is more dog-eat-dog than operating a business in such a competitive environment. This book is intended to provide a leg up to the business owner and trusted advisor. For sure, while the need is great, the demand is likely the 20 percent or fewer who are constantly seeking answers to the proverbial "splinter in my mind" challenge: "What could I be doing better and who is best suited to achieve better to best?"

Since the subject of this book is value creation, it makes sense to dwell on why it's relevant for owners and trusted advisors to have relationships with top-tier business appraisers. But, it's equally important for business appraisal organizations to raise the bar of intellectual rigor to have clients understand how risk and value starts the conversation. GRRK endeavors to continue the natural progression of identifying and measuring risk in determining equity value to the role of all constituents to build and manage value.

In *Business Valuation Body of Knowledge*, Dr. Shannon Pratt emphasizes the need for the use of supporting data. In the absence of this research and analysis, the determination of risk is more a guesstimate providing little support for conclusions of value.[1] Barry Schimel indicates 75 percent of closely held businesses are sold for less than their value! Yet, his book's emphasis is on profits, not on what changes the risk rate or price multiple.[2]

Thomas West shares in *Mergers and Acquisitions Handbook for Small and Midsize Companies* that buyers pay for opportunity, but not potential, as the latter is what is created by the acquirer and not the seller. While this is a point made in this book, it stands to reason the seller has the opportunity to prepare the business for sale to achieve the highest possible price. West states: "Identify the firm's uniqueness and hidden values.... Rules of thumb tend to be poor indicators of value..." because they rely on averages and not individual company-specific risks and opportunities.[3]

Rob Slee, author of the seminal treatise, *Private Capital Markets: Valuation, Capitalization and Transfer of Private Business Interests*,[4] and I have co-presented on issues of valuation and private capital liquidity. We agree with the "valuation as a range concept" as there are many optics of risk. His investment banking perspective for private companies ($5 to $350 million capitalization) is both elegant and eloquent. He dedicates his entire Chapter 10 to "Incremental Business Value," which demonstrates how to exceed the cost of capital—the focus of this book. We embrace Peter Drucker's statement: "Until a business returns a profit that is greater than its cost of capital, it operates at a loss."

This is because earning a return that is below the cost of capital lowers value despite a profit being reported, which is why this book emphasizes risks/opportunities and not solely revenues and profits. While this may cause chagrin for many CPAs and CFOs, the simple fact is accounting-focus does not require the measurement of the time-value of capital or consideration of risk. If it did, there would be rare occasions where debt funding wouldn't be part of value optimization considerations.

Many private equity acquisitions will include about 50 percent debt/50 percent cash in deal structure for this reason. Here is a simplistic reason why. Say 100 percent equity provides a 20 percent total return, meaning a 5× purchase price was paid. The PEG uses debt (pre-tax) at 5 percent for half the purchase price with the balance paid in cash. This means that $.05(.50) + .20(.50) = 12.5$ percent or the equivalent of an 8× multiple—a 60 percent increase over the 5× paid even before any other tax considerations, risk reductions, or operational performance improvements.

Slee indicates in Exhibits 10.11 (p. 159) and 35.7 (p. 562) of his book that reduced business risk is required to achieve equity value enhancement. This would also require knowledge of the capital structure of tangible and intangible assets, often with the latter being the domain of seasoned business valuation and financial experts. What private equity groups understand is their access to and cost of capital will likely differ from that available to the acquired company.

The compelling reason an owner and advisor would want to retain a strategic value architect is she will not only master debt/equity mix, but assist in lowering capital costs by lowering risks. This elevates price multiples and company value.

Thomson Reuters Private Equity Performance Index demonstrates that over the past 20 years buyouts have only achieved a 9 percent return with all private equity reporting 11.3 percent for the same period. Given the degree of skill and capital access available to PEGs, the level of risk compared to more passive investment returns is disparate.

Hence, even private equity groups and family offices that choose to directly invest in and operate private companies, would benefit from risk measurement and management assistance.

While not gospel, Slee segments the middle market with price multiples generally falling into lower ($5–$150 million in sales: 4–7× EBITDA); middle ($150–$500 million in sales: 8–9× EBITDA); and upper ($500–$1 billion in sales: 10–12× EBITDA).

Stated another way, due to perceived risks, equity investors often expect total returns of 30 to 40 percent compounded, especially for lower middle market companies. Clearly, the goal of boards, officers, and shareholders should be to scale a company size (growth) and increase its price multiple by lowering risk. The main point is that existing corporate finance theory tends to focus on modern portfolio theory of efficient markets. Most midmarket companies and their competitive environment are anything but efficient, which is part of the premise of this book. Slee examines cost of capital across a spectrum starting from traditional debt to venture capital and factoring, which is reflective of risks.

Where Slee leaves off on company-specific risks, this book hopes to triangulate with the premise the goal should be to measure the change (absolute gains) in value such as return on invested capital as a key metric of performance improvement.

Even lauded and oft-referenced Tax Court Judge David Laro, who outlined the valuation and discounting factors to be considered in the *Mandelbaum* court case, expresses the recognition of company-specific risk with an indicated range from −2 to +10 percent; however, "This adjustment is based entirely on the appraiser's analysis and judgment, so it should be well supported."[5] This begs the question, if most business valuation reports have nominal review of a company's operations, relationships, knowledge, and governance, can their assessment of risk and value be adequate?

Before delving further, it's necessary to understand what constitutes a top-tier business appraiser. Preferably, this is an individual in a firm or department that is an exclusive provider of valuation advisory services, one that hires only seasoned valuators who've performed 100 or more engagements. That number may seem arbitrary, but consider the fact that it would take a full-time appraiser approximately five years to reach it—and contrast that to working with someone who may complete 3 or 4 appraisals each year, which is typical of the industry.

A top-tier appraiser should be someone with mastery of valuation theory and practice—and preferably someone who's cut his teeth on providing litigation support (expert testimony). Nothing ruins a day more than opposing counsel and her seasoned valuation expert deconstructing one's work product.

It's a good idea to be cautious and inquire about specific experience within a given industry and for a specific purpose, as well as determine the appraiser's expertise in valuing equity versus solely enterprise value. It's also appropriate to ask for a redacted copy of a report to determine the degree of due diligence and analytical skills that differentiate between a passable work product and a superior one.

All trusted advisors should enhance their business appraiser relationships and knowledge to better understand the marketplace they serve. One issue that is all too commonly experienced by business appraisers is being seen as a commodity by other professional advisors due to the lack of time, effort, and interest fellow professionals apply to differentiate among the appraisers' skill level. This is often evidenced as the last and sometimes most painful check a client will write; Inevitably it's seen as a must-have transaction versus good-to-have investment. As a result, just like their own clients may do, advisors assume that hourly rates and lower fees equate to best work product value. This is proven by the assumption that a shorter report is often requested as it will lower fees. In truth, the lion's share of time ought not be in the report writing but in data analysis and research necessary to support value conclusions.

SOFTWARE AND RULES OF THUMB

It's become common for some practitioners (business appraisers, quasi-appraisers, and other professionals) to use software that generates a business value; or worse, they rely on some rule of thumb to come up with a result. This may be because in the pecking order, attorneys and accountants and occasionally wealth managers often enjoy the role of most trusted advisor—with an actual business appraiser seldom in sight.

Terms like *value*, *strategy*, and *equity discounts* are often expressed by these advisors despite most having a nominal understanding of the depth of expertise needed to master these concepts. They fall into the same trap they endure when their clients choose to use Legal Zoom, Turbo Tax, InsuranceQuotes.com, and/or e-Trade as an alternative to engaging (and paying) a professional.

There are many ways to demonstrate the inherent weaknesses of using a software-driven work product, including the fact that there are more than 800 factors, each with varying weights, that may influence a more thoughtful and supported result than software is presently capable of doing. In addition, consider this book, and the amount of time that has been expended on four specific categories that affect value.

While there are some more recent software companies claiming their product produces a high-caliber result, in discussions with their founders it becomes clear they don't use the myriad various data sources that are the benchmark of a superior work product. These products have charts and graphs that are admittedly appealing, but the intellectual rigor and degree of data analytics are often insufficient, with the possible exception of usually seven-figure or smaller companies where price multiples are commonly in the range from 2× to 5× of cash flows. In most cases, when someone other than a professional business appraiser determines a company's value, no one can explain how it was generated—it's like a mystery black box.

Software is one bane to the business appraiser's existence; so, too, is the use of rules of thumb—because no two companies are identical. For example, let's say two companies are identical in every respect, but one is in San Diego and the other is in Portland, Maine. Are their costs the same, their markets the same, and their competition the same? Presumably, no; since geographic location can influence value, this negates the notion that the same rule-of-thumb value could be applied to both companies.

Here are a few other scenarios (which were mentioned earlier but bear repeating here):

- Two identical companies, one that's been around for 5 years and other that's 20 years old. Many would say that the older company should have a higher value, but the truth is that the growth rate of the younger company is superior to that of its older cousin—so the values should not be the same.
- Let's say the rule of thumb is to value a company at 40 percent of its revenues. You have two companies with identical revenues, but one uses

debt and the other does not. It stands to reason that the values are not the same since it would be necessary to take into account how optimally the latter company's debt is used toward its performance and growth.
- If two companies have the same revenue but one has twice the profit margins—how can they have the same value?

If the rule of thumb is a multiple of earnings and income, many of the previous examples would apply.

More information would be needed to determine the respective values of two companies showing the same profit level, but one has twice the revenue. The same would be true if one company had twice the level of sales as another, but was less profitable.

These are things a rule of thumb does not take into account. Thus, while it's attractive to believe that software or a rule of thumb can replace the investment in a competent business appraiser, that's simply not the case. Somehow in the pecking order, the appraiser is likely to receive one of the last checks written by the client and fellow trusted advisors may try to justify their value to the client by identifying the least expensive alternative.

Sometimes (not as rare as you'd think), an accountant, attorney, or life insurance professional will provide their guesstimate of value—something to better justify the cost of their services. That practice is certainly not collaborative. At best it's a disservice to the client, and at worst it sets the stage for future liability.

A PERSONAL ASIDE

The previous content is not intended to be a rant. If anything, the process I've gone through has caused me to not only up my A-game, but also refer work to other business appraisers when the question of the fee becomes more pronounced. This frees me to work on more complex and lucrative matters and have a special niche of larger family businesses and family offices as well as private and public companies with revenues from 8 to 10 figures—a relative small market segment. I practice what I preach about selecting a niche and going deep. In addition, the science of equity value enhancement surpasses the art, and our offerings to include advisory services where certain retentions are 6 and 7 figures and more. This is one reason after 20+ years running a national boutique firm, I opted to merge my practice into a global firm going from a staff of 25 to ~900 at present count. Again, synergies of human and financial capital at work.

The fee levels are driven by determining value *plus* identifying and listing specific risks and value drivers that influence value at the asset, entity, and equity levels, such that the advice is often equity value enhancement—the premise of this book—and addresses how significant intangible asset values may be influenced by focusing on the human capital–related and other intangibles in the book: GRRK (governance, relationships, risk, and knowledge).

Our fees depend on the scope of work, duration of time, and number of individuals working on a strategic platform that creates a cultural and operational shift that can often result in a 50× return on investment of fees or greater.

COLLABORATION, COHESION, AND TRANSFORMATION

Other trusted advisors may benefit from thorough appraisals, as many of the issues found during due diligence give rise to increased professional services and products needs (e.g., insurance and investments as well as tax and legal advice). Existing relationships may also be further enhanced by working with an advisor whose aligned actions best serve the owner, as the owner in turn will undoubtedly share favorable experiences with peers—likely to propagate new work through referrals and a zealot for a client—making competitive risk highly unlikely.

Advisors who participate in these types of collaboration benefit their clients and themselves through this process as it also creates cohesion among advisors and clients. Fellow advisors will see how their peers' services are showcased and are likely to have other clients who would benefit from trusted advisors who go well beyond ad-hoc, tactical, technical, and transactional advice.

Business appraisers serve other advisors well by adhering to a higher standard and ensuring that professional services rendered are not commoditized. This is as much a responsibility of the industry accreditation bodies as it is of valuation firms and their practitioners.

Evidence of this is very poignant. The American Institute of Certified Public Accountants (AICPA) generated a whitepaper to its 400,000+ members noting that CPAs of the future must by 2025 transform to being trusted business advisors (TBAs) as an increased amount of the technical work will be performed offshore and/or replaced by software. This is evidenced by the concentration of industry revenues in the top 20 global and national accounting firms being, which are not in audit-related services but in advisory services. Keep in mind there are 1.28 million accountants in the United States according to the Bureau of Labor Statistics, as states license accountants and membership in the AICPA is not required.

The impact of this transformation is so profound; the value of a typical accounting firm declined from 150 percent of annual billings to 75 percent in the space of fewer than 10 years and is likely to be 33 percent as 2025 approaches. Therefore, accounting firms mostly based on tax return and financial statement transactions are not an adequate recipe for building a retirement nest egg.

Thomas Rawley and Gup Benton addressed: "Does value creation work?"[6] The authors shared almost 20 years ago that Warren Buffett had three key principles for executive compensation at Berkshire Hathaway's portfolio companies:

1. Goals tailored to how the specific operating business creates value
2. Simple metrics
3. Can be directly related to daily activities

According to the authors, there are four steps to incorporate value building:

1. Constant consideration and communication to workforce and shareholders of value metric results
2. Implementing compensation incentives and metrics that drive cash flow and reduce risk
3. Transparent reporting of both positive and negative results on a consistent basis
4. Actionable items to push for total returns of 20 percent or more

Many of the ideas in this book are not original. However, putting them into the present context offers a tool allowing for greater appreciation and utilization of brethren business appraisers' expertise. That is to say, values are more than numbers and risk identification and measurement are more than a paragraph in a report. Perhaps more importantly, equity value enhancement (EVE) requires a higher operating standard in order to have an actionable strategy to manage risk.

NOTES

1. Shannon Pratt, *Business Valuation Body of Knowledge* (New York: Wiley, 1998), 193–203.
2. Barry Schimel, *100 Ways to Win the Profit Game: Battle-Tested Business Strategies That Add Value to Your Business Now* (Washington, DC: Capital Books, 2000), 95.
3. Thomas West, *Mergers and Acquisitions Handbook for Small and Midsize Companies* (New York: Wiley, 1997), 29, 152.
4. Robert T. Slee, *Private Capital Markets: Valuation, Capitalization and Transfer of Private Business Interests*, 2nd ed. (Hoboken: Wiley, 2011), 6–7, 51, 143–164.
5. David Laro, *Business Valuation & Taxes* (Hoboken: Wiley, 2005), 192.
6. Thomas Rawley and Benton Gup, *The Valuation Handbook* (Hoboken: Wiley Finance, 2010), 37, 258.

CHAPTER 11

Putting It All Together—Four Vignettes

The intention of this book is not to simply impress the reader on what a thoughtful business valuation advisor or strategic value architect should look like. Rather, it is to stress that companies are confronted with the need to be dynamic and to have a strategy that allows the creation of enhanced value for shareholders. This requires leverage of both financial and human capital.

Focus by management, ownership, and advisors tends to be on revenues and profits (top and bottom line), which provide the economic benefit. Arguably, this benefit is more easily tracked. However, it is capital appreciation (growth) that most investors seek. Higher price multiples are the result of better-than-industry growth and reduction of operating risks. Therefore, each stakeholder needs to think like both a Main Street and a Wall Street investor who identifies, measures, manages, and mitigates risks.

Such activities may be lacking in large part as the concept of leveraging intangibles like governance, relationships, risks, and knowledge seems ethereal. Words like *strategy* are understood and spoken, but their application challenges many far wiser than the author. This is why solutions lie not within one individual, but within many. The challenge tends not to be persistance, passion, and purpose. Rather, it tends to be addressing resource gaps and not knowing where or how to start. The vignettes that follow provide some applications of these ideas.

Before we move to the vignettes, let me emphasize that all professionals can bring unique perspectives and benefits. I am blessed by having some high-quality and reciprocal relationships with top-tier attorneys, accountants, wealth, and insurance among other professionals; however, sincerely, I'd welcome more such relationships (after all running a ranch is like owning a boat, plane, or vineyard—you do it for the love of it—not necessarily that it is always a wise investment).

Be aware of narrow thinking. An example to illustrate is when a CPA, or the client, is thrilled with having "saved" taxes by receiving $10,000 or more in refunds. Unless you want the IRS/U.S. Treasury Department to act as your bank, paying no interest, the client has lost any return he would have otherwise received from having access to this capital had too much taxes not been overpaid.

It's this type of simplistic thinking without challenging conventional wisdom that leads to mediocre results. Another is selection of a professional. As shared earlier, accountants, economists, and finance professionals are not the same despite each dealing with figures, percentages, and dollars. However, there is crossover among the three.

Accounting is mainly concerned with the gathering, reporting, and analysis of business transaction data according to the principles of relevance, timeliness, reliability, comparability, and consistency of information or reports.

Finance has to do with making investment decisions and risk management. It is concerned with the time value of money (the value of future cash flows), rates of return, cost of capital, and optimal financial structures.

Economics is a social science that studies the production, consumption, and distribution of goods and services through the behaviors of persons, firms, industries, and nations to evaluate and quantify why they're doing what they're doing. Economics posits that capital should always be invested in a way that will produce the best risk-adjusted return; Finance actually figures that process out.

Even within each segment there are many subspecialties. There are CPAs who specialize in audit work; there are economists who focus on macro policy-making viewpoints; and there are finance professionals who focus solely on public companies.

Therefore, the notional 10,000 hours to achieve a degree of mastery has some merit. I have cautioned about the individual who spends a few hundred hours a year performing valuation work. How many years will it take to reach 10,000? Then there are subspecialties within valuation such as performing primarily intellectual property (such as patents) or financial reporting valuations. It is only because my background has always been in strategy, operations, and finance that during my first five years I sought to master comprehension of holding private equity interests. Then, the next five years was to primarily to understand how court rulings and legislative/regulatory issues impacted valuations associated with gift and estate tax. My next five years was dedicated toward understanding the transfers, transactions, and transitions of businesses and business interests and the optics of the owners, their families, and their advisors. The following five years was to go deeper into what caused disputes and how human capital had an impact on good companies becoming great ones.

My current five years has been dedicated to not only identifying and measuring the influences of all these factors, but also providing others the management services and tools to do so themselves or acting as a steward to maximize the process of value creation.

Dreams and innovations are simply not enough for success. Doing is—again and again, reviewing and revising along the way in a never ending cycle of enhancement. Why? Because if your competitors aren't quitting, you'll need to work smarter, not just harder.

VIGNETTE ONE: WHAT THE 2009 FINANCIAL CRISIS CAN TEACH US (IT'S ABOUT RELATIONSHIPS)

About six years ago, two other professionals and the author formed a concept called STAR, which stands for Strategic Trusted Advisor Roundtable. (We started with Group instead of Roundtable, but the PC police suggested this might be offensive to women.) The vision was simple and very subtle.

In 2008 through 2011, law and accounting firms were downsizing due to client fee sensitivity and concern for their own survival. The laws of economic Darwinism had kicked in. It was a mob, not even a herd—an "every man for himself" mentality as the veneer of civility due to fear had taken hold. Professional services firms were laying off support personnel like office management, receptionists, and assistants. They were thinning staff like legal secretaries, paralegals, and bookkeepers. Eventually some associates and even income partners were let go.

Most professional and business services firms' business models use leverage of junior staff time to bill profitable hours. It is a fundamental utilization model based upon hourly rates. Nevertheless, these two professions (law and accounting) often enjoy the client "inner circle" as most trusted advisors.

A common historic practice was senior partners maintaining their lifestyle in ensuring luxury car leases, one-plus house payments, kids' college, club memberships, and two-plus week vacations. These remained intact with the additional option of working fewer hours and socializing more.

Little thought went into the several flaws in this reasoning. First, if many of these firms had relied upon the founding partners' gravitas, goodwill, and relationships, then emerging managing partners focused upon technical and administrative skills. Being a rainmaker had less relevance. Cutting expenses does not in itself cause growth or stem billings' decline. Surgically cutting expenses versus using a broadsword is also an art form and often attrition of revenues is a result of poor rightsizing of staff. The next solution was reducing fees, which further commoditized services.

Simple supply and demand allowed clients to frame the issue of cost versus investment and frightened professional firm partners succumbed. As more and more of the firms did this, it created a further downward spiral on fees and cost cutting. Few knew how to articulate value-add selling where project fees could be shown to create client value.

This leads to a survival mindset, referenced earlier, of every man for himself: in short, a veneer of professionalism as finally kids were pulled from private school and/or upper-tier universities and sent to public school and state universities. And toys like motorcycles, jet skis, boats, and motorhomes were divested—as were second homes and timeshares.

The thing about most technical professions like law and accounting is that the technical education alone does little to teach how to operate a successful practice or to advise business owners on leveraging professional as well as business services. Law and tax often emphasize logic and exactness, which while attractive to some technicians, has little to do with the commerce of building brand and relationships. There are many hand-to-mouth, brilliant professionals who are in this position. Having a strategy that leverages their and others' knowledge and relationships is often a secondary thought, dismissed or foreign.

Yet, these same two professions often have a tight reciprocal arrangement as business owners' most trusted advisors. Does a business owner know what a good attorney or accountant looks like? Do the professions truly differentiate themselves? Compounding the commoditization problem is that some of these professions elevate their own importance by showing how much money they're "saving" the client with a "discounted" fee. The simple fact that the fee is the core metric makes the point. The true justification must be the value created, not the hours charged. These professions in turn expect the same from others they or their clients seek to retain.

Most have a passive practice, meaning they seldom actively seek to leverage new relationships. Relationships are from some external catalyst. Often worse, they occasionally succumb to the habit to mitigate their referral risk with a shallow bench of advisors by asking their clients to find their own. Does the attorney/CPA provide any guidance as to what a good advisor should look like? In my experience, the answer is a resounding "no."

This is akin to being an excellent surgeon but leaving a patient to select the anesthesiologist.

Occasionally, these professionals offer several names, but still their clients are on their own to differentiate with nominal understanding of what a good professional looks like. This is anything but professional guidance. A general practice physician would hardly say, "You need a cardiologist." They'd say, "If you were my brother, I'd recommend Dr. Yee Soh. He is the finest cardiologist in our healthcare system."

Then there are professions where commerce is as much a product of maintaining old relationships as actively pursuing new ones. These professions include banking, wealth, and insurance professionals. Because there are so many folks in these sectors, those who rise to the top are ones who best articulate their value message because there is often little distinction between what their firms can offer as viewed through the lens of clients as well as the advisors who refer them in. Thus, warm referrals increase odds of retention.

Being an approachable, likeable, and typical practitioner can still result in a fair amount of business. Preferably, having all the traits of a professional is so much better; however, knowing what good and great looks like is partially a time-attention-intention paradigm. Few take the time to really seek understanding what optimal looks like in order to provide clients best-in-class services and referrals.

Undoubtedly, nobody intentionally sets out to marginalize other professions, but it abounds. Doing so can result in the law of unintended consequences.

First, a brief segue to demonstrate how such professional behaviors have an impact that while preventable leads to less-than-optimal results. As this book is written, the Treasury Department (more specifically the Internal Revenue Service) with the possible help of the Executive Branch may seek to make permanent through regulation the concept of "family attribution." Simply put, the IRS contends that when families hold most or all the equity in a company, they would presumably be working in concert. Therefore, equity impairments ubiquitously referred to as "discounts" that would usually apply to lack of control and marketability should be disallowed, thereby raising taxes on sales and transfers.

Within the profession, the equity value is often adjusted by these "discounts" that lower the pro rata value of shares. In other words, if 100 percent of Mom's company was valued at $20 million and her brother held a 10 percent interest, the Service contends the value would be $2 million and the value of any gain to this amount should be taxed.

However, the standard of fair market value assumes a *notional investor* and not a known specific party who may or may not be a family member. In the investor's eyes, a concession to reflect the financial, operational, and structural risks associated with the 10 percent equity in the specific company or asset would need to be taken into account in the value of the equity.

As in all investments, a certain level of return is sought based upon the nature of the investment, holding period, and other factors. Further, having been retained to opine in over 100 shareholder disputes with many involving family members and trustees, the notion of attribution is farcical. The greater the sum, the greater the dysfunction.

So, why the commentary? As expressed elsewhere in this book, most business appraisals are prepared by accountants—many who perform only three or four annually with most assignments requested or recommended by a client's counsel. Compounding this specific issue is many attorneys are unable to fully understand how legal provisions, markets, and risks impact the equity that is being valued where the amount opined sometimes should be adjusted by less than −20 percent and often more than −35 percent.

So, almost 30 years earlier, the rules of forming partnerships were legislated into law, called Chapter 14, where sections 2701 through 2704 dealt almost exclusively with curtailing the abuses of forming partnerships and transferring equity with limited business purpose in an effort to reduce tax liabilities. While the law has little to do with what actually occurs between buyers and sellers, many legal practitioners gravitated to trusts as a partnership workaround to accomplish the same thing as the actual workings of a business, and finance was seldom understood much less mastered.

The elegance of the plan for its tax and asset protection perspective often trumped best applications for business reasons. Yet, which profession commonly instructs on valuation to lawyers? If you guessed attorneys, you'd be correct. So, needless to say the assumption was the work product could be universally prepared by most accountant-appraisers and that fees could be negotiated.

This *race to the bottom* created many reports, which on the face, to an untrained eye, appear to meet standard. The work product would be passed along to the IRS, which is overworked and often understaffed, so it often pursues the most likely targets of abuse. And that is the taxpayer, provided values with often no or nominal support for the asset-, entity-, or equity-level risks and their corresponding rates of return. So, taxpayer IRS examinations, audits and challenges, and subsequent negotiated settlements as well as (Tax and U.S. District) court "wins" and "losses" were often based upon to what degree the discount, value, or method was applied and accepted. Often the decisions had less to do with finance and more to do with other variables.

The point is, attorneys and accountants should know to differentiate between poor and good appraisal work products to vet poor results before they are sent to the IRS. Keep in mind the differential of the business appraisal fee versus higher taxes can often be millions of dollars in taxes! In other words, a $25,000 appraisal fee may yield a $5,000,000 tax savings and often more—a 200 to one return.

And history repeats itself. During the late 1980s and early 1990s, the savings and loan (S&L) sector was making some highly speculative loans on real property. Undoubtedly, there were some rotten real estate appraisers aiding and abetting this activity. The music stopped and many S&Ls went under and the federal government stepped in with the Resolution Trust Company to liquidate the S&Ls and sell off their assets.

The banking industry has a stronger lobbying group than the real estate appraisal industry with the latter thrown under the bus. The U.S. Congress established an enforcement entity and required the individual states to license and certify real estate appraisers to better regulate their activities.

Full circle back about a decade later, commercial banks are making big bets with depositors' funds and the public is buying homes they can ill-afford; yet, being qualified all the same. More regulation such as Dodd-Frank comes on line.

Is it any great surprise the abuses of some create greater regulation where the innocent are impacted due to overreach? If the business appraisal profession would better educate and be on more equal footing with the legal and tax professions, perhaps Chapter 14 Section 2704 and now the possibility of punitive regulations encroaching on business-owning families' rights would not have occurred. When the wound is self-inflicted it's egregious.

So, while I'm no great fan of how and how much of our tax dollars are collected and spent (and it's easy to blame the primary tax collector, IRS), the real issue is if greater importance were placed on *quality*, like 99.99999 percent of all U.S. mail gets delivered to the intended recipient, the professional services and their owner clients' focus would be less on *price* and more on quality. Therefore, there would be no workaround statutes to regulate mediocre performance that while not explicitly looking to game the system is nonetheless a catalyst in perpetuating a problem when a solution exists.

There can and should be mutual respect between the legal, tax, and valuation disciplines as they're all invaluable. Better to self-regulate than to wait for a government body to do it for our respective professions and the deliverables we produce. Yet, many of these deliverables are technical, tactical, and one-off transactions. The services are seldom designed to build more enduring relationships. This brings us back to STAR and the implications when such relationships are valued and leveraged.

If one were to state that going forward attorneys and accountants must learn relationship and business building skills, many would be offended. What if the banking, wealth, and insurance professionals were encouraged to leverage relationships with the attorneys and accountants? If these relationship-centric professions sought rapport with these most trusted client advisors in addition to cold-calling (going directly to business owners), then their prospect visits would be "warm" versus "cold." And the right accountant or lawyer might have a number of ideal business client relationships instead of just one, which provides greater advisor leverage in client contact when a fellow professional espouses your merits.

How do we leverage knowledge and relationships? Have a forum where one's barter is his or her knowledge and relationships: where the value-add is shortening the time between an introduction and a billable or commissionable event. STAR offered a lunch venue where seating at each table was by intentional design. The business transaction, trust and estate attorney(s), accountant, trust officer, and life insurance and private banker professionals would be seated at a table of six. Each would have a minimum of 10 years of experience and be a local community fixture with the assumption that the individual had been vetted by the marketplace such that they were surviving, if not thriving, in their own practice before and during 2009 and on. As introductions and summaries of what each did occurred around the table, their business cards would be passed around.

In turn, the listening individuals would be thinking about who in their professionals rolodex would be a quality introduction to the person currently sharing about their business and themselves, usually another advisor and occasionally a client. Each table participant would have a turn to share. Those who tended to focus on themselves did not fare well. If an attendee that was disposed to assisting others went to such gatherings each month, they stood the chance of meeting 60 new professionals each year with which they could further their relationships at subsequent STAR gatherings or more one-on-one meetings off-site.

The success of the model was fantastic as it allowed often close-to-the-vest attorneys and accountants to meet more relationship-driven professionals. Through observation and repetition, the more technical-driven professionals began to see the merits of timely follow-up and cease looking for a quick direct client referral. *Those who were most successful in this process were ones who followed up and made introductions to others.* By doing so, their actions, not lip-service, demonstrated they were collaborative and could be measured by their follow-up and the professional company they keep.

In short order, the attendance reached a monthly capacity of 110 at lunchtime, so a second group and then a third were formed. When operating on all eight cylinders, the second and third gatherings had 50 to 80 monthly attendees apiece. This meant those who attended regularly could meet almost 200 professionals each year!

During the peak, there were nearly a thousand STAR members. A second tier was then created and was referred to as Über groups. These groups were comprised of usually 20-plus-year seasoned professionals who exemplified the best of all worlds in technical mastery and were consummate connectors of other professionals (i.e., "givers gain").

A connector is more than just a referral source. This person keeps peers front of mind and makes intentional introductions to specific people while taking the time to provide thorough background summaries. If they see events that may hold interest to some or all of the Über group members, they will share. If assistance is sought or an ask is made, it commonly originates within the group. An example might be meeting a specific board member at a target company or an out-of-area professional. The referred can almost bank that the introduction will be a vetted, high-caliber client or contact.

Follow-up is mandatory. In the course of a year about 150 high-caliber Über group introductions can be made. A high-functioning group can generate millions of dollars of annual commerce while maintaining a deep and broad bench of professional talent. During the peak, there were seven such groups with an average of 8 to 15 professionals that met once monthly. I seldom attend STAR, but fairly religiously attend our original Über group.

To be fair, the method is imperfect. Many practitioners are often driven by feast and famine. There are some hunter-gathers in the professions who during more robust times excuse themselves from group attendance as the amount of their commerce is sufficiently robust, so the need for the group is secondary. This mindset defeats the purposeful planning and collaboration of the group. It erodes cohesion.

Finally, as new engagements slow, these less involved group participants are looking for new business and then reengage in the group. This type of behavior is common for younger professionals who are expected to develop their book of business to be on the partner track as well as to "cover their financial nut" (work to pay their college debt, car payments, rent, and other living expenses).

Not surprisingly, when such group members reemerge they often cease coming because other members who placed the group ahead of the individual have moved on to others who adhere to the same conviction of camaraderie. My wife has a simple saying: "If you have to explain the concept of team ahead of its individual players, there's little chance of change."

The point of this vignette is the "silo" or "what's in it for me" mentality is fairly common and it also occurs with business advisor prospects and clients. It can occur as daily firefighting replaces building a fireproof business model where the pipeline remains full. The myopia is often so common that only industry- or profession-focused events hold interest such as mandatory tradeshows or continuing education conferences and seminars. It narrows perspective.

Commerce occurs when disparate but complementary needs are integrated, and great business occurs when such activities are aligned and acted upon. It's akin to the difference between a marriage where the cornerstone is familiarity versus shared interests and aspirations. This vignette demonstrates nuanced shared relationships, and knowledge can be leveraged where uniqueness and action are the differentiation and provide client value-add.

If a client or fellow advisor's first question is "What is your hourly rate?" instead of "I'm looking for a solution," the request will always be a commodity-based transaction. In that exchange, the value differentiation is neither understood nor desired. The latter question is a well-schooled client or an advisor who understands that value-based projects are often a better investment in a relationship and a deliverable, which often serves three purposes: reduce risk, create value, and leverage human capital.

It's a win-win strategy again and again. I have made and received thousands of referrals and connections by making the time to help others succeed, which in turn has had similar benefits. It takes time and thick skin, as there will be a good number who are all too happy to take but are bewildered when asked to reciprocate.

And sometimes, when the organization doesn't exist to support leveraging knowledge and relationships, don't be afraid to be the solution. This has helped me as a group manager for LinkedIn's Trust & Estate Network, which has 21,000+ members as of this writing.

VIGNETTE TWO: THE TREES-AND-FOREST SYNDROME

A private healthcare information technology (HCIT) firm was the second success of a serial entrepreneur. He had made and lost much of his first $50 million and started the company about a dozen years ago. The company used a business process outsourcing model whereby hospitals and larger healthcare centers with somewhat antiquated legacy systems were being replaced by more efficient hardware and software.

Because of the amount and sensitivity of the data and the rapidly evolving push for healthcare to better leverage technology, the federal government was incentivizing significant investment to improve patient care, tens of billions of dollars a year. Every type of technology and consulting provider was posturing for a slice of the pie, so double digit growth during the race for the best software as a solution (SaaS) was in full gear.

The problem is older operating systems were often incompatible with newer ones, so a parallel program would be put in place just in case there was a glitch between the old and new systems transferring and managing data. This was as much as a technology mastery issue as it was having adequate type, level of personnel, and compensation. This industry issue is akin to the video console recorder (VCR) race between the VHS and the Betamax cartridge tape versions. Those age 30 and above know who won that race until both were replaced by the DVD and now streaming.

The point is there were many legacy systems and many SaaS options based upon budget and preference. The challenge was having the headcount strength to supply knowledge workers who were familiar with the old and new versions and who could facilitate the crossover as seamlessly as possible, while the current healthcare IT staff both worked on their day jobs as well as were trained on new hardware and software. Such engagements could be tens of millions of dollars and take years. Staffing needs would expand and contract, so maintaining appropriate headcount could be an issue.

For full disclosure, I try to wear many hats—the hat of the activist investor seeking the highest possible return; the hat of the C-suite; the hat of the financier; and the hat of the entrepreneur.

The truly successful entrepreneur wants more than just a large payday. She wants relevance and the time to enjoy and share financial success with others. Entrepreneurs often embrace the notion of entertainment, philanthropy, and obtaining a return on their human and financial capital, too. Candidly, they want access to the best ideas and the best deals, and while risk management is important, they didn't achieve concentrated wealth solely from risk aversion, but finding and seizing opportunities.

In a perfect world, the entrepreneur thinks like an investor. She might even wish to consider a private investment in a public equity (PIPE) or in a small-cap company so she can benefit from liquidity while having the skills or access to provide governance and leadership by holding one or more board seats, depending upon the amount of equity investment held.

This governing control can influence operating results. If she possessed the honed skills from owning a successful business, then she may have the human and financial capital knowhow needed. And if she doesn't like the operating results, she can threaten to pull equity or cull executives. Now, that's control. Conversely, the PIPE investor can always have an "operator" proxy sit on the board if she hasn't the time or inclination to do so. The point is any owner who is thinking like an investor, particularly an activist one, recognizes the best benchmark is high return on all invested capital.

Companies that are open to fresh perspectives are more likely to adapt and thrive. They may expect serious analytics when they may simply suffer from a trees-versus-forest conundrum. Productivity must be measured, managed, and mastered. Organic growth should be well above industry norms ("the pack").

Another attribute of a founder is that he has already learned what patient capital is, which is to say that there is a growth in value that occurs over many years, even a generation, so chasing after three-to-five-year returns may incentivize some private equity groups, but a longer perspective is often what differentiates the owner investor.

Keep in mind the activist investor is motivated to take an undervalued company, usually as a result of underperformance, and bring about the change that would usually only be permitted in a private company. This is why "operators" not only understand value, but how human and financial capital work together to unlock a company's and staff's potential. Occasionally, with this in mind and under the right circumstances, investors will take a public company private as the regulatory and quarter-by-quarter reporting and hitting forecasts are often shortsighted. This leads to occasional financial machinations so analysts don't downgrade the company's share price.

Finally, operators in the C-suite of a private company have to have a holistic strategy to have a broad perspective and to deploy capital so they're not one-trick ponies. Deploying capital in R&D and capital investment achieves better returns and allows all stakeholders to win as long as there is a balance of humility and hubris.

Regardless of industry, this means fostering innovation, which is more about human capital—the clients, the staff, and the market. Of course, the trusted advisors' perspectives should be sought. This means defined risk management and leveraged relationships that are an open pipeline of recruitment to attract and challenge the best minds. Only then can the C-suite drive value-based stewardship at the board level on down to the line staff and external to the organization.

In many ways, the HCIT was operating a model that had solid success. However, success without oversight can lead to operational issues when the wrong metrics are managed.

In this vignette, the business had a blend of professional management and family members. Some appeared ancillary (redundant) when examining the roles of subordinates reporting to family members. In and of itself, this is common, even with companies reporting hundreds of millions in annual revenues. The company did have a preexisting exit strategy; however, this was driven by private equity, which held a minority preferred equity position and two seats on the board of five.

The PEG's preferred rights converted to a control common position should the company sell a majority or all of its equity. The combined executive compensation was more than two times industry benchmark and was unnecessary given the level of stock options received by more senior personnel.

The CEO lived in Southern California; however, the headquarters were in the Midwest where one of his siblings was an executive in charge of human resources, administration, and technology, which overlapped with the role of the company CFO, who shared these duties. There was no executive vice president of operations or COO. There was an executive vice president of sales.

Growth was reported as double digit, and EBITDA profit margins were 27 percent of sales. What was not to love? The issue is there were other very similar competitors whose margins were nearer to 34 percent.

A deeper due diligence determined that the regional vice presidents of the northeastern and western United States were overseeing sales growth that was in the single digits. Both had been in their functions for two-plus years.

Analytics revealed that these two markets had the highest concentration of health facilities and among the highest year-over-year growth compared to most other regional markets. Simply put, there was insufficient disincentive for the two VPs to hustle and capture more market, and the EVP did not appear to be aware of their substandard performance or did nothing to resolve it. The largest finding was the majority of growth was occurring in the Midwest where the brand was best known. In addition, the company's labor expense was well above (+20%) that of its peer group.

The cause for bloated labor expense was a function of a conflicted policy in which technicians with specialized training would be benched for up to three months with pay in the hope the sales force would be awarded a new engagement necessitating their skillsets. There was no requirement for them to learn new skills during their idle time. Conversely, to incentivize staff to remain with the company, they were paid performance bonuses. The net result is the company still suffered high turnover as there were no assurances of which projects would require what types of technical skills.

Discussions to determine the nature of key client contracts (repeat business) and level of engagement by commercial bankers and attorneys and accountants, as well as by strategic partners, showed limited influence by these constituents. The net result is the company had $200 million in additional locked-up value that would have taken 6 to 18 months to free; however, management's focus was to pursue liquidity with a missed opportunity for some tax savings.

This scenario is common. It could have been a multibillion company if it possessed an overarching strategy: where governance supported oversight and metrics; where the brand was differentiated based upon unique relationships; and where knowledge could have been further harnessed to lower operating risks, better pursue available opportunities, and elevate the shareholder value.

Notwithstanding these shortcomings, success was defined as serious money made by the founder, the C-suite, family members, and his equity partners. The author, proving himself as an operator, was subsequently retained to evaluate a portfolio of companies held by the private equity group to apply the same type of assessment as described here.

VIGNETTE THREE: THE PATH NOT TAKEN

I perform a fair amount of risk mitigation (litigation, mediation, and arbitration) services and there are common themes. In duty-of-care or fiduciary duty breaches, it is often an ounce-of-prevention issue. As an example, the company CEO and/or board have not sought an independent opinion of the value and rights of controlling and/or preferred shareholders and as such the noncontrolling interests feel they have been slighted.

Similar issues arise in class action and damages cases, where at any time a trusted advisor could inquire about how the client is conducting business and whether it may run afoul of a regulatory or enforcement body, or how other potential parties may become harmed. Arguably, some acts are unintentional and others are weighed (cost of getting caught and ensuing dispute versus benefit).

It's when it's clear that a trusted advisor could or should have known of the consequences and chose not to advise that one should ask more questions. These questions are often about what are the merits of action versus inaction such as loss of income for tacitly or directly supporting undesirable actions. Yes, clients, jobs, and income can be lost. So?

The loss of marketplace goodwill and dispute costs over equity value far exceeds the insurance of obtaining an independent opinion beforehand. (Think Enron and the accounting firm performing their audits that rubber-stamped questionable accounting.) As there are inevitably advisors engaged in such matters, it begs to ask the question, after all the other tax and legal due diligence, why an independent fairness opinion wasn't sought. However, this vignette focuses on family businesses and the myriad issues that often lead to the dilution of their value and destruction of a legacy.

First, does the owner understand his or her role when there are multiple shareholders even when they're family? A common area of dispute is when two or more siblings or family members are involved in the operation of a business and then one chooses other pursuits. If that family member is also a shareholder, has she harmed the other family members by discontinuing their services for which they are presumably paid market-level compensation?

Where is the wisdom of the family and advisors when the remaining family members choose to elevate their compensation, reduce distributions, or enter into other related-party relationships at other than fair market (arm's-length) rates to penalize the member taking a different path? The family member is still a shareholder, so finding ways to reduce that member's economic benefit, as well as taking a second bite from the apple by claiming the departed family member's equity has limited value when it is from the financial machinations of the operating family members (and occasionally with the help of advisors), are all recipes for conflict.

Conversely, if one is a family member and shareholder and the active family members (shareholders, officers, and/or employees) are building capital and reinvesting in the business that may result in lower or no distributions, this does not mean, just because as a family member and shareholder you're dependent on the past income from distributions based upon your lifestyle, that the company or its management owes you more dividends.

Often the aggrieved have latent issues. Recently, there was a midmarket food manufacturer that had been a family business for over a century. One brother was more in the front office facing clients and the other was more operational. The operational brother chose to open up a restaurant and the other brother felt slighted.

The friction caused them not to speak to one another for many years. However, as they were siblings and saw each other during family gatherings, the hurt feelings finally mended. Often they don't. The brothers are now older and the brother involved in the manufacturer is involving two of his three children in the business with each of the children receiving equal distributions.

One day the non-operating sibling, who is also a board member, is helping her uncle at his restaurant at the cash register. Her father is visiting. An armed man comes into the restaurant and threatens her to turn over the cash. Her uncle and father try to subdue the robber and the uncle is fatally shot. Her father is inconsolable. His health deteriorates and his two operating children from the food manufacturer are allegedly too involved in the business to be of comfort. They, like their father, received many of their product sales paid in cash and skimmed about 5 percent of revenues as unreported. (This was not known to their sibling.)

The non-operating daughter had fond memories of her father's vigor and his purchasing an expensive luxury car every few years despite his advanced age. Father falls and strikes his head and needs physical and cognitive therapy. The costs and time investment were high, and his two children involved in the business did little to assist. Father dies.

Daughter's mother was father's best friend and confidant. She looked forward to family meals as food was a central part of the family's fabric. Once father passed, the two operating children became less involved in family gatherings and soon thereafter their increasingly frail mother passes away from grief. Once she does, the two siblings reduce director's compensation of the outside sibling, raise their salaries, and lower distributions.

The company, while having been in operation for 100+ years, had not grown much in the past 20 under the siblings as it was simply a cash cow. The siblings distrusted a third party to manage a separate Midwest location, which would have been very lucrative due to demand from several national clients. In their minds if it was not a family member, nobody could be trusted with the family secrets—the classic pennywise and pound foolish or projecting distrust by one's own somewhat unsavory actions.

Eventually, the brother allegedly forced the non-operating sister off the board and terminated her director's pay and shareholder distributions.

He and his sister that were involved in the business offered a remarkably low sum to buy the external sibling's shares. She refused. After about a decade of the past actions of her siblings, she sued under oppression rights and eventually received about 90 percent of what she was entitled to after over a year of bitterness and litigation expense which included my expert fees.

What she confided was she was beside herself in anger as she felt her siblings placed their personal enrichment over the family and the business, which was built in part by her father and uncle. She as much wanted to punish them for "killing" her parents prematurely, and the money was to exact the pain.

She also knew her brother, having gotten away with the bad-faith acts with the help of the family attorney and accountant, would undoubtedly do to her sister that which her sister and brother had done to her, so this brother did not have to share at all. Adding to fact being stranger than fiction, the two operating siblings had very little to do with running the daily activities of their business, so they could enjoy the funds derived from it.

There are several points here. If the siblings had allowed the company to be professionally managed and legitimate, it would have generated many times its current revenue and profit size. They would have the economic benefit and freedom of a passive investment even after tax. But the notion of control and greed have made it nearly impossible for another generation to continue the business's operations.

A similar dispute occurred between two New England brothers who had a very successful commercial cleaning business. One brother decides to leave and start investing in Florida as the real estate market was frothy and unbeknownst to him near peak. He claimed to the bank that he was still the company's president, which was untrue. This was done to access funding to leverage his purchases and have proof of external income to service the debt. Ironically, the brother involved in the daily operations was still paying him his salary despite no active involvement as president—brotherly love. The departing brother was previously active in company management, so the remaining brother was pulling double duty, yet receiving the same salary. The departed brother needs more funds to continue his investing lifestyle; discontinues reporting income to the taxing authorities; and ultimately sells a small block of his shares that then results in his operating brother, instead of having half the company, having over half and the control that comes with it.

The operating sibling fires his brother who has now not been involved in the company for over two years and takes his salary based upon the logic of holding both of their positions. The terminated brother sues despite the "at-will" clause in the company's bylaws. He also sues that it had not been his idea to sell his shares, making his brother a larger shareholder, but believed both would redeem stock, each keeping equal shares.

The "outside" brother in Florida runs afoul of the banks and files for bankruptcy and also has some ensuing issues with the IRS. He returns to New England and usurps his authority as a shareholder, but no longer a company officer in a sensitive negotiation with a labor union. Based upon his actions, the union obtains concessions that dramatically reduce the company's profits. This external brother alleges the operating brother is not adhering to his fiduciary duty by offering to pay a lower amount for his shares and wants to be paid based upon the share value when both brothers had visited selling the company four years earlier for an amount that found no offers. The brother relied upon the representation of an investment banker who would subsequently refuse to defend the earlier value.

The net result is the outside brother received about 25 percent of what he could have had he cooperated with his operating brother and sold the company at its market value. "I want it the way I want it" led to the brothers not only not being on speaking terms but having no involvement with each other's families despite each being the godparent to the other's kids. The wayward brother contributed to the decline of market value of the company as the union went on strike and picketed their job sites, causing them to lose long-time clients' goodwill. In trying to screw his brother, he ends up screwing himself as well.

I was retained by a very prominent attorney to investigate what looked like some questionable financial activities by a father and son who were operating a national company involved in cleaning solutions in the hospitality and eating establishment industries. This was a very profitable business.

As a 25 percent equity holder, the daughter and sister was concerned as her annual distributions went from north of $4 million to below $2.5 million. She lived on these distributions and was never involved in the family business.

Review of the financial statements reflected the company had recapitalized, stripping out equity and creating "NewCo" where the daughter was not a shareholder. NewCo renewed contracts which would eventually gut the pre-existing relationships of the original company.

Clearly, the two family members breached their fiduciary duty to the outside member, rationalizing that since she was not involved in the business, she should not receive as much benefit. The issues sometimes spread between family members, spouses, and generations, such as children suing their parents for causing a loss of value to their equity in a partnership where the founder(s) believe, since the equity was gifted, they can do as they wish. Wanting it so does not make it so.

In another case, members of a family who no longer wished to do the heavy lifting in a manufacturing business with many real property holdings were also unhappy they saw their distributions decline. They sued the family involved in the business for breach of duty because the revenues of the company had declined.

They failed to recognize that, although sales did in fact decline, the company had repositioned itself, which took capital investment and had subsequently resulted in much greater profits. The old business model simply was unsustainable. They also failed to understand that the demand for much of the land had significantly declined due to a lack of water right access, which caused the property to become fallow. A dose of reality didn't dampen the demands they had on the dough they previously had expected, and they did not want to have to return to working for a living.

In another case, a fairly common issue transpired. The founder of a global shipping business in an effort to minimize taxes created a very complicated tax structure prior to the sale of his company. The company's vice chairman and CFO had been with the founder from the beginning (30+ years) and had a very active role in the strategy and finances as they built this company from scratch. As such, the founder made him a trust protector of an irrevocable trust of which children from one marriage were the beneficiary and children from one marriage were not. The founder continued to expect that the friend and former CFO would perform as directed as trustee.

When he did not, he first tried to decant the trust (empty the trust of its assets) and sued the trustee for breach of duty, alleging he had invested in types of assets that were inconsistent with the settlor's intent. Once proving the assets and allocation were not only consistent with similar risk profile investments the founder had invested in currently and in the past, but were performing better than their industry peers by using hedging strategies and a balance of leverage and strong management skills, the trustee prevailed. Nevertheless, he had a tough time recovering his fees and lost a dear friend who placed greed over gratitude.

A chairman of a 100-plus-year-old large distribution company and his son ran the company and in addition they were co-trustees to the uncle's niece's and nephew's trusts. The chairman's sister (mother of the niece and nephew) died despite his demise being expected before her own. He carried some resentment that despite having more than doubled the company size during his multi-decade devotion to the company, he did not directly hold the controlling voting shares, but did so as trustee for the trust. The drafter of the trust was also the company and personal attorney of the settlors.

The company made numerous investments in what may be alleged to be interests and assets that had questionable contributory value to the core company. Restrictions had been placed on the beneficiaries (adult children), which severely hampered their rights.

The chairman had terminated his eldest son as company CEO and his second eldest is known to be more compliant, but not nearly as capable as the father. The uncle has done everything in his power to acquire the niece's and nephew's shares for well below market value while withholding distributions to create financial duress. The adult children are estranged from their uncle and unhappy with his actions to thwart their inheritance; however, they have not wished to select a litigious route. As a result they feel desperate despite having a likely claim of a breach of care and a conflict of interest by their uncle.

The uncle's goal appears to be to buy their shares at a significantly reduced value to be rid of them or to tighten his rights over their interests, such that he perceives he can unilaterally do as he wishes. The uncle is in his mid-seventies.

Should the uncle operate the company as a professional investor with the goal of optimizing shareholder value versus exploiting his heirs, the value of the company would be much greater than what it has been currently appraised. As family members do have shareholder rights, the uncle does have a duty of care; however, he does not appear to perceive that he does and has shown no inclination to acquire their shares at their market value or permit a third party to acquire either a minority, majority, or a controlling interest.

A review by several affluent families has shown an interest to acquire a minority block held by the niece and nephew and pay a premium to acquire a control position with the uncle still running the business after a company recapitalization. The uncle has shown no interest in visiting these options despite a duty to the shareholders (albeit family members) to consider such an option.

A few years ago a multigenerational major heavy construction firm lost the founder and one of his sons in the space of several months. The founder died from complications common for older folks—old age. The son, who was the company's chairman and CEO, died from too many marriages and girlfriends and as a result of wrapping his sports car around a phone pole, allegedly speeding from one girlfriend's home he had built to another awaiting girlfriend. The survivors were a twenty-something daughter and all the siblings, uncles, cousins, nieces, and nephews. The company's CFO was in his seventies and also was the steward of the family office activities, which was run from his office at the company.

The event occurred just as the residual impact of the 2009 financial crises was unfolding, and several subsidiary and labor union legal actions were on the horizon. At the same time, several of the money-losing subsidiaries and divisions were hemorrhaging millions of dollars as some family members had a range of no-show to no-skill jobs to maintain interfamily harmony. The annual cost to the family was tens of millions of dollars. In the absence of rightsizing the company and divesting underperforming business units and assets, the company would unlikely survive another year or two.

Despite the behaviors of key management, the company ultimately dodged a bullet, but decided to be more attentive to the clear delineation of the business and the family roles to ensure the business would remain viably in the family for generations to come. This activity took the involvement of family business advisors, insurance, banking, legal, and accounting teams to reimagine and reposition the company and clarify the roles and financial sums received by operator and nonoperating family members.

Each of these aforementioned cases involved control and money versus cohesion motivated parties. These issues do not happen overnight. They would be very hard to conceal from advisors. How do they occur? Do they have a corrosive impact on value? Do they blur the line of family member, employee, shareholder, officer, and director? You bet they do.

It's not just bad families or bad actors. Sometimes it's bad facts. In an all-too-common challenge by the IRS examiner, a decedent who had left $65 million in highly appreciated public securities and real estate had his estate audited. He held a 99 percent member interest, and a trust was the manager of the limited liability company. The service's position was the estate owed tens of millions of dollars in taxes.

Counsel for the estate retained our services. First, the service ignored that upon death the member interest, unless approved by the manager, was an assignee interest. This means an economic interest with no voting rights. Control was solely that of the manager upon the decedent's passing. Second, the LLC operating agreement had no put or call options (purchase obligations) nor a requirement to distribute the proceeds of the holdings if they were sold. The LLC had no debt and low yield. In effect, the economic benefit could not be realized by the notional 99% assignee investor.

Making matters worse, the decedent died January 2009. March 2009 was the very bottom of the stock market collapse. The IRS was emboldened by a recent Tax Court decision involving the *Estate of Holman* where the sole asset was millions of dollars of public stock in one company. The estate failed to demonstrate a non-business purpose and the judge ruled in favor of the Commissioner (IRS). In reviewing the record, there was no discussion of the legitimate business purpose of the asset protection entity. The court found that since the underlying asset was liquid, the "discounts" were disallowed and "grossed up" the estate, leaving the taxpayer a hefty bill. Arguably, this was more an issue with the advisors and less so the taxpayer as the same judge opined for a ~25 percent discount for an interest in an entity that held solely cash and CDs. The point is that a lack of financial and legal rigor was applied to the client case as well as the two Tax Court cases.

First, the analyst, through the estate's trust and litigation attorney (not the original T&E planning attorney), was able to show that if the theory is an immediate sale of the entire portfolio at the time of death, then the manager failed in his fiduciary duty to sell at various market peaks preceding the member's passing. In other words, we were framing the discussion for a subsequent argument about the reality of the financial markets and investor behavior. Second, the portfolio was not adequately diversified and the endowment funds of both Harvard and Yale holding billions of dollars had seen their portfolios drop value by more than 25 percent. These are funds that are professionally managed with teams of highly compensated sector managers. The LLC was not similar as was evidenced by no leverage on real property and below-market rent collection.

Third, the majority of the public securities invested were held in fund of funds, which have lock-up provisions requiring the manager to submit in writing in December a request for liquidation and affording the fund six months to unwind the specific holdings with a 10 percent holdback and a hefty liquidation fee. In addition, there was no liquidity in the market for the sale of the real estate holdings, which would require a duress sale concession. The early 1990s S&L crisis taught us that real property was being sold at discounts well north of 40 percent.

Fourth, the LLC had various provisions associated with the sale to a related and then a third party. Such provisions plus due diligence amounted to over one year holding period should every one of the steps be effectuated. Fifth, the manager did not have the obligation to distribute proceeds upon sale of underlying assets. Sixth, as the date of death was January, the notional sale should all the hoops be cleared would still require close to another year to make a request for liquidation.

Seventh, how many high-net-worth people exist who hold $65 million-plus and what does modern portfolio theory suggest? The notional investor would likely invest no more than 10 percent of wealth in any one opportunity. Fewer still would select fund of funds and an undiversified portfolio with the possibility of no voting rights. This means the investor would have to be worth $650 million and be perfectly happy with below-market returns and an unknown horizon where either a partial or full economic benefit would be realized should assets be sold and proceeds be distributed. The number of possible investors would likely be in the low thousands if any. Eighth, the portfolio had significant built-in gains (BIG), meaning a significant tax liability, which is counter to the notion of liquidity where the sale results in keeping cash or cash equivalent.

Further, the year-over-year return was below the blue-chip quality index (S&P 500) where an investment in Vanguard as a proxy would have resulted in over 450 net basis points (4.5%) greater than the portfolio held in large part due to the transparent and less transparent fees of the fund of funds. Given the decedent's age, the income allocation of the portfolio was lacking.

Ultimately, the IRS Regional Manager accepted a 37.5 percent aggregate discount, down from 42 percent that had been opined (counsel agreed with a 10% discount for lack of control—a *fait accomplis* for the IRS as it acknowledged no control, relying on a *Holman* decision measure, which has nothing to do with the empiricism of what the concession should have been).

What these examples demonstrate is even when ownership is held within a family, it doesn't mean they will necessarily be cohesive or agree. The issues are as much about legal provisions, risk management, and rates of return as they are about human capital (governance, relationships, knowledge, and behavior). Many tax and financial disputes could be resolved if the focus remained on what would the notional investor agree to on both the buy and sell side. If the investors are not contemplating an optimal holding period, then the risk becomes real that some wealth can be lost in the interim.

The point of Vignette Three is that both advisors and regulators must be privy and responsive to these issues whether these are 8- or 10-figure companies. Our role is not to enable exploitation just because the client is paying our bills, especially if the actions run afoul of the law or are morally repugnant.

Being independent will undoubtedly lose us some affluent clients who believe they have bought loyalty. Maintaining character and heading off problems by demonstrating the upside of being a benefactor and thinking long-term gain versus short-term advantage is usually the right thing to do. Clients don't always follow good advice and advisors don't have to keep those who won't.

VIGNETTE FOUR: PUTTING IT ALL TOGETHER (STRATEGY, HUMAN CAPITAL, AND FINANCE)

We have all heard that "those who can't do, teach." This book's intention is to emphasize that having the cultural mindset of a learning organization is a positive way to engage a company's most important resource—their people.

Leaders and advisors can leverage their knowledge and relationships. It is not easy. Those who are reliant on software to generate work product and lack the wisdom born of 50,000+ hours of experience should not be advising companies on how to take their operations to the next level. Neither should an entrepreneur who has had one successful company sale. There just are too many operational, industry, and market-related variables as this book has endeavored to share.

For the balance, the following example, graphics, and steps could be considered a framework for the application of GRRK to afford clients seeking fresh opportunities and options to be dynamic and disruptive in their markets.

Consider the possibilities for engaging staff and advisors as stewards of value creation. What are you waiting for?

Typically, valuation and advisory services are referred in by an attorney, followed by a wealth advisor and then an accountant. Occasionally, it is a family member or founder who has read one of my articles or seen a presentation or panel at a private capital market or family office event. Occasionally, what began as intake for a benchmark work product such as identify and measure risk to determine the value of equity evolves into a more comprehensive delineation of all the risks that are impacting equity value. This in turn may result in an engagement to manage and mitigate these risks.

A common question is how compensation is determined for such engagements. There is no one pat response. Typically, the identification and measurement of risks to prepare a value is project based. Fees are based upon timeframe, purpose, structure and industry complexity, and scope of work. A good start-point for smaller and uncomplicated matters is a $10,000 retainer; however, fees can run into the six figures depending upon retention purpose, the nature and complexity of assets, subsidiary relationships, and ownership. Occasionally, the work will require valuation of individual business units. The deeper the due diligence (time, research, data collection, and analytics), the greater the fees.

The second-tier project is, "So, now that we know the value and the opportunities and risks, what do we wish to do about it?" Frequently, this is where I may not be the best of salespeople, as more often than not the interest is there but action following it comes to a halt. This is commonly a result of the owner and advisor optics and occasionally key staff and family feeling threatened: "I don't have time," or "I'm unsure this is anything more than smoke and mirrors. How can you claim a value increase of 50 or 300 percent or more?"

First, there is no silver bullet. What reduces the procrastination is making the steps more bite-size. Think of coaching someone to run a marathon or lose 50 pounds. It would be ludicrous to suggest on day one the nascent runner is expected to complete 26.2 miles, so the first step might be to jog for 10 minutes and gradually build up endurance and strength over time. The same for dieting. Nobody should expect or want to lose 50 pounds in a month, but perhaps a pound a week is doable.

The point is that actionable items should not appear daunting; otherwise, there will be nominal buy-in. Conversely, entrepreneurial families want to see results quickly, and establishing an expectation of the here-to-there must be done or the issue of fees versus results will undoubtedly emerge.

So, assume the decision maker and/or family and/or advisor have some degree of buy-in to service retention. The intake needs to be established as early as possible. This means recognizing the company is part of an ecosystem and the roles of constituents will be needed as early as possible. This will often include first discussing wants, needs, and perceptions with the company founder and/or C-suite. Then the optics, awareness, and engagement of family, key staff, clients, and vendors is needed. Perhaps more importantly, the degree of involvement of bankers, accountants, family business advisors, attorneys, insurance professionals, and wealth managers needs to be determined.

This can take days, weeks, and sometimes months. The findings are then shared with key parties and prioritized for issues such as alignment and leverage. A one- to several-day (over several periods) workshop is needed that as a minimum will include key parties who are expected to influence outcomes.

The workshop is to identify resource gaps (time, talent, and temperament: human and financial capital). By doing so, the owner can determine whether he will be driving the charge or delegating the transformation to key staff and/or advisors (and that such individuals have the requisite abilities to effectuate the change sought). This step is critical as it provides for some degree of alignment across disciplines. It often unearths conflicts and capability concerns as well as opportunities. The previously identified risks are prioritized (no more than two or three addressed at a time, otherwise dilution of results is about certain).

At this point, the financial investment for the intake can be as low as five to seven figures with the latter usually being a national firm with substantial resources and requirements. The workshop(s) as well can also be in the low five to six figures. Again at this point, the notion of financial investment for a latter result causes much consternation by those writing the check as it is often perceived as "coming out of my pocket." While some amount of pain should be expected so the investment in services is more than lip service, the distrust of many advisors who have more sizzle than steak is a legitimate concern.

To make fees more palatable, often a retainer of $25,000 to $50,000 is paid up front and then more bite-sized monthly amounts against a project fee are charged. Again, this is based upon whether the company will be able to use its own staff and whether they will be using some of their trusted advisors or who the trusted advisors may recommend or whether my staff and external expertise will be utilized. Naturally, the more high-caliber professionals are deployed, the greater the investment and the higher the expected return.

This is usually when there is another conversation about skin-in-the-game. Should the client want to keep fees down, this may protract the process, so six months can extend to two years. Or, if time is a factor, then another option is lowering the up-front and monthly fees to a "participation" (success) fee for achieving milestones such as equity value enhancement, reduced costs, increased profits, or other measurable outcomes such as reduced risks. Invariably, the backend amounts paid are often many times greater than the up-front fee due to the percentage of new value creation.

I refer to this logic as the *casino mentality*. A patron goes into a casino and converts cash into chips. This is done as the pain of hard hundred dollar bills loss is dulled as chips subconsciously are not seen as money. The point is that many owners are hard-pressed to invest hundreds of thousands of dollars (and sometimes millions) to improve end results, but when they sell their company or equity stake and the same sums (and oftentimes more) are deducted from the sales proceeds, they are comfortable with this exchange as it's the "house's money" and they are somehow separate from it. This occasionally differs from larger private and public companies that often earmark significant professional fees budgeted to make operating improvements.

Key here is this is not an ad-hoc process. It must be strategic. It must engage the founder's commitment to influence an organizational culture to align to what is better, not simply familiar. Reactive is familiar. Dynamic is not.

While I'm not expecting the reader to embrace the notion of Zen or "flow," we know what superior performance looks like when we see it. Zen may be referred to as a philosophical practice of introspection and reflection where you may try to see or think through the meaning of any object of your attention in order to try to achieve some transcendence. It is common for professional athletes to be "in zone," thereby playing above their own game. This is also referred to as flow, where the mental state of operation in which a person performing an activity is fully immersed in a feeling of energized focus, full involvement, and enjoyment in the process of the activity. I think of it as ultra-focused passion, where the grind of blocking and tackling gives way to a greater purpose. A greater purpose cannot be achieved through tactics. This is why the governance in GRRK is so relevant and why optimal and dynamic performance is elusive.

And here is where the most time and attention is expended to modify how owners and advisors think about companies. This requires a framework with specific milestones that can take months and years to achieve. If it was simply a matter of throwing money at the obstacle or opportunity, then every deep-pocketed owner and company would have their version of the New York Yankees or Red Sox. It is more like moneyball with boring metrics when well-orchestrated result in a steady stream of wins. Batting consistent doubles isn't as exciting as homeruns. And as emphasized throughout this book, it is as much about human capital as it is financial.

That's very hard for most of us to wrap our minds around, because it's seldom expressed in the business media, in academia, or by our advisors. Why? It's more difficult to track and that which is difficult is often deferred or dropped. This is why most companies operate toward the reversion to the mean, which is mediocre.

Following is a pictorial and case example to better understand how this works.

At a Society of Trust & Estate Practitioners (STEP) event, I co-presented with a CPA on the notion of value creation (equity value enhancement—EVE) and that it was as beneficial to fellow trusted advisors serving affluent entrepreneurs as it is for their clients and prospects. The thesis emphasis is having a strategic plan to manage risk. The presentation prompted several subsequent meetings with a business attorney whose client was on the board of a fairly good-sized professional services firm. This in turn resulted in meeting with the C-suite and several of the firm's other trusted advisors.

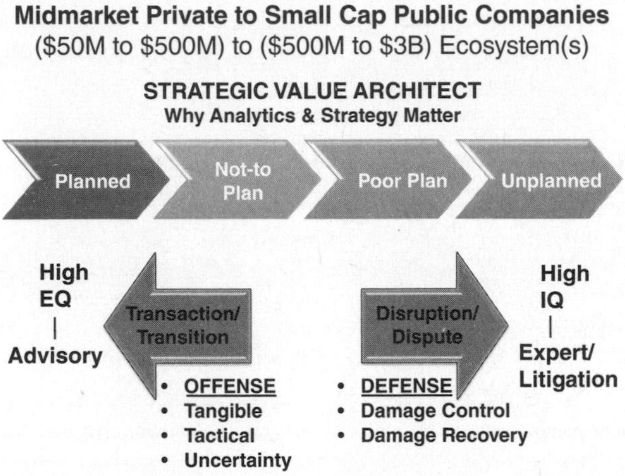

Midmarket Private to Small Cap Public Companies
($50M to $500M) to ($500M to $3B) Ecosystem(s)

STRATEGIC VALUE ARCHITECT
Why Analytics & Strategy Matter

Planned
Not-to Plan
Poor Plan
Unplanned

High EQ
|
Advisory

Transaction/ Transition

- OFFENSE
- Tangible
- Tactical
- Uncertainty

Disruption/ Dispute

- DEFENSE
- Damage Control
- Damage Recovery

High IQ
|
Expert/ Litigation

As I do with presentations, I endeavor to determine how sharp the folks are in the room and where influence lies. In this case it was the firm's CFO. His wife was an equestrian and he could relate with the sentiment that advisors' personalities run the gamut from high EQ (empathetic—people over processes) to high IQ, which is often more technical and transactional. I demonstrated that anyone in the room could be the steward; however, to have an advisory role one must solicit recommendations that ask tough questions like, "What will be the top three things we want to excel at in the North American market?" So, to be a strategic value architect, the plan must be birthed from an immutable and overarching strategy. Such plans tend to be proactive and produce both tangible and intangible results, whether it's build a market or buy one or both. Focus is on solving for uncertainty by addressing resource gaps. Sadly, as a plan becomes more ad hoc or is poorly conceived, the disruptions mount. This environment is often dominated by experts who may lack people skills, but whose focus is on damage control. There were blank stares when I inquired about who leadership thought was part of the firm's ecosystem.

This company had undergone numerous acquisitions; however, the synergies were not realized and the executive leadership recognized it suffered from a bureaucracy that did not support innovation. As an example, the three primary business units had in excess of 90,000 clients; however, cross-selling was not one of its strong suits nor was middle management incentivized to do something about it. Clearly, there were issues that impacted value creation such as relatively flat growth and well below-market return on invested capital.

Midmarket Private to Small Cap Public Companies
($50M to $500M) to ($500M to $3B) Ecosystem(s)

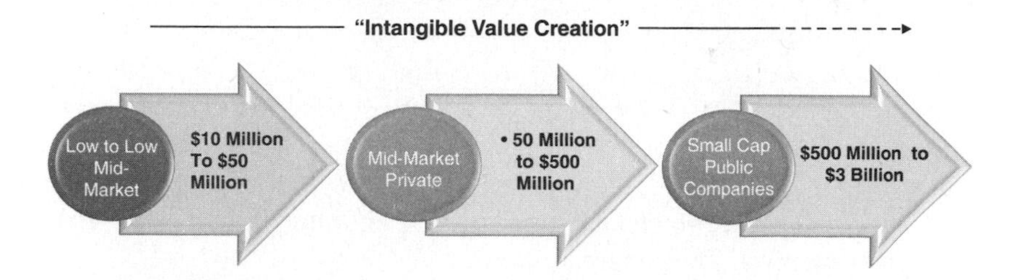

- **Options for the Business**
- **Opportunities for Owner & Family**
- **Transaction Support**

- **Value Creation/Intangibles**
- **Dynamic Capabilities/Opportunity to Act**
- **Sense—Seize—Transform**

The company fell within the higher range of revenue size; however, despite the significant staff size and a business model that presumably emphasized relationships and knowledge, management focused on cost cutting and growth through acquisition, which still was below organic growth of its peer group. We explored options to create intangible value and also discussed succession as there was a significant gap in age between senior and middle management and a different approach to dealing with risks and opportunities. Therefore, a discussion concerning unifying strategy together to produce dynamic capabilities (sense—seize—transform) held interest by both levels of management.

Advantage is *not* solely tactical, static, or business as usual

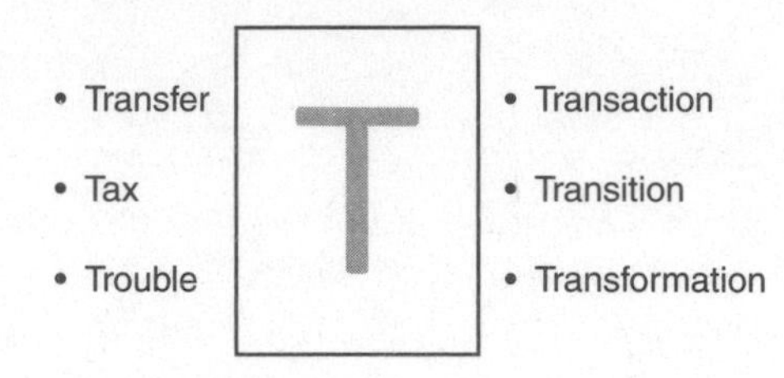

Those in the room were somewhat startled to learn that technical and transactional does not provide a competitive advantage in of itself. However, most concurred their focus on minimizing trouble and taxes and were not considering how a transition could end up being transformative. I sensed the discomfort as transformation translates to *change* through the optics of most people. However, markets are not static and the one guarantee is change is going to happen. It really is the catalyst—whether internal or external.

I indicated this is not a journey any one person had to take alone, nor did it require everyone row in unison. It did require rowing in the same direction and not necessarily on an identical path (albeit preferred). This is when the discussion of constituents and ecosystem reemerged. It's not a company operating in a vacuum nor are all the best ideas originated from the C-suite. Indoctrination to explore how the company might adapt raised as many questions as there were answers.

I. Governance

Think Culture.
Think Strategy.

A lot of information coming at one time, especially where old paradigms may need to be altered or shattered, started a secondary meeting as to what governance means. I can guarantee if there are a dozen people in a conference room, there'll be more than 12 answers and the same goes for the notion of strategy. Because the military indoctrinates its officers, I often use these analogies as an example of the blocking and tackling where everyone puts on armor and tries to prevail over their opposition. I liken that to UFC cage fighting. What is truly being sought is to recognize just how important culture can be to an organization. Doing the right things versus doing things right provides an ethos, which in the military vernacular is referred to as *esprit de corps* and *semper fidelis*. You'd better be able to trust that person who is fighting beside you whether in a bar or behind enemy lines.

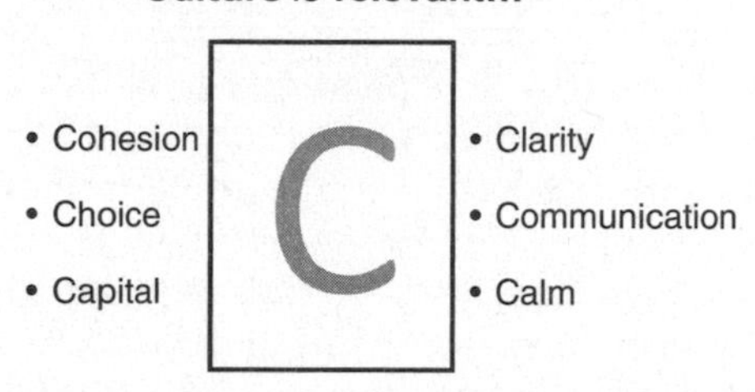

"Why do we exist?" Simply to sell more products and services is a nonstarter. It's a tougher question than it might sound. By breaking it down into some of the results of culture, it gets somewhat easier to achieve. Cohesion is not simply clans like warehousing and sales where each stays within their own group, but conduits and connections need to be created and those at every level must feel they have been involved in the resurrection of the company as something more than just financial capital, but human capital as well. This issue was readily apparent based upon the metrics used and the legacy staff retained as well as no fewer than 50 fiefdoms operating in their own silos where redundancy was rampant. When constituents are involved in the question, "How can we differentiate and be a market disruptor?," there is more clarity.

Memos and emails among the daily noise are insufficient. Management by walking around (MBWA) is often the only thing that ensures the vision is communicated internally and externally. Leadership must be patient and show a face of calm even when the transformation is occurring; otherwise, pushback is assured and new staff may not be the best solution. New leaders may be.

Strategy eats tactics for lunch.

The word strategy comes from *strategos*, the Greek word for a military general/leader. If you strategize, you are thinking and acting in the manner of a military general. It means you are ready to meet any challenge, you thrive during uncertainty, and you keep your mind focused on *both* risk and opportunities.

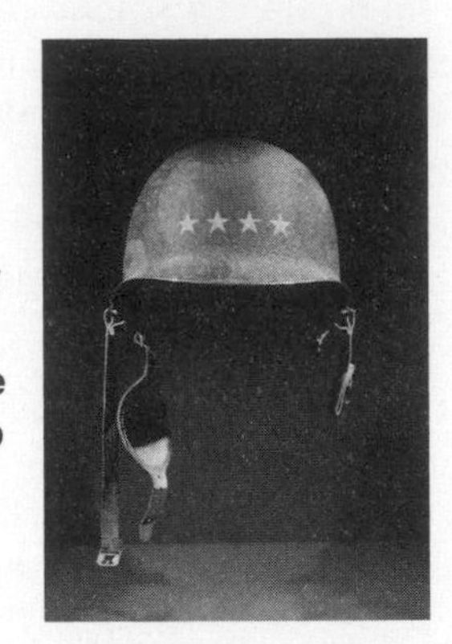

Part of the strategic overhaul is to examine whether the company is confusing tactics with strategy. It is amazing the sigh of relief division and department heads have when some of their observations are shared. Most uncertainty was self-inflicted by financial and information bottlenecks as well as tracking the wrong indicators. A strategy roadmap must be crafted to ensure the higher level thoughts have the resources to ensure their success. This means opportunities are seized and risks are minimized before they have significant costs and consequences. This process alone identified underperformance that was undetected as the metrics were previously almost exclusively financial. The result was after six months the increased savings were almost 600 basis points which would double within 18 months.

Coupling of Strategy & Dynamic Capabilities

Sensing	Senzing	Transforming
Identification of opportunities and risks proactively	Mobilization of resources to deliver value and shape markets	Continuous renewal and periodic major strategic shifts

"You have to be fast on your feet and adaptive or else a strategy is useless."

Charles de Gaulle, French general and statesman

One of the key issues was reimaging and outsourcing more mundane and redundant activities and providing a business process outsourcing

(BPO) model where more staff were embedded with the clients—boots on the ground to see firsthand the issues and opportunities. This has been common practice for many Department of Defense and Homeland Security contractors for many decades. The key is understanding just how relevant information (knowledge) is before it reaches the marketplace. This requires the *sensing* referred to earlier. The *seizing* means regardless of when, where, and who, the provider is nimble and responsive. This means answering the question, "Are you reacting to changes your clients are seeking or are you participating in, if not initiating and facilitating these changes?"

Transformation conveys that my existence is to serve your needs even before you might know or express those desires. This is the pinnacle role of a chief-of-staff, which I aim to be for clients and I want clients to aim to be for their existing and new patrons.

This requires an organizational change where review is near real time and delivery is shortened from six to eight weeks (sometimes quarterly) to having answers under some conditions as near to real time as possible. What would be the impact of being able to deliver in that manner? Would clients pay a premium for the additional value offered? If not, perhaps that is part of the discussion of whether a leaner and flatter organization would provide better results.

These activities resulted in the reduction of 7 percent of clients (which were a drain on resources) and an increase in service and product requests and associated revenues by 22 percent.

II. Relationships

Think advisors.
Think leverage.

Throughout this book I have emphasized the importance of relationships. I'm not referring to business transactions in which a client pays *X* for products and services and may do so again at given intervals. The relationships I'm referring to are not letting clients win at golf. I'm referencing elevating human interaction to more than you're on my side because you're buying from me and not when you're buying from my competitor. Relationships that convey, "I know you have a bottleneck and I'd like to send some of my best folks to brainstorm some solutions. Pay what you think the assistance is worth and by the way I heard that one of your competitors may be pulling out of the Southeast as they lost several key staff to competitors. Here's what I know."

These relationships whether internal or external offer eyes, ears, and hearts comparable to the courtship many of us pursued when we wanted to be betrothed to our significant other. Will resources and expectations enter into the equations? Surely, but consider the reciprocity when a favor is leveraged having more value than a transaction.

Think advisors.

- Alignment
- Best in class

It was illuminating to determine from interactions with key staff and board that the perception of advisory services was narrow given the subject company was itself in the professional services sector. The sole relationships that seemed enduring were with the law firm and a handful of investment bankers which they used to assist in acquisitions.

Their commercial banking relationship was an afterthought. Management did not seek relationships with vendors other than as part of transactions. This was costly and inefficient as much of purchasing was decentralized. Relationships with clients were ostensibly also transactional and reactive. Holiday and birthday cards, while a nice gesture, are far different than hosting small gatherings to have the executives from clients discuss the issues they confront and how they address them, which could create new opportunities between them and with the client company. These can be hosted roundtables or events recognizing best practices.

If high standards are expected from within the company, management could require the same from the constituents in their company's ecosystem. This requires an organizational transformation. It also requires the notion of embracing external perspectives that may offer a fresh approach to what may be seen as a given.

Each relationship based upon revenues and expenses/costs was revisited based upon criterion the company established. Conversely, clients and advisor/banker/vendor relationships were solicited to inquire what they considered an optimal outcome, and while some responses were no surprise, others were. The most common was, "We did not know you could do that for us."

Management was tasked with defining what would constitute an ideal relationship, which seems like an easy exercise. However, it can go much deeper. As shared earlier in this book, vendors can be asked, "What alternatives should we be thinking?" or "What practices do you find with your best customers?" Most importantly was, "What firm or person is considered the preeminent practitioner in this space and what is it that they do that differentiates themselves from others?" While the lists were long and differed depending upon subjective criteria, the common issue is very few were currently serving the company because "best" was confused with comfortable and familiar. Many such relationships were vestiges of personal preferences of past or current executives with no other real criteria established—which is very common.

So, while some relationships were enhanced and others jettisoned, the next most difficult task was to ensure that the flow of communication internally also included key external constituents. In some cases, costs increased, but the commensurate value received far exceeded the costs and in many occasions costs were reduced and responsiveness and engagement were amplified. The next result was additional and deeper relationships that would be difficult for competitors to undermine as they were seldom based upon solely financial metrics. The financial net result was increased revenues and a reduction of costs ranging between 3 and 25 percent.

The most difficult task was to achieve alignment between the advisors (including the board in this category, which had been primarily focused on regulatory and financial compliance rather than on requiring a strategy from the C-suite). What the C-suite learned was there was ostensibly no communication across advisors and their understanding of the company's mission and needs was anything but ideal. The company's EVP was tasked with outside assistance in creating project teams at the national, local, and business unit levels to ensure that advice was proactively sought and advisors were engaged in solving the challenges and pursuing opportunities. This was an almost two-year undertaking and ended up with ensuring a quarterly conference call where all the primary advisors were involved as part of an off-site annual meeting of executives to review past and future initiatives.

The Yin and Yang of Relationships

Process Management	People Management
Deals with the "mechanics" of the integration	Deals with the "personality" of the integration
Focus is on structure, order, and control—planning, accountability, org charts, process integration velocity, timelines, flowcharts	Focus is on the psychological, social, political, and cultural issues in play that represent critical risk factors
Involves administrative, operational, and technical matters	Involves the human side of organizational change
Concerned with the physical aspects of consolidating two organizations—e.g., technology, facilities, accounts, products, systems, equipment, etc.	Concerned with the intangibles, emotions, and atmospherics involved in consolidating two organizations—personal and cultural matters such as egos, ambitions, expectations, roles, power, status, values, beliefs, traditions, taboos, habits, etc.
Methodology-oriented; procedural, systematic, and analytical; logical, practical, and by-the-numbers	Attitudinal/behavioral-oriented; fluid, dynamic, and nonlinear; highly charged; combustible; many trigger points

Part of the conversation and subsequent self-assessment was to determine whether too much emphasis was placed upon processes. We have all been told "that's our policy" even when we know our situation may be unique. This conveys "take it or leave it." So, examination of processes and their history almost always found they were a workaround and a remnant of a legacy situation that may or may not be relevant anymore comparable to old laws that are still on the books. The heart of most processes was to centralize control or to standardize (even when it was more akin to pounding a square peg in a round hole). While this led to conformity, service organizations need to be adaptive to respond to both internal and external demands. This flattens organizations and limits the need for people who are administratively in charge of the process.

As expressed elsewhere in this book, the largest unique value an organization has is its people, their passion, and their innovation. By executives concentrating on company human capital, the notion of labor expense gives way to who works well within the ecosystem we're trying to create. This, too, is an extensive top-down assessment of how the culture will be built *of* and *by* the people with guidance and stewardship of principles being led by the company's leadership.

Dynamic vs. Ordinary Capabilities

- Accelerate the process
- Strive for maximum simplicity
- Make one poerson accountable for the integration
- Manage expectations

- Emphasize superior execution over fine-grained methodology
- Balance process management with people management
- Define and measure success carefully

One of the best exercises is to share the buzzwords and claims used by competitors and mix in those of the company and have constituents distinguish whose belong to which company's claims. Not surprisingly, differentiation is often indistinguishable, so the "emperor has no clothes" effect has an immediate impact. In large part this is because companies looking to increase sales often dilute their core competencies and are backward thinking as to "this has worked before, let's do more of it" versus inquiring whether a version 2.0 or an entirely new version is more appropriate. The latter examines what will be the needs not of tomorrow or next year, but years from now.

This is how strategy begins to drive the conversation of whether what is being done is ordinary or is dynamic. It takes all the discussions thus far in this vignette and requires actionable and measurable results that may be far different from the more traditional financial metrics relied upon. More importantly, it addresses the question of how will the company be disruptive in the marketplace and how will it need to act and look like in order to leapfrog ahead of its competitors. This does not mean duplicating what the best competitors are doing, but clearly addressing what they may not. The Avis-versus-Hertz battle where Hertz was #1 in rental cars and Avis addresses this by saying, "We try harder," is still akin to coming in second place in a baseball game.

If the board and C-suite are not committed to being so differentiated from their peers, achieving dynamic capabilities is elusive at best. This was an area of great discord among leadership based upon stylistic and optics preferences. The solution was finding the common ground from which emerged a leaner, meaner, and keener company that dominated in the service offerings by becoming its clients' concierge (go-to) resource.

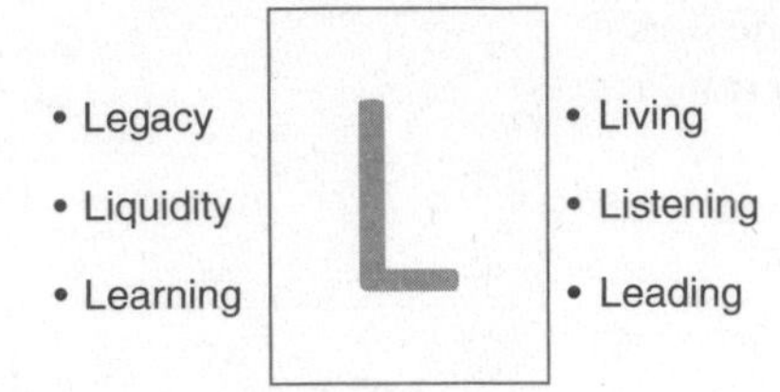

While the L words seem straightforward, sometimes a simple question of "How do we see the opportunities and risks *before* they happen?" requires a degree of reorientation and visioning. So, we must not only see things through our lens, but both see things through the lens of others and inquire when we cannot see, or the optics seem disparate. We are so attuned to making myriad assumptions when we make decisions, we don't reflect on just how many gaps there are or why they exist. It is hard for professionals to acknowledge that at best we often have only 60 percent of what we believe we need to know, which means gut-feel drives the unknown. Then there's what we "believe" to know. Anybody who has been to a jury trial knows there are a multitude of versions of what is seen; yet, all are presumed to see the same thing. Often this is based upon the notion of expedience and our own experiences. My wife sees species of birds and all I see is a blue, red, or gray bird, big or small based upon the relative importance to me. My personality is to think and review quickly and then reply, where my wife will ruminate for hours or days. Therefore, I have grown accustomed to this instead of thinking why are you procrastinating with a reply. Other than when issues we confront are time critical do we need an immediate response, recognizing people differ in the way they process information.

So, what if we could slow it down a little and ask more grounded questions like, "What will this mean to our company in one year or ten?" For a family business and many advisors the issue is conversion of part or all of their capital investment into liquidity; however, liquidity can also be a valuable discussion as to how capital is tied up and how it bottlenecks and its velocity.

Because the 1950s brick-and-mortar, top-down infrastructure does not lend itself to technological and generational differences in the twenty-first century, questions may need to be asked around "How do we provide the opportunity for a balance between family and career such that we provide a competitive advantage to attract top talent?" And while learning, listening, and leading are easy-to-understand concepts, they are often difficult to employ. Consider the executive who seldom solicits input and does little to recognize ideas of others. Being a listening and learning organization also requires a degree of stewardship.

As was the case of most, the subject company was process driven; however, it knew intuitively due to several adverse decisions that it was not extracting all it could from staff and constituents to obtain and respond to risks and embrace optics based upon the personalities and roles of those whose input was volunteered versus solicited.

III. Risks *(Opportunities)*

Think measure.
Think mastery.

It is not accidental that the largest section of this book concerns risks. Finance is in large part about risk management. So, among one of the first operational inquiries made is "What do you track and why?" Inevitably, gravitation is toward units of measure such as time and dollars. "We have had no accidents in 422 days" is fine for a manufacturer; however, as a professional service organization, it may require something more along the lines of "We have a third of employee turnover compared to our peers," or "Our corporate giving has contributed 1,000,000 volunteer hours in the past year."

The point is that until the identifiable risks are considered through deep due diligence and often an external audit (not simply a financial one), the areas of exposure are frequently unknown and often only supported partially as a cost center. However, when the company's board and key staff are tasked with establishing which risks would have the greatest impact on the company's intangible and tangible values on behalf of its stakeholders (not solely shareholders), then metrics are sure to follow. Since risk identification seldom comes naturally, the engagement of external firms such as, but not limited to, insurers makes sense.

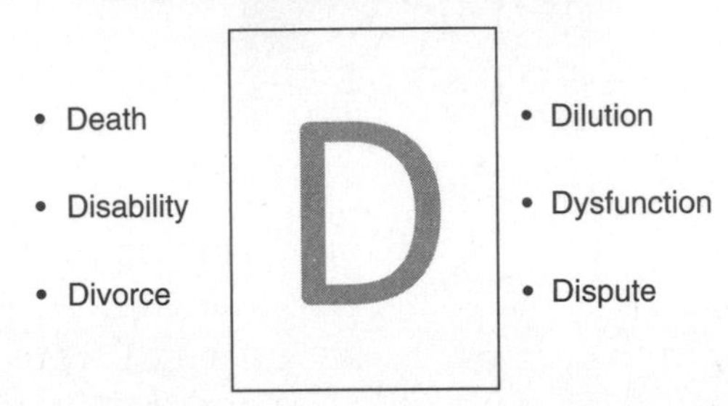

While often geared toward family businesses, "How do you determine if the business is healthy if you were not to look at just financial measures?" is relevant for most organizations. Contingencies should be part of any strategic and tactical planning as the disruptions they cause can be severe. Such risk management and mastery issues should become innate, from family and sick leave to vacations to death and disability. Absent this prior planning for unplanned events, the company, division, or unit becomes reactive and the response is often ad hoc, especially if the event is critical.

In a well-oiled machine, every component should be irreplaceable, otherwise there are excess parts; however, when a key issue causes dilution of activity results, or operational dysfunction, or may lead to internal or external disputes, an actionable result should have been on the shelf and then geared to the specific situation versus starting from scratch. (The author recognizes that there will occasionally be new twists and events that leadership may not have previously faced; however, how such events are confronted should have a "strike team" format that is tasked with identification, resources needed, and response in order that leadership can make a timely and reasonably informed decision.)

All issues cannot possibly be considered; however, the aftermath of 9/11 demonstrated that acts of God or war can be devastating to a company and its employees. These issues when given adequate time led to organizational cohesiveness, so all felt they are in it together versus "Better you than me," or "Your problem—deal with it." Management was able to identify several dozen items it did not currently track, and an additional dozen were suggested by staff and advisors that had not even been considered.

Think Risk Measurement

- Value = Economic Benefit/Return
- Value = Tangibles & Intangibles

The previous exercise takes many months to become second nature, as it is first seen as additional work and "What is the likelihood any of these things will ever happen to 'me' or 'us'?" This is where the design of value metrics becomes so critical, especially when examining what acts and events provide the greatest impact to company value. To avoid the perceived burden and dilution of the activity, no one individual was challenged with more than three elements for which she was responsible. Some functions were outsourced based upon expertise.

Actually seeing on a quarterly basis the economic value add (EVA), which is not an original concept here but is rarely understood or embraced by nonfinancial constituents, turns both cost and profit centers into ones that can reduce risk and increase value as a result.

Think Risk Mastery

"Getting from here to there" requires filling resource gaps

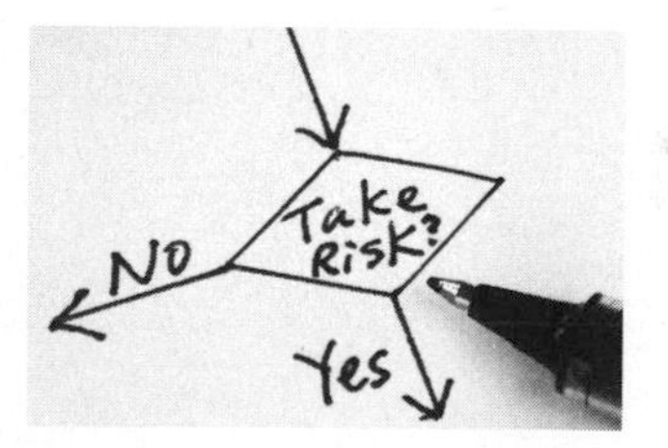

"If you want to do something new, you have to stop doing something old." *Peter Drucker*

As the last few slides reflect, not only do individuals have blind spots, but entire departments and divisions have them. If that is true, then companies that migrate to being learning organizations ask, "What don't we know and need to know?" and "Are resources available?" assuming the intent is there. From the corner office to the family and their advisor(s), I express this as "How do we get from here to there?"

As one who has had a copier, printer, and a facsimile machine on the fritz or an assistant on extended leave, I've learned just what I took for granted on how things worked behind the scenes. In the military, you had your "gunny" (E-7), a seasoned #2 who manifested what you sought and often did so behind the scenes to allow for plausible deniability. For fans of the television series, *Suits*, the attorney Harvey Spector has his executive assistant, Donna, who anticipates and knows who's doing what and when; this situational awareness is irreplaceable.

The point of strategic and tactical planning is to get granular down to the steps and tasks as ideas evolve to selected actions. This usually comes down to who is doing what, when, and for how much, and "How is 'success' going to be measured and managed?" Mastery comes when such questions become innate to all involved constituents. This is usually when innovations occur from some of the most unlikely sources.

In this engagement, it defined what executives and staff commitments and skills existed and which were absent. It required deeper discussions with the resources that trusted advisors from accountants to bankers to attorneys could provide. It almost always shows HR/IT gaps as these are often bolt-on functions that dilute the time a CFO has, especially when he is also wearing the hat of COO/EVP and possibly a board seat. Inevitably, the advisors know specialists with whom they are comfortable.

My role as chief-of-staff is to be the facilitator to ensure that all the flows and alignments are occurring and, where agreed, to provide some of my own company's staff to assist in some of the more facilitative, data- and analytics-driven areas, where either the function does not exist, the skillset does not exist; or the requisite time is insufficient to remain on schedule.

Most building contractors are well aware of the orchestration of these moving parts, which like a ballet performance looks easy but requires thousands of hours of preparation; thus, external partners are almost always called for to fill these resource gaps and build roadmaps. Once family (as applicable), staff, and advisors become truly second nature to the process, then mastery of risk management is part of the organizational DNA.

Because the process requires considerable focus on bringing the best to the table, a degree of intimacy occurs, making the bridge between governance, relationship, and knowledge like steel: very difficult to sever. "We're in this together" and "I help build that" are common refrains by those involved in this process.

The largest takeaway achieved by the client company was to introduce modeling and flowcharting to their decision trees. Executives actually sought books on topics we were discussing to up their A-game. They took a much deeper interest in their competitors and how the process worked from initial inquiry to completed transaction and follow-up.

IV. Knowledge

Think uncommon.
Think constituents.

"I don't know what I don't know" can arguably be the starting point of wisdom. The desire for knowledge should then demand something more than "here's how it's done"; otherwise, battles would be fought to attrition like World War I—an incredible waste of resources. So pushing and challenging internally, asking teams to reinvent and reimagine, is often a fruitful exercise, especially when they are not constrained by only looking at the past. And because advisors have exposure to other industries, they may see how novel solutions are applied to similar challenges that an insular organization may not.

Think Uncommon Knowledge

- Dynamic analytics
- Leveraged ecosystem

The military makes the distinction between information and intelligence, as the latter is independently confirmed and has undergone considerable analytics to address "what does this mean and how can we use this 'new' knowledge to enhance what we're doing now and in the future?" Putting industry clippings in the inbox for future review that then languishes is neither decisive nor an opportunity to be exploited. This is common practice, so support staff were tasked to spend part of their days summarizing events and findings and making recommendations based upon their research and their familiarity with what was being sought by leadership. This engagement by both staff and external sources allows an organization to collect and filter considerable information that after adequate analytics can provide considerable leverage.

Constituents' Knowledge

- ➢ Thought leaders
- ➢ Visionary stewards

A dynamic learning organization is what the client company wanted and what was delivered. In the space of 20 months (four months ahead of time and well under budget), the company's market value increased by 265 percent despite divesting several of its business units. Candidly, this also was as a result of a recapitalization and greater focus on organic growth and less dilution of time and resources of integrating companies with disparate cultures, agendas, and expectations into the mothership.

I applaud the board and the C-suite for trusting me enough to open their company's kimono and committing to a new direction, which they knew they needed and which I simply provided the tools and language to assist so they could tap into resources and passions that were already there. Grant you, the process started with a benchmark value and evolved into empowering the leadership to have a deeper vision of the "possible" and building an organization around that belief.

The highest takeaway was not the advisory fees; it was knowing the value brought from staff and advisors was harnessed and treasured. This in turn changed the way the company worked with its clients that became readily apparent to them. This resulted in inquiries that led to introductions to advisors and officers/owners of other companies and a new pipeline of fresh business.

Teaser Alert: What's in It for Me Answered

- Deeper strategic relationship—not a transaction
- Conduit for collaboration
- Perceived as SME—"You get it. You get me."
- More reciprocity and referrals
- Loyal clients become your advocate
- Much more business opportunities and $$$

Throughout this book I have tried to cajole, shame, and challenge advisors to consider how they presently serve clients. "Is there a better way?" seems to be less of an issue than "Why should I do it differently?" and the most ubiquitous and admittedly small-minded "What's in it for me?"

Deepening relationships brings untold commerce because valuing what others care about is what builds the cement around trust. This is where commerce comes from and, as the teaser alert demonstrates, can be the change for which your clients and you are hopefully seeking. Don't just provide a routine service any of your competitors can do and are doing the same way, but build a team around clients and the reciprocity and business will follow.

Getting from Here to There

- 30,000-foot view: a business has assets.
- Base value is book value—assets you can see.
- Focus is on revenues and profits, not risk.
- Risk is what primarily drives value. It's intangible.
- So are governance, relationships, and knowledge.
- Thriving businesses and families are dynamic.

I love the "getting from here to there" lead-in as it covers so much, and if silence is followed by the question, the advisor will often learn what keeps the company's owner/officer clients up at night.

The point of this book is rendering services as a transaction is so twentieth century. It's dead; the purveyors of "same" just don't know it yet. So, adding intangible value by reducing risks and sourcing opportunities is what gets both feet through the door; and then, closing it behind you, open it only with the consensus of clients. You are now the most trusted advisor and client gatekeeper.

Strategic Framework

- Founders and boards often lack a conceptual framework for assessing their company and for planning.
- They do not take advantage of modern analytical tools that can help them conquer the challenge of "family continuity" in firm or in family roles.
- Yet, strategic planning guides the firm and family.

GRRK is intended to start the conversation of why companies, owners, and advisors do what they do and challenge if there is a better way. The author does not have all the answers and not necessarily the best ones. What is known is that to drive the change a company is looking for (assuming it knows) is to have a strategic framework of which the strategic framework provides a simplified example. There are many versions and this is what has worked best for me.

I want clients and advisors to know I care passionately and protectively about their businesses and about what they're striving to build. But it always starts with a strategic plan and relationship building, not a one-off transaction. That will lose as much as 80 percent of potential clients, as most are looking for a cheap, fast silver bullet. Sadly, there are plenty of folks offering what the prospects say they want and selling it. It's like sugar. It tastes good and the high lasts for a while, and afterwards you're more lethargic and distrustful than before because the results often don't materialize as promised.

In the past, best practices was enough, but due to the volume and speed in which information flows, wasting resources isn't the competitive luxury it was once. Ask any print media company, "How's that working out for you?" Any content-rich e-commerce company knows the money is often not in the product or service offered; it is in the understanding of the behaviors of those visiting, shopping, and buying.

It is the analytics of these patterns that allows companies to gain a competitive advantage, so all stakeholders must access and seek knowledge and then leverage relationships to harness the knowledge into win-win actions. This is purposeful and part of a holistic strategy that is not easy for many, as it does require an emotional and unique approach to client service that is unfamiliar to many—even business valuators who are tasked with identifying and measuring the risk of company operations, not just simply evaluating financials. If nothing else, financials alone seldom offer adequate information to assess intellectual property/intangible assets, which is what drives enhanced value.

Strategic Framework

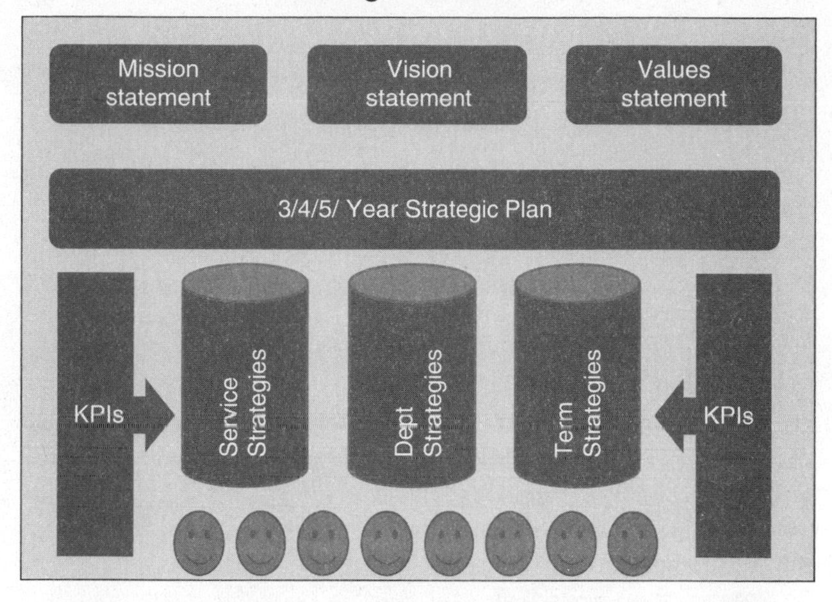

So, a firm and family often need to understand the framework in which metrics are created and how strategy flows from top down. Advisors and key constituents must be involved and understand the value of their roles.

Strategy & Transformation

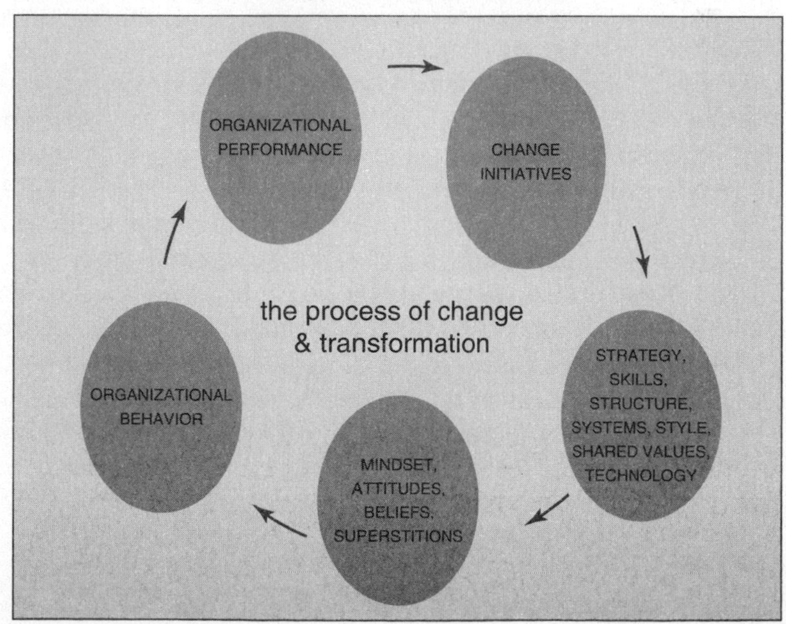

There is no magic bullet and change takes time. It is much more about human capital than about process alone.

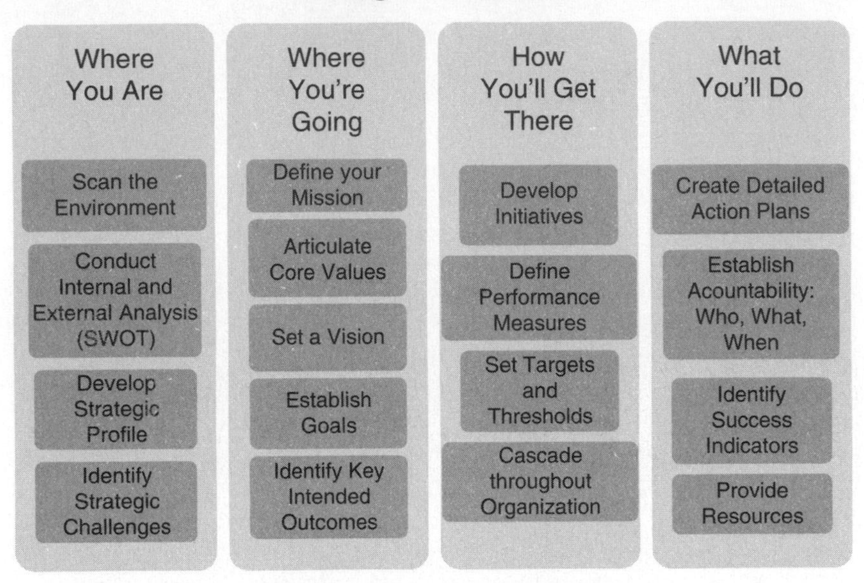

As a recap, knowing and understanding the underlying questions to challenge and guide are important not only to be an analyst but to be a change agent. Much of these elements are common to valuation professionals and can be articulated to families, firms, and their advisors. The net results are actionable items after questions tease out the most profound responses. Remember, it takes a village. No advisor or owner can be expected to go it alone. A battle tank is a formidable weapon system, but needs a loader, driver, gunner, and a commander working in concert within the tank as well as externally with the other tanks or combat units it is intended to support.

Strategic Management ~ Value Creation

Sheelerism: ***If synergies are not captured, you overpaid.***

To sum up, it takes a strategy to transform a company to orient itself toward value creation. This is particularly true when growth is through acquisition. In the absence of thoughtful pre- and post-integration examination, the accretion sought won't be realized. This is true as most acquisitions fail to realize the value for the price paid.

Strategic Framework Benefits

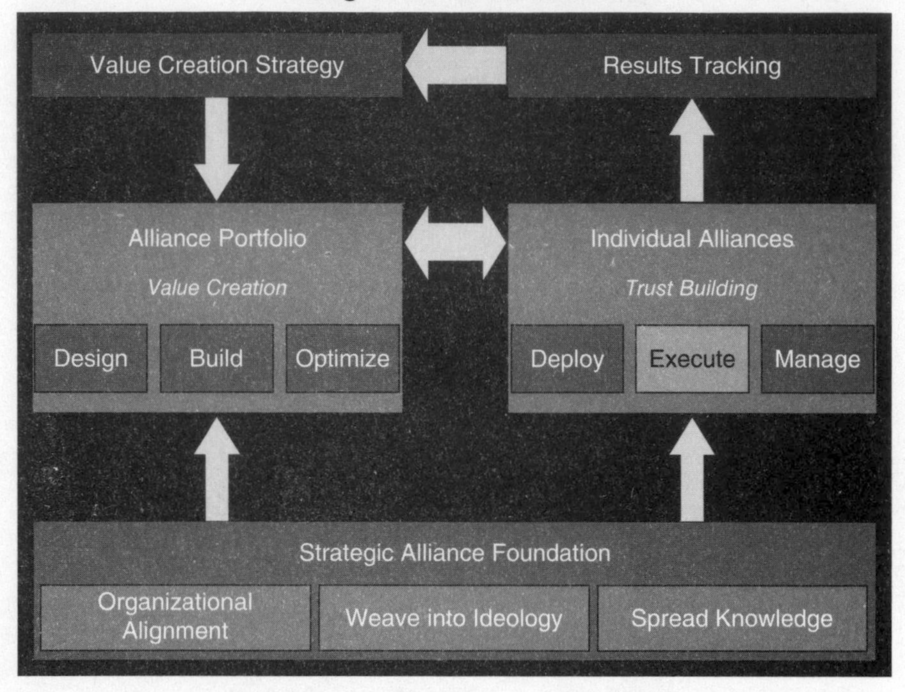

Therefore, innate to the constituents and ecosystem is a commitment to create value and develop the tools to identify, measure, manage, and mitigate risk as well as pursue opportunity faster and wiser than one's competitors. Optimally, the transformed company is a disruptor in the marketplace and clearly differentiated and almost impossible to replicate because the human capital and culture created are unique to the one organization.

What is important is that a strategic plan without a cultural shift and an actionable commitment is a temporal feel-good exercise that results in same stuff, different day.

V. Putting It Together

GRRK provides the strategy, metrics, and actions to allow firms and families to move from "success" to "significance."

It provides more time and clarity to leverage and align human and financial capital to pursue opportunities and reduce risk.

This way, firms and families retain control and sustain their legacy across generations, not just quarterly.

Therefore, *real* alpha can often be 2×, 5×, or more when measuring tangible and intangible assets.

These vignettes and this book are intended to raise the bar for the valuation profession, advisors, families, directors, owners, and officers. Most valuation (and for that matter most professional and business services) engagements are primarily one-off transactions meant to generate some additional revenue for practitioners, but in the absence of adequate skills, the companies retaining such talent are often poorly represented. This is in large part because the solutions are tactical and technical and not strategic. They lack a framework and ignore the important role of all constituents. They are often check-the-box and don't challenge those involved to know and seek the best relationships. They are formulaic.

This book begins the conversation of the necessity to better identify and measure company specific risk, and while there is no one formula in quantifying the result, the author invites his peers to pick up the mantle and provide new ways to better quantify the weight and measure of these risks.

By identifying, measuring, managing and mitigating risk as part of a holistic and strategic approach, equity value enhancement becomes an important role. The opportunity is as significant to increase the level of success for early stage companies as it is to facilitate transition of families and firms from one generation to the next. This is of mutual benefit to the strategic value architect as to the trusted advisors with whom he and she collaborates.

By leveraging both financial and human capital—governance, knowledge, and relationships while managing risks and sourcing opportunities, the reader can build significant new value into any enterprise. I wish you well.

Thanks for speaking GRRK!

NOTE: Questions, suggestions, speaking/writing, and retention inquiries are welcome. If you'd like to know more about Two Bears Ranch, equine, dog or veteran therapy, I invite you to contact me at carl@carlsheeler.com.

Recommended Reading

Barringer, Bruce. *Entrepreneurship: Successfully Launching New Ventures*. Upper Saddle River, NJ: Prentice Hall, 2006.

Barron, Robert. *Entrepreneurship: A Process Perspective*. Mason, Ohio: Thomson Southwestern, 2006.

Birley, Sue. *Mastering Entrepreneurship*. Upper Saddle River, NJ: Prentice Hall, 2000.

Bossidy, Larry. *Execution: The Discipline of Getting Things Done*. New York, NY: Crown Business, 2002.

Boulton, Richard. *Cracking the Value Code: How Successful Businesses Are Creating Wealth in the New Economy*. New York, NY: Harper Business, 2000.

Brandes, Charles, *Value Investing Today* (third edition), New York, NY: McGraw Hill, 2003

Brown Hartley, Bonnie. *Family Wealth Transition Planning: Advising Families of Small Businesses*. New York, NY: Bloomberg Press, 2009.

Bygrave, William. *The Portable MBA in Entrepreneurship*, 2nd ed. New York: John Wiley & Sons, 1997.

Cendrowski, Henry. *Private Equity: History, Governance and Operations*, 2nd ed. Hoboken: Wiley Finance, 2012.

Curtis, Gregory. *The Stewardship of Wealth*. Hoboken: John Wiley & Sons, 2013.

Dollinger, Marc. *Entrepreneurship: Strategies & Resources*, 2nd ed. Upper Saddle River, NJ: Prentice Hall, 1999.

Gerber, Michael. *Awakening the Entrepreneur Within*. New York, NY: Harper Collins, 2008.

Hangstefer, James. *Creating and Sustaining Company Growth*. Englewood Cliffs, NJ : Burton Merrill, 1997.

Harrington, James. *Total Improvement Management*. New York, NY: McGraw-Hill, 1995.

Hatten, Timothy. *Small Business Entrepreneurship and Beyond*. Upper Saddle River, NJ: Prentice Hall, 1997.

Helfert, Erich. *Techniques of Financial Analysis: A Guide to Value Creation*, 11th ed. New York, NY: McGraw-Hill Irwin, 2003.

Heriot, Kirk. *Cases in Entrepreneurship and Small Business Management*. Upper Saddle River, NJ: Pearson Prentice Hall, 2003.

Hisrich, Robert. *Entrepreneurship*, 6th ed. New York, NY: McGraw-Hill, 2005.

Hunt, Peter. *Structuring Mergers & Acquisitions: A Guide to Creating Shareholder Value*, 2nd ed. New York, NY: Aspen, 2004.

Jackim, Richard. *The $10 Trillion Opportunity: Designing Successful Exit Strategies for Middle Market Business Owners*. Cleveland, OH: Exit Planning Institute, 2005.

Jaffe, Dennis. *Working with the Ones You Love: Strategies for a Successful Family Business*. New York, NY: Relative Solutions, 2007.

Jaffe, Dennis. *Stewardship in Your Family Enterprise*. Carrollton, MS : Pioneer Imprints, 2010.

Jarvis, Christopher. *Wealth Secrets of the Affluent: Keys to Fortune Building and Asset Protection*. Hoboken: John Wiley & Sons, 2008.

Jones, Gareth. *Introduction to Business: How Companies Create Value for People*. New York, NY: McGraw-Hill Irwin, 2007.

Kaplan, Jack. *Patterns of Entrepreneurship*. New York: John Wiley & Sons, 2003.

Kim, W. Chan. *Blue Ocean Strategy*. Boston, MA: Harvard Business Press, 2005.

Koller, Tim. *Valuation: Measuring and Managing the Value of Companies*, 5th ed. Hoboken: Wiley, 2010.

Kourilsky, Marilyn. *The E-Generation*. Rancho Santa Margarita, CA: Kendall Hunt, 2000.

Kuratko, Donald. *Entrepreneurship: A Contemporary Approach*, 5th ed. New York, NY: Harcourt College, 2001.

___. *Strategic Entrepreneurial Growth*. New York, NY: Harcourt College, 2001.

Lambing, Peggy. *Entrepreneurship*, 2nd ed. Upper Saddle River, NJ: Prentice Hall, 2000.

Long, Mark. *Core Strategy*. Superlab, www.mysuperlab.com 2010.

Malkiel, Burton. *A Random Walk Down Wall Street: The Time Tested Strategy for Successful Investing*. New York, NY: W. W. Norton, 2012.

Meggision, Leon. *Small Business Management*, 5th ed. New York, NY: McGraw-Hill Irwin, 2006.

Miller, Warren. *Value Maps: Valuation Tools That Unlock Business Wealth*. Hoboken: Wiley, 2010.

Moorman, Jerry. *Successful Business Planning for Entrepreneur*. Mason, Ohio: Thomson Southwestern, 2006.

Ohlorst, Frank. *Big Data Analytics: Turning Big Data into Big Money*. Hoboken: John Wiley & Sons, 2011.

O'Neill, Martin. *Building Business Value: How to Command a Premium Price for Your Midsized Company*. Annapolis, MD: Third Bridge Press, 2009.

Parmenter, David. *Key Performance Indicators*. Hoboken: John Wiley & Sons, 2007.

Phelps, Edmund. *Mass Flourishing*. Princeton University Press, 2013.

Prince, Russ Alan. *The Private Client Lawyer*. Overland Park, KS: Wealth Management Press, 2003.

Prince, Russ Alan, *Profitable Brilliance*, New York, NY: Forbes Media, 2012

Rosplock, Kirby. *The Complete Family Office Handbook: A Guide for Affluent Families and the Advisors who Serve Them*. Hoboken: Wiley-Bloomberg Press, 2014.

Scarborough, Norman. *Effective Small Business Management*, 6th ed. Upper Saddle River, NJ: Prentice Hall, 2000.

Schimel, Barry. *100 Ways to Win the Profit Game: Battle-Tested Business Strategies That Add Value to Your Business Now*. Sterling, VA: Capital Books, 2000.

Schultz, Mike, and John Doerr. *Professional Services Marketing*. Hoboken: John Wiley & Sons, 2009.
Shane, Scott. *Finding Fertile Ground*. Upper Saddle River, NJ: Wharton School, 2005.
Slee, Robert T. *Private Capital Markets: Valuation, Capitalization and Transfer of Private Business Interests*, 2nd ed. Hoboken: John Wiley & Sons, 2011.
Stewart, Robert. *Value Optimization*. Hoboken: Wiley, 2010.
Timmons, Jerry. *New Venture Creation*, 6th ed. New York, NY: McGraw-Hill Irwin, 2004.
Trone, Donald, *LeaderMetrics: What Key Decision-Makers Need to Know When Serving in a Critical Leadership Role*. Mystic, CT: 3ethos, 2013
Urlacher, Lavern. *Small Business Entrepreneurship: An Ethics and Human Relations Perspective*. Upper Saddle River, NJ: Prentice Hall, 1999.
Vaugh, Donald. *Financial Planning for the Entrepreneur*. Upper Saddle River, NJ: Prentice Hall, 1997.
Voeller, Mark. *Exit Right: A Guided Tour of Succession Planning for Families-in-Business-Together,* Toronto, CN: Summit Run, 2002.
West, Thomas. *Mergers and Acquisitions Handbook for Small and Midsize Companies*. New York: John Wiley & Sons, 1997.
___. *Business Reference Guide: The Essential Guide to Pricing Businesses and Franchises*, 24th ed. Westford, MA: Business Brokerage Press, 2014.
Wilson, Richard. *The Single Family Office*. Author-published, 2014.
Wold, David. *Guide for Entrepreneurs*. Sandy, UT: NX Level Foundation for Education, 2004.
Zimmer, Thomas. *Essentials of Entrepreneurship*, 2nd ed. Upper Saddle River, NJ: Prentice Hall, 1998.

SUGGESTED TECHNICAL READING

Abrams, Jay. *Quantitative Business Valuation*. New York, NY: McGraw Hill, 2001.
Beaton, Neal. *Valuing Early Stage and Venture-Backed Companies*. Hoboken: Wiley Finance, 2010.
Blackman, Irving. *Valuing Your Privately Held Business*. New York: McGraw Hill, 1992.
Bogdanski, John. *Federal Tax Valuation*. New York, NY: Warren Gorman & Lamont, 1996.
Campbell, Ian. *The Valuation of Business Interests*. Montreal, CN: Canadian Institute of Chartered Accountants, 2001.
Damodaran, Aswath. *Damodaran on Valuation*. New York: John Wiley & Sons, 1994.
___. *The Dark Side of Valuation*. Upper Saddle River, NJ: Prentice Hall, 2001.
Feldman, Stanley. *Principles of Private Firm Valuation*. New York: John Wiley & Sons, 2005.
Hawkins, George. *Business Valuation Guide*. New York, NY: CCH, 2002.
Hitchner, James. *Financial Valuation*. New York: John Wiley & Sons, 2003.

Hood, L. Paul Jr,. A *Reviewer's Handbook to Business Valuation*. Hoboken: John Wiley & Sons, 2011.

Hunt, Peter. *Structuring Mergers & Acquisitions: A Guide to Creating Shareholder Value*, 2nd ed. New York, NY: Aspen, 2004.

Kasper, Larry. *Business Valuation: Advanced Topics*. Westport, CT: Quorum Books, 1997.

King, Alfred. *Valuation: What Assets Are Really Worth*. New York: John Wiley & Sons, 2002.

Koller, Tim. *Valuation: Measuring and Managing the Value of Companies*, 5th ed. Hoboken: John Wiley & Sons, 2010.

Laro, David. *Business Valuation & Taxes*. New York: John Wiley & Sons, 2005.

Mercer, Z. *Christopher. Quantifying Marketability Discounts*. Brockton, MA: Peabody, 1997.

Miles, Raymond. *Basic Business Appraisal*. New Smyrna Beach, FL: Institute of Business Appraisers, 1994.

Miller, Warren. *Value Maps: Valuation Tools That Unlock Business Wealth*. Hoboken: John Wiley & Sons, 2010.

O'Neill, Martin. *Building Business Value: How to Command a Premium Price for Your Midsized Company*. Annapolis, MD: Third Bridge Press, 2009.

Pratt, Shannon. *Business Valuation Body of Knowledge*. New York: John Wiley & Sons, 1998.

___. *Business Valuation: Discounts and Premiums*. New York: John Wiley & Sons, 2001.

___. *Valuing a Business: The Analysis and Appraisal of Closely Held Companies*, 5th ed. New York, NY: McGraw Hill, 2008.

___, and Roger Grabowski. *Cost of Capital*, 5th ed. Hoboken: John Wiley & Sons, 2014.

Rawley, Thomas, and Benton Gup. *The Valuation Handbook*. Hoboken: Wiley Finance, 2010.

Rosillo, Francisco. *Determination of Value*. Hoboken: John Wiley & Sons, 2013.

Reilly, Robert. *Valuing Intangible Assets*. New York, NY: McGraw Hill, 1999.

___. *The Handbook of Advanced Business Valuation*. New York, NY: McGraw Hill, 2000.

Roderick, Scott. *ESOP Valuation*. Oakland, CA: National Center for Employee Ownership, 1999.

Solomon, Lewis. *Valuation of Closely Held Businesses: Legal and Tax Aspects*. New York, NY: Aspen, 1998.

Slee, Robert T. *Private Capital Markets: Valuation, Capitalization and Transfer of Private Business Interests*, 2nd ed. Hoboken: John Wiley & Sons, 2011.

Stewart, Robert. *Value Optimization*. Hoboken: John Wiley & Sons, 2010.

West, Thomas. *Handbook of Business Valuation*. New York: John Wiley & Sons, 1992.

Yegge, Wilbur. *A Basic Guide for Valuing a Company*. New York: John Wiley & Sons, 1996.

Zukin, James. *Financial Valuation: Businesses and Business Interests*. New York: Warren Gorman & Lamont, 1990.

Index